THE PHILOSOPHICAL WORKS

OF

DESCARTES

RENDERED INTO ENGLISH BY

ELIZABETH S. HALDANE, C.H., LL.D.

AND

G. R. T. ROSS, M.A., D.Phil.

IN TWO VOLUMES

VOLUME II

CAMBRIDGE

AT THE UNIVERSITY PRESS

Published by the Syndics of the Cambridge University Press
The Pitt Building, Trumpington Street, Cambridge CB2 1RP
Bentley House, 200 Euston Road, London NW1 2DB
32 East 57th Street, New York 10022, USA
296 Beaconsfield Parade, Middle Park, Melbourne 3206, Australia

Standard Book No. 521 09417 8
First Edition 1911
Reprinted, with corrections 1931
Reprinted 1955, 1967, 1968,
1970, 1974, 1976,
1977

Reprinted in the United States of America
by Murray Printing Company

CONTENTS

INTRODUCTION

THE 'OBJECTIONS AND REPLIES.'

DESCARTES' friend, the Rev. Father Mersenne, circulated the *Meditations* in manuscript among various theologians and men of philosophic bent. Their criticisms (in Latin) were forwarded to Descartes, who in turn commented on them (in Latin), and published the whole discussion along with his *Meditations*. The first edition of the *Meditations*—that of 1641—had the first six sets of these *Objections and Replies* appended to them, viz. the objections by (i) the theologian Caterus, (ii) a group of theologians and philosophers, (iii) Hobbes, (iv) Arnauld, (v) Gassendi, and (vi) another group of theologians and philosophers, together with Descartes' replies.

The second edition of the *Meditations* (also in Latin) contained in addition the seventh set of objections—written by the Jesuit Bourdin—and Descartes' answer thereto, as well as Descartes' letter to Dinet, in which he complains of Bourdin's attack on him.

When the time came to prepare a French version of the *Objections and Replies*, Descartes wished to omit the discussion with Gassendi for the reasons set out on pp. 123–4. Clerselier, the translator, did actually publish a French version of the fifth set of *Objections and Replies*, but as this did not receive Descartes' sanction it has not been possible to use it in preparing the present English rendering of the whole of the *Objections and Replies*. A contemporaneous French version of *Objections and Replies* (vii) and of the letter to Dinet are lacking. Clerselier's version of sets (i—iv) and (vi) has therefore alone been used.

It will be found that in these discussions there are numerous and often long quotations from the *Meditations*. The reader will notice also that sometimes the rendering of these passages differs slightly from that given in Vol. I of the present work. This divergence of versions is inevitable, because the translation in Vol. I has been founded upon both the Latin and the French text of the *Meditations*—no doubt thus best representing Descartes' final thoughts on the subject. But Descartes' critics had before them only the original Latin text. It was but right therefore to translate directly from the Latin the excerpts they criticised, though an attempt has been made to keep the rendering here as uniform as possible with that in Vol. I. Besides the variations that are explained by the above cause there are others due to abridged quotation or paraphrase of the original passage both by Descartes and by his critics.

The works contained in this volume vary in importance. Thus the criticisms of Bourdin (*Objections VII*) are most tiresome and almost wholly worthless, while those by Hobbes, Arnauld, and Gassendi give us insight into the minds of those eminent thinkers, Gassendi's seeming materialism especially being of a most robust and interesting nature. In Descartes' replies there are several passages that are of importance in enabling us to understand his maturer doctrine. Thus in the *Reply to Objections I* we find an interesting discussion of efficient causality and 'causi sui' (pp. 13 sqq.), of the distinction between the infinite and the indefinite (pp. 17, 18), of the ontological proof of God's existence (see especially p. 21), and of the difference between a real and a formal distinction (pp. 22, 23). In the *Reply to Objections II* perhaps the passage on the difference between Synthesis and Analysis in proof is most noteworthy. The elucidation of the real distinction between body and mind is continued in the *Reply to Objections IV* (pp. 98 sqq.); that of efficient causality (on pp. 107 sqq.); while the question of the relation of Descartes' theory to the Roman doctrine of the Sacrament of the Eucharist comes up on pp. 116 sqq.

The *Reply to Objections V* (pp. 208–9) will yield some insight into Descartes' views about the dependence of mind on body. The derivation of ideas from sense is discussed on pp. 226 sqq.

The subject of the souls of brutes appears once more in the *Reply to Objections VI* (pp. 243 sqq.); the liberty and the indifference of the will in God and in man are discussed on pp. 247–9; Descartes' theory of matter is once more clearly stated on pp. 253 sqq.

In the *Reply to Objections VII* perhaps the most interesting passage is the illustration of the 'method of doubt' by the homely illustration of turning out all the apples in a basket and then picking out all that are not rotten for the purpose of putting them back once more (p. 282).

For the rest one feels that only Descartes' excessive desire to stand well with the Jesuits could have led him to reply in detail to the stupid misunderstandings of Bourdin.

G. R. T. ROSS.

OBJECTIONS URGED BY CERTAIN MEN OF LEARNING AGAINST THE PRECEDING MEDITATIONS; WITH THE AUTHOR'S REPLIES.

The First set of Objections[1].

Gentlemen,

As soon as I recognized that you were so anxious that I should make a thorough examination of the writings of M. Descartes, it seemed impossible for me, in duty, to disoblige in this matter friends so dear to me. My reason in complying was both that you might witness the extent of my esteem for you, and also that I might reveal my lack of power and intellectual endowment; hence, I hoped, you might in future allow me the more indulgence, if I require it, or, if I came short, be less exacting.

In my estimation M. Descartes is in truth a man who combines the highest intellectual endowments with an extreme modesty—one of whom even Momus, had he come to life, would approve. 'I think,' he says, 'hence I exist; nay, I am that very thinking, or the mind.' True. 'However, in thinking I have within me ideas of things, and firstly an idea of a being of extreme perfection and infinite.' I grant this. 'Moreover, I, not equalling the objective reality of this idea, am not its cause; hence it has some cause more perfect than I, and this immediately shows that there is something else besides me in existence, something more perfect than I am. This is a being who is an entity not in any indeterminate sense, but one which absolutely and with-

---

[1] The Author of these objections of the first group, is Caterus, a priest of Alkmaar, who sent them to Bannius and Bloemaert, two friends of Descartes. Cf. *Oeuvres*, Vol. III. p. 242, l. 4; p. 265, l. 20; p. 267, l. 9; p. 272, l. 27.

*out limitations embraces its whole reality wholly in itself, and is, as
it were, an anticipatory cause[1], as Dionysius[2] says (de divin. nom.
cap. 8[3]).'*

But here I am forced to stop a little, to avoid excessive exhaustion;
for already my mind fluctuates like the Euripus with its changing
tides. Now I consent, now I deny; I approve and once more dis-
approve. To disagree with the champion of this theory I do not care,
agree with him I cannot. But, pray, what sort of cause must an
idea have? or, tell me, what is an idea? It is the thing thought of
itself in so far as that is 'objectively' in the understanding. But explain what 'to be objectively in the understanding' is. As I was
taught, it is the determination of an act of mind by a modification due
to an object; but this is a merely external attribute of the thing and
nothing belonging to its reality. For, as 'being seen' is merely the
direction of the act of vision towards the percipient so 'being thought'
or 'being objectively in the understanding' is merely a standing still
of our thought within itself and ending there, which can occur whether
the thing is active or passive, indeed though it is even non-existent.
Hence, why should I ask for a cause of that which is nothing actual,
which is a mere name, a nonentity?*

Nevertheless, says our great philosopher,—'because a certain idea
has such and such an objective reality rather than another, it must
owe this to some cause[4].' *Nay it needs no cause, for its 'objective
reality' is a mere name and nothing actual. Further a cause exerts
some real and actual influence; but the objective existence which is
nothing actual can be the recipient of nothing, and hence cannot be
passively affected by the real activity of a cause, so far is it from
requiring a cause. My conclusion is that, though I have ideas, there
is no cause for their existence, so far from there being a cause for
them greater than me and infinite.*

' *But, if you do not assign some cause for ideas, you must, at least,
give some reason why this particular idea contains this particular
objective reality rather than that.' Quite right; it is not my way
to be niggardly with my friends but to be open-handed. I affirm
universally of all ideas what M. Descartes says at other times of the
triangle. He says:*—' Though possibly no such figure exists anywhere outside my thought or has at any time existed, yet is its

---

[1] The French phrase paraphrases this: 'One in which all things are included as in a universal and first cause.'

[2] The reference is to the writings attributed in mediaeval times to Dionysius—Dionysius the Areopagite.

[3] Chapitre cinquiesme. F. V.   [4] Cf. Med. III. Vol. I. p. 163, ll. 1—4.

nature something unconditionally determinate, an essence, or form that is immutable and eternal[1].' *It is hence an eternal verity which requires no cause. A boat is a boat, as Davus is Davus and not Œdipus. If, however, you drive me to assign a reason, I shall say it is the imperfection of the mind, which is not infinite; for, not clasping in a single embrace the whole which exists simultaneously and all together, it parcels out and divides the omni-present good. Thus, because it cannot bring forth the whole, it conceives it in a series of acts or, in technical language 'inadequately.'*

M. Descartes further asserts, ' Yet, however imperfect be the manner of the existence in which a thing is, by means of an idea, objectively in the understanding, nevertheless it is not merely nothing, nor, consequently, can it proceed from nothing.'

But this is equivocation; for, if 'nothing' is the same as 'an entity not actually existing,' it is entirely non-existent, because it does not actually exist, and hence it proceeds from nothing, i.e. *from no cause. But if by 'nothing' something imaginary is meant, something vulgarly styled* an 'ens rationis,' *it is not* 'nothing' *but something real which is distinctly conceived. But since it is merely conceived and is nothing actual, though it may be conceived, yet it cannot be caused* [*or banished from the mind*[2]].

But he proceeds, ' Further, I should like to ask, whether "I" who have this idea could exist, if no such being existed[3],' i.e. *if none existed,* 'from which the idea of a being more perfect than I proceeds,' *as he says immediately before.* 'For,' *says he,* 'from what should I proceed? From myself, from my parents, or from some other beings?...But, if I were self-originated, neither should I doubt, nor should I wish for anything, nor should I suffer lack of anything whatsoever, for I should have given myself all the perfections of which I have any idea, and should thus myself be God[4].' *'But, if I am derived from something else, the end of the series of beings from which I come will ultimately be one which is self-originated, and hence what would have held good for myself (if self-originated) will be true of this*[5].' *This is an argument that pursues the same path as that taken by St Thomas*[6], *and which he calls the proof from* 'the causality of an efficient cause.' *It is derived from Aristotle. But Aristotle and*

---

[1] Cf. Med. v. Vol. I. p. 180, ll. 4—7.   [2] French version.
[3] Cf. Vol. I. p. 167, sub fin.   [4] Cf. loc. cit. infra.
[5] Vol. I. p. 168, par. 2, sub fin.
[6] Thomas Aquinas, Summa totius Theologiae, Pars. I. Quaestio ii. De Deo, an Deus sit? Art. 3: Utrum Deus sit? p. 7, col. 2, Secunda via est ex ratione causae efficientis.

*St Thomas are not concerned with the causes of ideas.   Perhaps they
had no need to be, for might not the argument take a more direct and
less devious course?—I think, hence I exist; nay I am that very
thinking mind, that thinking.   But that mind, that thought, springs
either from itself or from something else.   On the latter alternative,
from what does that something else come?   If it is self-derived, it
must be God? for that which is self-originated will have no trouble in
conferring all things on itself.*

    *An entreaty I would press upon our author, is that he would not
hide his meaning from this Reader, one eager to comprehend him,
albeit perhaps lacking in acuteness.   'Self-originated[1]' has two senses,
firstly a positive meaning equivalent to—derived from its own self as
from a cause.   Hence anything which was self-originated and conferred its own existence on itself, would, if giving itself what it
desired by an act of choice involving premeditation, certainly give
itself everything and would thus be God.   Secondly, 'self-originated'
has a negative usage which equates it with 'by itself' or 'not derived
from anything else'; so far as my memory serves me, it is universally
employed in this sense.*

    *But now, if anything is self-derived, i.e. not due to something else,
how can I prove that it embraces all things and is infinite?   I shall
pay no heed to the reply that, if it is self-derived, it will have given
itself everything, for it does not depend on itself as on a cause, nor did
it anticipate its existence and so at a prior time choose what it should
afterwards be.   It is true I have heard this doctrine of Suarez 'All
limitations proceed from a cause, and the reason why anything is
finite and limited is, either that its cause could not, or that it would
not give it more being and perfection.   Hence, if anything is self-
derived and does not issue from a cause, it is necessarily unlimited
and infinite.'*

    *But I do not wholly agree.   For (be the thing ever so much self-
originated, i.e. not due to something else), if the limitation be due to
the thing's internal constitutional principles, i.e. to its very form and
essence, which, however, you have not yet proved to be infinite, what is
your answer?   It is certain that the hot, if you will concede that there
is such a thing, is hot and not cold in virtue of its own internal
constitutional principles, though you conceive that hot thing to derive
its existence from nothing else.   I doubt not that M. Descartes has no
lack of reasons for substantiating that which others perhaps have not
demonstrated with sufficient clearness.*

[1] a se.

*At last I find a point of agreement with my adversary. He has erected as a general rule, '*Whatever I know clearly and distinctly is something really true[1].' *Nay '*whatever I think is true; for almost from boyhood I have banished chimaeras and "entities of reason" from my mind. No faculty can be deflected from its proper object: the will if it moves at all tends towards good : indeed not even the senses themselves err ; sight sees what it sees, the ears hear what they hear : though what you see be tinsel there is nothing wrong with the vision ; the error comes in when your judgment decides that it is gold you are beholding.' Hence M. Descartes most properly assigns all error to the account of the will and judgment.*

*But now, from this cause infer what you wanted. '*I apprehend clearly and distinctly an infinite being; hence it is something true and real.' *But will not someone ask, '*Do you apprehend clearly and distinctly an infinite being?' *But what then is the meaning of that well-worn maxim known to all?*—The infinite quâ infinite is unknown. *For if, when I think of a chiliagon and have a confused representation of some figure, I do not have a distinct image of the chiliagon or know it, because I do not have its thousand sides evident and distinct before my mind, shall I not be asked,—how can the infinite be thought of distinctly and not confusedly, if the infinite perfections of which it is composed cannot be perceived clearly, and, as it were, with true distinctness of vision?*

*Perhaps this is what St Thomas meant when he denied that the proposition 'God is' is known "per se[2]." In objection to this he considers an argument drawn from Damascenus—'*God exists: the knowledge of this truth nature has implanted in all; hence the truth that God exists is known "*per se*.'" *His reply is* the knowledge of the existence of God is, in a general sense, and, *as he says*, in a confused manner, to wit, in so far as He is man's highest existence, implanted by nature in all. But this is not an unqualified apprehension of the existence of God, just as to know that someone is coming is not the same as to know Peter, though Peter be the man who is coming[3], etc. *This is tantamount to saying that God is known in so far as He falls under some general term or as final cause, or even as first and most perfect of beings, or finally as something which contains all things in a confused and generic manner, but not in respect of the precise notion which expresses His nature. I believe that M. Descartes will have no difficulty in replying to anyone who*

<hr>

[1] Vol. i. p. 158, l. 9.
[2] Summa Quaest. ii. Art. i.   [3] Summa loc. cit. p. 6, col. 2.

raises a question here. Yet I am sure that owing to what I here bring forward, merely for discussion's sake, he will call to mind the doctrine of Boethius: That there are certain common mental concep-tions which are only known 'per se' by the wise[1]. *Hence no one should marvel if those who desire to know more (than others) ask many questions, and for a long time linger over those topics which they know to have been laid down as the first principles of the whole subject, and in spite of this do not master it without strenuous intellectual effort.*

Let us then concede that someone has a clear and distinct idea of a highest and most perfect being; what further conclusion do you draw? That this infinite being exists, and that so certainly that the existence of God should have certitude, at least for my mind, as great as that which mathematical truths have hitherto enjoyed[2]. Hence there is no less[3] contradiction in thinking of a God (that is of a being of the highest perfection) who lacks existence (a particular perfection) than in thinking of a hill which is not relative to a valley[4]. *The whole dispute hinges on this; he who gives way here must admit defeat. Since my opponent is the stronger combatant I should like for a little to avoid engaging him at close quarters in order that, fated as I am to lose, I may yet postpone what I cannot avoid.*

Firstly then, though reason only and not authority is the arbiter in our discussion, yet, lest I be judged impertinent in gainsaying the contentions of such an illustrious philosopher, let me quote you what St Thomas says; it is an objection he urges against his own doctrine:— As soon as the intellect grasps the signification of the name God, it knows that God exists; for the meaning of His name is an object nothing greater than which can be conceived[5]. Now that which exists in fact as well as in the mind is greater than what exists in the mind alone. Hence, since the name 'God' being understood, God consequently exists in the mind, it follows that He really exists. *This argument formally expressed becomes—God is a being, a greater than which cannot be conceived; but that, a greater than which cannot be conceived, includes its existence; hence God by His very name or notion includes His existence, and as a direct consequence can neither be conceived as being, nor can be, devoid of existence. But now, kindly tell me is not this M. Descartes' own proof? St Thomas*

---

[1] Quotation in Thomas, loc. cit. p. 6, col. 2.
[2] Vol. I. p. 179, par. 1, sub fin.
[3] 'More,' Latin version.
[4] *Ibid.* par. 2.
[5] Significari.

defines God thus:—A being than which nothing greater can be conceived. **M. Descartes calls Him a being of extreme perfection;** *certainly nothing greater than this can be conceived.* St Thomas goes *on to argue*—That than which nothing greater can be conceived includes its existence; *otherwise a greater than it could be conceived,* *namely that which is conceived to contain its existence.* Now does not *M. Descartes bring up the same proposition as minor premise?* 'God *is the most perfect being, the most perfect being comprises within itself* *its existence, for otherwise it would not have the highest perfection.'* *St Thomas's conclusion is:*—Therefore since *God,* His name being understood, exists in the understanding, He exists in reality. *That* *is to say, owing to the very fact that in the very concept of the essence* *of an entity, nothing greater than which can be conceived, existence is* *involved, it follows that that very entity exists.* M. Descartes *draws the* *same inference:*—Yet, *says he,* owing to the fact that we cannot think of God as not existing, it follows that His existence is inseparable from Him, and hence that He in truth exists[1]. *But now let St Thomas* *reply both to himself and to M. Descartes.* Granted that everyone and anyone knows that by the name God is understood that which has been asserted, to wit, a being than which nothing greater can be thought, yet it does not follow that he understands that the thing signified by the name exists in reality, but only that it exists in the apprehension of the understanding. Nor can it be proved that it really exists, unless it be conceded that something really exists than which nothing greater can be thought—a proposition not granted by those who deny the existence of God. *This furnishes me with my* *reply, which will be brief—Though it be conceded that an entity of the* *highest perfection implies its existence by its very name, yet it does* *not follow that that very existence is anything actual in the real* *world, but merely that the concept of existence is inseparably united* *with the concept of highest being.* Hence you cannot infer that the *existence of God is anything actual, unless you assume that that* *highest being actually exists; for then it will actually contain all its* *perfections, together with this perfection of real existence.*

Pardon me, gentlemen, if now I plead fatigue; but here is something in a lighter vein. This complex existent Lion *includes both* *lion and the mode existence; and includes them essentially, for if you* *take away either it will not be the same complex.* But now, has not *God from all eternity had clear and distinct knowledge of this composite object?* *Does not also the idea of this composite, in so far as*

[1] Cf. Med. v. Vol. I. p. 181 sub fin.

it is composite, involve both its elements essentially? That is to say, does not its existence flow from the essence of this composite, existent Lion? *Yet, I affirm, the distinct cognition of it which God possesses, that which he has from all eternity does not constrain either part of the complex to exist, unless you assume that the complex does exist; for then, indeed, it will imply all its essential perfections and hence also that of actual existence. Therefore, also, even though you have a distinct knowledge of a highest being, and granted that a being of supreme perfection includes existence in the concept of its essence, yet it does not follow that its existence is anything actual, unless on the hypothesis that that highest being does exist; for then indeed along with its other perfections it will in actuality include this, its existence, also. Hence the proof of the existence of this highest being must be drawn from some other source.*

*I shall add but few words about the essence of the soul and the distinction between soul and body; for I confess that the speculations of this wonderful genius have so exhausted me that I can add but little more. It appears that the distinction between soul and body, if real, is proved by the fact that they can be conceived as distinct and as isolated from each other. Here I leave my opponent to contend with (Duns) Scotus, who says that—*In so far as one thing can be conceived as distinct and separate from another, the adequate distinction to draw between them is what he calls a *formal* and *objective* one, which is intermediate between a *real* distinction and a distinction of *reason*. *It is thus that he distinguishes between the Divine justice and the Divine pity.* They have, *he says,* concepts formally diverse prior to any operation of the understanding, so that, even then, the one is not the other: yet it does not follow that, because God's justice can be conceived apart from his pity, they can also exist apart.

But I see that I have far exceeded the bounds of a letter. These are the criticisms for which, to my mind, the subject calls. I leave it to you, gentlemen, to pick out any that may seem to you to have merit. If you take my part, it will be easy to prevail upon M. Descartes kindly not to bear me ill will in future for having in a few points contradicted him. If you uphold him, I yield, and own myself vanquished, the more eagerly from anxiety not to be overcome a second time. I send you greetings.

A REPLY BY THE AUTHOR TO THE FIRST SET OF OBJECTIONS.

Gentlemen,

You have certainly stirred up a stout antagonist against me, one whose ability and learning might have caused me serious perplexity, unless like a pious and Christian theologian he had preferred to befriend the cause of God and of its unworthy champion, rather than to make a serious attack on it. But, though this insincerity redounds only to his credit, to act in collusion with it would tend to draw down censure on me; and thus I prefer to unmask his device for rendering me assistance, rather than to answer him as an opponent.

To begin with, he has put in brief compass my chief argument for proving the existence of God, so that it should the more readily abide in the reader's memory; having briefly indicated his assent to what he thinks clearly enough demonstrated, and having thus strengthened that with his authority, he finally comes to the crux of the difficulty, and raises a question only as to what is to be here understood by the term *idea*, and what sort of cause this aforesaid idea demands.

Now I have written somewhere *an idea is the thing thought of itself, in so far as it is objectively in the understanding.* But these words he evidently prefers to understand in a sense quite different from that in which I use them, meaning to furnish me with an opportunity of explaining them more clearly. '*Objective existence in the mind is,*' he says, '*the determination of the act of mind by a modification due to an object, which is merely an extrinsic appellation and nothing belonging to the object,*' etc.[1] Now, here it must be noticed firstly that he refers to the thing itself, which is as it were placed outside the understanding and respecting which it is certainly an extrinsic

---

[1] Cf. above p. 2, par. 2.

attribute to be objectively in the understanding, and secondly, that
what I speak of is the idea, which at no time exists outside the mind,
and in the case of which '*objective existence*' is indistinguishable
from being in the understanding in that way in which objects are wont
to be there. Thus, for example, if someone asks what feature in the
sun's existence it is to exist in my mind, it will be quite right to
reply that this is a merely extrinsic attribute which affects it, and
to wit, one which determines an operation of the mind in the mode
due to the object. But if the question be, what the idea of the
sun is, and the reply is given, that it is the object thought of in
so far as that exists objectively in the understanding, he will not
understand that it is the sun itself, in so far as that extrinsic
attribute is in it ; neither will *objective existence in the understanding*
here signify that the mind's operation is here determined in the mode
due to an object, but that it is in the mind in the way in which
objects are wont to exist there. Hence the idea of the sun will
be the sun itself existing in the mind, not indeed formally, as it
exists in the sky, but objectively, i.e. in the way in which objects
are wont to exist in the mind ; and this mode of being is truly
much less perfect than that in which things exist outside the
mind, but it is not on that account mere nothing, as I have
already said.

When this learned theologian talks of *equivocation*, I think that
by this he means to warn me, and prevent me from forgetting that
which I have this moment mentioned. For, firstly, he says that a
thing existing in the mind through an idea, is not an *actual entity*,
i.e. is nothing situated outside the intellect ; and this is true.
Secondly he says that it is *not anything fictitious or an entity of
reason, but something real which is distinctly conceived* ; by which
words he admits all I have assumed. Yet he adds, *because it is
merely conceived and is nothing actual* (i.e. because it is merely an
idea, and nothing situated outside the mind), *it may be indeed
conceived, but by no means caused*[1] ; i.e. it does not require a cause
in order to exist outside the mind. Agreed ; but it does require
a cause to make it be conceived, and it is of this cause alone that
the question here is raised. Thus, if anyone has in his mind the
idea of any machine showing high skill in its construction, it is
certainly quite reasonable to ask what is the cause of that idea ;
and it is not sufficient to answer that the idea is nothing outside
the mind, and hence can have no cause, but can merely be con-

[1] Cf. p. 3, par. 3.

ceived; for here the whole question is—what is that which causes it to be conceived? Nor will it suffice to say that the mind itself is its cause, being the cause of its own acts; for this is not disputed, the question being the cause of the objective artifice which is in the idea. For there must be some definite cause of the fact that this idea of a machine displays this objective artifice rather than another, and its objective artifice bears to this cause the same relation that the objective reality of the idea of God bears to its cause. Various causes of such a contrivance might be assigned. It will be either a similar real machine already seen, the features of which are reproduced in the idea, or it will be great knowledge of mechanical science in the mind of him who thinks of it, or perchance a great intellectual acuteness, which has enabled the man to invent this device without previous scientific knowledge. We must note that every contrivance which in the idea has only objective existence, must necessarily exist in its cause, whatever that cause be, either formally or eminently. And we must apply the same rule to the objective reality which is in the idea of God. But in what will this exist unless in a God who really exists? My clear-sighted opponent, however, sees all this, and hence admits that we may ask *why this particular idea contains this particular objective reality rather than that*, and to this question he replies firstly: *that the same as what I have written about the idea of the triangle holds good of all ideas, viz. that though perchance the triangle nowhere exists, yet there does exist some determinate nature, or essence, or immutable and eternal form which belongs to it*[1]. Further he says *that this demands no cause*. But he sees well enough that this reply is nevertheless not satisfactory; for, although the nature of the triangle be immutable and eternal, that does not disallow the question why the idea exists in us. Hence he adds—'*If, however, you drive me to assign a reason, I shall say it is the imperfection of the mind,*' etc. But this reply seems to show merely that those who have desired to take exception to my views have no rejoinder to make that at all approaches the truth. For, sooth to say, there is no more probability that the imperfection of the human intellect is the cause of our possessing the idea of God, than that ignorance of mechanical science should be the cause of our imagining some machine showing highly intricate contrivance, rather than another less perfect one. On the contrary, clearly, if one possesses the idea of a machine which involves every

[1] Cf. pp. 2, 3.

contrivance that ingenuity can devise, it will be absolutely right to infer that it is the product of some cause, in which that extreme pitch of mechanical ingenuity was actually embodied, although in the idea it existed only objectively. By the same reasoning, when we have in us the idea of God, in which all thinkable perfection is contained, the evident conclusion is, that that idea depends upon some cause in which all that perfection also exists, to wit in the God who really exists. It is true that both cases would seem to be on the same footing, and that, just as all are not expert mechanicians, and hence cannot form the notion of a highly intricate machine, so all men might not have the same power of conceiving the idea of God; but since that idea is implanted in the same manner in the minds of all, and we perceive no source other than ourselves from which it comes, we suppose that it pertains to the nature of our mind. This indeed is not wrong, but we omit something else which principally merits consideration and on which the whole force and evidence of this argument depends, namely, that this power of having in one's self the idea of God could not belong to our intellect, if this intellect were merely a finite entity, as in fact it is, and did it not have God as the cause of its existence. Hence I have undertaken the further enquiry— *whether I could exist if God did not exist*[1]—not for the purpose of adducing a proof distinct from the preceding one, but rather in order to give a more thorough-going explanation of it.

At this point my opponent, through excess of courtesy, has put me in an awkward position, for he compares my argument with another drawn from St Thomas and from Aristotle, and thus he seems to compel me to explain why, having started with them on the same road, I have not kept to it at all points. But I beg him to excuse me from speaking of others, and to allow me to give an account only of what I have myself written.

Firstly then, I have not drawn my arguments from observing an order or succession of efficient causes in the realm of sensible things, partly because I deemed the existence of God to be much more evident than that of any sensible things, partly also because this succession of causes seemed to conduct merely to an acknowledgement of the imperfection of my intellect, because I could not understand how an infinity of such causes could have succeeded one another from all eternity in such a way that none of them has been absolutely first. For certainly, because I could

[1] Cf. Med. III. Vol. I. p. 167 sub fin.

not understand that, it does not follow that there *must* be a first cause, just as it does not follow that, because I cannot understand an infinity of divisions in a finite quantity, an ultimate atom can be arrived at, beyond which no further division is possible. The only consequence is that my intellect, which is finite, cannot comprehend the infinite. Therefore I prefer to use as the foundation of my proof my own existence, which is not dependent on any series of causes, and is so plain to my intelligence that nothing can be plainer; and about myself I do not so much ask, what was the original cause that produced me, as what it is that at present preserves me, the object of this being to disentangle myself from all question of the succession of causes.

Further, I have not asked what is the cause of my existence in so far as I consist of mind and body, but have limited myself definitely to my position in so far as I am merely a thing that thinks. And I think that this furthers my project in no small degree; for thus I have been able far better to free myself from prejudiced conclusions, to follow the dictates of the light of nature, to set questions to myself, and to affirm with certainty that there is nothing in me of which I am not in some way conscious. This clearly is quite different from judging that, because I was begotten by my father, he was the progeny of my grandfather, and, because in seeking out the parents of my parents I could not carry the process to infinity, deciding, in order to bring my quest to a conclusion, that hence there was some first cause of the series.

Moreover, I have not only asked what is the cause of my being in so far as I am a thinking thing, but chiefly in so far as I perceive that there exists in me, among other thoughts, the idea of a being of the highest perfection. For it is on this that the whole force of my demonstration depends; firstly because in that idea is contained the notion of what God is, at least in so far as I can comprehend Him, and according to the laws of true Logic, the question '*does a thing exist?*' must never be asked unless we already understand *what the thing is*; secondly, because it is this same idea that gives me the opportunity of enquiring whether I proceed from myself or from something else, and of recognising my defects; finally it is that which shows me not only that there is some cause of my existence, but that further in this cause all perfections are contained, and that hence it is God.

Finally, I have not said that it is impossible for anything to be its own efficient cause; for, although that statement is manifestly true when the meaning of efficient cause is restricted to those causes that are prior in time to their effects or different from them, yet it does not seem necessary to confine the term to this meaning in the present investigation. In the first place the question[1] would in such a case be unmeaning, for who does not know that the same thing can neither be prior to nor different from itself? Secondly, the light of nature does not require that the notion of an efficient cause should compel it to be prior to its effect; on the contrary, a thing does not properly conform to the notion of cause except during the time that it produces its effect, and hence is not prior to it. Moreover, the light of nature certainly tells us that nothing exists about which the question, why it exists, cannot be asked, whether we enquire for its efficient cause, or, if it does not possess one, demand why it does not have one. Hence, if I did not believe that anything could in some way be related to itself exactly as an efficient cause is related to its effect, so far should I be from concluding that any first cause existed, that, on the contrary, I should once more ask for the cause of that which had been called first, and so should never arrive at the first of all. But I frankly allow that something may exist in which there is such a great and inexhaustible power that it has needed no assistance in order to exist, and requires none for its preservation, and hence is in a certain way the cause of its own existence; such a cause I understand God to be. For, even though I had existed from all eternity and hence nothing had preceded my existence, none the less, seeing that I deem the various parts of time to be separable from each other, and hence that it does not follow that, because I now exist, I shall in future do so, unless some cause were so to speak to re-create me at each single moment, I should not hesitate to call that cause which preserves me an efficient cause. Thus, even though God has never been non-existent, yet because He is the very Being who actually preserves Himself in existence, it seems possible to call Him without undue impropriety the *cause of His own existence*. But it must be noted that here I do not mean a preservation which is effected by any positive operation of causal efficiency but one due merely to this fact, that the essential nature of God is such that He cannot be otherwise than always existent.

From these remarks it is easy for me to make my reply to the distinction in the use of the term 'self-originated' or *per se*[2], which,

[1] The question 'Can a thing be its own efficient cause?'
[2] Cf. above p. 4.

according to the counsel of my learned theological adversary, requires explanation. For, although those who, confining themselves to the peculiar and restricted meaning of efficient cause, think it impossible for a thing to be its own efficient cause, and do not discern here another species of cause analogous to an efficient cause, are accustomed to understand merely, when they say a thing exists *per se*, that it has no cause ; yet, if those people would look to the facts rather than the words, they would easily see that the negative meaning of the term ' self-originated ' proceeds merely from the imperfection of the human intellect, and has no foundation in reality, and that there is a certain other positive signification which is drawn from the truth of things and from which alone my argument issues. For if, e.g. anyone should imagine that some body was something *per se*, he can only mean that it has no cause, and he affirms this for no positive reason, but merely in a negative manner, because he knows no cause for it. But this shows some imperfection in his judgment[1], as he will easily recognize if he remembers that the several parts of time are not derived from one another, and that hence, though that body be supposed to have existed up to the present time *per se*, i.e. without any cause, that will not suffice to make it exist in future, unless there be some power contained in it which continually, as it were, re-creates it ; for then, when he sees that no such power is comprised in the idea of body, he will at once conclude that that body does not exist *per se*, taking the expression *per se* positively. Similarly when we say that God exists *per se*, we can indeed understand that negatively, our whole meaning being really that He has no cause. But, if we have previously enquired why He is or why He continues in being, and having regard to the immense and incomprehensible power which exists in the idea of Him we recognise that it is so exceedingly great that it is clearly the cause of His continuing to be, and that there can be nothing else besides it, we say that God exists *per se*, no longer negatively but in the highest positive sense. For, although we need not say that God is the efficient cause of His own self, lest, if we do so, we should be involved in a verbal dispute, yet, because we see that the fact of His existing *per se*, or having no cause other than Himself, issues, not from nothing, but from the real immensity of His power, it is quite permissible for us to think that in a certain sense He stands to Himself in the same way, as an

---

[1] French version. Latin version, in eo.

efficient cause does to its effect, and that hence He exists *per se* in a positive sense. Each one may also ask himself whether he exists *per se* in the same sense, and, having found no power in himself sufficient to preserve him through even a moment of time, he will rightly conclude that he depends on something else, and indeed on something else which exists *per se*, because since the matter here concerns the present, not the past or the future, there is no room for an infinite regress. Nay, here I will add a statement I have not hitherto made in writing—that we cannot arrive merely at a secondary cause, but that the cause which has power sufficient to conserve a thing external to it must with all the more reason conserve itself by its own proper power, and so exist *per se*[1].

Moreover when it is said that all limitation is due to a cause[2], while I hold that to be a real fact, I maintain that it is hardly expressed in proper terms, and that the difficulty is not solved ; for, properly speaking, limitation is only the negation of a greater perfection, and this negation does not come from a cause but is the very thing so limited. But though it be true that every limited thing depends on a cause, yet that is not self-evident, but must be deduced from something else ; for, as this subtle theologian well replies, a thing can be limited in two ways[3], either by that which produced it not having given it more perfection, or because its nature is such that it can only receive a certain amount, as e.g. in the case of the triangle, which by its nature can only have three sides. But it seems to me to be self-evident that everything that exists springs either from a cause or from itself considered as a cause ; for, since we understand not only what existence is, but also

[1] The French translation of 1661 inserts after this point a paragraph which exists neither in the Latin nor in the French edition of 1647. Though probably not original (Descartes died in 1650) but due to Clerselier, it is judged by the surviving editor of the standard modern French edition (M. Adam) to be important, and is inserted by him in a footnote (Vol. ix. Premières Réponses, p. 88). It is as follows :

"And, in order to anticipate here an objection which could be made, to wit that perhaps he who thus questions himself has the power of preserving himself without noticing it, I maintain that this cannot be, and that if he had this power, he would necessarily know it ; for as he considers himself at this moment only as a being that thinks, nothing can exist in him of which he does not have cognizance, because every action of a spirit (such as would be the act of self-preservation, if proceeding from him), being a thought and hence being present and known by the spirit, that particular action would, like the others, be present and be known, and by it he would come necessarily to know the powers which produced it, since every action points necessarily to the power which produces it."

[2] Cf. p. 4, par. 3.   [3] F. V. The Latin is more condensed.

what negation of existence is, we cannot feign that anything exists *per se* as to which no reason can be given regarding why it exists rather than does not exist; hence there is no reason for not interpreting self-originated in the sense in which it implies causal power, that power, to wit, which passes all bounds, and which, as we can easily prove, can be found in God alone.

As to what my opponent finally grants[1] me, it is a principle which, though admitting no question, is yet commonly so little taken into consideration and is so effective in rescuing all Philosophy from the obscurity of darkness, that by confirming it by his authority the learned Doctor does much to further my endeavour.

But prudently he here enquires *whether I know the infinite distinctly and clearly*[2]; and although I have tried to anticipate this objection, yet it occurs so spontaneously to each one, that it is worth while to give it a detailed reply. Therefore here, to start with, I shall say that the infinite *quâ* infinite is in nowise comprehended, but that nevertheless it is understood, in so far as clearly and distinctly to understand a thing to be such that no limits can be found in it is to understand clearly that it is infinite.

Here indeed I distinguish between *the indefinite* and *the infinite,* and that alone do I properly speaking call infinite in which nowhere are limits to be found; in this sense God alone is infinite. That moreover in which only in a certain aspect do I recognize no limit, as e.g. the extension of imaginary space, the many in number, or the divisibility of the parts of quantity, and other similar things, I call indeed *indefinite* but not *infinite,* because such things are not limitless in every respect.

Besides that, I distinguish between the formal notion[3] of the infinite or infinity and the thing which is infinite; for as for infinity, even though we understand it to have as much positive reality as may be, yet we understand it only in a certain negative fashion, from the fact, namely, that we perceive no limitation in the thing; but the thing itself which is infinite is indeed positively understood, though not adequately, i.e. we do not comprehend the whole of what is intelligible in it. But it is just as when gazing at the sea, we are said to behold it, though our sight does not cover it all nor measures its immensity; if indeed we view it from a distance in such a way as to take in the whole with a single glance, we see it only confusedly, as we have a confused image of a chiliagon, when

---

[1] p. 4, sub fin.   [2] p. 5, par. 2.   [3] Rationem.

taking in all its sides at the same time ; but if from near at hand
we fix our glance on one portion of the sea, this act of vision can be
clear and distinct, just as the image of a chiliagon may be, if it
takes in only one or two of the figure's sides.   By similar reasoning
I admit along with all theologians that God cannot be comprehended
by the human mind, and also that he cannot be distinctly known by
those who try mentally to grasp Him at once in His entirety, and
view Him, as it were, from a distance.   This was the sense in which,
in the words of St Thomas in the passage quoted[1], the knowledge of
God was said to be found in us only in a certain confused way.   But
those who try to attend to His perfections singly, and intend not so
much to comprehend them as to admire them and to employ all the
power of their mind in contemplating them[2], will assuredly find in
Him a much ampler and readier supply of the material for clear
and distinct cognition than in any created things.

Neither does St Thomas here deny this contention, as is clear
from his affirming in the following article that the existence of God
is demonstrable.   Moreover, wherever I have said that God can be
clearly and distinctly known, I have understood this to apply only
to this finite cognition of ours, which is proportionate to the diminu-
tive capacity of our minds.   Besides, there was no reason for understanding otherwise in order to prove the truth of the propositions I
have maintained, as will easily be noticed if people take heed that
I have affirmed the doctrine in dispute only in two places, to wit
where the question was asked whether, in the idea we form of God,
there is anything real or only the negation of reality[3], (as for
example in the idea of cold nothing else is found than the negation
of heat) a point which gives rise to no dispute [although we do not
comprehend the infinite][4]; and again this doctrine appeared in the
passage where I asserted that existence appertained to the notion of
a being of the highest perfection, just as much as three sides to the
notion of a triangle, a fact which can be understood without our
having an adequate knowledge of God.

My opponent here compares one[5] of my arguments with another

---

[1] Cf. Objections i. p. 5.
[2] Instead of this last phrase the French version has 'and to recognize how
far they are from all comprehension.'
[3] Rei.
[4] This clause occurs only in the French version.   The round brackets
above are also found only in F. V.   Taken together these two indications make
it clear that the ' point which gives rise to no dispute' is that ' there is reality in
the idea of God, whereas in the idea of cold there is none.'
[5] Above p. 6, par. 2.

of St Thomas's, so, as it were to force me to show which of the two has the more force. This I seem to be able to do with a good enough grace, because neither did St Thomas use that argument as his own, nor does he draw the same conclusion from it; consequently there is nothing here in which I am at variance with the Angelic Doctor. He himself asked whether the existence of God is in itself[1] known to man, i.e. whether it is obvious to each single individual; he denies this, and I along with him[2]. Now the argument to which he puts himself in opposition can be thus propounded. *When we understand what it is the word God signifies, we understand that it is that, than which nothing greater can be conceived*[3]; *but to exist in reality as well as in the mind is greater than to exist in the mind alone; hence, when the meaning of the word God is understood, it is understood that God exists in fact as well as in the understanding.* Here there is a manifest error in the form of the argument; for the only conclusion to be drawn is—*hence, when we understand what the word God means, we understand that it means that God exists in fact as well as in the mind*: but because a word implies something, that is no reason for this being true. My argument, however, was of the following kind—That which we clearly and distinctly understand to belong to the true and immutable nature of anything, its essence, or form, can be truly affirmed of that thing; but, after we have with sufficient accuracy investigated the nature of God, we clearly and distinctly understand that to exist belongs to His true and immutable nature; therefore we can with truth affirm of God that He exists. This is at least a legitimate conclusion. But besides this the major premise cannot be denied, because it was previously[4] conceded that *whatever we clearly and distinctly perceive is true.* The minor alone remains, and in it there is, I confess, no little difficulty. This is firstly because we are so much accustomed to distinguish existence from essence in the case of other things, that we do not with sufficient readiness notice how existence belongs to the essence of God in a greater degree than in the case of other things. Further, because we do not distinguish that which belongs to the true and immutable nature of a thing from that which we by a mental fiction assign to it, even if we do fairly clearly perceive that existence belongs to God's essence, we nevertheless do not conclude that God exists, because we do not know whether His essence is true and immutable or only a fiction we invent.

---

[1] So as not to need proof, F. V.
[2] F. V. merito, L. V.
[3] Significari, L. V.
[4] Cf. above p. 17, par. 2.

But, in order to remove the first part of this difficulty we must distinguish between possible and necessary existence, and note that in the concept or idea of everything that is clearly and distinctly conceived, possible existence is contained, but necessary existence never, except in the idea of God alone.   For I am sure that all who diligently attend to this diversity between the idea of God and that of all other things, will perceive that, even though other things are indeed conceived[1] only as existing, yet it does not thence follow that they do exist, but only that they may exist, because we do not conceive that there is any necessity for actual existence being conjoined with their other properties ; but, because we understand that actual existence is necessarily and at all times linked to God's other attributes, it follows certainly that God exists.

Further, to clear away the rest of the difficulty, we must observe that those ideas which do not contain a true and immutable nature, but only a fictitious one due to a mental synthesis, can be by that same mind analysed, not merely by abstraction (or restriction of the thought)[2] but by a clear and distinct mental operation ; hence it will be clear that those things which the understanding cannot so analyse have not been put together by it.   For example, when I think of a winged horse, or of a lion actually existing, or of a triangle inscribed in a square, I easily understand that I can on the contrary think of a horse without wings, of a lion as not existing and of a triangle apart from a square, and so forth, and that hence these things have no true and immutable nature.   But if I think of the triangle or the square (I pass by for the present the lion and the horse, because their natures are not wholly intelligible to us), then certainly whatever I recognise as being contained in the idea of the triangle, as that its angles are equal to right, etc., I shall truly affirm of the triangle ; and similarly I shall affirm of the square whatsoever I find in the idea of it.   For though I can think of the triangle, though stripping from it the equality of its angles to two right, yet I cannot deny that attribute of it by any clear and distinct mental operation, i.e. when I myself rightly understand what I say.   Besides, if I think of a triangle inscribed in a square, not meaning to ascribe to the square that which belongs to the triangle alone, or to assign to the triangle the properties of the square, but for the purpose only of examining that which arises from the conjunction of the two, the nature of that composite will be not less true and immutable than

[1] intelligamus.
[2] This phrase occurs only in the French version.

that of the square or triangle alone ; and hence it will be right to affirm that the square cannot be less than double the inscribed triangle, together with the similar properties which belong to the nature of this composite figure.

But if I think that existence is contained in the idea of a body of the highest perfection, because it is a greater perfection to exist in reality as well as in the mind than to exist in the intellect alone, I cannot then conclude that this utterly perfect body exists, but merely that it may exist ; for I can well enough recognize that that idea has been put together by my mind uniting together all corporeal perfections, and that existence does not arise out of its other corporeal perfections, because it (existence) can be equally well affirmed and denied of them.   Nay, because when I examine this idea of body I see in it no force by means of which it may produce or preserve itself, I rightly conclude that necessary existence, which alone is here in question, does not belong to the nature of a body, howsoever perfect it may be, any more than it belongs to the nature of a mountain not to have a valley, or any more than it pertains to the nature of a triangle to have its angles greater than two right angles. But now, if we ask not about a body but about a thing (of whatever sort this thing may turn out to be) which has all those perfections which can exist together, whether existence must be included in the number of these perfections we shall at first be in doubt, because our mind, being finite, and not accustomed to consider them unless separately, will perchance not at first see how necessary is the bond between them.   But yet if we attentively consider whether existence is congruous with a being of the highest perfection, and what sort of existence is so, we shall be able clearly and distinctly to perceive in the first place that possible existence is at least predicable of it, as it is of all other things of which we have a distinct idea, even of those things which are composed by a fiction of the mind.   Further, because we cannot think of God's existence as being possible, without at the same time, and by taking heed of His immeasurable power, acknowledging that He can exist by His own might, we hence conclude that He really exists and has existed from all eternity; for the light of nature makes it most plain that what can exist by its own power always exists.   And thus we shall understand that necessary existence is comprised in the idea of a being of the highest power, not by any intellectual fiction, but because it belongs to the true and immutable nature of that being to exist.   We shall at the same time easily perceive that that all-powerful being must comprise in himself all the other perfections that are contained in the idea of God, and hence these by their own nature and without any mental fiction are conjoined together and exist in God.

All this is manifest to one who considers the matter attentively, and it differs from what I have already written only in the method of explanation adopted, which I have intentionally altered in order to suit a diversity of intelligences. But I shall not deny that this argument is such that those who do not bethink themselves of all those considerations that go to prove it, will very readily take it for a sophism; hence at the outset I had much doubt as to whether I should use it, fearing that those who did not attain to it might be given an opportunity of cavilling about the rest. But since there are two ways only of proving the existence of God, one by means of the effects due to him, the other by his essence or nature, and as I gave the former explanation in the third Meditation as well as I could, I considered that I should not afterwards omit the other proof.

In the matter of the formal distinction which the learned Theologian claims to draw from Scotus[1], my reply is briefly to the effect that this distinction in no way differs from a modal one, and applies only to incomplete entities, which I have accurately demarcated from complete beings. This is sufficient to cause one thing to be conceived separately and as distinct from another by the abstracting action of a mind when it conceives the thing inadequately, without sufficing to cause two things to be thought of so distinctly and separately that we understand each to be an entity in itself and diverse from every other; in order that we may do this a real distinction is absolutely necessary. Thus, for example, there is a formal distinction between the motion and the figure of the same body, and I can quite well think of the motion without the figure and of the figure apart from the motion and of either apart from the body; but nevertheless I cannot think of the motion in a complete manner apart from the thing in which the motion exists nor of the figure in isolation from the object which has the figure; nor finally can I feign that anything incapable of having figure can possess motion, or that what is incapable of movement has figure. So it is also that neither can I understand justice apart from a just being, or compassion apart from the compassionate; nor may I imagine that the same being as is just cannot be compassionate. But yet I understand in a complete manner what body is [that is to say I conceive of body as a complete thing[2]], merely by thinking that

---

[1] Cf. p. 8.   [2] This clause is found only in the French version.

it is extended, has figure, can move, etc., and by denying[1] of it everything which belongs to the nature of mind. Conversely also I understand that mind is something complete which doubts, knows, wishes, etc., although I deny that anything belongs to it which is contained in the idea of body. But this could not be unless there were a real distinction between mind and body.

This is my answer, gentlemen, to your friend's subtle and most serviceable criticisms. If it still is defective, I ask to be informed about the omissions or the blunders it contains. To secure this from my critic through your good offices, would be to have a great kindness conferred upon me.

[1] L. V.   Encore que je nie, F. V.

THE SECOND SET OF OBJECTIONS[1].

Sir,

Your endeavour to maintain the cause of the Author of all things against a new race of rebellious giants has sped so well, that henceforth men of worth may hope that in future there will be none who, after attentive study of your Meditations, will not confess that an eternal divine Being does exist, on whom all things depend. Hence we have decided to draw your attention to certain passages noted beneath and to request you to shed such light upon them that nothing will remain in your work which, if at all demonstrable, is not clearly proved. For, since you have for so many years so exercised your mind by continual meditation, that matters which to others seem doubtful and obscure are to you most evident, and you perhaps know them by a simple intuitive act of mind, without[2] noticing the indistinctness that the same facts have for others, it will be well to bring before your notice those things which need to be more clearly and fully explained and demonstrated. This done, there will scarce remain anyone to deny that those arguments of yours, entered upon for the purpose of promoting the greater glory of God and vast benefit to all mankind, have the force of demonstrations.

In the first place, *pray remember that it was not as an actual fact and in reality, but merely by a mental fiction, that you so stoutly resisted the claim of all bodies to be more than phantasms, in order that you might draw the conclusion that you were merely a thinking being; for otherwise there is perhaps a risk you might believe that you could draw the conclusion that you were in truth nothing other than mind, or thought, or a thinking being. This we find worthy of mention only in connection with the first two*

---

[1] The title of the French translation is 'The Second Objections collected by the Rev. Father Mersenne from the utterances of divers Theologians and Philosophers.'

[2] I follow the French version here, the Latin is not so pointed.

Meditations, in which you show clearly that it is at least certain that you, who think, exist. But let us pause a little here. Up to this point you know that you are a being that thinks; but you do not know what this thinking thing is. What if that were a body which by its various motions and encounters produces that which we call thought? For, granted that you rejected the claim of every sort of body, you may have been deceived in this, because you did not rule out yourself, who are a body. For how will you prove that a body cannot think, or that its bodily motions are not thought itself? Possibly even, the whole bodily system, which you imagine you have rejected, or some of its parts, say the parts composing the brain, can unite to produce those motions which we call thoughts. 'I am a thinking thing,' you say; but who knows but you are a corporeal motion, or a body in motion?

Secondly, *from the idea of a supreme being, which, you contend, cannot be by you produced, you are bold enough to infer the necessary existence of the supreme being from which alone can come that idea that your mind perceives*[1]. *Yet we find in our own selves a sufficient basis on which alone to erect that said idea, even though that supreme being did not exist, or we were ignorant of its existence and did not even think of it though it did exist. Do I not see that I, in thinking, have some degree of perfection? And therefore I conclude that others besides me have a similar degree, and hence I have a basis on which to construct the thought of any number of degrees and so to add one degree of perfection to another to infinity, just as, given the existence of a single degree of light or heat, I can add and imagine fresh degrees up to infinity. Why, on similar reasoning, can I not add, to any degree of being*[2] *that I perceive in myself any other degree I please, and out of the whole number capable of addition construct the idea of a perfect being?* 'But,' you say, 'an effect can have no degree of perfection or reality which has not previously existed in its cause.' *In reply we urge (passing by the fact that experience shows us that flies and other animals, or even plants are produced by the sun, rain and the earth, in which life, a nobler thing than any merely corporeal grade of being, does not exist, and that hence an effect can derive from its cause some reality which yet is not found in the cause) that that idea is nothing but an entity of reason, which has no more nobility than your mind that thinks it. Besides this, how do you know that that idea would have come before your*

---

mind if you had not been nurtured among men of culture, but had passed all your life in some desert spot? Have you not derived it from reflections previously entertained, from books, from interchange of converse with your friends, etc., not from your own mind alone or from a supreme being who exists? You must therefore prove more clearly that that idea could not present itself to you unless a supreme being did exist; though when you show this we shall all confess ourselves vanquished. But it seems to be shown clearly that that idea springs from previous notions by the fact that the natives of Canada, the Hurons, and other savages, have no idea in their minds such as this, which is one that you can form from a previous survey of corporeal things, in such a way that your idea refers only to this corporeal world, which embraces all the perfections that you can imagine; hence you would have up to this point no grounds as yet for inferring more than an entirely perfect corporeal Entity, unless you were to add something else conducting us to the [knowledge of the] incorporeal or spiritual. Let us add that you can construct the idea of an angel (just as you can form the notion of a supremely perfect being) without that idea being caused in you by a [really existing] angel; though the angel has more perfection than you have. But you do not possess the idea of God any more than that of an infinite number or of an infinite line; and though you did possess this, yet there could be no such number. Put along with this the contention that the idea of the unity and simplicity of a sole perfection which embraces all other perfections, is merely the product of the reasoning mind, and is formed in the same way as other universal unities, which do not exist in fact but merely in the understanding, as is illustrated by the cases of generic, transcendental and other unities.

Thirdly, since you are not yet certain of the aforesaid existence of God, and yet according to your statement, cannot be certain of anything or know anything clearly and distinctly unless previously you know certainly and clearly that God exists, it follows that you cannot clearly and distinctly know that you are a thinking thing, since, according to you, that knowledge depends on the clear knowledge of the existence of God, the proof of which you have not yet reached at that point where you draw the conclusion that you have a clear knowledge of what you are.

Take this also, that while an Atheist knows clearly and distinctly that the three angles of a triangle are equal to two right, yet he is far from believing in the existence of God; in fact he denies it, because if God existed there would be a supreme existence, a highest

good, i.e. an infinite Being.   But the infinite in every type of perfec-
tion precludes the existence of anything else whatsoever it be, e.g. of
every variety of entity and good, nay even every sort of non-entity
and evil; whereas there are in existence many entities, many good
things, as well as many non-entities and many evil things.   We con-
sider that you should give a solution of this objection, lest the impious
should still have some case left them.

Fourthly, *you deny that God lies or deceives; whereas some*
schoolmen may be found who affirm this.   Thus Gabriel[1], Ariminensis[2],
and others think that in the absolute sense of the expression God does
utter falsehoods, i.e. what is the opposite of His intention and con-
trary to that which He has decreed; as when He unconditionally
announced to the people of Nineveh through the Prophet, Yet forty
days *and* Nineveh shall be destroyed; *and when in many other*
cases He declared things that by no means came to pass, because His
words were not meant to correspond with His intention or His decree.
But, if God could harden the heart of Pharaoh and blind his eyes, if
He communicated to His Prophets a spirit of lying, whence do you
conclude that we cannot be deceived by Him?   May not God so
deal with men as a physician treats his patients, or as a father his
children, dissimulation being employed in both cases, and that wisely
and with profit?   For if God showed to us His truth undimmed,
what eyes, what mental vision could endure it?

Yet it is true that it is not necessary for God to contrive deception
in order for you to be deceived in the things which you think you
clearly and distinctly perceive, if the cause of the illusion may reside
in you yourself, provided only that you are unaware of the fact.
What if your nature be such as to be continually, or at least very
frequently, deceived?   But what evidence is there that you are not
deceived and cannot be deceived in those matters whereof you have
clear and distinct knowledge?   How often have we not experienced
the fact that a man has been deceived in those matters of which he
believed that he had knowledge as plain as daylight?   Hence we think
that this principle of clear and distinct knowledge should be explained
so clearly and distinctly that no one of sound mind may ever be deceived
in matters that he believes himself to know clearly and distinctly;
apart from this condition we cannot yet make out that there is a
possibility of certitude in any degree attaching to your thinking or to
the thoughts of the human race.

[1] Gabriel Biel, 15th century, 'the last of the Scholastics.'
[2] Gregory of Rimini, 14th century.

Fifthly, *if the will never goes astray or errs, so long as it follows the clear and distinct knowledge of the mind that governs it*[1], *but exposes itself to danger if guided by a mental conception which is not clear and distinct, note that the following consequences ensue :— a Turk or any other infidel does not only not err because he does not embrace the Christian* [*and Catholic*] *Religion, but in addition to this he does err if he does embrace it, since he does not apprehend its truth either clearly or distinctly. Nay, if this canon of yours is true, there will be practically nothing which the will may permissibly embrace, since there is hardly anything known to us with that clearness and distinctness that you want for a certitude that no doubt can shake. Beware then lest, in your desire to befriend the truth you do not prove too much, and, instead of establishing it, overthrow it.*

Sixthly, *in your reply to the preceding*[2] *set of objections you appear to have gone astray in the drawing of your conclusion. This was how you propounded your argument*—We may truly affirm of anything, that which we clearly and distinctly perceive to belong to its true and immutable nature ; but (after we have investigated with sufficient accuracy what God is) we clearly and distinctly understand that to exist belongs to the nature of God[3]. *The proper conclusion would have been :*—therefore (after we have investigated with sufficient accuracy what God is) we can truly affirm that to exist belongs to God's nature. *Whence it does not follow that God actually exists, but only that He ought to exist if His nature were anything possible or not contradictory ; that is to say, that the nature or essence of God cannot be conceived apart from His existence and hence, as a consequence, if that essence is real, God exists as an actual fact. All this may be reduced to that argument which is stated by others in the following terms :*—If it is not a contradiction that God exists, it is certain that He exists ; but His existence is not a contradiction ; hence, etc. *But a difficulty occurs in the minor premise, which states that God's existence is not a contradiction, since our critics either profess to doubt the truth of this or deny it. Moreover that little clause in your argument* ('after we have sufficiently investigated the nature of God') *assumes as true something that all do not believe ; and you know that you yourself confess that you can apprehend the infinite only inadequately. The same thing must be said in the case of each and any of God's attributes ; for, since everything in God is utterly infinite, what mind can com-*

---

[1] F. V. mentis suae, L. V.   [2] F. V. Theologo (i.e. Catero), L. V.
[3] Cf. above p. 19, ll. 14 sqq.

prehend the smallest fragment of what exists in God except in a manner that is utterly inadequate ?   How then can you have 'investigated with sufficient clearness and distinctness what God is' ?

Seventhly, *you say not one word* [*in your Meditations*] *about the immortality of the human soul, which nevertheless you should above all things have proved and demonstrated as against those men—themselves unworthy of immortality—who completely deny it and perchance have an enmity against it.   But over and above this you do not seem to have sufficiently proved the distinctness of the soul from every species of body, as we have already said in our first criticism ; to which we now add that it does not seem to follow from the distinction you draw between it and the body that it is incorruptible or immortal.   What if its nature be limited by the duration of the life of the body, and God has granted it only such a supply of force and has so measured out its existence that, in the cessation of the corporeal life, it must come to an end ?*

These, Sir, are the difficulties on which we request you to shed light, in order that it may be profitable for each and all to read your Meditations, containing as they do so much subtlety and, in our opinion, so much truth.   This is why it would be well worth the doing if, hard upon your solution of the difficulties, you advanced as premises certain definitions, postulates and axioms, and thence drew conclusions, conducting the whole proof by the geometrical method, in the use of which you are so highly expert.   Thus would you cause each reader to have everything in his mind, as it were at a single glance, and to be penetrated throughout with a sense of the Divine being.

REPLY TO THE SECOND SET OF OBJECTIONS.

Gentlemen,

I had much pleasure in reading the criticisms you have passed on my little book dealing with First Philosophy; and I recognise the friendly disposition towards me that you display, united as it is with piety towards God and a zeal to promote His glory. I cannot be otherwise than glad not only that you should think my arguments worthy of your scrutiny, but also that you bring forward nothing in opposition to them to which I do not seem to be able quite easily to reply.

Firstly, you warn me *to remember that it was not actually but merely by a mental fiction that I rejected the claim of bodies to be more than phantasms, in order to draw the conclusion that I was merely a thinking being, so as to avoid thinking that it was a consequence of this that I was really nothing more than mind*[1]. But in the Second Meditation I have already shown that I bore this in mind sufficiently; here are the words :—*But perhaps it is the case that these very things, which I thus suppose to be non-existent because they are unknown to me, do not in very truth differ from that self which I know. I cannot tell; this is not the subject I am now discussing, etc.*[2] By these words I meant expressly to warn the reader that in that passage I did not as yet ask whether the mind was distinct from the body, but was merely investigating these properties of mind of which I am able to attain to sure and evident knowledge. And, since I discovered many such properties, I can only in a qualified sense admit what you subjoin, namely, *That I am yet ignorant as to what a thinking thing is*[3]. For though I confess that as yet I have not discovered whether that thinking thing is the same as the body or something diverse from it, I do not, on that account, admit

---

[1] p. 24.   [2] Cf. Med. ii. Vol. i. p. 152.   [3] p. 24.

that I have no knowledge of the mind. Who has ever had such an acquaintance with anything as to know that there was absolutely nothing in it of which he was not aware? But in proportion as we perceive more in anything, the better do we say we know it; thus we have more knowledge of those men with whom we have lived a long time, than of those whose face merely we have seen or whose name we have heard, even though they too are not said to be absolutely unknown. It is in this sense that I think I have demonstrated that the mind, considered apart from what is customarily attributed to the body, is better known than the body viewed as separate from the mind; and this alone was what I intended to maintain.

But I see what you hint at, namely, that since I have written only six Meditations on First Philosophy my readers will marvel that in the first two no further conclusion is reached than that I have just now mentioned, and that hence they will think the meditations to be too meagre, and unworthy of publication. To this I reply merely that I have no fear that anyone who reads with judgment what I have written should have occasion to suspect that my matter gave out; and moreover it appeared highly reasonable to confine to separate Meditations matters which demand a particular attention and must be considered apart from others.

Nothing conduces more to the obtaining of a secure knowledge of reality than a previous accustoming of ourselves to entertain doubts especially about corporeal things; and although I had long ago seen several books written by the Academics and Sceptics about this subject and felt some disgust in serving up again this stale dish, I could not for the above reasons refuse to allot to this subject one whole Meditation. I should be pleased also if my readers would expend not merely the little time which is required for reading it, in thinking over the matter of which the Meditation treats, but would give months, or at least weeks, to this, before going on further; for in this way the rest of the work will yield them a much richer harvest.

Further, since our previous ideas of what belongs to the mind have been wholly confused and mixed up with the ideas of sensible objects, and this was the first and chief reason why none of the propositions asserted of God and the soul could be understood with sufficient clearness, I thought I should perform something worth the doing if I showed how the properties or qualities of the soul are to be distinguished from those of the body. For although many have already maintained that, in order to understand the facts[1] of metaphysics, the mind must be abstracted from the senses, no one hitherto, so far as I know, has shown how this is to be done. The true, and in my judgment, the only way to do this is found in my Second Meditation, but such is its nature that it is not enough to have once seen how it goes; much time and many repetitions are required if we would, by forming the contrary habit of distinguishing intellectual from corporeal matters, for at least a few days, obliterate the life-long custom of confounding them. This appeared to me to be a very sound reason for treating of nothing further in the said Meditation.

But besides this you here ask *how I prove that a body cannot think*[2]. Pardon me if I reply that I have not yet given ground for the raising of this question, for I first treat of it in the Sixth Meditation. Here are the words :—*In order that I may be sure that one thing is diverse from another, it is sufficient that I should be able to conceive*[3] *the one apart from the other, etc.*, and shortly afterwards I say: *Although I have a body very closely conjoined with me, yet since, on the one hand, I have a clear and distinct idea of myself, in so far as I am a thinking thing and not extended; and, on the other hand, I have a distinct idea of the body in so far as it is an extended, not a thinking thing, it is certain that I* (that is the mind [or soul, by which I am what I am]) *am really distinct from my body and can exist without it*[4]. It is easy from this to pass to the following :—*everything that can think is mind or is called mind, but, since mind and body are really distinct, no body is a mind ; hence no body can think.*

I do not here see what you are able to deny. Do you deny that in order to recognise a real distinctness between objects it is sufficient for us to conceive one of them clearly apart from the other? If so, offer us some surer token of real distinction. I believe that none such can be found. What will you say? That those things are really distinct each of which can exist apart from the other. But once more I ask how you will know that one thing can be apart from the other; this, in order to be a sign of the distinctness, should be known. Perhaps you will say that it is given to you by the senses, since you can see, touch, etc., the one thing while the other is absent. But the trustworthiness of the senses is inferior to that of the intellect, and it is in many ways possible for

---

[1] L. V.   (Choses immaterielles ou metaphysiques, F. V.)   [2] Cf. p. 24.
[3] F. V.   intelligere, L. V.   [4] Vol. i. p. 190, par. 2.

one and the same thing to appear under various guises or in several places or in different manners, and so to be taken to be two things. And finally if you bear in mind what was said at •the end of the Second Meditation[1] about wax, you will see that properly speaking not even are bodies themselves perceived by sense, but that they are perceived by the intellect alone, so that there is no difference between perceiving by sense one thing apart from another, and having an idea of one thing and understanding that that idea is not the same as an idea of something else. Moreover, this knowledge can be drawn from no other source than the fact that the one thing is perceived apart from the other; nor can this be known with certainty unless the ideas in each case are clear and distinct. Hence that sign you offer of real distinctness must be reduced to my criterion in order to be infallible.

But if any people deny that they have distinct ideas of mind and body, I can do nothing further than ask them to give sufficient attention to what is said in the Second Meditation. I beg them to note that the opinion they perchance hold, namely, that the parts of the brain join their forces[2] with the soul[3] to form thoughts, has not arisen from any positive ground, but only from the fact that they have never had experience of separation from the body, and have not seldom been hindered by it in their operations, and that similarly if anyone had from infancy continually worn irons on his legs, he would think that those irons were part of his own body and that he needed them in order to walk.

Secondly, when you say that *in ourselves there is a sufficient foundation on which to construct the idea of God*, your assertion in no way conflicts with my opinion. I myself at the end of the Third Meditation have expressly said that *this idea is innate in me*[4], or alternatively that it comes to me from no other source than myself. I admit that *we could form this very idea, though we did not know that a supreme being existed*[5], but not that we could do so *if it were in fact non-existent*, for on the contrary I have notified that *the whole force of my argument lies in the fact that the capacity for constructing such an idea could not exist in me, unless I were created by God*[6].

Neither does what you say about flies, plants, etc., tend to prove that there can be any degree of perfection in the effect which has not antecedently existed in the cause. For it is certain that either

[1] Cf. Med. II. Vol. I. pp. 154 sqq.
[2] Concurrant.
[3] This phrase is only in the French version.
[4] Vol. I. p. 170, par. 3.
[5] p. 25.
[6] Vol. I. p. 170, foot.

there is no perfection in animals that lack reason, which does not exist also in inanimate bodies; or that, if such do exist, it comes to them from elsewhere, and that sun, rain and earth are not their adequate causes. It would also be highly irrat'nal for anyone, simply because he did not notice any cause co-operating in the production of a fly, which had as many degrees of perfection as the fly, though meanwhile he was not sure that no cause beyond those he has noticed is at work, to make this an occasion for doubting a truth which, as I shall directly explain in greater detail, the light of Nature itself makes manifest.

To this I add that what you say by way of objection about flies, being drawn from a consideration of material things, could not occur to people who, following my Meditations, withdraw their thoughts from the things of sense with a view to making a start with philosophical thinking.

There is also no more force in the objection you make in calling our idea of God an entity formed by thinking[1]. For, firstly, it is not true that it is an *ens rationis* in the sense in which that means something non-existent, but only in the sense in which every mental operation is an *ens rationis*, meaning by this something that issues from thought; this entire world also could be called an entity formed by the divine thought, i.e. an entity created by a simple act of the divine mind. Secondly, I have already sufficiently insisted in various places that what I am concerned with is only the perfection of the idea or its objective reality which, not less than the objective[2] artifice in the idea of a machine of highly ingenious device, requires a cause in which is actually contained everything that it, though only objectively, comprises.

I really do not see what can be added to make it clearer that that idea[3] could not be present in my consciousness unless a supreme being existed, except that the reader might by attending more diligently to what I have written, free himself of the prejudices that perchance overwhelm his natural light, and might accustom his mind to put trust in ultimate principles[4], than which nothing can be more true or more evident, rather than in the obscure and false opinions which, however, long usage has fixed in his mind.

That *there is nothing in the effect, that has not existed in a similar or in some higher[5] form in the cause*, is a first principle than which none clearer can be entertained. The common truth '*from*

---

[1] ens rationis.   [2] Objectif ou representé, F. V.
[3] The idea of God.   [4] primis notionibus.   [5] eminentiori modo.

nothing, nothing comes' is identical with it. For, if we allow that there is something in the effect which did not exist in the cause, we must grant also that this something has been created by nothing ; again the only reason why nothing cannot be the cause of a thing, is that in such a cause there would not be the same thing as existed in the effect.

It is a first principle *that the whole of the reality or perfection that exists only objectively in ideas must exist in them formally or in a superior manner*[1] *in their causes.* It is on this alone we wholly rely, when believing that things situated outside the mind have real existence; for what should have led us to suspect their existence except the fact that the ideas of them were borne in on the mind by means of the senses ?

But it will become clear to those who give sufficient attention to the matter and accompany me far in my reflections, that we possess the idea of a supreme and perfect being, and also that the objective reality of this idea exists in us neither formally nor eminently[1]. A truth, however, which depends solely on being grasped by another's thought, cannot be forced on a listless mind[2].

Now, from these arguments we derive it as a most evident conclusion that God exists. But for the sake of those whose natural light is so exceeding small that they do not see this first principle, viz. *that every perfection existing objectively in an idea must exist actually in something that causes that idea*, I have demonstrated in a way more easily grasped an identical conclusion, from the fact that the mind possessing that idea cannot be self-derived; and I cannot in consequence see what more is wanted to secure your admission that I have prevailed.

Moreover there is no force in your plea, that perchance the idea that conveys to me my knowledge of God has come *from notions previously entertained, from books, from conversations with friends, etc., not from my own mind alone*[3]. For the argument takes the same course as it follows in my own case, if I raise the question whether those from whom I am said to have acquired the idea have derived it from themselves or from any one else ; the conclusion will be always the same, that it is God from whom it first originated.

---

[1] eminenter.
[2] The French version makes Descartes say he cannot force truths on those who give his Meditations just as little serious thought as they give a novel read to pass the time.
[3] Cf. Obj. ii. p. 26. Descartes' quotation is not quite literal.

The objection you subjoin, *that the idea of God can be constructed out of a previous survey of corporeal things*[1], seems to be no nearer the truth than if you should say that we have no faculty of hearing, but have attained to a knowledge of sound from seeing colours alone; you can imagine a greater analogy and parity between colours and sounds than between corporeal things and God. When you ask me *to add something conducting us to [the knowledge of] an incorporeal and spiritual entity*[2], I can do nothing better than refer you back to my Second Meditation, so that you may at least see that it is not wholly useless. For what could I achieve here in one or two paragraphs, if the longer discourse to be found there, designed as it were with this very matter in view, and one on which I think I have expended as much care as on anything that I have ever written, has been wholly unsuccessful?

There is no drawback[3] in the fact that in that Meditation I dealt only with the human mind; most readily and gladly do I admit that the idea we have, e.g. of the Divine intellect, does not differ from that we have of our own, except merely as the idea of an infinite number differs from that of a number of the second or third power; and the same holds good of the various attributes of God, of which we find some trace in ourselves.

But, besides this, we have in the notion of God absolute immensity, simplicity, and a unity that embraces all other attributes; and of this idea we find no example in us: it is, as I have said before[4], *like the mark of the workman imprinted on his work*. By means of this, too, we recognise that none of the particular attributes which we, owing to the limitations of our minds, assign piecemeal to God, just as we find them in ourselves, belong to Him and to us in precisely the same sense. Also we recognise that of various particular indefinite[5] attributes of which we have ideas, as e.g. knowledge whether indefinite or infinite, likewise power, number, length, etc., and of various infinite attributes also, some are contained formally in the idea of God, e.g. knowledge and power, others only eminently, as number and length; and this would certainly not be so if that idea were nothing else than a figment in our minds.

If that were so it would not be so constantly conceived by all in

---

[1] Cf. Obj. II. p. 26, l. 13.   [2] Cf. Obj. II. p. 26, l. 18.

[3] Sc. to using Med. II. to establish the difference between God and matter. Cf. F. V.

[4] Cf. Med. III. Vol. I. p. 170, sub fin.

[5] The F. V. drops the distinction between indefinite and infinite.

the same way. It is most worthy of note that all metaphysicians are unanimous in their description of the attributes of God (those at least which can be grasped by the human mind unaided); and hence there is no physical or sensible object, nothing of which we have the most concrete and comprehensible idea, about the nature of which there is not more dispute among philosophers.

No man could go astray and fail to conceive that idea of God correctly if only he cared to attend to the nature of an all-perfect being. But those who confuse one thing with another, owing to this very fact utter contradictions; and constructing in their imagination a chimerical idea of God, not unreasonably afterwards deny that a God, who is represented by such an idea, exists. So here, when you talk of *a corporeal being of the highest perfection*, if you take the term 'of the highest perfection' absolutely, meaning that the corporeal thing is one in which all perfections are found, you utter a contradiction. For its very bodily nature involves many imperfections, as that a body is divisible into parts, that each of its parts is not the other, and other similar defects. For it is self-evident that it is a greater perfection not to be divided than to be divided, etc. But if you merely understand what is most perfect in the way of body, this will not be God.

I readily grant your further point, that *in the case of the idea of an angel, than which we are less perfect, there is certainly no need for that idea to be produced in us by an angel* ; I myself have already in the third Meditation[1] said that *the idea can be constructed out of those that we possess of God and of man.* There is no point against me here.

Further, those who maintain that they do not possess the idea of God, but in place of it form some image, etc., while they refuse the name concede the fact. I certainly do not think that that idea is of a nature akin to the images of material things depicted in the imagination, but that it is something that we are aware of by an apprehension or judgment or inference of the understanding alone. And I maintain that there is a necessary conclusion from the fact alone that, howsoever it come about, by thought or understanding, I attain to the notion of a perfection that is higher than I ; a result that may follow merely from the fact that in counting I cannot reach a highest of all numbers, and hence recognise that in enumeration there is something that exceeds my powers. And this conclusion is,

---

[1] Cf. Med. iii. Vol. i. p. 164.

not indeed to the effect that an infinite number does exist, nor yet that it implies a contradiction as you say[1], but that I have received the power of conceiving that a number is thinkable, that is higher than any that can ever be thought by me, and have received it not from myself but from some other entity more perfect than I.

It is of no account whether or not one gives the name idea to this concept of an indefinitely great number. But in order to understand what is that entity more perfect than I am, and to discover whether it is this very infinite number as an actually existing fact, or whether it is something else, we must take into account all the other attributes that can exist in the being from which the idea originates, over and above the power of giving me that idea; and the result is that it is found to be God.

Finally, when God is said to be *unthinkable*[2], that applies to the thought that grasps him adequately, and does not hold good of that inadequate thought which we possess and which suffices to let us know that he exists. It likewise does not matter though *the idea of the unity of all God's perfections is formed in the same way as 'Porphyrian*[3]*' universals.* Though there is this important difference, that it designates a peculiar and positive perfection in God, while generic unity adds nothing real to the nature of the single individuals it unites.

Thirdly, when I said that *we could know nothing with certainty unless we were first aware that God existed*, I announced in express terms that I referred only to the science apprehending such conclusions *as can recur in memory without attending further to the proofs which led me to make them*[4]. Further, knowledge of first principles is not usually called science by dialecticians. But when we become aware that we are thinking beings, this is a primitive act of knowledge derived from no syllogistic reasoning. He who says, '*I think, hence I am, or exist,*' does not deduce existence from thought by a syllogism, but, by a simple act of mental vision, recognises it as if it were a thing that is known *per se*. This is evident from the fact that if it were syllogistically deduced, the major premise, *that everything that thinks is, or exists,* would have to be known previously; but yet that has rather been learned from the experience of the individual—that unless he exists he cannot think. For our mind is so constituted by nature that general propositions are formed out of the knowledge of particulars.

---

[1] Cf. p. 26, par. 1, sub fin.   [2] inconcevable, F. V.
[3] E.g. generic unity, cf. Obj. II. loc. cit.   [4] Cf. Med. v. Vol. I. pp. 183, 184.

That *an atheist can know clearly that the three angles of a triangle are equal to two right angles,* I do not deny, I merely affirm that, on the other hand, such knowledge on his part cannot constitute true science, because no knowledge that can be rendered doubtful should be called science. Since he is, as supposed, an Atheist, he cannot be sure that he is not deceived in the things that seem most evident to him, as has been sufficiently shown ; and though perchance the doubt does not occur to him, nevertheless it may come up, if he examine the matter, or if another suggests it ; he can never be safe from it unless he first recognises the existence of a God.

And it does not matter though he think he has demonstrations proving that there is no God. Since they are by no means true, the errors in them can always be pointed out to him, and when this takes place he will be driven from his opinion.

This would certainly not be difficult to do, if to represent all his proofs he were to bring into play only that principle you here append, viz. *that what is infinite in every kind of perfection excludes every other entity whatsoever, etc.* [1]. For, in the first place, if he is asked whence comes his knowledge that that exclusion of all other entities is a characteristic of the infinite, there is nothing he can reasonably say in reply ; for by the word *infinite* neither is he wont to understand that which excludes the existence of finite things, nor can he know anything of the characteristic[2] of that which he deems to be nothing, and to have hence no characteristics at all, except what is contained merely in the meaning he has learned from others to attach to the word. Next, what could be the power of this imaginary infinite if it could never create anything ? Finally, because we are aware of some power of thinking within us, we easily conceive that the power of thinking can reside in some other being, and that it is greater than in us. But though we think of it as increased to infinity, we do not on that account fear that the power we have should become less. And the same holds good of all the other attributes we ascribe to God, even that of His might[3], provided that we assume that no such power exists in us except as subject to the Divine will. Hence evidently He can be known as infinite without any prejudice to the existence of created things.

Fourthly[4], *in denying that God lies, or is a deceiver,* I fancy

---

[1] Cf. Obj. ii. p. 27, ad init.   [2] naturam.
[3] His power of producing effects external to himself, F. V.
[4] Cf. Obj. p. 27.

that I am in agreement with all metaphysicians and theologians past and future. What you allege to the contrary refutes my position no more than, if I denied that anger existed in God, or that He was subject to other passions, you should bring forward in objection passages in Scripture where human attributes are ascribed to Him. Everyone knows the distinction between those modes of speaking of God that are suited to the vulgar understanding and do indeed contain some truth, a truth, however, relative to the human point of view,—modes of speaking which Holy Writ usually employs,—and those other expressions that give us the more bare and rigorous truth, though not that accommodated to the human mind. It is these latter that everyone should employ in philosophy, and it was my duty to use them specially in my Meditations, since not even there did I assume that there were as yet any men known to me, neither did I consider myself as consisting of mind and body, but as mind only. Hence, it is clear that I did not then speak of the lie that is expressed in words, but only of the internal formal ill-will which is contained in deception.

Therefore, though the words of the Prophet you bring forward '*Yet forty days and Nineveh shall be destroyed,*' did not constitute even a verbal lie but only a threat, the fulfilment of which depended on a condition; and again though when it is said that '*God hardened Pharaoh's heart,*' or something to the same effect, it must not be thought that this was a positive act, but only a negative one, viz. in not granting Pharaoh the grace necessary to make him repent; I should be loath to censure those who say that God can utter verbal deceptions through His prophets (deceptions which, like those that doctors use for the benefit of their patients, are lies in which there is no evil intention).

Nay, over and above this, there is the fact that sometimes we are really misled by the very natural instinct which God has given us, as in the case of the thirst of the dropsical patient. A man is moved to drink by a natural disposition[1] that is given him by God in order to preserve his body; but one afflicted with dropsy is deceived by this natural disposition, for drink is hurtful to him. But how this is compatible with the benevolence and truthfulness of God, I have explained in the sixth Meditation.

In cases, however, that cannot be thus explained, viz. in the case of our clearest and most accurate judgments which, if false,

---

[1] a natura.

could not be corrected by any that are clearer, or by any other natural faculty, I clearly affirm that we cannot be deceived. For, since God is the highest being He cannot be otherwise than the highest good and highest truth, and hence it is contradictory that anything should proceed from Him that positively tends towards falsity. But yet since there is nothing real in us that is not given by God (as was proved along with His existence) and we have, as well, a real faculty of recognising truth, and distinguishing it from falsehood (as the mere existence in us of true and false ideas makes manifest), unless this faculty tended towards truth, at least when properly employed (i.e. when we give assent to none but clear and distinct perceptions, for no other correct use of this faculty can be imagined), God, who has given it to us, must justly be held to be a deceiver.

Thus you see that, after becoming aware of the existence of God, it is incumbent on us to imagine that he is a deceiver if we wish to cast doubt upon our clear and distinct perceptions; and since we cannot imagine that he is a deceiver, we must admit them all as true and certain.

But since I here perceive that you are still entangled in the difficulties which I brought forward in the first Meditation, and which I thought I had in the succeeding Meditations removed with sufficient care, I shall here a second time expound what seems to me the only basis on which human certitude can rest.

To begin with, directly we think that we rightly perceive something[1], we spontaneously persuade ourselves that it is true. Further, if this conviction is so strong that we have no reason to doubt concerning that of the truth of which we have persuaded ourselves, there is nothing more to enquire about; we have here all the certainty that can reasonably be desired. What is it to us, though perchance some one feigns that that, of the truth of which we are so firmly persuaded, appears false to God or to an Angel, and hence is, absolutely speaking, false? What heed do we pay to that absolute falsity, when we by no means believe that it exists or even suspect its existence? We have assumed a conviction so strong that nothing can remove it, and this persuasion is clearly the same as perfect certitude.

But it may be doubted whether there is any such certitude, whether such firm and immutable conviction exists.

---

[1] concevoir clairement quelque verité, F. V.

It is indeed clear that no one possesses such certainty in those cases where there is the very least confusion and obscurity in our perception; for this obscurity, of whatsoever sort it be, is sufficient to make us doubt here. In matters perceived by sense alone, however clearly, certainty does not exist, because we have often noted that error can occur in sensation, as in the instance of the thirst of the dropsical man, or when one who is jaundiced sees snow as yellow; for he sees it thus with no less clearness and distinctness than we see it as white. If, then, any certitude does exist, it remains that it must be found only in the clear perceptions of the intellect.

But of these there are some so evident and at the same time so simple, that in their case we never doubt about believing them true: e.g. that I, while I think, exist; that what is once done cannot be undone, and other similar truths, about which clearly we can possess this certainty. For we cannot doubt them unless we think of them; but we cannot think of them without at the same time believing them to be true, the position taken up[1]. Hence we can never doubt them without at the same time believing them to be true; i.e. we can never doubt them.

No difficulty is caused by the objection that *we have often found that others have been deceived in matters in which they believed they had knowledge as plain as daylight*[2]. For we have never noticed that this has occurred, nor could anyone find it to occur with these persons who have sought to draw the clearness of their vision from the intellect alone, but only with those who have made either the senses or some erroneous preconception the source from which they derived that evidence.

Again there is no difficulty though some one feign that the truth appear false to God or to an Angel, because the evidence of our perception does not allow us to pay any attention to such a fiction.

There are other matters that are indeed perceived very clearly by our intellect, when we attend sufficiently closely to the reasons on which our knowledge of them depends, and hence we cannot then be in doubt about them; but since we can forget those reasons, and yet remember the conclusions deduced from them, the question is raised whether we can entertain the same firm and immutable certainty as to these conclusions, during the time that we recollect that they have been deduced from first principles that are evident; for this remembrance must be assumed in order that they may be

---

[1] Ut assumptum est, L. V., comme je viens de dire, F. V.
[2] Cf. Obj. II. p. 27, par. 3.

called conclusions. My answer is that those possess it who, in virtue of their knowledge of God, are aware that the faculty of understanding given by Him must tend towards truth; but that this certainty is not shared by others. But the subject has been so clearly explained at the end of the fifth Meditation that there seems to be nothing to add here.

Fifthly, I marvel that you deny that *the will runs into danger if guided by a mental conception that lacks clearness and distinctness*[1]. For what can give it certainty, if what guides it has not been clearly perceived? And whoever, whether philosopher, theologian or merely man employing reason, fails to admit that there is the less risk of error in our actions in proportion to the greater clearness with which we understand anything before giving our assent to it; while error occurs with those who pass judgment in ignorance of its grounds? Moreover no concept is said to be obscure or confused, except for the reason that it contains something of which we are in ignorance.

Consequently your objection about *the faith one should embrace*[1] affects me no more than it does any others who have at any time cultivated the human power of reason; and in truth it has no force against anyone. For although the things are dark of which our faith is said to treat, yet the grounds on which we embrace it are not obscure, but clearer than any natural light. Nay, we must distinguish between the matter or fact to which we assent, and the formal reason that constrains our will to assent to that. For it is in this reason alone that we require clearness. And as to the matter, no one has ever denied that it may be obscure, indeed obscurity itself; for when I affirm that our concepts must be divested of obscurity in order that we may give credence to them without any danger of going astray, it is concerning this very obscurity that I form a clear judgment. Further it should be noted that the clearness or evidence by which our will can be constrained to assent, is twofold, one sort proceeding from our natural light, the other from divine grace. But though the matters be obscure with which our faith is said to deal, nevertheless this is understood to hold only of the fact or matter of which it treats, and it is not meant that the formal reason on account of which we assent to matters of faith is obscure; for, on the other hand, this formal reason consists in a certain internal light, and it is when God supernaturally fills us with this illumination that we are confident that what is proposed for our belief has been revealed by Him, Himself, and that it is

[1] Cf. Obj. II. p. 28.

clearly impossible that He should lie: a fact more certain than any natural light and often indeed more evident than it on account of the light of grace.

But certainly the sin that Turks and other infidels commit in not embracing the Christian religion is not due to their refusal to assent to obscure doctrines as being obscure, but arises either because they strive against the divine grace that moves them internally, or because by other sins they make themselves unworthy of grace. I boldly affirm that an infidel who, destitute of all supernatural grace, and plainly ignoring all that we Christians believe to have been revealed by God, embraces the faith to him obscure, impelled thereto by certain fallacious reasonings, will not be a true believer, but will the rather commit a sin in not using his reason properly. I believe that no orthodox Theologian has ever had any other opinion than this, nor will those who read my works be able to imagine that I have not recognised this supernatural light, since in the fourth Meditation, in which I have investigated the cause of falsity, I expressly said that '*it inclines our inmost thought to will without yet diminishing our liberty*[1].'

But I should like you to remember here that, in matters that may be embraced by the will, I made a very strict distinction between the practical life and the contemplation of truth. For to the extent to which the practical life is involved, so far am I from thinking that assent must be given only to what is clearly seen, that on the contrary I believe that we need not always expect to find even probable truths there; rather it is often the case that we must choose one out of a number of alternatives about which we are quite ignorant, and cleave to this none the less firmly after we have decided for it, as long as no arguments hostile to it can be entertained, than if it had been selected for reasons of the highest evidence, as I have explained on p. 26 of my Discourse on Method[2]. But where only the contemplation of truth is involved, who has ever denied that assent must be refused when the matter is obscure and cannot be perceived with sufficient distinctness? But that this latter question alone is the subject of discussion in my Meditations is proved both by the very passages in debate, and by the fact that at the end of the first Meditation I made a statement in express terms to the following effect '*that I could not at this point yield too much to distrust, since my object was not action, but knowledge*[3].'

---

[1] Cf. Med. iv. Vol. i. p. 175.   [2] Cf. Discourse, Part iii. Vol. i. p. 96.
[3] Vol. i. p. 148, par. 2, sub fin.

Sixthly, at the point where you criticise the conclusion of a syllogism constructed by me, you yourselves seem to make a blunder in the form of the argument. In order to derive the conclusion you desire, you should have worded the major premise thus : *that which we clearly understand to belong to the nature of anything, can truthfully be asserted to belong to its nature*; and consequently nothing but an unprofitable tautology will be contained in it. But my major premise was as follows—*that which we clearly understand to belong to the nature of anything can truly be affirmed of that thing.* Thus, if to be an animal belongs to the nature of man it can be asserted that man is animal : if to have its three angles equal to two right angles belongs to the nature of the triangle, it can be asserted that the triangle has its three angles equal to two right angles : if existence belongs to the nature of God, it can be affirmed that God exists, etc. But my minor premise was *yet existence does belong to the nature of God.* Whence it is evident that the conclusion must be drawn as I drew it : *hence it can be truly affirmed of God that He exists*; but not as you wish : *hence we can truthfully affirm that existence belongs to the nature of God.*

Thus, in order to make use of the exception that you append, you should have denied the major and said : *that which we clearly understand to belong to the nature of anything, cannot on that account be ascribed to it, unless the nature of that thing be possible, or not contradictory.* But notice, kindly, how little value this exception has. By *possible* either you mean, as all commonly do, whatever does not disagree with human thought; and in this sense it is manifest that the nature of God, as I have described it, is possible, because I have assigned nothing to it that we did not clearly and distinctly perceive ought to belong to it, and consequently it cannot be in disagreement with our thought. Or surely you imagine some other kind of possibility, one proceeding from the object itself, but which, unless it agrees with the preceding variety can never be known by the human mind. But on this account it tells quite as much against everything else that man may know as against the nature or existence of God. For that which entitles us to deny that God's nature is possible though there is no impossibility on the part of its concept, (but on the contrary all the things included in that concept of the divine nature are so connected that there seems to be a contradiction[1] in saying that any one of them does not belong to

---

[1] ut implicare nobis videatur.

God), will permit us to deny that it is possible for the three angles of a triangle to be equal to two right angles, or that he, who actually thinks, exists. Much more right will there be to deny that anything we apprehend by our senses is true, and thus the whole of human knowledge will be overturned, though for no good reason.

To take the argument you compare with mine : *if there is no contradiction in God's existence, it is certain that He exists; but there is no contradiction; therefore,* etc., it is true materially though formally a sophism. For in the major premise the expression '*there is contradiction*' stands in relation to the concept of the cause by virtue of which God's existence is possible; but in the minor it applies merely to the concept of the divine nature and existence itself. As is evident; for if the major be denied the proof will have to go thus : *if God has not yet existed, His existence is a contradiction, because no sufficient cause for bringing Him into existence can be assigned : but,* as was assumed, *His existence is not contradictory, hence,* etc. If, on the other hand, the minor be denied, the proof must thus be stated : *that is not contradictory in the formal concept of which there is nothing involving contradiction; but in the formal concept of the divine existence or nature there is nothing involving contradiction; therefore,* etc. Now these two proofs are very diverse. For it is possible that in a certain thing nothing may be conceived that prevents the existence of that thing, though meanwhile on the side of the cause there is known to be something that opposes its coming into being.

But though we conceive God only inadequately, or, if you prefer to put it thus, *in an utterly inadequate manner*[1], this does not prevent its being certain that His nature is possible, or not contradictory; nor does it prevent our affirming truly that we have examined it with sufficient precision (i.e. with as much as is required in order to attain to this knowledge, and in order to know that necessary existence appertains to this same Divine nature). For all contradictoriness[2] or impossibility is constituted by our thought, which cannot join together ideas that disagree with each other; it cannot reside in anything external to the mind, because by the very fact that a thing is outside the mind it is clear that it is not contradictory, but is possible. Moreover, contradictoriness in our concepts arises merely from their obscurity and confusion; there can be none in the case of clear and distinct ideas. Hence it suffices us to under-

[1] Cf. Obj. ii. p. 29.
[2] Implicantia, a 'mot d'école' according to F. V.

stand clearly and distinctly those few things that we perceive about God, though they form a quite inadequate knowledge, and to note that among the other constituents of this idea, however inadequate it be, necessary existence is found, in order to be able to affirm that we have examined the nature of God with sufficient precision, and to maintain that it contains no contradiction.

Seventhly, in the synopsis of my Meditations[1] I stated the reason why I have said nothing about the immortality of the soul. That I have sufficiently proved its distinctness from any body, I have shown above. But I admit that I cannot refute your further contention, viz. that *the immortality of the soul does not follow from its distinctness from the body, because that does not prevent its being said that God in creating it has given the soul a nature such that its period of existence must terminate simultaneously with that of the corporeal life*[2]. For I do not presume so far as to attempt to settle by the power of human reason any of the questions that depend upon the free-will of God. Natural knowledge shows that the mind is different from the body, and that it is likewise a substance; but that the human body, in so far as it differs from other bodies, is constituted entirely by the configuration of its parts and other similar accidents, and finally that the death of the body depends wholly on some division or change of figure. But we know no argument or example such as to convince us that the death or the annihilation of a substance such as the mind is, should follow from so light a cause as is a change in figure, which is no more than a mode, and indeed not a mode of mind, but of body that is really distinct from mind. Nor indeed is there any argument or example calculated to convince us that any substance can perish. But this is sufficient to let us conclude that the mind, so far as it can be known by aid of a natural philosophy, is immortal.

But if the question, which asks whether human souls cease to exist at the same time as the bodies which God has united to them are destroyed, is one affecting the Divine power, it is for God alone to reply. And since He has revealed to us that this will not happen, there should be not even the slightest doubt remaining.

It remains for me to thank you for your courtesy and candour in deigning to bring to my notice not only the difficulties that have occurred to you, but also those that can be brought forward by Atheists and people of hostile intent. I see nothing in what you

[1] Cf. Vol. I p. 141, ll. 9 sqq.   [2] Cf. Obj. II. p. 29.

have brought forward of which I have not already in my Meditations given a solution and ruled out of court. (For those objections *about insects bred by the sun, about the natives of Canada, the people of Nineveh, the Turks, etc.,* cannot occur to those who follow the way I have pointed out, and abstract for a time from everything due to the senses, in order to pay heed to the dictates of the pure and un-corrupted reason, and consequently I thought that I had adequately barred them out.) But though this is so, I consider that these objections of yours will aid my purpose. For I scarce expect to have any readers who will care to attend so accurately to all that I have written as to bear in memory all that has gone before, when they have come to the end ; and those who do not do so will easily fall into certain perplexities, which they will either find to be satisfactorily explained in this reply of mine, or which will occasion them to examine into the truth still further.

Further, in the matter of the counsel you give me about *propounding my arguments in geometrical fashion, in order that the reader may perceive them as it were with a single glance*[1], it is worth while setting forth here the extent to which I have followed this method and that to which I intend in future to follow it. Now there are two things that I distinguish in the geometrical mode of writing, viz. the order and the method of proof.

The order consists merely in putting forward those things first that should be known without the aid of what comes subsequently, and arranging all other matters so that their proof depends solely on what precedes them. I certainly tried to follow this order as accurately as possible in my Meditations; and it was through keeping to this that I treated of the distinction between the mind and the body, not in the second Meditation, but finally in the sixth, and deliberately and consciously omitted much, because it required an explanation of much else besides.

Further, the method of proof is two-fold, one being analytic, the other synthetic.

Analysis shows the true way by which a thing was methodically discovered and derived, as it were effect from cause[2], so that, if the reader care to follow it and give sufficient attention to everything, he understands the matter no less perfectly and makes it as much his own as if he had himself discovered it. But it contains nothing to incite belief in an inattentive or hostile reader ; for if the very

Cf. Obj. II. sub fin.   [2] tanquam a priori.

least thing brought forward escapes his notice, the necessity of the conclusions is lost; and on many matters which, nevertheless, should be specially noted, it often scarcely touches, because they are clear to anyone who gives sufficient attention to them.

Synthesis contrariwise employs an opposite procedure, one in which the search goes as it were from effect to cause[1] (though often here the proof itself is from cause to effect to a greater extent than in the former case). It does indeed clearly demonstrate its conclusions, and it employs a long series of definitions, postulates, axioms, theorems and problems, so that if one of the conclusions that follow is denied, it may at once be shown to be contained in what has gone before. Thus the reader, however hostile and obstinate, is compelled to render his assent. Yet this method is not so satisfactory as the other and does not equally well content the eager learner, because it does not show the way in which the matter taught was discovered.

It was this synthesis alone that the ancient Geometers employed in their writings, not because they were wholly ignorant of the analytic method, but, in my opinion, because they set so high a value on it that they wished to keep it to themselves as an important secret.

But I have used in my Meditations only analysis, which is the best and truest method of teaching. On the other hand synthesis, doubtless the method you here ask me to use, though it very suitably finds a place after analysis in the domain of geometry, nevertheless cannot so conveniently be applied to these metaphysical matters we are discussing.

For there is this difference between the two cases, viz. that the primary notions that are the presuppositions of geometrical proofs harmonize with the use of our senses, and are readily granted by all. Hence, no difficulty is involved in this case, except in the proper deduction of the consequences. But this may be performed by people of all sorts, even by the inattentive, if only they remember what has gone before; and the minute subdivisions of propositions is designed for the purpose of rendering citation easy and thus making people recollect even against their will.

On the contrary, nothing in metaphysics causes more trouble than the making the perception of its primary notions clear and distinct. For, though in their own nature they are as intelligible as,

---

[1] tanquam a posteriori quaesitam.

or even more intelligible than those the geometricians study, yet being contradicted by the many preconceptions of our senses to which we have since our earliest years been accustomed, they cannot be perfectly apprehended except by those who give strenuous attention and study to them, and withdraw their minds as far as possible from matters corporeal. Hence if they alone were brought forward it would be easy for anyone with a zeal for contradiction to deny them.

This is why my writing took the form of Meditations rather than that of Philosophical Disputations or the theorems and problems of a geometer; so that hence I might by this very fact testify that I had no dealings except with those who will not shrink from joining me in giving the matter attentive care and meditation. For from the very fact that anyone girds himself up for an attack upon the truth, he makes himself less capable of perceiving the truth itself, since he withdraws his mind from the consideration of those reasons that tend to convince him of it, in order to discover others that have the opposite effect.

But[1] perhaps some one will here raise the objection, that, while indeed a man ought not to seek for hostile arguments when he knows that it is the truth that is set before him, yet, so long as this is in doubt, it is right that he should fully explore all the arguments on either side, in order to find out which are the stronger. According to this objection it is unfair of me to want to have the truth of my contentions admitted before they have been fully scrutinised, while prohibiting any consideration of those reasonings that oppose them.

This would certainly be a just criticism if any of the matters in which I desire attention and absence of hostility in my reader were capable of withdrawing him from the consideration of any others in which there was the least hope of finding greater truth than in mine. But consider that in what I bring forward you find the most extreme doubt about all matters, and that there is nothing I more strongly urge than that every single thing should be most carefully examined and that nothing should be admitted but what has been rendered so clear and distinct to our scrutiny that we cannot withhold our assent from it. Consider too that, on the other hand, there is nothing else from which I wish to divert the minds of my readers, save beliefs which they have never properly examined and which are derived from

---

[1] The French version here comes to an end, adding only a short paragraph of seven lines by way of formal conclusion.

no sound reasoning, but from the senses alone. Therefore I hardly think that anyone will believe that there is much risk in confining his attention to my statement of the case; the danger will be no more than that of turning his gaze away from it towards other things which in some measure conflict with it and only darken counsel (i.e. to the prejudices of the senses).

Hence, in the first place, I rightly require singular attention on the part of my readers and have specially selected the style of writing which I thought would best secure it and which, I am convinced, will bring my readers more profit than they would acquire if I had used the synthetic method, one which would have made them appear to have learned more than they really had. But besides this I deem it quite fair to ignore wholly and to despise as of no account the criticisms of those who refuse to accompany me in my Meditations and cling to their preconceived opinions.

But I know how difficult it will be, even for one who does attend and seriously attempt to discover the truth, to have before his mind the entire bulk of what is contained in my Meditations, and at the same time to have distinct knowledge of each part of the argument; and yet, in my opinion, one who is to reap the full benefit from my work must know it both as a whole and in detail. Consequently I append here something in the synthetic style that may I hope be somewhat to my readers' profit. I should, however, like them kindly to notice that I have not cared to include here so much as comes into my Meditations, for that would have caused me to be much more prolix than in the Meditations themselves, nor shall I explain in such accurate detail that which I do include; this is partly for brevity and partly to prevent anyone, believing that what is here written is sufficient, examining without adequate care the actual Meditations, a work from which, I am convinced, much more profit will be derived.

ARGUMENTS DEMONSTRATING THE EXISTENCE OF GOD AND THE DISTINCTION BETWEEN SOUL AND BODY, DRAWN UP IN GEOMETRICAL FASHION.

DEFINITIONS.

I. *Thought* is a word that covers everything that exists in us in such a way that we are immediately conscious of it. Thus all the operations of will, intellect, imagination, and of the senses are thoughts. But I have added *immediately*, for the purpose of excluding that which is a consequence of our thought; for example, voluntary movement, which, though indeed depending on thought as on a causal principle[1], is yet itself not thought.

II. *Idea* is a word by which I understand the form of any thought, that form by the immediate awareness of which I am conscious of that said thought; in such a way that, when understanding what I say, I can express nothing in words, without that very fact making it certain that I possess the idea of that which these words signify. And thus it is not only images depicted in the imagination that I call ideas; nay, to such images I here decidedly refuse the title of ideas, in so far as they are pictures in the corporeal imagination, i.e. in some part of the brain. They are ideas only in so far as they constitute the form of the mind itself that is directed towards[2] that part of the brain.

III. By the *objective reality of an idea* I mean that in respect of which the thing represented in the idea is an entity[3], in so far as that exists in the idea; and in the same way we can talk of

---

[1] cogitationem quidem pro principio habet. 'volonté pour son principe,' F. V., which is not so pointed.
[2] conversam in. [3] entitatem rei representatae per ideam.

objective perfection, objective device, etc. For whatever we perceive as being as it were in the objects of our ideas, exists in the ideas themselves objectively.

IV. To exist *formally* is the term applied where the same thing exists in the object of an idea in such a manner that the way in which it exists in the object is exactly like what we know of it when aware of it; it exists *eminently* when, though not indeed of identical quality, it is yet of such amount as to be able to fulfil the function of an exact counterpart.

V. Everything in which there resides immediately, as in a subject, or by means of which there exists anything that we perceive, i.e. any property, quality, or attribute, of which we have a real idea, is called a *Substance*; neither do we have any other idea of substance itself, precisely taken, than that it is a thing in which this something that we perceive or which is present objectively in some of our ideas, exists formally or eminently. For by means of our natural light we know that a real attribute cannot be an attribute of nothing.

VI. That substance in which thought immediately resides, I call *Mind*[1]. I use the term 'mind' here rather than 'spirit,' as 'spirit' is equivocal and is frequently applied to what is corporeal.

VII. That substance, which is the immediate subject of extension in space[2] and of the accidents that presuppose extension, e.g. figure, situation, movement in space etc., is called *Body*. But we must postpone till later on the inquiry as to whether it is one and the same substance or whether there are two diverse substances to which the names Mind and Body apply.

VIII. That substance which we understand to be supremely perfect and in which we conceive absolutely nothing involving defect or limitation of its perfection, is called *God*.

IX. When we say that any attribute[3] is contained in the nature or concept of anything, that is precisely the same as saying that it is true of that thing or can be affirmed of it.

X. Two substances are said to be really distinct, when each of them can exist apart from the other.

---

[1] The French cannot convey the distinction between Mens and Anima. Hence *esprit* has to do duty for both. F. V. simply points out the ambiguity of the term.

[2] extensionis localis.   [3] F. V. quid, L. V.

POSTULATES.

The *First* request I press upon my readers is a recognition of the weakness of the reasons on account of which they have hitherto trusted their senses, and the insecurity of all the judgments they have based upon them. I beg them to revolve this in their minds so long and so frequently that at length they will acquire the habit of no longer reposing too much trust in them. For I deem that this is necessary in order to attain to a perception of the certainty of metaphysical truths [not dependent on the senses].

Secondly, I ask them to make an object of study of their own mind and all the attributes attaching to it, of which they find they cannot doubt, notwithstanding it be supposed that whatever they have at any time derived from their senses is false; and I beg them not to desist from attending to it, until they have acquired the habit of perceiving it distinctly and of believing that it can be more readily known than any corporeal thing.

Thirdly, I bid them carefully rehearse those propositions, intelligible *per se*, which they find they possess, e.g. *that the same thing cannot at the same time both be and not be; that nothing cannot be the efficient cause of anything*, and so forth; and thus employ in its purity, and in freedom from the interference of the senses, that clarity of understanding that nature has implanted in them, but which sensuous objects are wont to disturb and obscure. For by this means the truth of the following Axioms will easily become evident to them.

Fourthly, I postulate an examination of the ideas of those natures in which there is a complex of many coexistent attributes, such as e.g. the nature of the triangle or of the square, or of any other figure; and so too the nature of Mind, the nature of Body, and above all the nature of God, or of a supremely perfect entity. My readers must also notice that everything which we perceive to be contained in these natures can be truly predicated of the things themselves. For example, because the equality of its three angles to two right angles is contained in the idea of the Triangle, and divisibility is contained in the nature of Body or of extended thing (for we can conceive nothing that is extended as being so small as not to be capable of being divided in thought at least), we constantly assert that in every Triangle the angles are equal to two right angles, and that every Body is divisible.

Fifthly, I require my readers to dwell long and much in contemplation of the nature of the supremely perfect Being. Among other things they must reflect that while possible existence indeed attaches to the ideas of all other natures, in the case of the idea of God that existence is not possible but wholly necessary. For from this alone and without any train of reasoning they will learn that God exists, and it will be not less self evident to them than the fact that number two is even and number three odd, and similar truths. For there are certain truths evident to some people, without proof, that can be made intelligible to others only by a train of reasoning.

Sixthly, I ask people to go carefully over all the examples of clear and distinct perception, and likewise those that illustrate that which is obscure and confused, mentioned in my Meditations, and so accustom themselves to distinguish what is clearly known from what is obscure. For examples teach us better than rules how to do this; and I think that I have there either explained or at least to some extent touched upon all the instances of this subject.

Seventhly and finally, I require them, in virtue of their consciousness that falsity has never been found in matters of clear perception, while, on the contrary, amidst what is only obscurely comprehended they have never come upon the truth, except accidentally, to consider it wholly irrational to regard as doubtful matters that are perceived clearly and distinctly by the understanding in its purity, on account of mere prejudices of the senses and hypotheses in which there is an element of the unknown. By doing so they will readily admit the truth and certainty of the following axioms. Yet I admit that several of them might have been much better explained and should have been brought forward as theorems if I had wished to be more exact.

Axioms or Common Principles[1].

I. Nothing exists concerning which the question may not be raised—'what is the cause of its existence?' For this question may be asked even concerning God. Not that He requires any cause in order to exist, but because in the very immensity of His being[2] lies the cause or reason why He needs no cause in order to exist.

---

[1] notiones. [2] naturae.

II. The present time has no causal dependence on the time immediately preceding it. Hence, in order to secure the continued existence[1] of a thing, no less a cause is required than that needed to produce it at the first.

III. A thing, and likewise an actually existing perfection belonging to anything, can never have *nothing*, or a non-existent thing, as the cause of its existence.

IV. Whatever reality or perfection exists in a thing, exists formally or else eminently in its first and adequate[2] cause.

V. Whence it follows also that the objective reality of our ideas requires a cause in which the same reality is contained not indeed objectively, but formally or else eminently. We have to note that the admission of this axiom is highly necessary for the reason that we must account for our knowledge of all things, both of sensuous and of non-sensuous objects, and do so by means of it alone. For whence, e.g., comes our knowledge that there is a heaven? Because we behold it? But that vision does not reach the mind, except in so far as it is an idea, an idea, I say, inhering in the mind itself, and not an image depicted in the phantasy. But neither can we, in virtue of this idea, assert that there is a heaven, except because every idea needs to have some really existing cause of its objective reality; and this cause we judge to be the heaven itself, and so in other cases.

VI. There are diverse degrees of reality or (the quality of being an) entity. For substance has more reality than accident or mode; and infinite substance has more than finite substance. Hence there is more objective reality in the idea of substance than in that of accident; more in the idea of an infinite than in that of a finite substance.

VII. The will of a thinking being is borne, willingly indeed and freely (for that is of the essence of will), but none the less infallibly, towards the good that it clearly knows. Hence, if it knows certain perfections that it lacks, it will immediately give them to itself if they are in its power [for it will know that it is a greater good for it to possess them, than not to possess them].

VIII. That which can effect what is greater or more difficult, can also accomplish what is less.

---

[1] ad rem conservandam.　　　　[2] totale, F. V.

IX. It is a greater thing to create or conserve substance than the attributes or properties of substance; it is not, moreover, a greater thing to create that than to conserve its existence, as I have already said.

X. Existence is contained in the idea or concept of everything, because we can conceive nothing except as existent[1], with this difference, that possible or contingent existence is contained in the concept of a limited thing, but necessary and perfect existence in the concept of a supremely perfect being.

PROPOSITION I.

THE KNOWLEDGE OF THE EXISTENCE OF GOD PROCEEDS FROM THE MERE CONSIDERATION OF HIS NATURE.

Demonstration.

To say that something[2] is contained in the nature or concept of anything is the same as to say that it is true of that thing (Def. IX). But necessary existence is contained in the concept of God (Ax. X). Hence it is true to affirm of God that necessary existence exists in Him, or that God Himself exists.

And this is the syllogism of which I made use above, in replying to the sixth objection[3]. Its conclusion is self-evident to those who are free from prejudices, as was said in the fifth postulate. But, because it is not easy to arrive at such clearness of mind, we seek to establish it by other methods.

PROPOSITION II.

A POSTERIORI[4] DEMONSTRATION OF GOD'S EXISTENCE FROM THE MERE FACT THAT THE IDEA OF GOD EXISTS IN US.

Demonstration.

The objective reality of any of our ideas must have a cause, in which the very same reality is contained, not merely objectively but formally, or else eminently (Ax. V). But we do possess the idea of God (Deff. II and VIII), and the objective reality of this idea is contained in us neither formally nor eminently (Ax. VI), nor can it be contained in anything other than God Himself (Def. VIII). Hence this idea of God, which exists in us, must have God as its cause, and hence God exists (Ax. III).

---

[1] nisi sub ratione existentis.
[2] quelque attribut, F. V.
[3] Cf. supra, p. 45.
[4] par ses effets, F. V.

PROPOSITION III.

THE EXISTENCE OF GOD IS PROVED BY THE FACT THAT WE, WHO
POSSESS THIS IDEA, OURSELVES EXIST.

Demonstration.

If I had the power of conserving my own existence, I should
have had a proportionately greater power of giving myself the
perfections that I lack (Axx. VIII and IX); for they are only
attributes of substance, whereas I am a substance. But I do not
have the power of giving myself these perfections; otherwise I should
already possess them (Ax. VII). Therefore I do not have the power
of conserving myself.

Further, I cannot exist without being conserved, whilst I exist,
either by myself, if I have that power, or by some other one who
has that power (Axx. I and II); yet, though I do exist, I have not
the power of conserving myself, as has just been proved. Consequently it is another being that conserves my existence.

Besides, He to whom my conservation is due contains within
Himself formally or eminently everything that is in me (Ax. IV).
But there exists in me the perception of many perfections that I do-
not possess, as well as of the idea of God (Deff. II and VIII).
Therefore the perception of the same perfections exists in Him by
whom I am conserved.

Finally this same Being cannot possess the perception of any
perfections of which He is lacking, or which He does not possess-
within Himself either formally or eminently (Ax. VII). For, since
He has the power of conserving me, as has been already said, He
would have the power of bestowing these upon Himself, if He lacked
them (Axx. VIII and IX). But He possesses the perception of all
those that I lack, and which I conceive can exist in God alone, as
has been lately proved. Therefore He possesses those formally or
eminently within Himself, and hence is God.

COROLLARY.

GOD HAS CREATED THE HEAVEN AND THE EARTH AND ALL THAT
IN THEM IS. MOREOVER HE CAN BRING TO PASS WHATEVER
WE CLEARLY CONCEIVE, EXACTLY AS WE CONCEIVE IT.

Demonstration.

This all follows clearly from the previous proposition. For in it
we prove that God exists, from the fact that some one must exist in
whom are formally or eminently all the perfections of which we

have any idea. But we possess the idea of a power so great that by Him and Him alone, in whom this power is found, must heaven and earth be created, and a power such that likewise whatever else is apprehended by me as possible must be created by Him too. Hence concurrently with God's existence we have proved all this likewise about him.

PROPOSITION IV.

THERE IS A REAL DISTINCTION BETWEEN MIND AND BODY.

Demonstration.

God can effect whatever we clearly perceive just as we perceive it (preceding Corollary). But we clearly perceive the mind, i.e. a thinking substance, apart from the body, i.e. apart from any extended substance (Post. II); and *vice versa* we can (as all admit) perceive body apart from mind. Hence, at least through the instrumentality of the Divine power, mind can exist apart from body, and body apart from mind.

But now, substances that can exist apart from each other, are really distinct (Def. X). But mind and body are substances (Deff. V, VI and VII), that can exist apart from each other (just proved). Hence there is a real distinction between mind and body.

Here it must be noted that I employed the Divine power as a means[1], not because any extraordinary power was needed to effect the separation of mind and body, but because, treating as I did of God alone in what precedes, there was nothing else for me to use[1]. But our knowledge of the real distinctness of two things is unaffected by any question as to the power that disunites them.

---

[1] As a means for proving my point, F. V.

THE THIRD SET OF OBJECTIONS[1]
WITH THE AUTHOR'S REPLY.

FIRST OBJECTION.

(In reference to Meditation I, *Concerning those matters that may be brought within the sphere of the doubtful.*)[2]

It is sufficiently obvious from what is said in this Meditation, that we have no criterion[3] for distinguishing dreaming from waking and from what the senses truly tell us; and that hence the images present to us when we are awake and using our senses are not accidents inhering in external objects, and fail to prove that such external objects do as a fact exist. And therefore, if we follow our senses without using any train of reasoning, we shall be justified in doubting whether or not anything exists. Hence we acknowledge the truth of this Meditation. But, since Plato and other ancient Philosophers have talked about this want of certitude in the matters of sense, and since the difficulty in distinguishing the waking state from dreams is a matter of common observation, I should have been glad if our author, so distinguished in the handling of modern speculations, had refrained from publishing those matters of ancient lore.

REPLY.

The reasons for doubt here admitted as true by this Philosopher were propounded by me only as possessing verisimilitude, and my reason for employing them was not that I might retail them as new, but partly that I might prepare my readers' minds for the study of intellectual matters and for distinguishing them from matters corporeal, a purpose for which such arguments seem wholly necessary; in part also because I intended to reply to these very

---

[1] F. V. adds ' urged by a Celebrated English Philosopher,' i.e. Hobbes.

[2] What I have here enclosed within brackets is a marginal title in both the Latin and the French text of the standard French edition.

[3] L. V. uses the Greek word κριτήριον.

arguments in the subsequent Meditations; and partly in order to show the strength of the truths I afterwards propound, by the fact that such metaphysical doubts cannot shake them. Hence, while I have sought no praise from their rehearsal, I believe that it was impossible for me to omit them, as impossible as it would be for a medical writer to omit the description of a disease when trying to teach the method of curing it.

OBJECTION II.

(In opposition to the Second Meditation, *Concerning the nature of the Human Mind.*)

I am a thing that thinks; *quite correct.* *From the fact that I think, or have an image*[1], *whether sleeping or waking, it is inferred that I am exercising thought*[2]; *for* I think and I am exercising thought *mean the same thing.* *From the fact that I am exercising thought it follows that* I am, *since that which thinks is not nothing.* *But, where it is added,* this is the mind, the spirit, the understanding, the reason, *a doubt arises.* *For it does not seem to be good reasoning to say,* I am exercising thought, *hence* I am thought; *or* I am using my intellect, *hence* I am intellect. *For in the same way I might say,* I am walking; *hence* I am the walking[3]. *It is hence an assumption on the part of M. Descartes that that which understands is the same as the exercise of understanding*[4] *which is an act of that which understands, or, at least, that that which understands is the same as the understanding, which is a power possessed by that which thinks.* *Yet all Philosophers distinguish a subject from its faculties and activities, i.e. from its properties and essences; for the* entity *itself is one thing, its* essence *another.* *Hence it is possible for a thing that thinks to be the subject of the mind, reason, or understanding, and hence to be something corporeal; and the opposite of this has been assumed, not proved.* *Yet this inference is the basis of the conclusion that M. Descartes seems to wish to establish.*

In the same place he says, I know that I exist; the question is, who am I—the being that I know? It is certain that the knowledge of this being thus accurately determined does not depend on those things which I do not yet know to exist[5].

---

[1] phantasma, L. V. une idée, F. V.   [2] quod sum cogitans.
[3] sum ambulans, *ergo* sum ambulatio.   [4] intellectionem.
[5] Cf. Med. II. vol. I. p. 152.

*It is quite certain that the knowledge of this proposition, I exist,
depends upon that other one, I think, as he has himself correctly
shown us. But whence comes our knowledge of this proposition,
I think? Certainly from that fact alone, that we can conceive no
activity whatsoever apart from its subject, e.g. we cannot think of
leaping[1] apart from that which leaps, of knowing apart from a
knower, or of thinking without a thinker.*

*And hence it seems to follow that that which thinks is something
corporeal; for, as it appears, the subjects of all activities can be
conceived only after a corporeal fashion, or as in material guise,
as M. Descartes himself afterwards shows, when he illustrates by
means of wax[2], this wax was understood to be always the same thing,
i.e. the identical matter underlying the many successive changes,
though its colour, consistency, figure and other activities were
altered. Moreover it is not by another thought that I infer that
I think; for though anyone may think that he has thought (to think
so is precisely the same as remembering), yet we cannot think that
we are thinking, nor similarly know that we know. For this would
entail the repetition of the question an infinite number of times;
whence do you know, that you know, that you know, that you know?*

*Hence, since the knowledge of this proposition, I exist, depends
upon the knowledge of that other, I think, and the knowledge of it
upon the fact that we cannot separate thought from a matter that
thinks, the proper inference seems to be that that which thinks is
material rather than immaterial.*

Reply.

Where I have said, *this is the mind, the spirit, the intellect, or
the reason,* I understood by these names not merely faculties,
but rather what is endowed with the faculty of thinking, and this
sense the two former terms commonly, the latter frequently bear.
But I used them in this sense so expressly and in so many places
that I cannot see what occasion there was for any doubt about their
meaning.

Further, there is here no parity between walking[3] and thinking;
for walking is usually held to refer only to that action itself, while
thinking[4] applies now to the action, now to the faculty of thinking,
and again to that in which the faculty exists.

---

[1] walking, in F. V., cf. Reply also.   [2] Cf. vol. I. p. 154.
[3] ambulatio.   [4] cogitatio.

Again I do not assert that that which understands and the activity of understanding are the same thing, nor indeed do I mean that the thing that understands and the understanding are the same, if the term understanding be taken to refer to the faculty of understanding; they are identical only when the understanding means the thing itself that understands. I admit also quite gladly that, in order to designate that thing or substance, which I wished to strip of everything that did not belong to it, I employed the most highly abstract terms I could; just as, on the contrary this Philosopher uses terms that are as concrete as possible, e.g. *subject, matter, body,* to signify that which thinks, fearing to let it be sundered from the body.

But I have no fear of anyone thinking that his method of coupling diverse things together is better adapted to the discovery of the truth than mine, that gives the greatest possible distinctness to every single thing. But, dropping the verbal controversy, let us look to the facts in dispute.

A thing that thinks, he says, *may be something corporeal; and the opposite of this has been assumed; not proved.* But really I did not assume the opposite, neither did I use it as a basis for my argument; I left it wholly undetermined until Meditation VI, in which its proof is given.

Next he quite correctly says, that *we cannot conceive any activity apart from its subject,* e.g. thought apart from that which thinks, since that which thinks is not nothing. But, wholly without any reason, and in opposition to the ordinary use of language and good Logic, he adds, *hence it seems to follow that that which thinks is something corporeal;* for *the subjects*[1] *of all activities are* indeed *understood as falling within the sphere of substance* (or even, if you care, *as wearing the guise of matter,* viz. metaphysical matter), but not on that account are they to be defined as bodies.

On the other hand both logicians and as a rule all men are wont to say that substances are of two kinds, spiritual and corporeal. And all that I proved, when I took wax as an example, was that its colour, hardness, and figure did not belong to the formal nature[2] of the wax itself [i.e. that we can comprehend everything that exists necessarily in the wax, without thinking of these]. I did not there treat either of the formal nature[3] of the mind, or even of the formal nature of body.

---

[1] L. V. italicizes too many of the words in the rest of the sentence; F. V. none at all. I have effected a compromise.

[2] rationem. [3] ratione.

Again it is irrelevant to say, as this Philosopher here does, that one thought cannot be the subject of another thought. Who, except my antagonist himself, ever imagined that it could? But now, for a brief explanation of the matter,—it is certain that no thought can exist apart from a thing that thinks; no activity, no accident can be without a substance in which to exist. Moreover, since we do not apprehend the substance itself immediately through itself, but by means only of the fact that it is the subject of certain activities, it is highly rational, and a requirement forced on us by custom, to give diverse names to those substances that we recognize to be the subjects of clearly diverse activities or accidents, and afterwards to inquire whether those diverse names refer to one and the same or to diverse things. But there are *certain* activities[1], which we call *corporeal*, e.g. magnitude, figure, motion, and all those that cannot be thought of apart from extension in space[2]; and the substance in which they exist is called *body*. It cannot be pretended that the substance that is the subject of figure is different from that which is the subject of spatial motion, etc., since all these activities agree in presupposing extension[3]. Further, there are other activities, which we call *thinking*[4] activities, e.g. understanding, willing, imagining, feeling, etc., which agree in falling under the description of thought, perception, or consciousness. The substance in which they reside we call a *thinking thing* or *the mind*, or any other name we care, provided only we do not confound it with corporeal substance, since thinking activities have no affinity with corporeal activities, and thought, which is the common nature[5] in which the former agree, is totally different from extension, the common term[5] for describing the latter.

But after we have formed two distinct concepts of those two substances, it is easy, from what has been said in the sixth Meditation, to determine whether they are one and the same or distinct.

OBJECTION III.

What[6] then is there distinct from my thought? What can be said to be separate from me myself?

Perchance some one will answer the question thus—I, the very self that thinks, am held to be distinct from my own thought; and, though it is not really separate from me, my thought is held to be

---

[1] actus.   [2] absque extensione locali.
[3] F. V. conveniunt sub una communi ratione extensionis, L. V.
[4] cogitativos.   [5] ratio communis.
[6] Quotation from Med. II. vol. I. p. 153, par. 3.

diverse from me, just in the way (as has been said before) that leaping[1] is distinguished from the leaper. But if M. Descartes shows that he who understands and the understanding are identical we shall lapse back into the scholastic mode of speaking. The understanding understands, the vision sees, will wills, and by exact analogy, walking, or at least the faculty of walking will walk. Now all this is obscure, incorrect, and quite unworthy of M. Descartes' wonted clearness.

Reply.

I do not deny that I, the thinker, am distinct from my own thought, in the way in which a thing is distinct from its mode. But when I ask, *what then is there distinct from my thought*, this is to be taken to refer to the various modes of thought there recounted, not to my substance; and when I add, *what can be said to be separate from me myself*, I mean only that these modes of thinking exist entirely in me. I cannot see on what pretext the imputation here of doubt and obscurity rests.

Objection IV.

Hence it is left for me to concede that I do not even understand by the imagination what this wax is, but conceive[2] it by the mind alone[3].

There is a great difference between imagining, i.e. having some idea, and conceiving with the mind, i.e. inferring, as the result of a train of reasoning, that something is, or exists. But M. Descartes has not explained to us the sense in which they differ. The ancient peripatetics also have taught clearly enough that substance is not perceived by the senses, but is known as a result of reasoning.

But what shall we now say, if reasoning chance to be nothing more than the uniting and stringing together of names or designations by the word is*? It will be a consequence of this that reason gives us no conclusion about the nature of things, but only about the terms that designate them, whether, indeed, or not there is a convention (arbitrarily made about their meanings) according to which we join these names together. If this be so, as is possible, reasoning will depend on names, names on the imagination, and imagination, perchance, as I think, on the motion of the corporeal organs. Thus mind will be nothing but the motions in certain parts of an organic body.*

---

[1] walking, F. V.   [2] concipere. In Med. II. it is *percipere.*
[3] Cf. Med. II. vol. I. p. 155, l. 11.

REPLY.

I have here explained the difference between imagination and a pure mental concept, as when in my illustration I enumerated the features in wax that were given by the imagination and those solely due to a conception of the mind. But elsewhere also I have explained how it is that one and the same thing, e.g. a pentagon, is in one way an object of the understanding, in another way of the imagination [for example how in order to imagine a pentagon a particular mental act is required which gives us this figure (i.e. its five sides and the space they enclose) which we dispense with wholly in our conception]. Moreover, in reasoning we unite not names but the things signified by the names; and I marvel that the opposite can occur to anyone. For who doubts whether a Frenchman and a German are able to reason in exactly the same way about the same things, though they yet conceive the words in an entirely diverse way? And has not my opponent condemned himself in talking of conventions arbitrarily made about the meanings of words? For, if he admits that words signify anything, why will he not allow our reasonings to refer to this something that is signified, rather than to the words alone? But, really, it will be as correct to infer that earth is heaven or anything else that is desired, as to conclude that mind is motion [for there are no other two things in the world between which there is not as much agreement as there is between motion and spirit, which are of two entirely different natures].

OBJECTION V.

In reference to the third Meditation—concerning God—some of these (thoughts of man) are, so to speak, images of things, and to these alone is the title 'idea' properly applied; examples are my thought of a man, or of a Chimera, of Heavens, of an Angel, or [even] of God[1].

When I think of a man, I recognize an idea, or image, with figure and colour as its constituents; and concerning this I can raise the question whether or not it is the likeness of a man. So it is also when I think of the heavens. When I think of the chimera, I recognize an idea or image, being able at the same time to doubt whether or not it is the likeness of an animal, which, though it does not exist, may yet exist or has at some other time existed.

---

[1] Cf. Med. III. vol. I. p. 159, par. 2.

But, when one thinks of an Angel, what is noticed in the mind is now the image of a flame, now that of a fair winged child, and this, I may be sure, has no likeness to an Angel, and hence is not the idea of an Angel. But believing[1] that created beings exist that are the ministers of God, invisible and immaterial, we give[1] the name of Angel to this object of belief, this supposed being, though the idea used in imagining an Angel is, nevertheless, constructed out of the ideas of visible things.

It is the same way with the most holy name of God; we have no image, no idea corresponding to it. Hence we are forbidden to worship God in the form of an image, lest we should think we could conceive Him who is inconceivable.

Hence it appears that we have no idea of God. But just as one born blind who has frequently been brought close to a fire and has felt himself growing warm, recognizes that there is something which made him warm, and, if he hears it called fire, concludes that fire exists, though he has no acquaintance with its shape or colour, and has no idea of fire nor image that he can discover in his mind; so[2] a man, recognizing that there must be some cause of his images and ideas, and another previous cause of this cause and so on continuously, is finally carried on to a conclusion, or to the supposition of some eternal cause, which, never having begun to be, can have no cause prior to it: and hence he necessarily concludes that something eternal exists. But nevertheless he has no idea that he can assert to be that of this eternal being, and he merely gives a name to the object of his faith or reasoning and calls it God.

Since now it is from this position, viz. that there is an idea of God in our soul, that M. Descartes proceeds to prove the theorem that God (an all-powerful, all-wise Being, the creator of the world) exists, he should have explained this idea of God better, and he should have deduced from it not only God's existence, but also the creation of the world.

REPLY.

Here the meaning assigned to the term idea is merely that of images depicted in the corporeal imagination[3]; and, that being agreed on, it is easy for my critic to prove that there is no proper idea of Angel or of God. But I have, everywhere, from time to time, and principally in this place, shown that I take the term idea to

---

[1] credens (sic)...imponimus.
[2] itaque (sic), L. V.   de mesme, F. V.   [3] phantasia.

stand for whatever the mind directly perceives; and so when I
will or when I fear, since at the same time I perceive that I will
and fear, that very volition and apprehension are ranked among my
ideas. I employed this term because it was the term currently used
by Philosophers for the forms of perception of the Divine mind,
though we can discover no imagery in God; besides I had no other
more suitable term. But I think I have sufficiently well explained
what the idea of God is for those who care to follow my meaning;
those who prefer to wrest my words from the sense I give them, I
can never satisfy. The objection that here follows, relative to the
creation of the world, is plainly irrelevant [for I proved that God
exists, before asking whether there is a world created by him, and
from the mere fact that God, i.e. a supremely perfect being exists,
it follows that if there be a world it must have been created by
him].

OBJECTION VI.

But other (*thoughts*) possess other forms as well. For example,
in willing, fearing, affirming, denying, though I always perceive
something as the subject of my thought, yet in my thought I
embrace something more than the similitude[1] of that thing; and,
of the thoughts of this kind, some are called volitions or affections,
and others judgments[2].

*When a man wills or fears, he has indeed an image of the thing
he fears or of the action he wills; but no explanation is given of what
is further embraced in the thought of him who wills or fears. If
indeed fearing be thinking, I fail to see how it can be anything other
than the thought of the thing feared. In what respect does the fear
produced by the onrush of a lion differ from the idea of the lion as it
rushes on us, together with its effect (produced by such an idea in the
heart), which impels the fearful man towards that animal motion we
call flight? Now this motion of flight is not thought; whence we are
left to infer that in fearing there is no thinking save that which
consists in the representation[3] of the thing feared. The same account
holds true of volition.*

*Further you do not have affirmation and negation without words
and names; consequently brute creatures cannot affirm or deny, not
even in thought, and hence are likewise unable to judge. Yet a man
and a beast may have similar thoughts. For, when we assert that*

---

[1] add to the idea, F. V.   [2] Cf. vol. I. p. 159, par. 2.
[3] similitudine translated 'idea' in previous note.

*a man runs, our thought does not differ from that which a dog has
when it sees its master running. Hence neither affirmation nor
negation add anything to the bare thought, unless that increment be
our thinking that the names of which the affirmation consists are the
names of the same thing in [the mind of] him who affirms. But this
does not mean that anything more is contained in our thought than
the representation of the thing, but merely that that representation is
there twice over.*

REPLY.

It is self-evident that seeing a lion and fearing it at the same
time is different from merely seeing it. So, too, it is one thing to
see a man running, another thing to affirm to oneself that one sees
it, an act that needs no language[1]. I can see nothing here that
needs an answer.

OBJECTION VII.

It remains for me to examine in what way I have received that
idea from God. I have neither derived it from the senses; nor has
it ever come to me contrary to my expectation[2], as the ideas of
sensible things are wont to do, when these very things present
themselves to the external organs of sense or seem to do so.
Neither also has it been constructed as a fictitious idea by me, for I
can take nothing from it and am quite unable to add to it. Hence
the conclusion is left that it is innate in me, just as the idea of my
own self is innate in me[3].

*If there is no idea of God (now it has not been proved that it
exists), as seems to be the case, the whole of this argument collapses.
Further (if it is my body that is being considered) the idea of my own
self proceeds [principally] from sight; but (if it is a question of the
soul) there is no idea of the soul. We only infer by means of the
reason that there is something internal in the human body, which
imparts to it its animal motion, and by means of which it feels and
moves; and this, whatever it be, we name the soul, without employing
any idea.*

REPLY.

If there is an idea of God (as it is manifest there is), the whole
of this objection collapses. When it is said further that we have no

---

[1] This clause does not appear in F. V.
[2] nec unquam expectanti mihi advenit, L.V., non omitted, A. and T. vol. VII.
p. 183.
[3] Cf. Med. II. vol. I. p. 170, par. 3.

idea of the soul but that we arrive at it by an inference of reason, that is the same as saying that there is no image of the soul depicted in the imagination, but that that which I have called its idea does, nevertheless, exist.

OBJECTION VIII.

But the other idea of the sun is derived from astronomical reasonings, i.e. is elicited from certain notions that are innate in me[1].

It seems that at one and the same time the idea of the sun must be single whether it is beheld by the eyes, or is given by our intelligence as many times larger than it appears. For this latter thought is not an idea of the sun, but an inference by argument that the idea of the sun would be many times larger if we viewed the sun from a much nearer distance.

But at different times the ideas of the sun may differ, e.g. when one looks at it with the naked eye and through a telescope. But astronomical reasonings do not increase or decrease the idea of the sun; rather they show that the sensible idea is misleading.

REPLY.

Here too what is said not to be an idea of the sun, but is, nevertheless, described, is exactly what I call an idea. [But as long as my critic refuses to come to terms with me about the meaning of words, none of his objections can be other than frivolous.]

OBJECTION IX.

For without doubt those ideas, which reveal substance to me, are something greater, and, so to speak, contain within them more objective reality than those which represent only modes or accidents. And again, that by means of which I apprehend a supreme God who is eternal, infinite, omniscient, all-powerful, and the creator of all else there is besides, assuredly possesses more objective reality than those ideas that reveal to us finite substances[2].

I have frequently remarked above that there is no idea either of God or of the soul; I now add that there is no idea of substance. For substance (the substance that is a material, subject to accidents

---

[1] Cf. Med. III. vol. I. p. 161, par. 3.
[2] *Ibid.* p. 162, par. 1.

and changes) is perceived[1] and demonstrated by the reason alone,
without yet being conceived by us, or furnishing us with any idea[2].
If that is true, how can it be maintained that the ideas which reveal
substance to me are anything greater or possess more objective reality
than those revealing accidents to us? Further I pray M. Descartes
to investigate the meaning of more reality. Does reality admit of
more and less? Or, if he thinks that one thing can be more a thing
than another, let him see how he is to explain it to our intelligence
with the clearness called for in demonstration, and such as he himself
has at other times employed.

REPLY.

I have frequently remarked that I give the name idea to that
with which reason makes us acquainted just as I also do to anything
else that is in any way perceived[3] by us. I have likewise explained
how reality admits of more and less: viz. in the way in which
substance is greater than mode; and if there be real qualities or
incomplete substances, they are things to a greater extent than
modes are, but less than complete substances. Finally, if there
be an infinite and independent substance, it is more a thing than
a substance that is finite and dependent. Now all this is quite
self-evident [and so needs no further explanation].

OBJECTION X.

Hence there remains alone the idea of God, concerning which
we must consider whether it is not something that is capable of
proceeding from me myself. By the name God I understand a
substance that is infinite [eternal, immutable], independent, all-
knowing, all-powerful, and by which both I myself and everything
else, if anything else does exist, have been created. Now all these
characteristics are such that, the more diligently I attend to them,
the less do they appear capable of proceeding from me alone; hence,
from what has been already said, we must conclude that God
necessarily exists[4].

When I consider the attributes of God, in order to gather thence
the idea of God, and see whether there is anything contained in it
that cannot proceed from ourselves, I find, unless I am mistaken,
that what we assign in thought to the name of God neither proceeds

---

[1] F. V. evincitur, L. V.   [2] without our having any idea of it, F. V.
[3] conceived, F. V.   [4] Cf. Med. III. vol. I. p. 165, par. 3.

from ourselves nor needs to come from any other source than external objects. For by the word God I mean a substance, i.e. I understand that God exists (not by means of an idea but by reasoning). This substance is infinite (i.e. I can neither conceive nor imagine its boundaries or extreme parts, without imagining further parts beyond them): whence it follows that corresponding to the term infinite there arises an idea not of the Divine infinity, but of my own bounds or limitations. It is also independent, i.e. I have no conception of a cause from which God originates; whence it is evident that I have no idea corresponding to the term independent, save the memory of my own ideas with their commencement at divers times and their consequent dependence.

Wherefore to say that God is independent, is merely to say that God is to be reckoned among the number of those things, of the origin of which we have no image. Similarly to say that God is infinite, is identical with saying that He is among those objects of the limits of which we have no conception. Thus any idea of God is ruled out; for what sort of idea is that which has neither origin nor termination?

Take the term all-knowing. *Here I ask: what idea does M. Descartes employ in apprehending the intellectual activity of God?*

All-powerful. So too, what is the idea by which we apprehend power, which is relative to that which lies in the future, i.e. does not exist? I certainly understand what power is by means of an image, or memory of past events, inferring it in this wise—Thus did He, hence thus was He able to do; therefore as long as the same agent exists He will be able to act so again, i.e. He has the power of acting. Now these are all ideas that can arise from external objects.

Creator of everything that exists. *Of creation some image can be constructed by me out of the objects I behold, e.g. the birth of a human being or its growth from something small as a point to the size and figure it now possesses. We have no other idea than this corresponding to the term creator. But in order to prove creation it is not enough to be able to imagine the creation of the world. Hence although it had been demonstrated that an* infinite, *inde-pendent, all-powerful, etc. being exists, nevertheless it does not follow that a creator exists. Unless anyone thinks that it is correct to infer, from the fact that there is a being which we believe to have created everything, that hence the world was at some time created by him.*

Further, when M. Descartes says that the idea of God and that of the soul are innate in us, I should like to know whether the minds of those who are in a profound and dreamless sleep yet think. If not, they have at that time no ideas. Whence no idea is innate, for what is innate is always present.

REPLY.

Nothing that we attribute to God can come from external objects as a copy proceeds from its exemplar, because in God there is nothing similar to what is found in external things, i.e. in corporeal objects. But whatever is unlike them in our thought [of God], must come manifestly not from them, but from the cause of that diversity existing in our thought [of God].

Further I ask how my critic derives the intellectual comprehension of God from external things. But I can easily explain the idea which I have of it, by saying that by idea I mean whatever is the form of any perception. For does anyone who understands something not perceive that he does so? and hence does he not possess that form or idea of mental action? It is by extending this indefinitely that we form the idea of the intellectual activity of God; similarly also with God's other attributes.

But, since we have employed the idea of God existing in us for the purpose of proving His existence, and such mighty power is comprised in this idea, that we comprehend that it would be contradictory, if God exists, for anything besides Him to exist, unless it were created by Him ; it clearly follows, from the fact that His existence has been demonstrated, that it has been also proved that the whole world, or whatever things other than God exist, have been created by Him.

Finally when I say that an idea is innate in us [or imprinted in our souls by nature], I do not mean that it is always present to us. This would make no idea innate. I mean merely that we possess the faculty of summoning up this idea.

OBJECTION XI.

The whole force o the argument lies in this—that I know I could not exist, and possess the nature I have, that nature which puts me in possession of the idea of God, unless God did really exist, the God, I repeat, the idea of whom is found in me[1].

Since, then, it has not been proved that we possess an idea of God, and the Christian religion obliges us to believe that God is

[1] Cf. Med. III. vol. I. pp. 170, 171.

inconceivable, which amounts, in my opinion, to saying that we have no idea of Him, it follows that no proof of His existence has been effected, much less of His work of creation.

REPLY.

When it is said that we cannot conceive God, to conceive means to comprehend adequately. For the rest, I am tired of repeating how it is that we can have an idea of God. There is nothing in these objections that invalidates my demonstrations.

OBJECTION XII.

(Directed against the fourth Meditation, *Concerning the true and the false.*)

And thus I am quite sure that error, in so far as it is error, is nothing real, but merely defect. Hence in order to go astray, it is not necessary for me to have a faculty specially assigned to me by God for this purpose[1].

It is true that ignorance is merely a defect, and that we stand in need of no special positive faculty in order to be ignorant; but about error the case is not so clear. For it appears that stones and inanimate things are unable to err solely because they have no faculty of reasoning, or imagining. Hence it is a very direct inference that, in order to err, a faculty of reasoning, or at least of imagination is required; now both of these are positive faculties with which all beings that err, and only beings that err, have been endowed.

Further, M. Descartes says—I perceive that they (*viz. my mistakes*) depend upon the cooperation of two causes, viz. my faculty of cognition, and my faculty of choice, or the freedom of my will[2]. *But this seems to be contradictory to what went before. And we must note here also that the freedom of the will has been assumed without proof, and in opposition to the opinion of the Calvinists.*

REPLY.

Although in order to err the faculty of reasoning (or rather of judging, or affirming and denying) is required, because error is a lack of this power it does not hence follow that this defect is anything real, just as it does not follow that blindness is anything real, although stones are not said to be blind merely because they

---

[1] Med. IV. vol. I. p. 173, l. 2.　　　　[2] Cf. Med. IV. vol. I. p. 174, l. 11.

are incapable of vision.   I marvel that in these objections I have as yet found nothing that is properly argued out.   Further I made no assumption concerning freedom which is not a matter of universal experience ;   our natural light makes this most evident and I cannot make out why it is said to be contradictory to previous statements.

But though there are many who, looking to the Divine fore-ordination, cannot conceive how that is compatible with liberty on our part, nevertheless no one, when he considers himself alone, fails to experience the fact that to will and to be free are the same thing [or rather that there is no difference between what is voluntary and what is free].   But this is no place for examining other people's[1] opinions about this matter.

OBJECTION XIII.

For example, whilst I, during these days, sought to discuss whether anything at all existed, and noted that, from the very fact that I raised this question, it was an evident consequence that I myself existed, I could not indeed refrain from judging that what I understood so clearly was true ; this was not owing to compulsion by some external force, but because the consequence of the great mental illumination was a strong inclination of the will, and I believed the above truth the more willingly and freely, the less indifferent I was towards it[2].

This term, great mental illumination, *is metaphorical, and consequently is not adapted to the purposes of argument.   Moreover everyone who is free from doubt claims to possess a similar illumina-tion, and in his will there is the same inclination to believe that of which he does not doubt, as in that of one who truly knows.   Hence while this illumination may be the cause that makes a man obstinately defend or hold some opinion, it is not the cause of his knowing it to be true.*

Further, not only to know a thing to be true, but also to believe it or give assent to it, have nothing to do with the will.   For, what is proved by valid argument or is recounted as credible, is believed by us whether we will or no.   It is true that affirming and denying, maintaining or refuting propositions, are acts of will; but it does not follow on that account that internal assent depends upon the will.

Therefore the demonstration of the truth that follows is not

---

[1] The Calvinists', F. V.   [2] Cf. Med. IV. vol. I. p. 176, par. 2.

adequate—and it is in this misuse of our free-will, that this privation consists that constitutes the form of error[1].

REPLY.

It does not at all matter whether or not the term *great illumination* is proper to argument, so long as it is serviceable for explanation, as in fact it is. For no one can be unaware that by mental illumination is meant clearness of cognition, which perhaps is not possessed by everyone who thinks he possesses it. But this does not prevent it from being very different from a bigoted opinion, to the formation of which there goes no perceptual evidence.

Moreover when it is here said that when a thing is clearly perceived[2] we give our assent whether we will or no, that is the same as saying that we desire what we clearly know to be good whether willing or unwilling ; for the word *unwilling* finds no entrance in such circumstances, implying as it does that we will and do not will the same thing.

OBJECTION XIV.

(To the fifth Meditation, *On the essence of material things*.)

As, for example, when I imagine a triangle, though perhaps such a figure does not exist at all outside my thought, or never has existed, it has nevertheless a determinate nature, or essence, or immutable and eternal form, which is not a fiction of my construction, and does not depend on my mind, as is evident from the fact that various properties of that triangle may be demonstrated[3].

If the triangle exists nowhere at all, I do not understand how it ᶜan have any nature ; for that which exists nowhere does not exist. Hence it has no existence or nature. The triangle[4] in the mind comes from the triangle[5] we have seen, or from one imaginatively constructed out of triangles we have beheld. Now when we have once called the thing (from which we think that the idea of triangle originates) by the name triangle, although the triangle itself perishes, yet the name remains. In the same way if, in our thought, we have once conceived that the angles of a triangle are together all equal to two right angles, and have given this other name to the triangle — possessed of three angles equal to two right angles—*although there*

---

[1] Vol. I. p. 177, l. 1.   [2] perspectis; conceived, F. V.
[3] Vol. I. p. 180, ll. 4 sqq.
[4] idea that the mind conceives of triangle, F. V.
[5] un autre triangle, F. V.

were no angle[1] *at all in existence, yet the name would remain; and the truth of this proposition will be of eternal duration*—a triangle is possessed of three angles equal to two right angles. *But the nature of the triangle will not be of eternal duration, if it should chance that triangle perished*[2].

In like manner the proposition, man is animal, *will be eternally true, because the names it employs are eternal, but if the human race were to perish there would no longer be a human nature.*

Whence it is evident that essence in so far as it is distinguished from existence is nothing else than a union of names by means of the verb is. *And thus essence without existence is a fiction of our mind. And it appears that as the image of a man in the mind is to the man so is essence to existence; or that the essence of Socrates bears to his existence the relation that this proposition*, Socrates is a man, *to this other*, Socrates is or exists. *Now the proposition*, Socrates is a man, *means, when Socrates does not exist, merely the connection of its terms; and* is, *or to be*, *has underlying it the image of the unity of a thing designated by two names.*

REPLY.

The distinction between essence and existence is known to all; and all that is here said about eternal names in place of concepts or ideas of an eternal truth, has been already satisfactorily refuted.

OBJECTION XV.

(Directed against the sixth Meditation—*Concerning the existence of material things.*)

For since God has evidently given me no faculty by which to know this (*whether or not our ideas proceed from bodies*[3]), but on the contrary has given me a strong propensity towards the belief that they do proceed from corporeal things, I fail to see how it could be made out that He is not a deceiver, if our ideas proceeded from some other source than corporeal things. Consequently corporeal objects must exist[4].

It is the common belief that no fault is committed by medical men who deceive sick people for their health's sake, nor by parents who mislead their children for their good; and that the evil in deception

---

[1] triangle, F. V.

[2] for if every triangle whatsoever perished, it also would cease to be, F. V.

[3] L. V., that God by himself or by the intermediation of some created thing more noble than body, conveys to us the ideas of bodies, F. V.

[4] Vol. I. p. 191, middle.

*lies not in the falsity of what is said, but in the bad intent of those
who practise it.* M. *Descartes must therefore look to this proposition,*
God can in no case deceive us, *taken universally, and see whether it
is true; for if it is not true, thus universally taken, the conclusion,*
hence corporeal things exist, *does not follow.*

REPLY.

For the security of my conclusion we do not need to assume
that we can never be deceived (for I have gladly admitted that we
are often deceived), but that we are not deceived when that error
of ours would argue an intention to deceive on the part of God, an
intention it is contradictory to impute to Him.   Once more this
is bad reasoning on my critic's part.

FINAL OBJECTION.

For now I perceive how great the difference is between the two
(i.e. between waking and dreaming) from the fact that our dreams
are never conjoined by our memory [with each other and] with the
whole of the rest of our life's action [as happens with the things
which occur in waking moments][1].

*I ask whether it is really the case that one, who dreams he doubts
whether he dreams or no, is unable to dream that his dream is
connected with the idea of a long series of past events.   If he can,
those things which to the dreamer appear to be the actions of his past
life may be regarded as true just as though he had been awake.
Besides, since, as M. Descartes himself asserts, all certitude and
truth in knowledge depend alone upon our knowing the true God,
either it will be impossible for an Atheist to infer from the memory of
his previous life that he wakes, or it will be possible for a man to
know that he is awake, apart from knowledge of the true God.*

REPLY.

One who dreams cannot effect a real connection between what
he dreams and the ideas of past events, though he can dream that
he does connect them.   For who denies that in his sleep a man
may be deceived? But yet when he has awakened he will easily
detect his error.

But an Atheist is able to infer from the memory of his past life
that he is awake; still he cannot know that this sign is sufficient to
give him the certainty that he is not in error, unless he knows that
it has been created by a God who does not deceive.

[1] Vol. I. p. 199, ll. 2 sqq.

FOURTH SET OF OBJECTIONS[1].

LETTER TO A MAN OF NOTE[2].

Sir[3],

    The favour you have done me[4] *I acknowledge, though I note that you expect a return for it.* Kind though your action was, yet to let me share in the enjoyment of reading that most acute work only on condition I should disclose what I think of it, was to demand a requital, and surely a heavy one. Truly a hard condition, compliance with which the desire to acquaint myself with a fine piece of work has wrung from me, but one against which I should gladly protest if an exception could be claimed for one who 'has committed a deed through the urgency of pleasure,' and added to the concessions recognized by the Praetor of old, who excused acts 'done under the influence of violence or fear.'

    What would you have ? It is not my estimate of the author that you look for; you already know how much I appreciate the force of his genius and his distinguished learning. Likewise you are not unaware of the troublesome matters that at present take up my time and, if you have too exalted an opinion of me, it does not follow that I am unaware of my own inadequacy. And yet what you submit to me for examination demands both intellectual powers of no ordinary nature and above all a mind set free from care, in order that it may, by its disengagement from all external turmoil, have leisure for self-contemplation; and as you see, this is impossible without intent meditation and complete mental self-absorption Nevertheless, if it is your bidding, I obey. The blame for my shortcomings will fall

---

  1 Fourth set of Objections brought forward by M. Arnauld, Doctor in Theology. F. V.

    2 Letter of the said M. Arnauld written to the Rev. Father Mersenne. F. V.

    3 Mon Réverend Père, F. V.; vir clarissime, L. V.

    4 In sending to him the ' Meditations' of·Descartes, cf. F. V.

*upon you, who compel me to take up my pen. But though Philosophy
could arrogate to itself the whole of this work, yet since its author
with great modesty of his own accord appears before the tribunal of
the Theologians, I shall here play a double rôle. I shall first propound the chief objections that, in my opinion, philosophers can adduce
in connection with the outstanding problems as to the nature of the
human mind and [the existence] of God; secondly, I shall unfold
certain difficulties which a theologian can detect in the whole work.*

The Nature of the Human Mind.

*The first thing that here occurs to me to be worthy of remark is
that our distinguished author should have taken as the foundation of
the whole of his philosophy the doctrine laid down [before him] by
St Augustine, a man of most penetrating intellect and of much note,
not only in the sphere of theology, but in that of philosophy as well.
In 'De Libero arbitrio,' Book II, chap. 3., Alipius, when disputing
with Euodius, setting about a proof of the existence of God, says:*
Firstly, to start with the things that are most evident, I ask you
whether you yourself exist, or are you apprehensive lest in [answer-
ing] this question you are in error, when in any case, if you did
not exist you could never be in error? *Similar to this are the
words of our author:* But perhaps there exists an all-powerful being,
extremely cunning, who deceives me, who intentionally at all times
deceives me. There is then no doubt that I exist, if he deceives
me. *But let us proceed, and, to pursue something more relevant to
our purpose, let us discover how, from this principle, we can demonstrate the fact that our mind is [distinct and] separate from our
body.*

*I am able to doubt whether I have a body, nay, whether any body
exists at all; yet I have no right to doubt whether I am, or exist, so
long as I doubt or think.*

*Hence I, who doubt and think, am not a body; otherwise in enter-
taining doubt concerning body, I should doubt about myself.*

*Nay, even though I obstinately maintain that no body at all
exists, the position taken up is unshaken: I am something, hence I
am not a body.*

*This is really very acute, but someone could bring up the objection
which our author urges against himself; the fact that I doubt about
body or deny that body exists, does not bring it about that no body
exists.* Hence perhaps it happens that these very things which
I suppose to be nothing, because they are unknown to me, yet do

not in truth differ from that self which I do know. I know nothing about it, *he says*, I do not dispute this matter; [I can judge only about things that are known to me.] I know that I exist; I enquire who I, the known self, am; it is quite certain that the knowledge of this self thus precisely taken, does not depend on those things of the existence of which I am not yet acquainted[1].

But he admits in consonance with the argument laid down in the Method, that the proof has proceeded only so far as to exclude from the nature of the human mind whatsoever is corporeal, not from the point of view of the ultimate truth, but relatively only to his consciousness[2] (the meaning being that nothing at all was known to him to belong to his essential nature, beyond the fact that he was a thinking being)[3]. *Hence it is evident from this reply that the argument is exactly where it was, and that therefore the problem which he promises to solve remains entirely untouched. The problem is:* how it follows, from the fact that one is unaware that anything else [(except the fact of being a thinking thing)] belongs to one's essence, that nothing else really belongs to one's essence[3]. *But, not to conceal my dullness, I have been unable to discover in the whole of Meditation II where he has shown this. Yet so far as I can conjecture, he, attempts this proof in Meditation VI, because he believes that it is dependent on the possession of the clear knowledge of God to which in Meditation II he has not yet attained. Here is his proof:*

Because I know that all the things I clearly and distinctly understand can be created by God just as I conceive them to exist, it is sufficient for me to be able to comprehend one thing clearly and distinctly apart from another, in order to be sure that the one is diverse from the other, because at least God can isolate them; and it does not matter by what power that isolation is effected, in order that I may be obliged to think them different from one another. Hence because, on the one hand, I have a clear and distinct idea of myself in so far as I am a thinking being, and not extended, and on the other hand, a distinct idea of body, in so far as it is only an extended thing, not one that thinks, it is certain that I am in reality distinct from my body and can exist apart from it[4].

Here we must halt awhile; for on these few words the whole of the difficulty seems to hinge.

Firstly, in order to be true, the major premiss of that syllogism

---

[1] Cf. Med. II. vol. I. p. 152.   [2] Perceptionem.
[3] Cf. Preface, vol. I. pp. 138, 139.   [4] Cf. Med. VI. vol. I. p. 190.

must be held to refer to the adequate notion of a thing [(i.e. the notion which comprises everything which may be known of the thing)], not to any notion, even a clear and distinct one.   For M.   Descartes in his reply to his theological critic[1] *admits that it is sufficient to have a* formal *distinction* and that a real *one is not required*, to cause one thing to be conceived separately and as distinct from another by the abstracting action of the mind when it conceives a thing inadequately[2].   *Whence in the same passage he draws the conclusion* which he adds:—But still I understand in a complete manner what body is [(i.e. I conceive body as a complete thing)], merely by thinking that it is extended, has figure, can move, etc., and by denying of it everything which belongs to the nature of mind. Conversely also, I understand that mind is something complete, which doubts, knows, wishes, etc., although I deny that anything belongs to it which is contained in the idea of body.   Hence[3] there is a real distinction between mind and body[4].

But, if anyone casts doubt on the (minor) premiss here assumed, and contends that it is merely that your conception is inadequate when you conceive yourself [(i.e. your mind)] *as being a thinking but not an extended thing, and similarly when you conceive yourself* [(i.e. your body)] *as being an extended and not a thinking thing, we must look to its proof in the previous part of the argument.   For I do not reckon a matter like this to be so clear as to warrant us in assuming it as an indemonstrable first principle and in dispensing with proof.*

Now as to the first part of the statement, namely, that you completely understand what body is, merely by thinking that it is extended, has figure, can move, etc., and by denying of it everything which belongs to the nature of mind, *this is of little value. For one who contends that the human mind is corporeal does not on that account believe that every body is a mind.   Hence body would be so related to mind as genus is to species.   But the genus can be conceived without the species, even although one deny of it whatsoever is proper and peculiar to the species; whence comes the common dictum of Logicians, ' the negation of the species does not negate the genus.' Thus, I can conceive figure without conceiving any of the attributes proper to the circle.   Therefore, we must prove over and above this that the mind can be completely and adequately conceived apart from the body.*

---

[1] Reply to Objections I.   [2] Above, p. 22, par. 3.
[3] This slightly abridges the passage quoted.   [4] pp. 22, 23.

*I can discover no passage in the whole work capable of effecting this proof, save the proposition laid down at the outset :—*I can deny that there is any body or that any extended thing exists, but yet it is certain that I exist, so long as I make this denial, or think ; hence I am a thing that thinks and not a body, and the body does not pertain to the knowledge of myself.

But the only result that I can see this to give, is that a certain knowledge of myself be obtained without a knowledge of the body. But it is not yet quite clear to me that this knowledge is complete and adequate, so as to make me sure that I am not in error in excluding the body from my essence. I shall explain by means of an example :—

Let us assume that a certain man is quite sure that the angle in a semicircle is a right angle and that hence the triangle made by this angle and the diameter is right-angled; but suppose he questions and has not yet firmly apprehended, nay, let us imagine that, misled by some fallacy, he denies that the square on its base is equal to the squares on the sides of the right-angled triangle. Now, according to our author's reasoning, he will see himself confirmed in his false belief. For, *he will argue,* while I clearly and distinctly perceive that this triangle is right-angled, I yet doubt whether the square on its base is equal to the square on its sides. Hence the equality of the square on the base to those on the sides does not belong to its essence.

Further, even though I deny that the square on its base is equal to the squares on its sides, I yet remain certain that it is right-angled, and the knowledge that one of its angles is a right angle remains clear and distinct in my mind ; and this remaining so, not God himself could cause it not to be right-angled.

Hence, that of which I doubt, or the removal of which leaves me with the idea still, cannot belong to its essence.

Besides, since I know that all things I clearly and distinctly understand can be created by God just as I conceive them to exist, it is sufficient for me, in order to be sure that one thing is distinct from another, to be able to comprehend the one clearly and distinctly apart from the other, because it can be isolated by God. *But I clearly and distinctly understand that this triangle is right-angled, without comprehending that the square on its base is equal to the squares on its sides. Hence God at least can create a right-angled triangle, the square on the base of which is not equal to the squares on its sides.*

I do not see what reply can here be made, except that the man in question does not perceive clearly that the triangle is right-angled. But whence do I obtain any perception of the nature of my mind clearer than that which he has of the nature of the triangle? He is as sure that the triangle in a semicircle has one right angle (which is the notion of a right-angled triangle) as I am in believing that I exist because I think.

Hence, just as a man errs in not believing that the equality of the square on its base to the squares on its sides belongs to the nature of that triangle, which he clearly and distinctly knows to be right-angled, so why am I not perhaps in the wrong in thinking that nothing else belongs to my nature, which I clearly and distinctly know to be something that thinks, except the fact that I am this thinking being? Perhaps it also belongs to my essence to be something extended.

And certainly, some one will say it is no marvel if, in deducing my existence from the fact that I think, the idea that I form of the self, which is in this way an object of thought, represent me to my mind as merely a thinking being, since it has been derived from my thinking alone. And hence from this idea, no argument can be drawn to prove that nothing more belongs to my essence than what the idea contains.

In addition, it can be maintained that the argument proves too much and conducts us to the Platonic doctrine (refuted nevertheless by our author) that nothing corporeal belongs to the essence of man, who is hence entirely spirit, while his body is merely the vehicle of spirit; whence follows the definition of man as a spirit that makes use of a body.

But if you reply that body is not absolutely excluded from my essence, but merely in so far precisely as I am a thinking being, the fear seems likely to arise that some one will entertain a suspicion that the knowledge of myself, in so far as I am a thinking being, is not the knowledge of anything fully and adequately conceived, but is known only inadequately and by a certain intellectual abstraction.

Hence, just as geometers conceive of a line as length without breadth, and of a surface as length and breadth together without depth, although there is no length apart from breadth, no breadth without depth, some one may perhaps doubt whether everything that thinks is not likewise something extended; a thing in which, nevertheless, over and above the attributes common to other extended things, e.g. the possession of figure, motion, etc., is found this unique[1] faculty of thinking. Whence it follows that while by an intellectual

---

[1] peculiaris cogitandi virtus.

abstraction, it can be apprehended by means of this character alone and unaided as a thing that thinks, it is quite possible that in reality corporeal attributes are compatible with a thinking being; just as quantity can be mentally conceived by means of length alone, while it is possible that in reality breadth and depth go along with length in every quantity.

The difficulty is increased by the fact that this power of thinking seems to be attached to corporeal organs, since we can believe it to be asleep in infants, extinguished in the case of lunatics; and this is an objection strongly urged by those impious men whose aim is the soul's slaughter.

Thus far I have dealt with the distinction between mind and body in real existence. But since M. Descartes has undertaken to prove the immortality of souls, it is right to ask whether that follows evidently from this separateness of existence. According to the principles of the vulgar philosophy that conclusion by no means can be drawn, for the common opinion is that the souls of animals are distinct from their bodies, but nevertheless perish with them.

I had carried my criticism to this point and was intending to show how, according to our author's principles, which I believed I had gathered from his method of philosophical enquiry, the immortality of the soul[1] could be easily inferred from its distinctness from the body, when a new work[2], a little treatise bearing the fruit of our author's reflections, came into my hands; and this work not only throws much light on the whole, but in connection with this passage brings forward exactly what I was to adduce with a view to the solution of the above problem.

For in the matter of the souls of animals, in other passages he lets us know sufficiently well that they have no soul, but merely a body disposed in a certain manner and so compounded of various organs that all the actions we see them perform can be effected in it and by its means.

But I fear that this belief will not carry persuasion into men's minds, unless supported by the strongest evidence. For at the first blush, it seems incredible that there is any way by which, without any intervention of the soul, it can come to pass that the light reflected from the body of a wolf into the eyes of a sheep should excite into motion the minute fibres of the optic nerves and by the penetration of

---

[1] Mentis.
[2] The *Synopsis of the Meditations* (cf. vol. i. pp. 140—143) sent by Descartes to Mersenne, Dec. 31, 1640, fifty days after the *Meditations* (A. et T.).

this movement to the brain, discharge the animal spirits into the nerves in the manner requisite to make the sheep run off.

One thing which I here shall add is, that I wholly approve of M. Descartes' teaching, relative to the distinction between the imagination and thought or intelligence, and of the greater certainty attaching to that which we grasp by the reason than to what is perceived by the senses. For long ago, I learned from St Augustine, De Animae Quantitate, ch. 15, *that we must give no countenance to those who would persuade us that what we discern by the intellect is less certain than what comes by the bodily eyes, vexed as they ever are with rheum. Whence also,* in Solil, bk. I. ch. 4, *he says that he has found that in the matter of geometry the senses are like a ship. For, he says,* when they had brought me to the destination I was making for, after I had quitted them and had begun on firm land to repeat all that they had taught me, for a long time my footsteps tottered[1]. Wherefore, I believe that one could more readily learn navigation on land than understand geometry by the use of the senses (alone)[2] although they seem to give some help to us when first we begin to learn.

Concerning God.

The first proof of the existence of God, that unfolded by our author in Meditation III, falls into two parts. The former is, that God exists, if the idea of Him exists in me; the second shows that I, in possessing this idea, can derive my existence only from God.

In the earlier part there is only one thing that does not secure my approval, and that is, that though M. Descartes had asserted that strictly speaking falsity was to be found in judgments only, *he yet admits shortly afterwards that* ideas may be false, not formally indeed, but materially[3]. *Now this seems to me to disagree with his first principles.*

But I fear I may not be able to explain my thought with sufficient lucidity in a matter of such obscurity; an example will make it clearer. If, he says, cold is merely privation of heat, the idea of cold which represents it as though it were something positive, is false materially[3].

Nay, if cold is merely the privation of heat, there can be no

---

[1] F. V. adds 'as do the steps of those who set foot on land after a long voyage.'

[2] This appears in the F. V. and is not in the original Latin of St Augustine.

[3] Cf. Med. III. vol. I. p. 164, par. 3.

idea of cold which represents it as a positive thing, and our author here confuses idea with judgment.

For what is the idea of cold? It is cold itself in so far as it is objectively in the understanding. But if cold is a privation, it cannot exist objectively in the mind by the instrumentality of an idea, the objective existence of which is a positive entity. Hence, if cold is merely privation, there can be no positive idea of it, and hence no idea materially false.

This is confirmed by the argument by which M. Descartes proves that the idea of an infinite being cannot be otherwise than true; for, although it can be pretended that such a being does not exist, it cannot be pretended that the idea of it displays nothing real to me.

Obviously, the same may be affirmed of every positive idea. For, although it can be imagined that the cold, which I believe to be represented by a positive idea, is not positive, yet I cannot pretend that a positive idea represents to me nothing real and positive; since a positive idea is not so styled by reason of the existence it has as a mode of thinking (in that sense all ideas would be positive), but from the objective existence which it contains and displays to our intellect. Hence, though that idea is possibly not the idea of cold, it cannot be a false idea.

But, you rejoin, its falsity consists in the very fact that it is not the idea of cold. Nay, it is your judgment that is false, if you deem it to be the idea of cold; but it, itself, is in itself[1] most true. Similarly, the idea of God should not be called false, even materially, though some one transfer it to something which is not God, as idolaters have done.

Finally, what does that idea of cold, which you say is false materially, represent to your mind? Privation? In that case it is true. A positive entity? Then it is not the idea of cold. Further, what is the cause of that positive objective being, which makes you conclude that that idea is materially false? It is, you reply, myself, in so far as I participate[2] in non-existence. Therefore the positive objective existence of a certain idea may proceed from nothing, a conclusion which upsets the most important fundamental principles of M. Descartes.

But let us proceed now to the second part of the argument where

---

[1] *In te* A. et T. misprint for *in se*? Mais pour elle, il est certain qu'elle est tres vraye! F. V.

[2] F. V. a nihilo sum, L. V.

he asks, whether I myself, who possess the idea of an infinite being, can proceed from anything other than an infinite being, and especially whether I can be self-caused. *M. Descartes contends that I cannot be self-caused owing to the fact that,* if I myself had given myself existence, I should have given myself also all those perfections, the ideas of which I perceive in myself[1]. *But his theological critic acutely replies:*—'self-originated' should be taken not in a positive but in a negative sense which identifies it with 'not derived from anything else[2].' But now, *he says,* if anything is self-derived, i.e. not due to something else, how can I prove that it embraces all things and is infinite? I shall pay no heed to the reply that, if it is self-derived it will have given itself everything; for it does not depend on itself as on a cause, nor did it anticipate its existence and so at a prior time choose what it should afterwards be[3].

To refute this argument, M. Descartes contends that existence per se should be taken not negatively but positively[4], especially in so far as it refers to God. So that God in a certain sense stands to Himself in the same way as an efficient cause does to its effect. Now this seems to me to be a strong[5] assertion and to be untrue.

Hence, while in part I agree with M. Descartes, I partly differ from him. I admit that I cannot be self-derived except in a positive sense, but I deny that the same should be said of God. Nay, I think that it is a manifest contradiction that anything should be positively self-derived in the sense of proceeding from itself as a cause. Hence I come to the same conclusion as our author, but by quite another route, as I shall here set forth:—

In order to be self-derived, I should have to proceed from myself positively and in the sense of coming from myself as a cause: hence I cannot be self-derived.

To prove the major premiss of this syllogism, I rely on the grounds of my antagonist drawn from the doctrine that, since the various parts of time can all be dissevered from each other, from the fact that I exist it does not follow that I shall in future exist, unless some cause, as it were, re-creates me at every single moment[6].

In the matter of the minor, [viz. that I cannot proceed from myself positively and as it were from a cause] I deem it to be so

[1] Med. III. vol. I. pp. 167, 168 (not accurately quoted).
[2] Objj. I. p. 4, par. 2. [3] Objj. I. *loc. cit. infra.*
[4] pp. 15, 16 above. [5] Durum; hardy, F. V.
[6] Med. III. vol. I. p. 168.

*evident to the light of nature that its proof would be vain, a proving
of the known by the less known. Indeed, our author seems to have
acknowledged its truth, since he has not dared openly to deny it.
Consider, I pray, those words in his reply to his theological opponent.*

I have not, *so run his words*, said that it is impossible for anything to be its own efficient cause : for, although that statement is
manifestly true when the meaning of efficient cause is restricted to
those causes that are prior to their effects or different from them,
yet it does not seem necessary to confine the term to this meaning
in the present investigation, for the light of nature does not require
that the notion of an efficient cause should compel it to be prior to
its effect[1].

*This is excellent so far as the first part goes, but why has he
omitted the second? Has he not omitted to add that the same light
of nature does not require that the notion of an efficient cause should
compel it to be different from its effect, only because the light of
nature does not permit him to assert that?*

*Now surely, if every effect depends upon a cause and receives its
existence from a cause, is it not clear that the same thing cannot
depend upon itself, cannot receive its existence from itself?*

*Further, every cause is the cause of an effect, every effect the effect
of a cause; hence there is a mutual relation between cause and effect.
But a mutual relation can be possessed only by two things.*

*Again, it is merely absurd to conceive of a thing as receiving
existence and yet possessing that very existence before the time at
which we conceive that it received it; but that would be the result if
we attributed the notions of cause and effect to the same thing in
respect of itself. What is the notion of cause? The conferring of
existence. What is the notion of effect? The receiving of existence.
Moreover, the notion of cause is prior in nature to that of effect.*

*But we cannot conceive a thing by means of the notion of cause as
giving existence, unless we conceive it as possessing existence. Hence
we should have to conceive that a thing possessed existence before
conceiving it to receive existence; yet when anything receives, the
receiving precedes the possessing.*

*This reasoning may be otherwise couched thus :—no one gives
what he does not possess; hence no one can give himself existence
unless he already possess it, but, if he already possess it, why should
he give it to himself?*

Finally, M. Descartes asserts that the light of nature lets us

---

[1] p. 13 *sub fin.*—p. 14, l. 8, abbreviated.

know that the distinction between creation and conservation is solely a distinction of the reason[1]. *But this self-same light of nature lets us know that nothing can create itself, and that hence nothing can conserve itself.*

But to pass down from the general thesis to the particular one[2] concerning God, it will now, in my opinion, be more evident that God can be self-derived not in the positive sense, *but only* negatively, *i.e., in the sense of* not proceeding from anything else.

And firstly, it clearly follows from the premiss that M. Descartes advances in order to prove that if a body exists per se, *it must be per se* in the positive sense. For, *he says*, the several parts of time are not derived from one another, and hence, though that body be supposed to have existed up to the present time *per se,* i.e. without any cause, that will not suffice to make it exist in future, unless there be some power contained in it which, as it were, re-creates it continually[3].

But, far from this argument being applicable to the case of a supremely perfect and infinite being, the opposite rather can clearly be inferred, and for opposite reasons. For the idea of an infinite being contains within it that of infinite duration, i.e. a duration bounded by no limits, and hence indivisible, unchanging, and existing all at once; one in which it is only erroneously and by reason of the imperfection of our intellect that the conception of prior and posterior can be applied.

Whence it manifestly follows that the infinite Being cannot be thought to exist even for one moment without our conceiving at the same time that it always has and always will exist (a fact that our author himself elsewhere proves); hence it is idle to ask why it continues in existence.

Nay, as Augustine frequently shows (an author whom none since the time of the sacred writers have surpassed in the worthiness and sublimity of what they say concerning God), in God there is no past or future, but always present existence [which clearly shows that we cannot without absurdity ask why God continues to exist[4]].

Further, God cannot be thought to be self-derived in the positive sense, as if He originally brought Himself into existence, for in that case He would have existed before He existed. He is said to be self-derived merely because, as our author frequently declares, as a fact He maintains Himself in existence.

---

[1] Med. III. vol. I. p. 168 *sub fin.* 　　　　[2] hypothesim, L. V.
[3] p. 15 above. 　　　　[4] Abridgement of a long clause added in F. V.

Yet, in the case of an infinite being, conservation must be denied no less than creation. For what, pray, is conservation but the continual reproduction of some things? Hence, all conservation implies some initial production. Another reason is that the very term continuation, just like that of conservation, implies something of potentiality. But an infinite being is pure actuality without any potentiality.

Hence, let us conclude that God cannot be conceived to be self-originated in the positive *sense, except by reason of the imperfection of our intellect, that thinks of God as existing after the fashion of created things. This conclusion will be rendered more evident by the following argument.*

We seek to discover the efficient cause of a thing only with respect to its existence, not with respect to its essence. For example, if I see a triangle, I may enquire about the efficient cause that brought this triangle into existence, but it will be absurd for me to ask what is the efficient cause by reason of which the triangle has its three angles equal to two right angles. The correct reply to such a question would not be to assign an efficient cause, but to say merely, 'because such is the nature of the triangle.' This is why the mathematicians, not concerning themselves with the existence of their objects, do not employ efficient and final causes in their proofs. But existence, nay, if you like, continuance in existence, is involved in the essence of an infinite being, no less than the equality of its three angles to two right angles is involved in that of a triangle. Therefore, just as the reply to the question why the triangle has its three angles equal to two right angles should not be in terms of an efficient cause, but the reason assigned should be the eternal and immutable nature of the triangle; so when we ask why God exists, or continues in existence, we must seek for no efficient cause, either within God or without Him, and for nothing similar to an efficient cause (for my contention touches the thing not the name for it): we should state as our reason this alone, 'because such is the nature of a supremely perfect being.'

Hence in opposition to what M. Descartes says: the light of nature tells us that nothing exists about which the question, why it exists, cannot be asked, whether we enquire for its efficient cause, or, if it does not possess one, demand why it does not have one[1], *I reply that the answer to the question why God exists should not be in terms of efficient causality, but merely 'because He is God,' i.e. an*

---

*infinite Being.   And when we are asked for the efficient cause of
God, we must reply that He needs no efficient cause.   And if our
interrogator plies us with the question why no efficient cause is
required, we must answer 'because He is an infinite Being, and in
such a case existence and essence are identical'; for only those things,
the actual existence of which can be distinguished from their essence,
require an efficient cause.*

*Therefore the doctrine collapses that is contained in the immediately
subsequent passage, which here I quote:*—Hence if I did not believe
that anything could in some way be related to itself exactly as an
efficient cause is related to its effect, so far should I be from concluding that any first cause existed, that, on the contrary, I should
once more ask for the cause of that which had been called first, and
so should never arrive at the first cause of all.

*By no means; if I thought that I must enquire for the efficient
cause of anything whatsoever, or for something analogous to the
efficient cause, I should seek for a cause of that given thing whatsoever it was, different from it, because to me it is most manifest that
nothing can in any way be so related to itself as is an efficient cause
towards its effect.*

*I think I am right in bringing this to the notice of M. Descartes
in order that he may give careful and attentive consideration to these
matters, because I am sure that theologians, almost without exception,
must take offence at the doctrine that God is self-originated in a*
positive *sense, and proceeds, as it were, from a cause.*

*The only remaining scruple I have is an uncertainty as to how a
circular reasoning is to be avoided in saying:* the only secure reason
we have for believing that what we clearly and distinctly perceive
is true, is the fact that God exists[1].

*But we can be sure that God exists, only because we clearly and
evidently perceive that; therefore prior to being certain that God
exists, we should be certain that whatever we clearly and evidently
perceive is true.*

*Something which had escaped me I now add, viz., that I believe
that M. Descartes is in error, though he affirms it as certain, when
he makes the statement that* nothing can exist in him, in so far as he
is a thinking being, of which he is not conscious[2].   *By the* self *in so
far as it is a thinking being, nothing more is meant than the mind,
in so far as it is distinct from the body.   But who does not see that*

---

[1] Med. v. vol. I. p. 183, par. 3.
[2] Med. III. vol. I. p. 169 *ad init.* (paraphrased).

much may be in the mind, of the existence of which the mind is not conscious? The mind of an infant in its mother's womb possesses the faculty of thought without being conscious of it. There are innumerable similar instances that I pass by in silence.

Matters likely to cause difficulty to Theologians.

Here, in order to curtail a discussion that has already grown wearisome, I prefer to aim at brevity and to indicate my points rather than to debate them in detail.

First I am apprehensive lest offence may be caused by our author's free method of speculation, which renders everything doubtful. He does, in fact, admit in the Method[1] that this style of thinking is dangerous for a mediocre intelligence; I confess, however, that in the Synopsis this cause of alarm is somewhat mitigated.

Nevertheless, this Meditation should appear equipped with a slight preface in which it is pointed out that the doubt entertained about these matters is not really serious, and that the intention is merely to set on one side for a little those matters which give rise to the very least and most hyperbolical[2] doubt, *as our author in another place phrases it, in order to discover something so firm and steadfast that no one, however perverse in his opinions, can have any doubt about it. Consequently, when it comes to the place at which these words appear:*—that since I was ignorant of the author of my being[3], *I deem that it would be better to write instead:*—I feigned that I was ignorant.

In Meditation IV, which treats of the True and the False, I greatly desire, for reasons that it would be tedious to recount, that he would explain, and that, either in this Meditation itself or in the Synopsis, two particular matters.

The first is why in enquiring into the cause of error, while treating copiously of the mistakes made in distinguishing between the true and the false, he does not also treat of the error that occurs in the pursuit of good and evil.

For, since that former enquiry sufficiently promotes our author's design and object, and what is here said of the source of error may arouse the gravest objections, if it is extended to the pursuit of good and evil, prudence, to my mind, requires, nay, the correct order

---

[1] Cf. Method, vol. i. p. 90.   [2] Vol. i. p. 198 *sub fin.*
[3] Vol. i. p. 189, middle.

of exposition, about which our author is so careful, demands the omission of certain irrelevancies that may give rise to contention, lest the reader quarrel over inessentials and be prevented from perceiving what is important.

The second point I wish to bring to our author's notice is that he, when he maintains that we should assent only to what we clearly and distinctly know, deals only with such matters as pertain to the sciences and fall in within the province of theory[1], *and not with those things that concern our faith, and the conduct of life ; and this is why he censures the rashness of the opinionative* [i.e. of those who think they understand matters of which they have no knowledge], *but not the just persuasion of those who accept with caution what they believe.*

For there are three things in the soul of man, *as St Augustine, in De Utilit. Credendi, ch.* 15, *with great sagacity reminds us,* that seem to stand in close proximity to each other [and appear to be virtually the same thing], but which are well worthy of being distinguished : viz. knowing, believing, opining.

He knows, whose comprehension of anything is based on sure grounds. *He believes* who, influenced by some strong authority, thinks something to be true without having sure grounds on which to base his comprehension. *The opinionative man is* he who thinks he understands that of which he has no knowledge.

To be opinionative is moreover a grave fault, and that for two reasons : firstly, he who is convinced that he already knows is thereby debarred from being able to learn, if indeed the matter is one that can be comprehended : further, his presumption is in itself a sign of an ill-disposed mind.

Hence, what we know we owe to reason ; what we believe, to *authority ;* while our mere opinions are born of *error.* All this has been said in order that we may understand how, while clinging to our faith in matters we do not as yet comprehend, we are exempt from the charge of opinionative presumption.

For those who say that we should believe nothing that we do not know to be true, stand in dread only of the imputation of opinionativeness, for it is disgraceful and calamitous to fall into this error. But anyone who after serious consideration sees the great difference between one who fancies that he knows [what he does not know] and one who, understanding that he does not

---

[1] sub intelligentiam cadunt.

understand a certain matter, yet believes it owing to the influence of some authority, will at once feel himself freed from the peril of error, the charge of an inhuman lack of assurance and the imputation of arrogance.

A little later[1] *St Augustine in ch.* 12, *adds* : many arguments could be brought to show that nothing at all in human society will remain secure, if we make up our minds to believe nothing that we cannot regard as fully comprehended. *So far St Augustine.*

M. Descartes can well enough judge how important it is to point out this distinction; but the many people who in these days are prone to impiety may make a bad use of his words, for the purpose of shattering the faith.

But the chief ground of offence to theologians that I anticipate is that, according to M. Descartes' doctrines, the teachings of the Church relative to the sacred mysteries of the Eucharist cannot remain unaffected and intact.

For it is an article of our faith that the substance of the bread passes out of the bread of the Eucharist, and that only its accidents remain. Now these are extension, figure, colour, odour, savour and the other sensible qualities.

But M. Descartes recognizes no sense-qualities, but only certain motions of the minute bodies that surround us, by means of which we perceive the different impressions to which we afterwards give the names of colour, savour, and odour. Hence there remain figure, extension and mobility. But M. Descartes denies that those powers can be comprehended apart from the substance in which they inhere and that hence they cannot exist apart from it; and this is repeated in the reply to his theological critic[2].

Likewise he acknowledges only a formal[3] *distinction between these affections and substance, but a formal difference seems not to allow things so distinguished to be sundered from each other even by the Divine power.*

I am confident that M. Descartes, whose piety is so well known to us, will weigh this with diligence and attention and will judge that he must take the greatest pains, lest, while meaning to maintain the cause of God against the attacks of the impious, he appears to have at all endangered that faith, which God's own authority has founded, and by the grace of which he hopes to obtain that eternal life, of which he has undertaken to convince the world.

---

[1] This must be wrong, as the previous citation refers to ch. 15.
[2] Cf. above, p. 22.   [3] *Ibid.*

REPLY TO THE FOURTH SET
OF OBJECTIONS[1].

I could not possibly desire any one to examine my writings who could show more insight and courtesy than the opponent whose criticisms you have forwarded. The gentleness with which he has treated me lets me see that he is well-disposed both to me and to the cause I maintain. Yet so accurately has he reconnoitred the positions he attacks, so thoroughly has he scrutinized them, that I am confident that nothing in the rest of the field has escaped his keen gaze. Further so acutely has he contested the points from which he has decided to withhold his approval, that I have no apprehension lest it be thought that complaisance has made him conceal anything. The result is, that instead of my being disturbed by his objections, my feeling is rather one of gratification at not meeting with opposition in a greater number of places.

REPLY TO THE FIRST PART.

The Nature of the Human Mind.

I shall not take up time here by thanking my distinguished critic for bringing to my aid the authority of St Augustine, and for expounding my arguments in a way which betokened a fear that others might not deem them strong enough.

I come first of all to the passage where my demonstration commences of how, *from the fact that I knew that nothing belongs to my essence* (i.e. to the essence of the mind alone) *beyond the fact that I am a thinking being, it follows that in actual truth nothing else does belong to it*[2]. That was, to be sure, the place where I proved that God exists, that God, to wit, who can accomplish whatever I clearly and distinctly know to be possible.

---

[1] F. V. adds 'urged by M. Arnauld, Doctor of Theology.' Then beneath is the title 'Letter from the author to the Rev. Father Mersenne.'

[2] Above, p. 81.

For although much exists in me of which I am not yet conscious (for example in that passage I did, as a fact, assume that I was not yet aware that my mind had the power of moving the body, and that it was substantially united with it), yet since that which I do perceive is adequate to allow of my existing with it as my sole possession, I am certain that God could have created me without putting me in possession of those other attributes of which I am unaware. Hence it was that those additional attributes were judged not to belong to the essence of the mind.

For in my opinion nothing without which a thing can still exist is comprised in its essence, and although mind belongs to the essence of man, to be united to a human body is in the proper sense no part of the essence of mind.

I must also explain what my meaning was in saying *that a real distinction cannot be inferred from the fact that one thing is conceived apart from another by means of the abstracting action of the mind when it conceives a thing inadequately, but only from the fact that each of them is comprehended apart from the other in a complete manner, or as a complete thing*[1].

For I do not think that an adequate knowledge of the thing is, in this case, required, as M. Arnauld assumes ; nay, we have here the difference that if any knowledge is to be *adequate*, it must embrace all the properties which exist in the thing known. Hence, there is none but God who knows that He has adequate cognition of all things.

But a created mind actually possessed of adequate knowledge in many cases can never know that this is in its possession unless God give it a private revelation of the fact. But in order to have adequate knowledge of anything, it requires merely to have in itself a power of knowing what is adequate for that thing. And this can easily occur. But in order to know that he has this knowledge, or that God has put nothing in the thing in question over and above what he has knowledge of, a man's power of knowing would need to equal the infinite capacity of God—an obvious absurdity.

But now, in order to apprehend a real distinction between two things, we do not need to have adequate knowledge of them, unless we can be aware that it is adequate ; but this being unattainable, as has just been said, it follows that an adequate knowledge is not required.

[1] Above, p. 82.

Hence, when I said that *to apprehend one thing apart from another by means of an act of abstraction on the part of the intellect when its conceptions are inadequate, is not sufficient*, I did not think that it would be thence inferred that an *adequate* cognition was required for the purpose of inferring a real distinction, but merely a cognition which we had not, by an intellectual abstraction, rendered *inadequate*.

It is one thing for a cognition to be entirely adequate, of which fact we could never be sure unless it were revealed by God; it is quite another for our knowledge to have sufficient adequacy to let us see that we have not rendered it inadequate by an intellectual abstraction.

Similarly, when I said that a thing must be comprehended in a *complete* manner, I meant not that the intellectual operation must be adequate, but merely that we must have a knowledge of the thing sufficient to let us know that it is *complete*.

I thought this had been sufficiently plain from previous and subsequent passages alike; for, shortly before I had distinguished *incomplete* from *complete entities* and had said that *each single thing that has a really distinct existence, must be understood to be an entity in itself and diverse from every other*[1].

But afterwards, preserving the same meaning as when I said that *I understood in a complete manner what body is*, I immediately added that *I understood also that mind is something complete*[2]; I thus took 'to understand in a complete manner' and 'to understand that a thing is something complete' in one and the same sense.

But at this point a question may justly be raised as to what I understand by *a complete thing*, and how I prove that, *understanding two things to be complete in isolation from one another is sufficient to establish a real distinction between them*.

Therefore, to the first query I reply that by *a complete thing* I mean merely a substance endowed with those forms or attributes which suffice to let me recognise that it is a substance.

For we do not have immediate cognition of substances, as has been elsewhere noted; rather from the mere fact that we perceive certain forms or attributes which must inhere in something in order to have existence, we name the thing in which they exist a *substance*.

But if, afterwards, we desired to strip that substance of those attributes by which we apprehend it, we should utterly destroy our

---

[1] Cf. Reply to Objections I. *sub fin.*   [2] *Ibid. infra.*

knowledge of it; and thus, while we might indeed apply words to it, they would not be words of the meaning of which we had a clear and distinct perception.

I do not ignore the fact that certain substances are popularly called *incomplete substances*. But if they are said to be incomplete, because they cannot exist by themselves [and unsupported by other things], I confess it seems to me to be a contradiction for them to be substances ; i.e. for them to be things subsisting by themselves and at the same time incomplete, i.e. not capable of subsisting by themselves. But it is true that in another sense they can be called incomplete substances ; viz. in a sense which allows that, in so far as they are substances, they have no lack of completeness, and merely asserts that they are incomplete in so far as they are referred to some other substance, in unison with which they form a single self-subsistent thing [distinct from everything else].

Thus, the hand is an incomplete substance, when taken in relation with the body, of which it is a part ; but, regarded alone, it is a complete substance. Quite in the same way mind and body are incomplete substances viewed in relation to the man who is the unity which together they form ; but, taken alone, they are complete.

For, as to be extended, divisible, possessed of figure, etc. are the forms or attributes by which I recognise that substance called *body* ; so, to be a knowing, willing, doubting being, etc. are the forms by which I recognize the substance called *mind* ; and I know that thinking substance is a complete thing, no less than that which is extended.

But it can nowise be maintained that, in the words of M. Arnauld, *body is related to mind as genus is to species*[1] ; for, although the genus can be apprehended apart from this or that specific difference, the species can by no means be thought apart from the genus.

For, to illustrate, we easily apprehend figure, without thinking at all of a circle (although that mental act is not distinct unless we refer to some specific figure, and it does not give us a complete thing, unless it embraces the nature of the body) ; but we are cognisant of no specific difference belonging to the circle, unless at the same time we think of figure.

But mind can be perceived clearly and distinctly, or sufficiently so to let it be considered to be a complete thing without any of those forms or attributes by which we recognize that body is a

[1] Above, p. 82.

substance, as I think I have sufficiently shown in the Second Meditation ; and body is understood distinctly and as a complete thing apart from the attributes attaching to the mind.

Nevertheless M. Arnauld here urges that *although a certain notion of myself can be obtained without a knowledge of the body, it yet does not thence result that this knowledge is complete and adequate, so as to make me sure that I am not in error in excluding the body from my essence*[1]. He elucidates his meaning by taking as an illustration the triangle inscribed in a semicircle, which we can clearly and distinctly know to be right-angled, though we do not know, or even deny, that the square on its base is equal to the squares on its sides ; and nevertheless we cannot thence infer that we can have a [right-angled] triangle, the square on the base of which is not equal to the squares on the sides.

But, as to this illustration, the example differs in many respects from the case in hand.

For firstly, although perhaps a triangle may be taken in the concrete as a substance possessing triangular shape, certainly the property of having the square on the base equal to the squares on the sides is not a substance ; so too, neither can either of these two things be understood to be a complete thing in the sense in which *Mind and Body* are ; indeed, they cannot be called *things* in the sense in which I used the word when I said *that I might comprehend one thing* (i.e. one complete thing) *apart from the other, etc.*[2] as is evident from the succeeding words—*Besides, I discover in myself faculties, etc.*[3] For I did not assert these faculties to be *things*, but distinguished them accurately from things or substances[4].

Secondly, although we can clearly and distinctly understand that the triangle in the semicircle is right-angled, without noting that the square on its base equals those on its sides, we yet cannot clearly apprehend a triangle in which the square on the base is equal to those on the sides, without at the same time perceiving that it is right-angled. But we do clearly and distinctly perceive mind without body and body without mind.

Thirdly, although our concept of the triangle inscribed in the semicircle may be such as not to comprise the equality between the square on its base and those on its sides, it cannot be such that no ratio between the square on the base and those on the sides is held

---

[1] Cf. above, p. 83.   [2] Cf. Med. vi. vol. i. p. 190, *ad init.*   [3] *Ibid. infra.*
[4] For this last clause F. V. has 'rather I wished to make a distinction between things, i.e. between substances, and the modes of these things, i.e. the faculties of these substances.'

to prevail in the triangle in question; and hence, so long as we remain ignorant of what the ratio is, nothing can be denied of the triangle other than what we clearly know not to belong to it: but to know this in the case of the equality of the ratio is entirely impossible. Now, on the other hand, there is nothing included in the concept of body that belongs to the mind; and nothing in that of mind that belongs to the body.

Therefore, though I said that *it was sufficient to be able to apprehend one thing clearly and distinctly apart from another, etc.*, we cannot go on to complete the argument thus:—*but I clearly and distinctly apprehend this triangle*[1], *etc.* Firstly, because the ratio between the square on the base and those on the sides is not a complete thing. Secondly, because that ratio is clearly understood only in the case of the right-angled triangle. Thirdly, because the triangle itself cannot be distinctly apprehended if the ratio between the squares on the base and on the sides is denied.

But now I must explain how it is that, *from the mere fact that I apprehend one substance clearly and distinctly apart from another, I am sure that the one excludes the other*[2].

Really the notion of *substance* is just this—that which can exist by itself, without the aid of any other substance. No one who perceives two substances by means of two diverse concepts ever doubts that they are really distinct.

Consequently, if I had not been in search of a certitude greater than the vulgar, I should have been satisfied with showing in the Second Meditation that *Mind* was apprehended as a thing that subsists, although nothing belonging to the body be ascribed to it, and conversely that *Body* was understood to be something subsistent without anything being attributed to it that pertains to the mind. And I should have added nothing more in order to prove that there was a real distinction between mind and body: because commonly we judge that all things stand to each other in respect to their actual relations in the same way as they are related in our consciousness[3]. But, since one of those hyperbolical doubts adduced in the First Meditation went so far as to prevent me from being sure of this very fact (viz. that things are in their true nature[4] exactly as we perceive them to be), so long as I supposed that I had no knowledge of the author of my being, all that I have said about God and about truth in the Third, Fourth and Fifth Meditations

---

[1] Cf. above, p. 83, *sub fin.*
[2] Cf. Med. vi. vol. i, p. 190.
[3] perceptionem, L. V., pensée, F. V.
[4] juxta veritatem.

serves to further the conclusion as to the real distinction between *mind* and *body*, which is finally completed in Meditation VI.

My opponent, however, says, *I apprehend the triangle inscribed in the semicircle without knowing that the square on its base is equal to the squares on the sides*[1]. True, that triangle may indeed be apprehended although there is no thought of the ratio prevailing between the squares on the base and sides; but we can never think that this ratio must be denied. It is quite otherwise in the case of the mind where, not only do we understand that it exists apart from the body, but also that all the attributes of body may be denied of it; for reciprocal exclusion of one another belongs to the nature of substances.

There is no conflict between my theory and the point M. Arnauld next brings up, *that it is no marvel if, in deducing my existence from the fact that I think, the idea I thus form of myself represents me merely as a thinking being*[2]. For, similarly when I examine the nature of body I find nothing at all in it that savours of thought; and there is no better proof of the distinctness of two things than if, when we study each separately, we find nothing in the one that does not differ from what we find in the other.

Further, I fail to see how this argument *proves too much*[3]. For, in order to prove that one thing is really distinct from another, nothing less can be said, than that the divine power is able to separate one from the other. I thought I took sufficient care to prevent anyone thence inferring that *man was* merely *a spirit that makes use of a body*; for in this very Sixth Meditation in which I have dealt with the distinction between mind and body, I have at the same time proved that mind was substantially united with body; and I employed arguments, the efficacy of which in establishing this proof I cannot remember to have seen in any other case surpassed. Likewise, just as one who said that a man's arm was a substance really distinct from the rest of his body, would not therefore deny that it belonged to the nature of the complete man, and as in saying that the arm belongs to the nature of the complete man no suspicion is raised that it cannot subsist by itself, so I think that I have neither proved too much in showing that mind can exist apart from body, nor yet too little in saying that it is substantially united to the body, because that substantial union does not prevent the formation of a clear and distinct concept of the

---

[1] Cf. above, p. 83, *sub fin.*   [2] p. 84, par. 3.
[3] Objj. IV., *ibid. infra.*

mind alone as of a complete thing. Hence this differs greatly from the concept of a superficies or of a line, which cannot be apprehended as complete things unless, in addition to length and breadth, depth be ascribed to them.

Finally, the fact that *the power of thinking is asleep in infants and in maniacs*—though not indeed *extinct*[1], yet troubled—should not make us believe that it is conjoined with the corporeal organs in such a way as to be incapable of existing apart from them. The fact that our thought is often in our experience impeded by them, does not allow us to infer that it is produced by them; for this there is not even the slightest proof.

I do not, however, deny that the close conjunction between soul and body of which our senses constantly give us experience, is the cause of our not perceiving their real distinction without attentive reflection. But, in my judgment, those who frequently revolve in their thought what was said in the Second Meditation, will easily persuade themselves that mind is distinguished from body not by a mere fiction or intellectual abstraction, but is known as a distinct thing because it is really distinct.

I make no reply to M. Arnauld's additions[2] about the immortality of the soul, because they are not in conflict with my doctrine. As for the matter of the souls of brutes[3], this is not the place to treat the subject, and I could not, without taking in the whole of Physics, say more about them than in the explanations given in the fifth part of the discourse on Method[4]. Yet, not to pass over the matter altogether, I should point out that the chief thing to note appears to me to be that motion is impossible alike in our own bodies and in those of the brutes, unless all the organs or instruments are present, by means of which it can be effected in a machine. Hence in our very selves the mind [(or the soul)] by no means moves the external limbs immediately, but merely directs the subtle fluid styled the animal spirits[5], that passes from the heart through the brain towards the muscles, and determines this fluid to perform definite motions, these animal spirits being in their own nature capable of being utilized with equal facility for many distinct actions. But the greater part of our motions do not depend on the mind at all. Such are the beating of the heart, the digestion of our food, nutrition, respiration when we are asleep, and even walking, singing

---

[1] p. 85, par. 2.   [2] *Ibid. infra.*   [3] *Ibid. infra.*
[4] Meth. v. vol. i. pp. 115 sqq.   [5] F. V., spiritus, L. V.

and similar acts when we are awake, if performed without the mind attending to them. When a man in falling thrusts out his hand to save his head he does that without his reason counselling him so to act, but merely because the sight of the impending fall penetrating to his brain, drives the animal spirits into the nerves in the manner necessary for this motion, and for producing it without the mind's desiring it, and as though it were the working of a machine. Now, when we experience this as a fact in ourselves, why should we marvel so greatly *if the light reflected from the body of a wolf into the eyes of a sheep*[1] should be equally capable of exciting in it the motion of flight?

But if we wish by reasoning to determine whether any of the motions of brutes are similar to those which we accomplish with the aid of the mind, or whether they resemble those that depend alone upon the *influxus* of the animal spirits and the disposition of the organs, we must pay heed to the differences that prevail between the two classes : viz. those differences explained in the fifth part of the Discourse on Method, for I have been able to discover no others. Then it will be seen that all the actions of brutes resemble only those of ours that occur without the aid of the mind. Whence we are driven to conclude that we can recognize no principle of motion in them beyond the disposition of their organs and the continual discharge[2] of the animal spirits that are produced by the beat of the heart as it rarefies the blood. At the same time we shall perceive that we have had no cause for ascribing anything more to them, beyond that, not distinguishing these two principles of motion, when previously we have noted that the principle depending solely on the animal spirits and organs exists in ourselves and in the brutes alike, we have inadvisedly believed that the other principle, that consisting wholly of mind and thought, also existed in them. And it is true that a persuasion held from our earliest years, though afterwards shown by argument to be false, is not easily and only by long and frequent attention to these arguments expelled from our belief[3].

Reply to the second part, concerning God.

Up to this point I have attempted to refute M. Arnauld's arguments and to withstand his attack ; for the rest, as they are wont who combat with a stronger antagonist, I shall not oppose myself directly to his onslaught, but rather avoid the blow.

---

[1] Cf. p. 85, *sub fin.*　　　　　　　[2] affluxus.
[3] The F. V. paraphrases this last sentence at considerable length.

In this section only three points are raised; and these may be readily admitted in the sense in which he understands them. But I attached a different meaning to what I wrote, a meaning that appears to me to be also correct.

The first assertion is *that certain ideas are false materially*[1], i.e. according to my interpretation, that they supply the judgment with material for error. But my critic, taking ideas in their formal aspect, contends that falsity never resides in them.

The second is, that God is self-originated *in a positive sense, the sense implying as it were derivation from a cause*[2]. Here I had in mind merely that the reason why God requires no efficient cause in order to exist, is based on something positive, to wit, the very immensity of God, than which nothing can be more positive. M. Arnauld, however, shows that God is neither self-produced nor conserved by Himself by any positive activity belonging to an efficient cause; and this I likewise clearly affirm.

The third controverted statement is *that nothing can exist in the mind of which we are not conscious*[3]; which I in affirming held to refer to the acts of the mind, while it is of the mental faculties that he denies it.

But, to trace things out one by one, when he says, *if cold be merely a privation, there can be no idea which represents that as something positive*, it is clear that he treats of this idea only in its *formal* aspect. For, since ideas themselves are forms, and are never composed of any matter, when we take them as representing something, we regard them not *in a material guise* but *formally*; but if we were to consider them not in so far as they represent this or that other thing, but in the respect in which they are operations of the intellect, it might be said that they were taken materially, but then they would have no reference to the truth or falsity of objects. Hence it seems to me that ideas cannot be said to be materially false in any other sense than that which I have just explained. Thus, whether cold be something positive or a privation, my idea of it does not differ; it remains in me exactly the same as I have always had it. And I say that it furnishes me with material for error, if as a fact cold is a privation and does not possess so much reality as heat, because in considering either of the ideas of heat and cold just as I received them both from my senses, I am unable to perceive that more reality is revealed to me by one than by the other.

---

[1] Cf. above, p. 86.   [2] Cf. p. 88.   [3] Cf. p. 92.

But it is not the case that I have *confused judgment and idea*[1] ; for I have stated that in the latter the falsity we find is *material*, while in the former it can only be *formal*.

Moreover, when my critic asserts that *the idea of cold is cold itself in so far as that is objectively present in the understanding*[2] ; I think that his distinction is of value. For, in the case of obscure and confused ideas, among which those of heat and cold must be enumerated, it often happens that they are referred to something other than that of which they are in truth the ideas. Thus, if cold is really a privation, the idea of cold is not cold itself in so far as that is objectively present in the understanding, but something else which I wrongly take for that privation, to wit, some sensation[3] that has no existence outside the understanding.

But the same does not hold of the idea of God, at least of the idea of Him that is clear and distinct, because it cannot be said that this refers to something with which it is not in conformity. Touching the confused ideas of the gods that idolaters fashion, I do not see why they cannot be said to be materially false, in so far as they furnish those who employ them with false judgments. Though indeed ideas that give the judgment little or no occasion for error cannot, it seems, be said with equal reason to be materially false as those that give it much opportunity; moreover, it is easy by example to show that some ideas do give much more occasion for error than others. For this does not exist to such an extent in the confused ideas fashioned by the caprice of the mind (such as those of false gods) as in those that the senses give us in a confused way, such as the ideas of heat and cold; if indeed, as I said, it is true that they reveal to us nothing real. But opportunity for error is greatest in ideas that come from the appetites of sense; e.g. does not the thirst of the dropsical patient give him much material for error, in occasioning him to judge that the drink, that really will be harmful to him, will do him good?

But M. Arnauld asks what that idea of cold reveals to me, that I said was materially false. *For*, he says, *if it reveals privation, it is thereby true; if it display to him some positive entity it is not the idea of cold*[4]. Quite right; but the only reason why I call that idea materially false is because, since it is obscure and confused, I cannot decide whether it displays to me something outside my

---

[1] Cf. above, p. 87, par. 5.　　[2] Cf. *loc. cit.* par. 2.
[3] Sensus. F. V. sentiment.　　[4] Cf. *loc. cit.* par. 6.

sensation or not ; and this is why I have an opportunity for judging that it is something positive, although perchance it is only a privation.

Hence it must not be asked, *what the cause is of that positive objective entity, from which I say it results that this idea is false materially*[1] ; because I do not assert that its material falsity proceeds from any positive entity, but merely from its obscurity, which, to be sure, does have something positive as its underlying subject, viz. the sensation itself.

In very truth, that positive entity exists in me in so far as I am something real ; but the obscurity which alone causes me to think that that idea of the sensation of cold represents an object external to me, called cold, has no real cause, but arises merely from the fact that my nature is not in every respect perfect.

My chief principles are in no way shaken by this objection. But I should have more dread lest, not having spent much time in reading the writings of philosophers, I might not have followed sufficiently their fashion of speaking, in calling ideas that give the judgment occasion for error *materially* false, unless in the first author on whom I have chanced, I had found the term *materially* used with the same meaning : viz. Fr. Suarez, *Metaphysical Disputations*, 9, section 2, no. 4.

Let us now turn to the chief charge my distinguished critic brings against me. To me, indeed, there seems to be nothing worthy of censure in the passage mentioned, viz. where I said *that it is quite permissible for us to think that God in a certain sense stands to Himself in the same way as an efficient cause does to its effect*[2]. For by this very statement I have denied that doctrine which M. Arnauld thinks *bold and untrue*, viz. that God is His own efficient cause. In saying that *in a certain sense God stood so to Himself*, I showed that I did not think the relation to be identical in both cases ; and in introducing what I said with these words— *it is quite permissible for us to think*, I showed that the matter could only be explained by the imperfection of the human understanding. But in the rest of what I wrote I have confirmed this at every point ; for at the very beginning, where I said that *nothing existed as to the efficient cause of which we might not inquire*, I added, *or, if it does not possess an efficient cause, demand why that is awanting*[3]. The words sufficiently show that I believed something did exist which does not require an efficient cause. Moreover, what else

[1] Cf *loc. cit.* par. 6. [2] Cf. above, p. 88, par. 2.
[3] Above, p. 14, ll. 10—14.

could that be than God? Shortly afterwards I said that *in God there is such a great and inexhaustible power, that He has needed no assistance in order to exist, and requires none for His preservation, and hence He is in a certain way the cause of His own existence*[1]. Here the expression *cause of His own existence* can by no means be understood as efficient cause; it merely means that the inexhaustible power of God is the cause or reason why He needs no cause. It was because that inexhaustible power, or immensity of His essence, is as highly *positive* as is possible, that I said that the reason or cause why God does not require a cause was *a positive one*. This I could not have affirmed of any finite thing however perfect in its own kind; if it were alleged to be *self-derived*, this could be understood only *in a negative sense*, since no reason could be derived from its positive nature on account of which we could understand that it did not require an efficient cause.

In the same way I have at all points compared the formal cause or reason derived from God's essential nature, which explains why He Himself does not need any cause in order to exist, with the efficient cause, without which finite things cannot exist; consequently the difference between the two may be learned from my very words. Nor have I anywhere said that God conserves Himself by any positive transeunt action[2], in the way in which created beings are preserved in existence by Him; I have said merely that the immensity of the power, or essence, on account of which He needs no one to preserve Him in existence, is something *positive*.

Therefore I can readily admit everything M. Arnauld brings forward in order to prove that God is not His own efficient cause, and that He does not conserve Himself by any transeunt action, or any continual reproduction of Himself; and this is the sole conclusion of his argument. But, as I hope, even he will not deny that that immensity of power, on account of which God needs no cause in order to exist, is in Him something *positive*, and that nothing *positive* of this type could be conceived in any other thing, on account of which it should require no cause in order to exist; and this alone was what I meant to express in saying that nothing could be understood to be *self-derived* unless *in a negative sense*, except God alone. I had no need to assume more than this, in order to resolve the difficulty that had been brought forward.

But since my critic warns me with such seriousness that *Theo-*

---

[1] Above, p. 14, ll. 10—14.   [2] Influxus; influence, F. V.

logians, almost without exception, must take offence at the doctrine that God is self-originated in a positive sense, and proceeds, as it were, from a cause, I shall explain in more detail why this fashion of speech is in this question exceedingly useful, and even necessary, and why it seems to me to be quite free from any suspicion of being likely to cause offence.

I am aware that the Theologians of the Latin[1] church do not employ the word 'cause' in matters of divinity, where they treat of the procession of persons in the Holy Trinity, and that where the Greeks used αἴτιον and ἀρχή indifferently, they have preferred to employ the word *principium* alone taken in its most general sense, lest from the usage anyone might infer that the Son was not so great as the Father. But where no such danger of error can come in, and the question relates to God not as a trinity but as a unity, I see no reason why the word *cause* should be so much shunned, especially when we have come to the point when it seems very useful and almost necessary to employ the term.

No term can have a higher utility than to prove the existence of God; and none can be more necessary than this if, without it, God's existence cannot be clearly demonstrated.

But I think that it is manifest to all, that to consider the efficient cause is the primary and principal, not to say the only means of proving the existence of God. We shall not be able to pursue this proof with accuracy, if we do not grant our mind the liberty of asking for an efficient cause in every case, even in that of God; for with what right should we exclude God, before we have proved that He exists? Hence in every single case we must inquire whether it is *derived from itself or from something else*; and indeed by this means the existence of God may be inferred, although it be not expressly explained what is the meaning of anything being *self-derived*. For those who follow the guidance of the light of nature alone, spontaneously form here a concept common to efficient and formal cause alike. Hence, when a thing is *derived from something else* it is derived from that as from an efficient cause; but what is *self-derived* comes as it were from a formal cause; it results from having an essential nature which renders it independent of an efficient cause. On this account I did not explain that matter in my Meditations, assuming that it was self-evident.

But when those who are accustomed to judge in accordance

---

[1] Latinos Theologos: nos Theologiens, F. V.

with the notion that nothing can be its own efficient cause, and are familiar with the accurate distinction between formal and efficient cause, see the question raised whether anything is self-derived, it easily follows that, taking that to apply only to the efficient cause properly so styled, they think that the expression *self-derived* should not be held to mean derived from itself *as from a cause*, but merely in a negative sense and as *not having a cause*; and so consequently it results that the existence of something is implied, into the cause of the existence of which we ought not to inquire. But if this interpretation of *self-derived* were admitted, there would be no reason by which to prove God's existence from His effects, as was shown correctly by the author of the first Objections; hence we must on no account sanction it.

But in order to reply expressly to this, let me say that I think we must show that, intermediate ₁between *efficient cause*, in the proper sense, and *no cause*, there is something else, viz. *the positive essence of a thing*, to which the concept of efficient cause can be extended in the way in which in Geometry we are wont to extend the concept of a circular line, that is as long as possible, to that of a straight line; or the concept of a rectilinear polygon with an indefinite number of sides to that of a circle. I see no better way of explaining this than in saying, as I did, *that the meaning of efficient cause was in the present investigation not to be confined to those causes which are prior in time to their effects, or different from them; in the first place because the question (whether a thing can be its own efficient cause) would be unmeaning, since no one is unaware that the same thing cannot be prior to or different from itself; secondly because the former of these two conditions can be omitted from the concept without impairing the integrity of the notion of efficient cause*[1].

For the fact that the cause need not be prior in time is evident from its not having the character[2] of a cause except while it produces its effect, as I have said.

But from the fact that the second condition cannot also be annulled, we may only infer that it is not an efficient cause in the proper sense of the term, which I admit. We cannot, however, conclude that it is in no sense a positive cause, which may be held to be analogous to an efficient cause; and this is all that my argument requires. For by the very light of nature by which I perceive

---

[1] Cf. above, pp. 14, 89.   [2] rationem; le nom et la nature, F. V.

that I should have given myself all the perfections of which I have any idea, if I had indeed given myself existence, I am aware also that nothing can give itself existence in that way which is implied by the meaning to which we restrict the term efficient cause, viz. in a way such that the same thing, in so far as it gives itself being, is different from itself in so far as it receives being; for to be the same thing and not the same thing, i.e. a different thing, is a contradiction.

Thus it comes that when the question is raised whether anything can give itself existence, this must be understood merely to mean whether anything has a nature or essence such that it does not need to have any efficient cause in order to exist.

When the statement is added *that if anything is such it will give itself all the perfections of which it has any idea, if indeed it does not as yet possess them*[1], the meaning is that it cannot fail to have in actuality all the perfections that it knows, because by the light of nature we perceive that a thing, the essence of which is so limitless that it does not stand in need of an efficient cause in order that it may exist, does not require an efficient cause either, in order to possess all the perfections of which it is aware, and that its own essential nature gives to it eminently[2] whatever we can think that an efficient cause is able to bestow on anything else.

These words also, *it will give them to itself, if it does not as yet possess them*, are merely explanatory. For the same light of nature lets us know that the thing does not at the present moment have the power and desire to give itself anything new, but that its essential nature is such that from all eternity it is in possession of everything which we can imagine it would bestow on itself if it did not already possess it.

Nevertheless, all the above forms of expression which are derived from the analogy of efficient causation are highly necessary in order to guide the light of nature so as to give us a clear comprehension of those matters; they are exactly parallel to the way in which Archimedes, by comparing the sphere and other curvilinear figures with rectilinear figures, demonstrates of the former properties that could hardly otherwise be understood. And, just as no exception is taken to such proofs, though they make us regard the sphere as similar to a polyhedron, so, in my opinion, I cannot here be blamed for using the analogy of efficient causality in order to explain

---

[1] p. 88, par. 1 (not quoted exactly).   [2] Eminenter.

matters that appertain to the formal cause, i.e. to the very essence of God.

Nor can any danger of error be apprehended at this point, since that single feature peculiar to an efficient cause and incapable of being extended to the formal cause involves a manifest contradiction, and hence such a thought can be entertained by no one, viz. that anything should be different from itself, i.e. the same thing and not the same thing.

We must mark here, too, that my language ascribes to God the dignity implied by the word cause in a way that does not require that He should have the imperfection[1] attached to being an effect. For, exactly as Theologians, though styling the Father the *originating principle*[2] of the Son, do not on that account admit that the Son is something *originated*[3], so, though admitting that God is, in a sense, *His own cause*, I have nevertheless nowhere called him similarly *His own effect;* for, in truth, effect is used chiefly when speaking of an efficient cause and is regarded as of inferior[4] nature to it, though often higher than other causes.

Moreover, in taking the entire essence of a thing as its formal cause here, I merely follow the footsteps of Aristotle. For in *Post. Anal.* Bk II. ch. 11, after passing over the material cause, he names as αἰτία[5] primarily τὸ τί ἦν εἶναι[6], or, as it is rendered in philosophical Latin, *the formal cause*; and he extends this to all the essential natures of all things, since at that point he is not treating of the causes of a physical compound (as neither do I in this place), but generally of the causes from which knowledge of any kind may be derived.

But it can be shown that it was hardly possible for me to refrain in this inquiry from ascribing to God the character of a cause, from the fact that, though my distinguished critic has tried to perform in another way the same task as I undertook, he has quite failed in his attempt, at least, as it appears to me. For after taking many words to show that God is not His own efficient cause, because the concept of an efficient cause requires diversity between it and its effect, after showing that God is not self-originated in the positive sense (where positive is taken to imply the positive transeunt action of a cause), after likewise maintaining that God does not conserve Himself in the sense in which conservation means the continuous

---

[1] indignitas, V. L.
[2] principium.
[3] principiatum.
[4] ignobilior.
[5] cause.
[6] a thing's essential nature.

production of a thing, all of which contentions I gladly admit; after all this he once more hastens to prove that God should not be called the efficient cause of Himself, *because we seek to discover the efficient cause of a thing only with respect to its existence and not at all with respect to its essence. But existence is involved in the essence of an infinite being, no less than the equality of its angles to two right angles is involved in that of a triangle. Therefore when we ask why God exists, we must not attempt to reply by assigning an efficient cause any more than we should do if asked why the triangle has its three angles equal to two right angles*[1]. But this syllogism can easily be manipulated so as to tell against its author; thus, although we do not enquire for an efficient cause with respect to a thing's essence, nevertheless we can do so with regard to its existence; but in God essence and existence are not distinguished; hence we may enquire about the efficient cause of God.

But in order to reconcile those two matters, we should reply to the question as to why God exists, not indeed by assigning an efficient cause in the proper sense, but only by giving the essence of the thing or formal cause, which, owing to the very fact that in God existence is not distinguished from essence, has a strong analogy with the efficient cause, and may on this ground be called similar to an efficient cause.

Finally, M. Arnauld adds that *when we are asked for the efficient cause of God, we must reply that He needs no efficient cause. And if our interrogator plies us with the question why no efficient cause is required, we must answer, 'because He is an infinite Being, and in such a case existence and essence are identical*[2], *for only those things, the existence of which can be distinguished from their essence require an efficient cause.'* He thinks that this overthrows my contention that *if I did not believe that anything could in some way be related to itself exactly as an efficient cause is related towards its effect, in enquiring into the causes of things I should never arrive at a first cause of all*[3]. But to me it seems that this reasoning is neither overthrown nor in any way shaken or enfeebled. The main force not only of my argument but of all demonstrations that may be brought up to prove the existence of God from the effects that flow from Him, depends on this. Moreover, there is no argument advanced by practically any theologian that is not based on the effects of God's causality.

[1] Cf. above, p. 91 (abridged).   [2] Cf. p. 92, par. 1.
[3] Cf. *ibid. infra* (abridged).

Therefore, far from making intelligible the proof of God's existence, when he does not permit us to assign to the relation He has towards Himself the analogy of efficient causation, it is rather the case that M. Arnauld prevents his reader from understanding it, especially at the end, where he draws the conclusion :—*that if he thought he must enquire for the efficient cause of anything whatsoever, or for something analogous to the efficient cause, he would seek for as cause of that given thing, whatsoever it was, something that was different from it.* For how could those who have not as yet known God enquire into the efficient cause of other things, in order thus to arrive at the knowledge of God, unless they believed that it was possible to enquire for the efficient cause of everything whatsoever? And how could they make God, as being the first cause, the end of their investigation if they thought that things must in all cases have a cause distinct from themselves?

My opponent here seems to act as if (following Archimedes, who, in speaking about the properties he has demonstrated of the sphere, taking it as analogous to rectilinear figures inscribed within it, had said : 'If I imagined that the sphere could not be taken for a rectilinear figure or as after the fashion of a rectilinear figure with an infinite number of sides, I should attach no force to this proof, because properly it holds not of the sphere as a curvilinear figure, but applies to it merely as a rectilinear figure with an infinite number of sides'); it seems, I repeat, as if, at once unwilling to take the sphere in this way, but at the same time desirous of retaining the proof of Archimedes, he said : 'If I thought that the conclusion here drawn must be judged to be true of a rectilinear figure with an infinite number of sides, I should not admit that it holds good of the sphere, because I know quite certainly that the sphere is by no means a rectilinear figure.' But so saying he could not arrive at the same result as Archimedes, but on the contrary, would quite prevent himself and others from properly understanding the proof.

I have pursued this topic at somewhat greater length than the subject demanded, in order to prove that it is a matter of great anxiety to me to prevent anything from appearing in my writings capable of giving just offence to theologians.

Finally, to prove that I have not argued in a circle in saying, *that the only secure reason we have for believing that what we clearly and distinctly perceive is true, is the fact that God exists; but that clearly we can be sure that God exists only because we perceive that*[1],

---

[1] p. 92, parr. 6 and 7.

I may cite the explanations that I have already given at sufficient length in my reply to the second set of Objections, numbers 3 and 4. There I distinguished those matters that in actual truth we clearly perceive from those we remember to have formerly perceived. For first, we are sure that God exists because we have attended to the proofs that established this fact; but afterwards it is enough for us to remember that we have perceived something clearly, in order to be sure that it is true; but this would not suffice, unless we knew that God existed and that he did not deceive us.

The fact *that nothing can exist in the mind, in so far as it is a thinking thing, of which it is not conscious*[1], seems to me self-evident, because we conceive nothing to exist in it, viewed in this light, that is not thought, and something dependent on thought; for otherwise it would not belong to the mind, in so far as it is a thinking thing. But there can exist in us no thought of which, at the very moment that it is present in us, we are not conscious. Wherefore I have no doubt that the mind begins to think at the same time as it is infused into the body of an infant, and is at the same time conscious of its own thought, though afterwards it does not remember that, because the specific forms of these thoughts do not live in the memory.

But it has to be noted that, while indeed we are always in actuality conscious of acts or operations of the mind, that is not the case with the faculties or powers of mind, except potentially. So that when we dispose ourselves to the exercise of any faculty, if the faculty reside in us, we are immediately actually conscious of it; and hence we can deny that it exists in the mind, if we can form no consciousness of it.

Reply relative to those matters likely to cause difficulty to Theologians.

Whilst I have combated M. Arnauld's first objections and have avoided any collision with his second, I am quite willing to agree to the next set of criticisms, except in the case of the final one; and here I hope without great difficulty to get him himself to yield his assent to me.

Hence I quite admit that what is found in the first Meditation and even in the others is not suited to the capacity of every understanding, and this I have avouched on every possible occasion and

---

[1] Cf. p. 93, *sub fin.*

always shall proclaim. This was the reason why I did not discuss the same matters in the Discourse on Method, which was written in French, but reserved them for the Meditations which, I announced, should be read only by intellectual and educated persons. No one should say that I had better have refrained from penning matters, the reading of which many people ought to avoid ; for I believe these things to be necessary to such an extent, that nothing stable or firm in philosophy can, I am convinced, be ever established without them. And though fire and steel may not be handled without danger by children or careless people, yet they are so important for life that no one thinks that we should for the above reason do without them.

Now, as to the fact that in the fourth Meditation I treated only *of the mistakes made in distinguishing between the true and the false, but not of the error that occurs in the pursuit of good and evil*[1], *and touching the fact that I always excluded those things that concern our faith and the conduct of life,* when I asserted that *we should assent only to what we clearly and distinctly know;* with these two facts the whole context of my works manifests agreement. I explained this also expressly in my reply to the second set of Objections, no. 5[2], and I set it forth also in the Synopsis. I make this statement in order to show how much value I attach to M. Arnauld's judgment and how much I esteem his advice.

The remaining matter is the Sacrament of the Eucharist. M. Arnauld believes that my doctrines are in conflict with this, *because it is an article of our faith that the substance of the bread passes out of the bread of the Eucharist, and that only its accidents remain*[3]; *further he believes that I recognise no real accidents, but only modes which cannot be comprehended apart from the substance in which they inhere, and hence cannot exist apart from it*[4].

But I have no difficulty in parrying this objection when I say that I have never as yet denied the existence of real accidents. For, though in the Dioptric and the work on Meteors I did not employ them in explaining the matters of which I treated, nevertheless, in the Meteors, p. 164, I expressly said that I did not deny their reality. But in these Meditations, while I assumed indeed that I was as yet unaware of their existence, I did not on that account deny their reality. For the analytic style of composition which I adopted allows us sometimes to make certain assumptions

---

[1] Cf. above, p. 93. [2] Cf. above, pp. 43, 44.
[3] p. 95, par. 5. [4] *Ibid. infra* (abridged).

without their being as yet sufficiently investigated, as was evident in the first Meditation, in which I provisionally assumed many doctrines that I afterwards refuted. Further, it was not my purpose at this point to formulate any doctrine about the nature of accidents; I simply brought forward what seemed at a preliminary survey to be true of them. Finally, from the fact that I alleged that modes could not be conceived apart from some substance in which they inhered, it should not be inferred that I deny that they can be held apart from it by the divine power, because I firmly hold and believe that God is able to accomplish many things that we are incapable of comprehending.

But I shall here express myself more frankly and shall not conceal the fact that I am convinced that the only thing by which our senses are stimulated is that superficies which forms the boundary of the dimensions of the perceived body. For contact takes place only at the surface. Likewise, not I alone, but practically all philosophers along with Aristotle himself, affirm that no sense is stimulated otherwise than by contact. Thus, for example, bread or wine cannot be perceived except in so far as its surface is in contact with the organ of sense, either immediately or by the mediation of air or other bodies, as I believe, or as many philosophers allege, by the intervention of 'intentional forms [1].'

But we must note that we should not form our idea of that surface merely from the external figure of bodies that is felt by the fingers; we should take into account also those tiny crevices that are found between the minute grains of the flour of which the bread is composed, as well as between the particles of spirit, water, vinegar and lees or tartar that combine or constitute the wine, and so in the case of the particles of other bodies also. For, as a fact, these particles, possessing diverse figures and motions are never so closely united with each other as not to leave many interstices between them, which are not vacant, but filled with air or some other material. Thus in bread we can see with the naked eye fairly large spaces, which may be filled not merely with air, but with water, wine and other liquids. But since the bread remains always self-identical, although the air or other material contained in its pores changes, it is clear that these things do not belong to its substance; hence we see that its surface is not that superficies that traces the

[1] mediantibus speciebus intentionalibus—the theory that the 'form' or sensible character of the object propagated copies of itself through the medium and that those alone were directly perceived.

briefest outline round it, but that which immediately envelopes its
separate particles.

We must likewise observe that not only does the whole of this
superficies move when the whole piece of bread is transferred from
one place to another, but that it also has a partial movement, as
happens when some of the particles of bread are set in motion by
the entrance of air or other bodies into its pores. Hence, if there
are any bodies such that any or all of their parts are in continual
motion (which I think holds of many of the constituent parts of
bread and in the case of all the particles in wine), we must believe
that the superficies of these things are continually in some sort of
motion.

Finally, we must note that, by the superficies of bread or of
wine or of any other body, is meant not any part of their substance,
nor indeed any part of the quantity of the body, nor even a part of
the circumjacent bodies, but merely *that limit which is conceived
to lie between the single particles of a body and the bodies that
surround it, a boundary which has absolutely none but a modal
reality*[1].

But now, since contact is effected at this boundary alone and
nothing is perceived unless by contact, it is clear that from the
single statement that the substance of the bread and wine is changed
into the substance of some other body in such a way that this new
substance is entirely contained within the same limits as those
within which the other substances previously were, or in precisely
the same place as that in which the bread and wine previously
existed, or rather (since these boundaries are continually moving)
in that in which they would exist if they were present, it necessarily
follows that that new substance would act on our senses in entirely
the same way as that in which the bread and wine would act, if no
transubstantiation had occurred.

Moreover, it is the teaching of the Church in the Council of
Trent, session 13, canons 2 and 4, *that the whole substance of the
bread is changed into the substance of the body of Christ our Lord,
while only the semblance of the bread remains unaltered.* Here I do
not see what can be meant by the appearance of the bread, except
that superficies which intervenes between its single particles and
the bodies surrounding them.

For, as has already been said, it is at this superficies alone that
contact occurs ; and Aristotle himself supports us in saying that

[1] entitatem.

not only that sense which is in special called *touch*, but the other senses also perceive by touching :—*De Anima*, Book III. chap. 13 : καὶ τὰ ἄλλα αἰσθητήρια ἁφῇ αἰσθάνεται.

Further, there is no one who thinks that here by species is meant anything else than exactly what is required for acting on the senses. There is no one, too, who believes in the conversion of the bread into the body of Christ, that does not at the same time believe that this body of Christ is accurately comprised within that superficies beneath which the bread, if it were present, would be found ; and this even though it is not there in the proper sense of being in a place, *but sacramentally and with that form of existence which, though we have a difficulty in expressing it in words, yet when our thought is illumined by faith, we can still believe to be possible with God, and ought always firmly so to believe.* Now, all these matters are so conveniently and correctly explained by my principles that not only have I nothing here to fear in the way of giving the slightest cause of offence to orthodox theologians, but on the contrary I confidently anticipate reaping gratitude from them, because in my Physics I propound those doctrines which agree with Theology much better than the common opinions. As a matter of fact, never, to my knowledge at least, has the Church in any passage taught that the semblances[1] of the wine and bread that remain in the Sacrament of the Eucharist are real accidents of any sort which, when the substance in which they inhered is removed, miraculously subsist by themselves.

But[2] perhaps because the theologians who first tried to explain this matter in a philosophical way were so firmly convinced that the accidents that stimulate our senses are something real and distinct from substance, that they did not even remark that doubt might in conceivable circumstances be cast on their opinion ; the semblances[1] manifested by the bread were likewise believed by them without any scrutiny or valid reason to be real accidents of this kind. Thenceforward, they were wholly taken up with explaining how the accidents could exist without their subject. But here they found such difficulty that (like wayfarers who have arrived among thickets that seem to offer no clear thoroughfare) from the difficulty of the situation alone they were bound to infer that they had wandered from the straight road.

[1] Species.
[2] The whole of what follows up to p. 122 appeared only in the second edition of the *Objections*.

For, firstly they seem to contradict themselves; at least those do who admit that all sense-perception is effected by contact, when they suppose that in objects something other than the various disposition of their superficies is required for the purpose of stimulating the senses; for it is self-evident that in order to effect contact surface alone is necessary. Those, on the other hand, who do not make the above admission are unable to describe what happens with any appearance of verisimilitude.

Further, the human mind is unable to think that the accidents of bread are realities and yet exist apart from the substance of the bread, without thinking of them after the fashion of a substance. Hence there seems to be a contradiction in believing with the Church that the whole substance of the bread is changed, and meanwhile thinking that something real remains, which previously was in the bread, for nothing real can be conceived to remain, except what subsists, and though it is called an accident, we nevertheless conceive it as a substance. Hence, in reality, it is the same as to say that while indeed the whole of the substance of the bread is changed, there yet remains that part of its substance that is called a real accident, and this, if not verbally, is at any rate in thought a contradiction.

And this seems to be the chief reason why certain people have at this point disagreed with the Roman Church. Does anyone not believe that when we are free to choose, and there is no reason, either theological or indeed philosophical, compelling us to embrace certain particular opinions, we should most readily select those beliefs that can give others no opportunity or pretext for turning aside from the truth of the faith? But I think I have here shown with sufficient clearness that the doctrine that assumes the existence of real accidents does not harmonize with theological reasoning; that it is wholly in conflict with philosophical thought I hope clearly to demonstrate in a treatise on the principles[1] of philosophy on which I am now engaged. Then I shall show how colour, savour, weight and whatever else stimulates the sense, depend wholly upon the exterior surface of bodies.

Finally, if we assume the existence of real accidents, it follows that by the miracle of transubstantiation, which alone can be inferred from the words of consecration, something new and indeed incomprehensible is gratuitously added, something that permits

---

[1] in summâ philosophiae.

those real accidents to exist apart from the substance of the bread, without themselves in the meantime being substances. But this not only conflicts with human reason, but also with the theological axiom that says that the words of consecration effect nothing beyond what they signify; the theologians refuse to assign to miraculous causes what can be explained by the natural reason. But my explanation of the matter removes all their difficulties. For, far from its postulating some miraculous agency in order to explain the conservation of the accidents after the substance is removed, it refuses to admit that without a new miracle (such as might alter the dimensions in question) could they be annulled. It has been related that such an event has happened and that at such times the priest has found in his hand flesh or a tiny child. But this confirms my contention, for it has never been believed that what happened was due to a cessation of the miracle; it has always been ascribed to a new miracle.

Besides this, there is nothing incomprehensible or difficult in the idea of God, the creator of all things, being able to change one substance into another, and the second substance remaining comprised within the same superficies as that which bounded the former. For nothing can be more consonant with reason, no statement better received in the general ranks of the philosophers, than the assertion that not only all sensation, but generally all action of body on body, is effected by contact, and that this contact can occur only at the surface. Whence it evidently follows that the same substance, whatever be the change in the substance that lies beneath it, must always act and be acted on in the same way.

Wherefore, if I here may speak the truth freely and without offence, I avow that I venture to hope that a time will some day come when the doctrine that postulates the existence of real accidents will be banished by theologians as being foreign to rational thought, incomprehensible, and causing uncertainty in the faith; and mine will be accepted in its place as being certain and indubitable. I have purposely made no concealment here, in order that I may combat to the best of my ability the calumnies of those who, wishing to be thought more learned than others, are never so much enraged as when some new scientific doctrine, of which they cannot pretend they previously had knowledge, is brought forward. Frequently, their opposition is more bitter in proportion as they believe that the doctrine is true and important, and when unable to refute it by argument, they maintain without a shadow of reason that it is contrary to Holy Scripture and the verities of the faith[1]. This truly is impiety—to attempt to employ the authority of the Church in order to overthrow the truth[2]. But I appeal from such people to the judgment of pious and orthodox theologians, to whose opinion and decision I willingly submit myself.

[1] This is abridged in the F. V.
[2] This sentence is not in the F. V.

ANNOUNCEMENT BY THE AUTHOR RELATIVE TO THE FIFTH SET OF OBJECTIONS[1].

BEFORE the appearance of the first edition of these Meditations[2] I wished to have them examined not only by the learned Doctors of the Sorbonne, but also by all other men of science who should care to take the trouble of reading them. I thus hoped that by causing these objections and my replies to be printed as a continuation of the Meditations, each in the order in which they were composed, I should thereby render the truth much more evident. And though the objections that were sent to me fifth in order did not appear to me to be the most important and are very lengthy, I did not fail to have them printed in their proper order, so as not to disoblige their author. I likewise caused him to be furnished with a proof of the impression lest anything should be set down as his, of which he did not approve. But as he has since composed a work of great size[3], containing these same objections, together with several new counter-arguments or answers to my replies, and since he there complains of me for having published them, as if I had done so against his wishes, and says that he sent them to me only for my private instruction, I shall henceforth gladly comply with his desire and so relieve this volume of their presence. This was the reason why, on learning that M. Clerselier was taking the trouble to translate the other Objections, I begged him to omit these latter ones. And in order that he may have no cause to regret their absence, I have to inform the reader at this place that I have lately read them a second time, and that I have read also all the new counter-arguments in the huge volume containing them, with the

[1] In the first French edition of the Meditations with Objections and Replies.
[2] i.e. the Latin edition of 1641.
[3] Petri Gassendi, *Disquisitio metaphysica*, Amsterdam, 1644.

purpose of extracting thence all the points I should judge to stand in need of a reply; but I have been unable to discover one, to which, in my opinion, those who have at all understood the meaning of my Meditations will not be able to reply without any aid from me. As to those who judge books only by their size or by their title, I have no ambition to secure praise from them.

LETTER FROM M. DESCARTES TO M. CLERSELIER

TO SERVE AS A REPLY TO A SELECTION OF THE PRINCIPAL OBJECTIONS TAKEN BY M. GASSENDI TO THE PRECEDING REPLIES[1].

[12th January, 1646.]

SIR,

I owe you a deep debt of gratitude for noticing that I have neglected to reply to the huge volume of hostile arguments which the Author of the fifth set of Objections has composed in answer to my Replies, and for having asked some of your friends to extract the strongest arguments from this book, as well as for sending me the selection[2] which they have made. In this you have shown more anxiety for my reputation than I myself possess ; for I assure you that to me it is a matter of indifference whether I am esteemed or contemned by the people with whom such arguments have weight. Those of my friends who have read his book, and the best heads among them, have declared to me that they have found nothing in it to arrest their attention ; now I am content to have satisfied them alone. I know that the greater part of mankind seize on appearance more readily than on the truth, judge wrongly more frequently than aright. This is why I hold that their approval is not worth the trouble I should incur in doing all that might be required in order to secure it. But none the less I am pleased with the selection you have sent me, and I feel myself obliged to reply to it, more in order to express my gratitude to your friends for their trouble, than because I need to defend myself. For I believe that those who have taken the trouble to make it must

---

[1] i.e. to the Replies to Objections V.
[2] This selection is not extant. MM. Adam et Tannery refer their readers to the index (which they print) of Gassendi's *Disquisitio metaphysica*.

now believe, as I do, that all the objections that this book contains are founded solely on the misunderstanding of certain terms or on certain false suppositions. But though all the objections they have remarked on are of that sort, yet they have been so diligent as even to have added certain ones which I do not remember to have previously read.

They notice three criticisms directed against the first Meditation : 1. *That I demand an impossibility in desiring the abandonment of every kind of prejudice.* 2. *That in thinking one has given up every prejudice one acquires other beliefs of a still more prejudiced kind.* 3. *That the method I have proposed of doubting everything does not promote the discovery of any single truth.*

The first of these criticisms is due to the author of this book not having reflected that the word prejudice does not apply to all the notions in our mind, of which it is impossible for us to divest ourselves, but only to all those opinions our belief in which is a result of previous judgments. And since judging or refraining from judgment is an act of the will, as I have explained in the appropriate place, it is evident that it is under our control; for in order to rid one's self of all prejudice, nothing needs to be done except to resolve to affirm or deny none of the matters we have previously affirmed or denied, unless after a fresh examination. But yet we do not on that account cease to retain all these same notions in the memory. Nevertheless I have said that there was a difficulty in expelling from our belief everything that had been put there previously, partly because we need to have some reason for doubting before determining to do so ; it was for this cause that I propounded the chief reasons for doubting in my first Meditation. Another source also of the difficulty is that whatever be the resolution we have formed of denying or affirming nothing, it is easy to forget, if we have not impressed it firmly on the memory ; and this was why I recommended that this should be thought of earnestly.

The second objection is nothing but a manifest falsity; for though I said that we must even compel ourselves to deny the things we had previously affirmed with too great assurance, I expressly limited the period during which we should so behave to the time in which we bend our thought to the discovery of something more certain than what we had been able thus to deny: and during this time it is evident that we could not entertain any belief of a prejudicial character.

The third criticism is mere cavilling. True, mere doubt alone does not suffice to establish any truth ; but that does not prevent it from being useful in preparing the mind for the subsequent establishment of truth. This is the sole purpose for which I have employed it.

Your friends mark six objections to Meditation II. The first is that in the statement, *I think, hence I exist*, the author of these criticisms will have it that I imply the assumption of this major premiss, *he who thinks, exists*, and that I have thus already espoused a prejudice. Here he once more mishandles the word *prejudice*: for though we may apply this term to that proposition when it is brought forward without scrutiny, and we believe it merely because we remember we have made this same judgment previously, we cannot maintain on every occasion that it is a prejudice, i.e. when we subject it to examination, the cause being that it appears to be so evident to the understanding that we should fail to disbelieve it even on the first occasion in our life on which it occurred to us, on which occasion it would not be a prejudice. But the greater error here is our critic's assumption that the knowledge of particular truths is always deduced from universal propositions in consonance with the order of the sequence observed in the syllogism of dialectic. This shows that he is but little acquainted with the method by which truth should be investigated. For it is certain that in order to discover the truth we should always start with particular notions, in order to arrive at general conceptions subsequently, though we may also in the reverse way, after having discovered the universals, deduce other particulars from them. Thus in teaching a child the elements of geometry we shall certainly not make him understand the general truth that '*when equals are taken from equals the remainders are equal,*' or that '*the whole is greater than its parts,*' unless by showing him examples in particular cases. For want of guarding against this error our author has been led astray into the many fallacious reasonings which have gone to swell his book. He has merely constructed false major premisses according to his whim, as though I had deduced from these the truths I have explained.

The second objection which your friends remark is : *that, in order to know that I think, I must know what thought is; which I certainly do not know*, they say, *because I have denied everything.* But I have denied nothing but prejudices, and by no means notions like these, which are known without any affirmation or denial.

Thirdly : *Thought cannot lack an object, for example the body.*

Here we must keep clear of the ambiguity in the word thought ; it can be taken either for the thing that thinks or for that thing's activity. Now I deny that the thing that thinks needs any object other than itself in order to exercise its activity, though it can also reach out to material things when it examines them.

Fourthly : *Even though I have a thought of myself, I do not know whether that thought is a corporeal action or a self-moved atom, rather than an immaterial substance.* Here we have once more the ambiguity in the word thought, and, apart from this, I see nothing but a baseless question somewhat of this kind—you esteem that you are a man, because you perceive in yourself all the things on account of which you bestow the name of men on all who possess them ; but how do you know that you are not an elephant rather than a man, owing to some other causes which you cannot perceive? After the substance which thinks has judged that it is an intelligence because it has remarked in itself all the properties of thinking substances, and has been unable to recognise any of those belonging to body, once more it is asked how it knows that it is not a body, rather than an immaterial substance.

Similar to this is the fifth objection : *That though I find nothing extended in my thought, it does not follow that it is really not extended, because my thought is not the rule of the truth of things.* Likewise the sixth : *That possibly the distinction drawn by my thought between thought and body, is false.* But here we must particularly notice the equivocation in the words :—*my thought is not the rule of the truth of things.* For, if anyone care to allege that my thought ought not to be the rule for others, so as to make them believe something because I think it true, I entirely agree. But that is not at all to the point here. For I have never wished to force anyone to follow my authority ; on the contrary I have announced in divers places that one should never let one's self be persuaded except by received proofs. Further, if the word thought be taken indifferently for every psychical operation, it is certain that we can have many thoughts, from which we can infer nothing relative to the truth of matters outside of us. But that also is not to the point here, where the question concerns only those thoughts that form clear and distinct perceptions, and the judgments which everyone can make on his own account in the train of these perceptions. This is why, in the sense in which these words should be here understood, I say that each individual's thought, i.e. the perception or knowledge which he has of a thing, ought to be for him the rule for the truth of that thing ; that is to say, that all the judgments he makes should be conformable with that perception in order to be correct. Even in the matter of the truths of the faith, we should perceive some reason persuading us that they have been revealed by God, before determining ourselves to believe them ; and though those who are ignorant do well to follow the judgment of the more capable, touching those matters that are difficult of apprehension, it must nevertheless be their own perception that tells them that they are ignorant and that those whose judgments they wish to follow are less ignorant, otherwise they would do ill to follow them, and would act as automata or as mere animals rather than as men. Hence it is the most absurd and extravagant error that a philosopher can commit, to wish to make judgments which have no relation to his perception of things. Yet I fail to see how my critic can avoid the censure of having fallen into this error, in the greater part of his objections ; for he does not wish each individual to stand firmly by his own perceptions, but claims that we should rather believe the opinions or fancies he pleases to set before us, though we wholly fail to grasp them as perceptions.

In opposition to the third Meditation your friends have re-marked :—1. *That not everyone has experience of the presence of the idea of God within him.* 2. *That if I had this idea I should comprehend it.* 3. *That several people have read my arguments, whom they have failed to persuade.* 4. *That it does not follow from the fact that I know myself to be imperfect, that God exists.* But, if we take the word idea in the way in which I expressly said I took it, without getting out of the difficulty by the equivocation practised by those who restrict it to the images of material things, likenesses formed in the imagination, we shall be unable to deny that we have some idea of God, except by saying that we do not understand the words—*that thing which is the most perfect that we can conceive ;* for that is what all men call God. But to go so far as to assert that they do not understand the words which are the commonest in the mouths of men, is to have recourse to strange extremes in order to find objections. Besides, it is the most impious confession one can make, to say of one's own accord, in the sense in which I have taken the word idea, that one has no idea of God : for this is not merely to say that one does not know it by means of the natural reason, but also that neither by faith nor by any other means could one have any knowledge of it, because if one has no idea, i.e. no perception corresponding to the signification of the word *God*, it is vain to say one believes that *God* exists; it would be the same as saying that one believes that *nothing* exists, and thus one would remain plunged in the abyss of impiety and the extremity of ignorance.

What they add—*that if I had this idea I should comprehend it*—is alleged without grounds. For, because the word *comprehend* conveys a sense of limitation, a finite spirit cannot comprehend God, who is infinite. But that does not prevent him from apprehending[1] Him, just as one can touch a mountain without being able to embrace it.

Their statement about my arguments—*that several people have read them without being persuaded by them*—can easily be refuted; for there are others who have understood them and have been satisfied with them. For more credence should be attached to what one man (who does not mean to lie) says, if he alleges that he has seen or learned something, than one should give to a thousand others who deny it, for the mere reason that it was impossible for them to see it or become aware of it. Thus at the discovery of the Antipodes the report of a few sailors who had circumnavigated the earth was believed rather than the thousands of philosophers who had not believed the earth to be round. Further, though they here cite as confirmation the Elements of Euclid, saying that everyone finds them easy to apprehend, I beg my critics to consider that among those men who are counted the most learned in the Philosophy of the Schools, there is not one in a hundred who understands them, and that there is not one in ten thousand who understands all the demonstrations of Apollonius or Archimedes, though they are as evident and as certain as those of Euclid.

Finally, when they say *that it does not follow from the fact that I recognise some imperfections in myself that God exists*, they prove nothing. For I do not deduce this conclusion from that premiss alone, without adding something else; they merely remind me of the artifice of my critic who has the habit of mutilating my arguments and reporting only parts of them, in order to make them appear to be imperfect.

I see nothing in these remarks touching the three other meditations to which I have not elsewhere given an ample reply, e.g. to their objection :—1. *That I have reasoned in a circle in drawing my proofs of the existence of God from certain notions that exist in*

---

[1] aperçoive.

us, and afterwards saying that we can be certain of nothing unless we already know that God exists. 2. *That the knowledge of God's existence contributes nothing to the acquisition of a knowledge of the truths of mathematics.* 3. *That God may deceive us.* On this subject consult my reply to the second set of objections, numbers 3 and 4, and the end of part 2 of the reply to the fourth set of objections[1].

But at the end my critics add a reflection which is not, to my knowledge, to be found in the book of counter arguments[2] written by this Author, though it is very similar to his criticisms. *Many people of great acumen,* they say, *believe that they clearly see that the mathematical extension, which I take as the basal principle of my Physics, is nothing but my thought, and that it has and can have no subsistence outside of my mind, being merely an abstraction that I form from a physical body; that consequently the whole of my Physics is but imaginary and fictitious, as is likewise all pure mathematics: and that the physical nature of the real things that God has created requires a matter that is real, solid, and not imaginary.* Here we have the objection of objections, and the sum of the whole doctrine of these men of great acumen who are here brought into evidence. Everything that we are able to understand and conceive, is, according to their story, but imagination—the fictitious creation of our mind, and can have no real subsistence : whence it follows that nothing exists which we can comprehend, conceive, or imagine, or admit as true, and that we must close the door against reason, and content ourselves with being Monkeys or Parrots, and no longer be Men, if we wish to place ourselves on a level with these acute intelligences. For, if the things which we conceive must be esteemed to be false merely because we can conceive them, what is there left for us but to accept as true the things we do not conceive, and to make our system of belief out of them, imitating others without knowing why we do so, like the Monkeys, and uttering only those words which we do not understand, like Parrots ? But I have something substantial wherewith to console myself, inasmuch as my critics here conjoin my Physics with pure Mathematics, which it is my deepest wish my Physics should resemble.

As for the two questions added at the end, viz.—*how the soul moves the body if it is not material?* and *how it can receive the specific*

---

[1] Cf. pp. 38—43 and p. 115.   [2] Instances.

forms[1] *of corporeal objects?* these give me here merely the opportunity
of declaring that our Author had no right, under pretext of criticising
me, to propound a mass of questions like this, the solution of which
was not necessary for the proof of what I have written, questions of
which the most ignorant man might raise more in a quarter of an hour
than the wisest could solve in a lifetime. Thus I do not feel called
upon to answer any of them. Likewise these objections, among
other things, presuppose an explanation of the nature of the union
between soul and body, a matter of which I have not yet treated.
But to you, for your own benefit, I declare that the whole of the
perplexity involved in these questions arises entirely from a false
supposition that can by no manner of means be proved, viz. that if
the soul and the body are two substances of diverse nature, that
prevents them from being capable of acting on one another; for, on
the contrary, those who admit the existence of real accidents, like
heat, weight, and so forth, do not doubt that these accidents have
the power of acting on the body, and nevertheless there is more
difference between them and it, i.e. between accidents and a
substance, than there is between two substances.

For the rest, since I have my pen in my hand, I may call
attention here to two of the ambiguities which I have found in
this book of counter-arguments, because they are such as to my
mind, might most easily entrap an inattentive reader, and I desire
in this way to testify to you that if I had found anything else
worthy of a reply I should not have passed it over.

The first is on page 63[2], where because I have said in one

---

[1] espèces.
[2] *Metaphysical Disquisitions* etc., pp. 62—64, i.e. the third part of the
Counter-argument which follows 'Doubt 4' directed against Meditation II and
the Reply. (For these two passages cf. Objj. v, pp. 140—142 and pp. 147, 148):
' and especially since it has been shewn that you have either assumed your conclusion or failed to prove it when you draw this inference: *I am then strictly taken
only a thing that thinks.* It would be better to make a frank confession, and, as,
close upon my "Doubt," I urge you once more to do, remember that after you
have said, *I am then strictly taken only a thing that thinks,* you have declared
that you do not know, and do not at this point dispute, *whether you are that
complex system of members, styled the human body, or a subtle air infused into
those members, or fire, or vapour, or breath, etc.* For thence two conclusions
follow. One is that when we arrive at your demonstration in Meditation VI,
you will be convicted of having failed to prove at any point that you are not a
complex system of members, or a subtle air, or vapour, etc., and that you will
not be able to take that as granted or proved. Secondly it will follow that it
was unjustifiable to draw the conclusion: *I am then strictly taken only a thing
that thinks.* What does that word *only* mean? Is it not restriction (so to
speak) to something thinking solely, and exclusive of all other things, among
which we find a system of members, a subtle air, fire, vapour, breath, and other
bodies? Since you are a thinking thing, do you know that you are none of
these as well? You reply clearly that you do not know. *I do not know,* you

place[1], that while the soul is in doubt of the existence of all material things it knows itself precisely, *in the strict sense, only*[2], as an immaterial substance; and seven or eight lines lower down, in order to show that, by using the words *in the strict sense, only* I do not mean an entire exclusion or negation, but only an abstraction from material things, I said that, in spite of that, I was not sure that there was nothing corporeal in the soul, although nothing of such a nature was known to exist in it; my opponents are so unjust to me as to wish to persuade the reader that in saying *in the strict sense, only* I wished to exclude the body, and have thus contradicted myself afterwards in saying that I did not wish to exclude it. I make no reply to the subsequent accusation of having assumed something in the Sixth Meditation that I had not previously proved, and of having thus committed a fallacy. It is easy to detect the falsity of this charge, which is only too common in the whole of this book, and might make me suspect that its Author had not acted in good faith, if I had not known his character and did not believe he has been the first to be entrapped by so false a belief.

say, *I do not now dispute it.* Why then do you say *that you are only a thing that thinks?* Are you not asserting something of which you are not certain? Is it not an inference that you do not prove? Have you not destroyed something you imagined you had established? Look, here is your reasoning:

He who knows that he is a thinking thing and is unaware whether he is anything else as well, whether a system of members, a subtle air, etc., is, in the strict sense, only a thing that thinks.

But I know that I am a thing that thinks, and am unaware whether I am anything else as well, whether a system of members, a subtle air, etc.

Therefore I am, in the strict sense, only a thing that thinks.

There is nothing added in my presentation of the matter; nay, it is enough to propound your argument as it stands. I merely append the remark that, since as propounded it is evidently so absurd, it was not without reason that I urged you above to be cautious, not only lest you should assume something unadvisedly in place of yourself, but lest you should not assume enough, and knowing something about yourself, should think that this was the whole of your nature. Whence I now also declare that you could have argued correctly provided you had reasoned in this way:

He who knows that he is a thing that thinks, and is unaware whether he is anything else, whether a system of members, a subtle air, etc., knows in the strict sense only that he is a thinking thing:

But I know that I am a thing that thinks, and am unaware whether I am anything else as well, whether a system of members, a subtle air, etc.

Therefore I know in the strict sense only that I am a thinking thing.

This indeed would have been a true and legitimate conclusion and no one would have been indignant with you; we should have attended only to the conclusions you were able to draw. But now since there is such a difference between these two conclusions—*I am, in the strict sense, only a thing that thinks,* and *I know in the strict sense only that I am a thing that thinks*—can anyone tolerate the fallacy you commit in passing from that which you know to that which you are?'

[1] Med. II, Vol. I. p. 152.

[2] praecise tantum.

The other ambiguity is on p. 84[1], where he wishes to make *to abstract* and *to distinguish* have the same meaning, though all the time there is a great difference between them : for in distinguishing a substance from its accidents, we must consider both one and the other, and this helps greatly in becoming acquainted with substance ; whereas if instead one only separates by abstraction this substance from these accidents, i.e. if one considers it quite alone without thinking of them, that prevents one from knowing it well, because it is by its accidents that substance is manifested.

Here, my dear Sir, is the whole of the reply for which this great book of counter-arguments calls ; for, though perhaps I should better content my critic's friends if I reported every hostile argument one after the other, I believe I should not please my own friends, who would have cause to reprove me for having occupied time with a task for which there was little need, and of thus putting my leisure at the disposal of all those who might care to squander theirs in plying me with useless questions. But I give you my thanks for your kind attentions. Adieu.

[1] *Metaphysical Disquisitions*, p. 84, i.e. the first part of the counter-argument following 'Doubt 8' directed against Med. II, and the Reply (cf. Objj. v, pp. 147, 148): 'If now any reader be so patient as to read over my "Doubt" again, I ask him to judge of it and of the Reply at the same time. You say *that you have not abstracted the concept of wax from the concept of its accidents.* I concede your good faith in the matter! Are not these your very words—*I distinguish wax from its external forms, and consider it in naked isolation, as it were divested of the garments that cover it?* What else is the abstraction of the concept of one thing from the concept of others but the considering of it apart from them? what else but to consider it in naked isolation, with the covering vestments stripped off? Is there any other way of abstracting the concept of human nature from the concepts of individual men, than by distinguishing it from the so-called individuating differences, and considering it in isolation and stripped of that which invests it? But it is a task I little relish to argue about a point, ignorance of which would ensure a boy disputant a beating from his master. You say *that you rather wished to show how the substance of wax is manifested by its accidents.* It was *that* you wished to point out, *that* which you clearly announced. Is not this a neat way of getting out of the difficulty? And when you wished to point it out, what means did you employ for doing so, or how did you make the wax manifest, if not by looking to its accidents, first as to its garments, and then stripping these off and considering it in isolation?'

THE FIFTH SET OF OBJECTIONS[1].

LETTER FROM P. GASSENDI TO M. DESCARTES[2].

Sir[3],

　　Our friend Mersenne did me a great kindness in communicating to me your magnificent work—your Meditations on First Philosophy.　The excellence of your arguments, the perspicuity of your intellect, and the brilliance of your expression have caused me extraordinary delight.　It gives me great pleasure to compliment you on the sublimity and felicity with which your mind assails the task of extending the boundaries of the sciences and bringing to light those matters that preceding ages have found most difficult to drag from their obscurity.　To me it has proved hard to comply, as friendship obliged me to do, with the request M. Mersenne also made, and let you know if I took any exception to your doctrine and had any scruple unsatisfied.　Especially I foresaw that, if I did not agree with your arguments, I should merely display my own lack of acuteness, or rather should merely manifest rashness, if I dared to utter my dissent in the smallest matter, and appear to oppose you.　Nevertheless I have yielded to my friend, thinking besides that you would approve of his plan rather than of mine; since indeed your candour will easily let you see that my intention is solely to display to you without disguise the reasons I have for doubting.　I testify that this will be amply confirmed if you have patience to scrutinize them thoroughly; for as to any influence they may have in causing you the slightest sense of insecurity in your reasonings, or in causing you to consume, in replying, any time destined for more valuable

---

[1] The French translation by Clerselier was published contrary to the advice of Descartes in the edition sanctioned by him, consequently MM. Adam and Tannery do not include it in their edition of the works of Descartes. The translation was not revised by Descartes. Instead of this is substituted the brief letter translated above (pp. 125—134).

[2] Eximio viro Renato Cartesio P. Gassendus S.

[3] Vir eximie.

*studies, I declare myself not responsible for this. Nay, I cannot
without shame-facedness expose my difficulties to your gaze, sure as
I am that there is none of them that has not often suggested itself to
you in your reflections, and which you have not with full consciousness dismissed as of no account, or determined to keep out of sight.
Consequently, though I bring forward certain hypotheses, I bring
them forward merely as hypotheses, and they are hypotheses that
affect not the truths themselves of which you have undertaken the
proof, but the method and the cogency of your proof. I unaffectedly
acknowledge the existence of Almighty God and the immortality of
our souls; my doubts concern merely the validity[1] of the reasoning
by which you prove those matters, as well as other things involved in
the scheme of Metaphysical science.*

RELATIVE TO MEDITATION I.

Of the things which may be brought within the sphere of the doubtful.

*In the matter of the first Meditation, there is really little for me
to linger over; I agree with your plan of freeing your mind from
every prejudice. On one point only I am not clear; that is, why
you should not have preferred to indicate simply and with few words
that what you previously knew was uncertain, in order subsequently
to choose what might be found to be true, rather than by regarding
everything as false, not so much to dismiss an old prejudice, as to
take up with a new one. Thus, for example, it became necessary to
feign that God was a deceiver, or some evil spirit that mocks us, in
order to convince yourself; whereas it would have seemed to be sufficient to ascribe that to the obscurity of the human mind and the
weakness of its nature alone. Further, you feign that you are
dreaming in order to cast doubt on everything, and consider that
everything that happens is done to make sport of us. But will that
compel you to believe that you are not awake and to deem uncertain
and false the events that occur before your eyes? Say what you will,
no one will be convinced that you have convinced yourself that none
of the things you have learned are true, and that your senses, or a
dream, or God, or an evil spirit have imposed on you. Would it
not have been better and more consonant with philosophic candour
and the love of the truth to state the actual facts in a straightforward
and simple manner, rather than to incur the possible objection of*

[1] Energiam.

having recourse to an artifice, of eagerness for verbal trickery and seeking evasions? Yet, since you have been pleased to take this way, I shall make no further criticism on it.

RELATIVE TO MEDITATION II.

Of the Nature of the Human Mind; and that it is more easily known than the Body.

1. *When it comes to the second Meditation, I see that you still persist in keeping up the game of pretence, and yet that you recognize at least that* you exist; *which thus establishes the* conclusion that this proposition:—I am, I exist, is true each time that you pronounce it, or that you mentally conceive it[1]. *But I don't see that you needed all this mechanism, when you had other grounds for being sure, and it was true, that you existed. You might have inferred that from any other activity, since our natural light informs us that whatever acts also exists.*

You add that this does not yet let you know clearly enough what you are[2]. *But this is admitted, and in quite a serious spirit; we grant it quite willingly: to know this requires toil and exertion. But surely this knowledge might have been sought for without all that circumlocution and all those suppositions.*

You next wish to contemplate yourself as what you have believed yourself to be, in such a way that, when every doubtful element is withdrawn, nothing may be left beyond what is absolutely certain and indubitable[3]. *But you will do this with the approval of everyone. You tackle the matter; and believing that you are a man, you ask,* what is man? *Purposely dismissing the common definition you select those characteristics* which at the first glance presented themselves to you, e.g. that you had a face, hands, and other members which you designated by the name body; and likewise that you were nourished, that you walked, that you felt, that you thought, features which you referred to the soul[4]. *So far, so good, only what becomes of the distinction you draw between the soul and the body? You say* that you did not then perceive what the soul was, but imagined merely that it was like a wind, a flame, or an ether, which was spread throughout your grosser parts[5]. *That is worth noting.* But body you did not doubt to have a nature identical with whatever can be defined by figure, or can be confined in a certain place, can fill a space from which it can exclude every other body, can be

---

[1] Vol. I. p. 150, par. 1.   [2] *Ibid.* par. 2.   [3] *Ibid.*
   Ibid. p. 151, par. 1.   [5] *Ibid.*

perceived by touch, sight, hearing, smell or taste, and can be moved in many ways[1]. *But these things you can even at present attribute to bodies, provided you do not attribute all of them to every corporeal thing; inasmuch as wind is a body, and yet is not perceived by sight. And you cannot exclude the other attributes which you mention next in order, for wind, fire, also move many things. Moreover, what you subjoin, viz. that you denied to body the power of moving itself, cannot, so far as it appears, be successfully maintained; for this implies that every body must by its own nature be without motion, and that all its motions must proceed from an incorporeal principle; and it must be thought that neither can water flow nor an animal move, unless through the agency of some incorporeal mover.*

2. *Next you investigate whether,* the existence of a deceiving agent being up to this point supposed, you can affirm that any of the things which you judged to belong to the nature of body exist in you. You say that after the most careful scrutiny nothing of such a sort can be found in you[2]. *Already at this point you consider yourself not as a complete human being, but as that inner and more hidden part, such as you deemed the soul to be. Wherefore I ask thee, O soul, or whatever the name be by which you choose to be addressed, have you by this time corrected that notion in virtue of which you previously imagined that you were something similar to wind, or a like substance, diffused throughout the members of the body? You certainly have not. Why then, cannot you be a wind, or rather a very subtle spirit, which, by means of the heat of the heart, is distilled from the purest of the blood or from some other source; or may there not be some other cause by which you are evoked and preserved; and may you not, being diffused throughout the members, attribute life to them, and see with the eye, hear with the ear, think by means of the brain and discharge the other functions which by common consent are ascribed to you? If that be so, why may you not have the same figure as the whole of this body has, just as the air takes the shape of the vessel which contains it? Why may you not believe that you are bounded too by the same circumambient medium as surrounds the body, or by the bodily epidermis? May you not occupy space, or those parts of space which the solid body or its parts do not completely fill? In truth, the solid body possesses pores through which you yourself may be diffused, in such a way that, where the parts of which you consist are found none of its parts*

---

[1] Vol. I. p. 151.   [2] *Ibid.* par. 2.

*exist; just as in a mixture of wine and water, where the particles
of the former are, the parts of the second are not found, howsoever
much sight be unable to distinguish between the two.* Why will it
be impossible for you to exclude another body from the same space as
you occupy, when the parts composing the solid body are incapable of
existing in the same tiny portions of space in which you are found?
Why cannot you participate in many motions? For when you
assign many motions to the members themselves, how can you move
them unless you yourself are moved? Certainly you must not be
unmoved if you are to cause movement, where exertion is called for;
nor can you rest immoveable when the body itself is moved. If this
be so, why do you say that none of those things exist in you which
are relative to the nature of the body?

3. *You proceed to say* that, of the things ascribed to soul,
neither nourishment nor walking belong to·you[1]. *But, in the first
place, a thing may be a body and yet not be nourished. Secondly, if
you are such a body as we have described breath to be, why, if your
more solid members are nourished by more solid substance, may you—
a more rarefied one—not be also nourished by a rarer substance?
Further, are you not young and vigorous when that body, of which
these are the parts, is in the vigour of youth? And when it is weak,
are you not yourself weak? In the matter of moving, when it is
owing to you that your members move and never pass into any position
except you move and transport them thither, how can that be possible
without movement on your part? But, you say,* if now I do not
possess a body, these are nothing but figments[1]. *But whether you
are making game of us or playing with yourself, there is no reason
for our delaying here. If, however, you are speaking seriously, you
must prove that you neither have any body which you inform, nor are
of such a nature as to be nourished and to move along with it.*

You proceed, saying that you are without sensation[1]. *But yourself assuredly are such as to see colour, hear sounds, etc.* This, *you
say,* cannot occur apart from the body. *I grant you that; but, in
the first place, a body is present to you and you yourself reside within
the eye, which certainly does not see without you; and secondly you
may be a rarefied body operating by means of the sense-organs.* You
say I have thought I perceived many things during sleep that
subsequently I recognised as not having been experienced at all.
*But though you go wrong if, without using the eye, you seemed to
have experiences which do not occur without the eye coming into play,*

[1] Vol. I. p. 151, par. 2.

*nevertheless so to err is not your universal experience, nor have you
not employed your eye, by which you perceive and by which you take
in the images, which now you can use without employing the eye.*

At length you come to the conclusion that thought belongs to you.
*True, that is not to be denied; but you still have to prove that the
power of thinking is so much superior to the nature of body, that
neither breath nor any other mobile, pure, and rarefied body, can by
any means be so adapted as to be capable of exercising thought. You
will have to prove at the same time that the souls of the brutes are
incorporeal inasmuch as they think, or, over and above the functioning
of the external senses, are aware of something internal, not only while
awake, but when dreaming. Again, you must prove that this solid
body contributes absolutely nothing to your thinking (though you have
never existed without it nor have ever hitherto had any thought in
isolation from it), and that your thinking is hence independent of it;
so that you can neither be impeded nor disturbed by the foul and
dense vapours or fumes, which sometimes so afflict the brain.*

4. *Your conclusion is:* I am, to speak accurately, a Thing
which thinks, that is to say, a mind or a soul, or an understanding,
or a reason[1]. *Here I confess that I have been suffering from a
deception. For I believed that I was addressing the human soul,
or that internal principle, by which a man lives, feels, moves from
place to place and understands, and after all I was only speaking to
a mind, which has divested itself not only of the body but of the soul
itself. Have you, my worthy sir, in attaining to this result, followed
the example of those ancients, who, though they thought that the soul
was diffused throughout the whole body, believed that its principal
part—the dominating part[2]—was located in a determinate region of
the body, e.g. in the brain, or in the heart? Not that they judged
that the soul was not also to be found there, but that they believed
that the mind was, as it were, added to the soul existing there, was
linked to it, and along with it informed that region. I ought really
to have remembered that from the discussion in your Discourse on
Method. There you appeared to decide that all those offices, ascribed
both to the vegetative and to the sensitive soul, do not depend on the
rational soul and can be exercised without it before it is introduced
into the body, as does happen in the case of the brutes, in whom your
contention is that no reason is found. I do not know how I managed
to forget this, except for the reason that I remained in doubt as to
whether that principle by means of which we and the brutes alike*

---

[1] Vol. I. p. 152, par. 1.   [2] τὸ ἡγεμονικόν.

exercise the vegetative function and feel, was not according to your nomenclature to be styled soul, soul being exclusively reserved for the human mind.　Yet since it is that principle that is properly said to animate us, mind is capable of no other function than to make us think, as you indeed assert.　And, since this is so, call it now Mind, *and let it be, taken precisely,* a Thing which thinks.

You add that it is thought alone which cannot be separated from you.　*Truly it is impossible to deny this of you, if you are primarily Mind alone and refuse to allow that your substance can be distinguished from the substance of the soul except in thought; though here I pause and ask whether, when you say that* thought cannot be separated from you, *you mean that you, as long as you exist, think to an indefinite extent.　This is indeed in conformity with the pronouncement of those celebrated philosophers who, in order to prove your immortality, assumed that you were in perpetual motion, or, as I interpret it, thought continuously.　But this will not gain the adhesion of those who cannot comprehend how you can think during a lethargic sleep, or while in the womb.　Besides, I have a difficulty here as to whether you think that you have been infused into the body or one of its parts during the uterine stage of existence or at birth. But I should be loth to be troublesome with my enquiries, or to reflect whether you remember what your thoughts were when in the womb, or in the days, months, and years succeeding your birth; or, if you replied that you had forgotten, to ask why this was so.　Yet I suggest that you should remember how obscure, how meagre, how nearly nonexistent your thought must have been during those periods of life.*

Proceeding, you maintain that you are not the complex of members which we call the human body[1].　*But that must be admitted because you are considering yourself solely as a thing which thinks, as a part of the concrete human whole, distinct from this exterior and more solid part.*　'I am not,' *you say*, 'a subtle air distributed through these members, I am not a wind, a fire, a vapour, nor a breath, nor anything which I can construct in imagination. For I have assumed that all these were nothing; and let that supposition be unchanged.'　*But halt here, O Mind, and let those suppositions or rather those fictions take themselves off.　You say,* 'I am not air or anything of such a nature.'　*But, if the total soul be something of the kind, wherefore may not you who are thought to be the noblest part of the soul, be deemed to be, as it were, the flower, or the subtlest, purest, and most active part of it.　You say*

[1] Vol. I. p. 152, par. 2.

'perhaps those same things which I supposed were non-existent, are real things and are not different from the self which I know? I do not know about this, I shall not dispute about it now.' *But if you do not know, if you do not dispute the matter, why do you assume that you are none of these things?* 'I know,' *you say,* 'that I exist; but the knowledge of my existence taken in its precise significance cannot depend on that which I do not know.' *Granted, but remember that you have not proved that you are not air, or a vapour, or many other things.*

5. *In sequence to this you describe that which you call the imagination.* You say that to imagine is nothing else than to contemplate the figure or image of a corporeal thing, *obviously for the purpose of inferring that you are aware of your own nature by means of some other species of thought than imagination. But, though it is permissible for you to define imagination in accordance with your own opinions, I ask you why, if you are corporeal (the contradictory of which you have not proved), you cannot contemplate yourself in the guise of some corporeal figure or image? And I ask you, when you so regard yourself, if you are conscious of or observe anything other than a pure, transparent, and rarefied substance like wind[1], which pervades the whole body or at least the brain or a part of it, animating you, and discharging your vital functions through the body.* 'I know,' you say, 'that nothing at all that I can understand by means of the imagination belongs to this knowledge which I have of myself.' *But you do not state how you know this; and since a short time ago you had decided that you did not know whether or not these things belonged to you, I ask you whence you now derive your conclusion?*

6. *Your next point is:* that it is necessary to recall the mind from these modes of thought with the utmost diligence, in order that it may be able to know its own nature with perfect distinctness[2]. *Very sound advice; but, after having thus with the utmost diligence recalled yourself, report, I pray you, how distinctly you have perceived your own nature. For all that you record is that you are a Thing which thinks, a truth we all previously believed; but you do not reveal to us what the nature of this operative substance is, how it coheres, and how it adapts itself for discharging such various functions in such various ways, and many other such things about which we have hitherto been in ignorance.*

You allege that intellect can perceive that which imagination is

---

[1] aurae instar. [2] Vol. I. p. 153 *ad init.*

incapable of discerning (*the imagination which you identify with the 'common sense'*). *But, my worthy Mind, can you prove that there are many internal faculties and not a single, simple faculty by means of which we are conscious of everything whatsoever it be? When I behold the sun with open eyes, sensation most manifestly occurs. When, subsequently, I bethink myself of the sun, keeping my eyes closed, internal cognition manifestly occurs. But how, in fine, shall I be able to discern that I perceive the sun with the common sense, or faculty of imagination, and not really with the mind, or understanding, and so at pleasure apprehend the sun, now by the activity of the understanding, which is other than the imagination, now by the act of the imagination which is different from that of the understanding? True, if it were possible for an understanding to exist after cerebral trouble had set in, and injury to the imagination, an understanding which discharged all its peculiar and incommunicable[1] functions, then understanding could be said to be as easily distinguishable from imagination as imagination from external sense. But since the reverse of this is true, we have certainly no ready means of setting up this distinction.*

When it is said, as you will have it, that imagination occurs when we contemplate the image of a corporeal object, *you see that, since there is no other way of contemplating corporeal things, bodies must be apprehended by the imagination alone, or, at least that no other faculty of knowing can be discerned.*

You mention that you still cannot prevent yourself thinking that corporeal things, the images of which are framed by thought, which are made known by the activity of the senses, are more distinctly known than that obscure and unknown part of you which does not come under the imagination: so that it seems strange to you that you should know and understand more distinctly things the existence of which is dubious and which seem foreign to you[2]. *To begin with, that is an excellent saying* 'that unknown part of you.' *For in truth you do not know what it is nor what is its nature; nor hence can you come to know that it is of such a sort as to be incapable of entering the imagination. Further, all our knowledge seems to find its source in the senses; and although you deny that whatever is* in the understanding must have existed previously in the sense, *my contention seems to be none the less true, since unless knowledge enters by a sort of invasion alone,—at a stroke[3], as it were it must yet be elaborated and perfected by analogy, by composition, by division, by*

---

[1] puras.   [2] Vol. I. p. 153, *sub fin.*   [3] κατὰ περίπτωσιν.

amplification, by attenuation (of the things of sense[1]*) and other similar
devices which it is unnecessary to recount. Hence it is by no means
strange that those things which of themselves rush in and excite the
sense make a more lively impression on the mind than that made by
objects which the mind itself constructs out of the material that chances
to meet its senses and which it grasps, being receptive in so far only
as it is given the opportunity of so acting. Also you indeed call
material things doubtful; but if you cared to confess the truth, you
would acknowledge that you are not less certain of the existence of the
body which you inhabit, and of all the things that surround you, than
of your own existence. And if you manifest yourself to yourself by
that operation alone which is called thought, how does that compare
with the manifestations of things of this sort? They indeed are
made manifest not only by various operations, but also by many
other highly convincing circumstances, by their magnitude, figure,
solidity, colour, savour, etc., so that, though they are external to you,
it is by no means strange that you should know and comprehend them
more distinctly than yourself. But you ask how it is possible to
understand something foreign to you better than yourself. I reply
that the case of the eye, which sees other things but does not see itself,
illustrates how this is possible.*

7. 'But,' *you ask,* 'what then am I? A thing which thinks.
What is a thing which thinks? It is a thing which doubts, understands, affirms, denies, wills, refuses, which also imagines and feels.'
*You mention many things here which in themselves cause me no
difficulty. This alone makes me pause, your saying that you are a
thing which feels. It is indeed strange, for you had previously
maintained the opposite; or perchance did you mean that in addition
to yourself there is a corporeal faculty residing in the eye, in the
ear, and in the other organs, which receiving the semblance of things,
gives rise to the act of sensation in a way that allows you thereupon
to complete it, and brings it to pass that you are really the very self
which sees, hears and perceives other things? It is for this reason, in
my opinion, that you make sensation as well as imagination a species
of thought. So be it; but look to it, nevertheless, that that sensation
which exists in the brutes, since it is not dissimilar to your sensation,
be not capable of earning the title of thought also, and that thus the
brutes themselves may have a mind not dissimilar to your own.*

You will say, I, holding the citadel in the brain, receive whatsoever is sent me by the (animal[2]) spirits which permeate the

---

[1] Tr.　　　　　　　[2] Tr.

nerves, and thus the act of sense which is said to be effected by the whole body is transacted in my presence. Good; *but in the brutes there are nerves, (animal) spirits, a brain, and a conscious principle residing therein, which in a similar manner receives the messages sent by the animal spirits and accomplishes the act of sensation. You will say that* that principle in the brain of brutes is nothing other than the Fancy[1] or faculty of imagination. *But kindly show that the principle in the human brain is other than the Fancy or imaginative faculty. I asked you a little while back for a criterion by means of which you could prove that it was different, a criterion which, in my opinion, you are not likely to offer me.* True, you *assert that the operations of the human principle far surpass those which are to be obtained in brutes. But, in the same way as man may be the most outstanding of all the animals, yet without being detached from his place in the number of the animals, so, though you are for the above reasons proved to be the most excellent of imaginative faculties or Fancies, you do not lose your place in the ranks of such faculties. For even that self which you specially style the mind, though it may very well imply a higher[2] nature, cannot be anything of a diverse type. Indeed, in order to prove that you are of a diverse (i.e. as you contend of an incorporeal) nature, you ought to display some operation in a way different from that in which the brutes act, and to carry this on, if not without the brain, at least in independence of it; but this is not complied with. (Indeed the reverse happens[3]), if, as a matter of fact, you are troubled when the brain is troubled, are overwhelmed when it is overcome, and if you yourself are unable to retain any trace of the semblances of things which it has lost.* You say that in the brutes everything takes place through a blind impulsion of the (animal) spirits and the other organs, just in the same way as motion is achieved in a clock or any other machine. *But however true this be in the case of the other functions, like nutrition, the pulsation of the arteries, and so forth, which very functions take place in man in precisely the same way as in brutes, can it be said that either the operations of sense, or what are called the emotions[4] of the soul are effected in brutes by means of a blind impulse, and not in our case also? A morsel of food discharges a semblance of itself into the eye of the dog, and this being transferred to the brain, attaches itself to the soul, as it were, by means of hooks; and the soul itself thenceforth and the whole body, which coheres with it, is haled to that food, as it were, by chains of*

---

[1] Phantasiam.   [2] Dignioris.   [3] Tr.   [4] passiones.

the most delicate contriving. The stone also which someone picks up threateningly sends forth a semblance of itself, which, acting like a lever, gives a propulsion to the soul and reverses the course of the body and compels it to take flight. But does not the very same thing happen in man? Perhaps you know of some other way in which this can take place; if so, I should be much indebted if you would explain it to me.

You say 'I (the soul)[1] am free and there is a power within me by means of which I can turn a man equally from fleeing and from going forward.' *But the imaginative principle does as much in a brute; a dog may for the time disregard blows and threats and rush at the food it sees (and man often does much the same thing!).* You say that the dog barks by mere impulsion and not owing to resolve, as in the case of men speaking. *But in the case of man there are causes at work too, and hence we might deem that his speaking was due to impulsion; for that also which we attribute to choice is due to the stronger impulse, and the brute also exercises his own choice when one impulse is greater than the others. I have indeed witnessed a dog attuning its barks to the sound of a trumpet in such a way as to imitate all the changes in its notes, sharp or flat, slow and quick, however much more frequent and prolonged the sounds were made, capriciously and suddenly.* You say brutes lack reason. *But while doubtless they are without human reason, they do have a reason of their own. Hence evidently they cannot be called irrational[2] except in comparison with us, or relatively to our species of reason, since in any case* λόγος *or ratio[3] seems to be as general in its significance, and can be as easily ascribed to them, as the term cognitive faculty or internal sense.* You say that they do not reason to conclusions[4]. *But though they do not reason so perfectly and about so many things as man, they still do reason; and the difference seems to be merely one of more or less.* You say that they do not speak. *But though they do not utter human expressions (as is natural seeing they are not man) yet they emit their own peculiar cries, and employ them just as we do our vocal sounds.* You say that a man in delirium can weave together a number of cries in order to signify something; while the cleverest of the animals cannot do so. *But consider whether it is fair of you to demand human sounds in the brute, and not to attend to its own proper cries. But this discussion would take too much time if pursued further.*

---

[1] Tr.   [2] ἄλογα.
[3] Greek and Latin terms for Reason.   [4] ratiociuari.

8. *Next you adduce* the instance of a piece of wax, *and concerning it you have much to say, in order to show* that what are called the accidents of the wax are one thing, the wax itself or the substance of the wax another, and that we require only the mind or understanding, but not sense or imagination in order to perceive distinctly the wax itself, and its substance[1]. *But firstly that itself is what everyone commonly allows, namely, that the concept of wax or of its substance can be abstracted from the concept of its accidents. But is it the case that this secures a distinct perception of the substance or nature of the wax? We indeed conceive that besides the colour, the figure, the capacity for being liquefied, etc., there is something which is the subject of the accidents and the observed changes of the wax; but as to what that is or what is its nature, we are ignorant. Nay, it always eludes our apprehension and it is only by conjecture that we think that there must be some substratum. Hence I marvel how you can maintain that, after you have finished stripping off those forms, as it were the vestures, of the wax, you perceive perfectly and very clearly what the wax is. For you do indeed perceive that the wax or its substance is something over and above such forms; but what that is you do not perceive, unless you are deceiving us. It is not revealed to you, as a man can be revealed to sight whose clothing and hat alone we have previously beheld, if we strip him of these in order to discover who and what he is. Further, when you think you perceive that in some way or other, how, I pray, do you perceive it? Is it not as something continuous[2] and extended? For you do not conceive it as a point, though it is of such a nature as to be now more widely, now less extended. And since extension of this kind is not infinite, but has a limit, do you not conceive it as in some way possessing figure? Further, when you seem as it were to see it, do you not attach some colour to it, albeit confused? You certainly take it to be something more of a bodily nature, and so equally more visible than the mere void. Whence even the activity of your understanding is imagination of a kind Tell us in good faith whether you maintain that you conceive it apart from any extension, figure and colour? If so, then what is it?*

What you have to say about seeing men, or perceiving them by the mind, men, however, whose hats and cloaks we alone behold[3] *does not prove that the mind is anything more than a faculty of imagination which is capable of passing judgment. For certainly*

---

[1] Cf. Med. II. Vol. I. pp. 154, 155.
[2] fusum.   [3] Cf. Vol. I. p. 155 *sub fin.*

*the dog, in which you do not admit the presence of a mind similar to
yours, judges in a similar manner, when it sees, not its master, but
his hat or clothes [and yet recognises him]*[1]. *Nay more. Although
his master stand or sit, lie down, recline, draw himself together or
stretch himself out, it yet recognises him always as its master, who
can exist under all these forms, though nevertheless he does not
[preserve the same proportions and]*[2] *exist under one form rather
than another, as wax does. And when it chases the hare that runs
from it, do you not believe it thinks that it is throughout the same
hare which it sees both intact and dead, and subsequently skinned
and chopped into pieces?* Your next point, that the perception of
colour, hardness, and so forth, is not an act of vision or of touch,
but only an intuition of the mind, *may be granted, as long as mind
is not taken to be something different from the imaginative faculty
itself. But when you add,* that that act of intuition may be imperfect and confused, or perfect and distinct in proportion as we attend
more or less closely to the elements of which the wax is composed ;
*this certainly shows, not that the mental intuition of this we know not
what over and above all the forms of the wax, is a clear and distinct
knowledge of the wax, but that it is a survey effected by the senses, of
all, so far as that is possible, the accidents and mutations which the
wax can sustain. From these we shall assuredly be able to conceive
and explain what it is we mean by the term wax ; but we shall not
be able either to conceive by itself or explain to others that naked, or
rather that inscrutable substance.*

9.   *You next add :* But what should I say of this mind, that is
of myself, for up to this point I do not admit in myself anything
but mind ? What then am I who seem to perceive this wax so
distinctly, do I not know myself not only with much more truth,
and certainty, but also with much more distinctness and clearness ?
For, if I judged that the wax is or exists from the fact that I see
it, how much more clearly does it follow that I exist ? For it may
be that what I see is not really wax. It may also happen that I do
not even possess eyes with which to see anything. But it cannot
be that when I see, or (for I do not now take account of the distinction), when I think I see, that I myself who think am nought.
So if I judge that wax exists from the fact that I touch it, the
same thing will follow, to wit, that I am ; and so if I judge from
the fact that I imagine it, or from any other cause, the same result

[1] Added in Clerselier's French version.
[2] Omitted in Clerselier's French version.

will follow.   But what I have here remarked of wax may be applied
to all other things which are external to me[1].   *These are your own
words ; and I here repeat them in order to let you see that while they
indeed prove that you distinctly perceive that you exist, from the fact
that you distinctly see and are aware of the existence of wax and those
accidents of it, they yet do not prove that you for this reason know
what or of what nature you are, either distinctly or indistinctly.
Yet to do so had been worth your while, for of your existence there is
no doubt.   Notice meanwhile, though I do not mean to dwell on the
point, that neither have I previously raised the objection that, since
you do not admit the existence in you of anything beyond mind alone,
and therefore rule out eyes, hands and the rest of the organs, it is
vain to talk of wax and its accidents, which you see, touch, etc.; you
certainly cannot see them without using your eyes, touch them without
employing the hands (or, to adopt your mode of expression, think that
you see and touch them).*

    You proceed : If the perception of wax has seemed to me clearer
and more distinct not only after the sight and touch, but also after
many other causes have rendered it quite manifest to me, with how
much more distinctness must it be said that I now know myself, since
all the reasons which contribute to the knowledge of wax, or to any
other body whatever, are yet better proof of the nature of my mind ?[2]
*But, just as your conclusions about wax prove only the perception of
the existence of mind, and fail to reveal its nature, so will all other
examples fail to prove anything more.   But, if you wish to deduce
something more from the perception of the substance of wax and other
things, the only conclusion you can arrive at will be that just as we
conceive that substance confusedly only and as an unknown somewhat,
so we must also conceive of the mind.   Hence you may well repeat
that phrase of yours—that* obscure and unknown part of me.

    Your conclusion is : And finally, behold I have without pre-
meditation reverted to the point I desired.   For, since it is now
manifest that the mind[3] itself and bodies are not, properly speaking,
known by the senses or by the faculty of imagination, but by the
understanding only ; and since they are not known owing to the
fact that they are seen and touched, I see clearly that there is
nothing which is easier for me to know than my mind.   *So you
have it ; but I do not see how you deduce or are clearly aware, that*

---

[1] Vol. I. p. 158, par. 3.   [2] Vol. I. p. 153 *sub fin.*
[3] Gassendi inserted Mentem, reading ipsam et corpora instead of D.'s ipsamet
corpora, cf. Med. II. p. 157, where the trans. occurs—'that even bodies are
not,' etc.

*anything else can be known of your Mind than that it exists.
Whence that also which was promised by the very title of the Meditation, viz. that the human mind considered by itself would be shown
to be better known than the body, cannot in my estimation be complied with.   For it was not your project to prove that the human
mind existed and that its existence was better known than that of the
body, when really no one disputed its existence; rather you doubtless
wished to make its nature better known than that of the body and
this is what you, however, have not achieved.   Truly, O Mind, you
have recounted of corporeal nature the very things, the list of which
we know, viz. extension, figure, occupation of space, etc.   But what
about yourself?   You are not a material complex, not air, not wind,
not a fire, or one of many other things.   To grant you these results
(though some of them you yourself refuted), they are not however
what we expected.   They are forsooth negatives and we want to
know, not what you are not, but what you really are.   Hence, you
refer us to your main conclusion, viz. that you are a* Thing *which
thinks, i.e. doubts, affirms, etc.   But first, to say that you are a
Thing is to say nothing which is known.   For "thing" is a general
term, undifferentiated and vague and not applying to you more than
to anything else in the entire world, to anything which is not wholly
non-existent.   You are a Thing?   That is to say, you are not
nothing; or, what is precisely the same, you are something.   But a
stone is not nothing, i.e. is something; and so is a fly, and so on
with everything else.   Next, in saying that you are a Thinking
being, though you do assign a predicate known to us, yet it was not
previously unknown and was not the object of your enquiry.   Who
doubts your thinking?   That which baffles us, that which we seek to
discover is that inner substance belonging to you, the property of
which is to think.   Wherefore, your conclusion should correspond
with your quest, and that is to discover, not that you are a Thinking
thing, but of what nature you, the thing which thinks, are.   Is it
not the case that it will not be sufficient for you to say, when a knowledge of wine superior to the vulgar is sought for: wine is a thing
which is liquid, extracted from grapes, is white or red, is sweet,
intoxicating and so on?   Rather you will try to discover and to
declare how that internal substance, in accordance with what you
have observed of its fabrication, has been compounded out of a
mixture of spirits, humour*[1]*, tartar and other elements, in some or
other particular quantity and proportion.   Hence, similarly, since a*

[1] Phlegmate.

*knowledge of yourself superior to the vulgar, i.e. to what you pre-
viously possessed, is called for, you see quite clearly that it is not
enough to inform us that you are a thing which thinks, doubts, understands, etc., but that you ought to scrutinise yourself, as it were, by
a chemical method of procedure in order to be able to reveal and
demonstrate to us your internal substance. If you accomplish this,
we shall certainly ourselves discover by investigation whether you are
better known than the body itself, of which anatomy, chemistry and
many other sciences, many senses and numbers of experiments of all
kinds tell us so much.*

Relative to Meditation III.

Of God: That He exists.

1. *In your Third Meditation, from the fact that your clear and
distinct knowledge of the proposition,* I am a thing which thinks, *was
recognized by you to be the cause of your certainty of its truth, you
infer that you are able to set up this general Rule:* that all things
which I perceive very clearly and very distinctly are true[1]. *But
though amid the obscurity that surrounds us, there may very well be
no better Rule obtainable, yet when we see that many minds of the
first rank, which seem to have perceived many things so clearly and
distinctly, have judged that the truth of things is hidden either in
God or in a well, may it not be open to us to suspect that the Rule is
perhaps fallacious? And really, since you are not ignorant of the
argument of the Sceptics, tell me what else can we infer to be true as
being clearly and distinctly perceived, except that that which appears
to anyone does appear? Thus it is true that the taste of a melon
appears to me to be of this precise kind. But how shall I persuade
myself that therefore it is true that such a savour exists in the melon?
When as a boy and in enjoyment of good health, I thought otherwise,
indeed, perceiving clearly and distinctly that the melon had another
taste. Likewise, I see that many men think otherwise also, as well as
many animals that are well equipped in respect of the sense of taste
and are quite healthy. Does then one truth conflict with another?
Or is it rather the case that it is not because a thing is clearly and
distinctly perceived that it is of itself true, but that that only is true
which is clearly and distinctly perceived to be so. Practically the
same account must be given of those things that are relative to the
mind. I could have sworn at other times that we cannot pass from
a lesser to a greater quantity without passing through the stage of*

[1] Vol. i. p. 158, par. 1, *sub fin.*

equality (to a fixed quantity)[1]: *that two lines which continually approach one another cannot fail to meet if produced to infinity. I seemed to myself to perceive those truths so clearly and distinctly that I took them for the truest and most indubitable of axioms: nevertheless arguments subsequently presented themselves which convinced me of the opposite, seeming to make me perceive that more clearly and more distinctly. But when I now again consider the nature of Mathematical assumptions I once more waver. Whence it may indeed be said that it is true that I acknowledge the truth of such and such propositions, in so far as I assume or conceive that quantity, lines and so forth are constituted in this way; but that they are for this reason of themselves true, cannot be safely advanced. But whatever may be the case in mathematical matters, I ask you, as regards the other matters which we are now investigating, what is the reason that men's opinions about them are so many and so various? Each person thinks that he clearly and distinctly perceives that proposition which he defends. To prevent you from saying that many people either imitate or feign belief, I direct your attention to those people who face even death for the sake of the opinions they hold, even though they see others facing it for the sake of the opposite cause: surely, you do not believe that at that point the cries they utter are not authentic. You yourself indeed experience this difficulty,* because previously you admitted many things to be altogether certain and manifest, which you afterwards discovered to be dubious[2]. *In this passage, however, you neither refute nor confirm your Rule, but merely snatch the opportunity of expatiating about the Ideas by which you may be deceived, in so far as they represent something as being external to you, which is, nevertheless, perhaps not external to you; and once more you treat of a God who may deceive, and by whom you may be led into error respecting these propositions:—"* two and three are five," "the square has not more than four sides[3]." *Evidently you thus suggest that the proof of the rule is to be expected, waiting until you have shown that a God exists who cannot be a deceiver. Yet to throw out this warning hint, you ought not so much to take pains to substantiate this Rule, following which we so readily mistake the false for the true, as to propound a method which will direct us and show us when we are in error and when not, so often as we think that we clearly and distinctly perceive anything.*

2. *You next distinguish* Ideas (*by which you mean thoughts in so far as they resemble images*) as innate, adventitious and factitious.

---

[1] Tr.   [2] Vol. I. p. 158, par. 2, *ad init.*   [3] *Ibid.* par. 3.

In the first class you put, your understanding of what a thing, what truth, what thought is; *in the second,* your hearing of a noise, seeing the sun, feeling (the heat of)[1] the fire; *in the third,* the Sirens and Hippogryphs you construct imaginatively. *You add also* that perhaps these may be all adventitious or all innate or all made by yourself, inasmuch as you have not yet clearly grasped their origin. *Further, lest meanwhile, before you have grasped this, some fallacy creep in, it is well to note that all Ideas seem to be adventitious, and proceed from things existing outside the mind and falling under some sense faculty. Thus the mind has a power (or rather is itself the power) not only of perceiving the adventitious Ideas themselves or of perceiving those which things convey to it by means of the senses, I repeat, bare and distinct, and wholly such as it receives them within itself; but also of uniting, dividing, diminishing, enlarging, arranging, and of performing other operations of this description.*

Hence the third class of Ideas at least is not distinct from the second; for the Idea of a chimaera is nothing else than the idea of the head of a lion, the belly of a goat and the tail of a serpent, out of which the mind forms a single Idea, though apart or singly they are adventitious. So the Idea of a Giant or a man conceived as being like a mountain or the whole world, is merely adventitious. It is the idea of a man of the common stature, amplified at pleasure by the mind, though presented with greater confusedness in proportion as it is amplified in thought. So, too, the Idea of a Pyramid, of a city, or of anything else which one has not seen, is merely the Idea of a Pyramid, city or another thing previously seen, somewhat altered in form and consequently multiplied and arranged in some confused way.

As for the forms which you say are innate, they certainly seem to be non-existent, and any that are said to be of such character appear also to have an adventitious origin. You say, my nature is the source of my power of understanding what a thing is[2]. *But I do not think that you mean to speak of the power of understanding itself, which is not in doubt, and is not the subject of investigation here; but rather of the Idea of a Thing. Neither do you mean the Idea of any particular Thing; for the Sun, this stone and all single things are Things, the Ideas of which you say are not innate. Hence you speak of the Idea of Thing taken universally and as practically synonymous with "entity" and extending as widely as it. But I ask you, how can this Idea be in the mind, without all the single things being there also, together with their genera, from which it abstracts and forms a conception which is proper to none of the particulars and yet agrees with them all? If the Idea of Thing is innate, the Idea of animal, of plant, stone, of all universals will have to be innate also. There will be no need for us to give ourselves the labour of discriminating from each other the many particulars, which enables us, after again making a number of distinctions, to retain that alone which is common to all, or, what amounts to the same thing, frame the Idea of a genus.*

You say also that it is your nature which enables you to understand what truth is, *or, as I interpret,* gives you the Idea of truth. *But if truth is merely the conformity of a judgment with the thing about which the judgment is passed, truth is a certain relation, and hence not to be distinguished from that very thing and that Idea as related to each other, or what is the same thing, from the very Idea of the thing; for the Idea represents both itself and the thing in so far as it has such and such a character. Whence the Idea of Truth is merely the Idea of a thing in so far as it is conformable to that thing, or represents it as having the nature it possesses. The consequence is that if the Idea of the thing is not innate but adventitious, the Idea of truth is also adventitious, and not innate. If this holds of each particular truth, it must also hold of truth universally, the notion of which, or Idea (as has already been maintained in the case of the idea of thing) is constructed out of particular notions or Ideas.*

You allege that it is to your nature you owe your comprehension of what thought is (*I continue to interpret once more* the Idea of thought). *But, just as the mind can, out of the Idea of one city, construct in imagination the Idea of another, so can it, out of the Idea of one operation, say, seeing or tasting, construct the Idea of another, e.g. of thought. Surely, there is a recognised analogy between the cognitive faculties, and each readily conduces to a knowledge of the other. Though there is no need for much expenditure of labour in connection with the Idea of thought; it should rather be reserved for that of mind, and to the same extent for that of the soul; for if that is acknowledged to be innate, there will be no harm in admitting that the Idea of thought is also innate. Hence we must wait until you have proved your thesis in the case of the mind or the soul.*

3.   *You seem* afterwards to make it doubtful not only whether any

Ideas proceed from external things, but also whether there are any external objects at all. *And you seem thence to infer* that although there exist in you the Ideas of things said to be external, those Ideas nevertheless do not prove that the things exist, since they do not necessarily proceed from them, but may be due to yourself or to some other cause, I know not what. *It was for this reason I fancy, that you previously continued to say:* That you had not previously perceived earth, sky, or stars, but the Ideas of earth, sky and stars, which might possibly be a source of delusion. *Therefore, if you are not yet convinced of the existence of earth, sky, stars, and other objects, why, pray, do you walk about on the earth or alter the position of your body in order to behold the sun? Why do you approach the fire in order to feel its heat? Why sit down at table to a meal, in order to satisfy your hunger? Why move your tongue in order to speak, or your hand in order to send this writing to us? Certainly the doubts you express may be asserted or subtly derived from our thought, but they do not advance the matter in hand, and since you are not really in doubt about the existence of things external to you, let us act seriously and in good faith and talk about things just as they really are. But if, assuming the existence of external objects, you think that it has been properly proved that the Ideas we have of them cannot be derived from them themselves, you will have to dispose not only of the objections you yourself bring, but of additional difficulties which can be raised.*

Thus you do recognise that ideas appear admittedly to proceed from objects, because we seem to be taught this lesson by nature and because we are sensible that those ideas do not depend on us, or on our will[1]. *But, not to mention either these arguments or their solution, you ought also among other things to have brought up and solved the objection in which it is asked:—why one born blind has no idea of colour or one born deaf of sound, if it is not because external things have not been able to convey from themselves any semblance of themselves into the mind of the afflicted individual? For the inlets have been closed since birth, and obstacles placed there for all time, which prevent anything from passing through them.*

Afterwards you press the example of the Sun, of which you have two ideas, one derived from the senses, viz. that in accordance with which the sun seems to be extremely small; while the other is derived from astronomical reasonings, and represents the sun to be of great size. That idea is true and more similar (to its object)[2]

---

[1] Vol. I. p. 160, par. 3.   [2] Tr.

which is not drawn from the senses, but is elicited from your innate notions, or achieved by some other means. *But each of that pair of ideas of the Sun is true, similar to, and in conformity with the Sun; only one is less, the other more so. In precisely the same way the two ideas we have of a man, the one proceeding from him at ten yards' distance, the other at a hundred or a thousand, are similar to him, true, and in conformity with him. But the one has these qualities in a greater degree than the others, in respect that the idea which we have when the man is near is to a slight degree impaired, while that which proceeds from a distance suffers to a greater extent. All this might be explained in a few words if it were permitted, or if you did not grasp it sufficiently yourself.*

Moreover, though it is by the mind alone that we are aware of that vast idea of the sun, the idea is not on that account elicited from any innate notion. Rather what occurs is, that in so far as experience proves and reason, supporting it, confirms the belief that things at a distance appear smaller than when they are near, the idea which finds entrance by the channels of sense is merely amplified by the mind's own power, and so much the more in proportion to what is known to be the sun's distance from us and the precise number of semi-diameters of the earth to which its diameter is equal.

Do you wish to infer that no part of this idea is implanted in us by nature? Ask what it is in one born blind. You will find in the first place that in his mind it has neither colour nor brilliance; secondly, that neither is it round[2], unless someone has told him that it is round and he himself has previously handled round bodies. Finally you will discover that it is not of such great magnitude unless the blind person has either by reasoning or owing to the influence of authority amplified his previously received notion.

Yet—allow me to interpose this reflection—I ask you: have we ourselves, we who have seen the Sun so often, who have so many times beheld its apparent diameter, and have as frequently reasoned as to its true diameter, have we, I say, any other than the common image of the sun? It is true that by reason we infer that the sun exceeds the earth in size more than a hundred and sixty times; but do we on that account possess the idea of a body of such a vast extent? It is true we amplify this idea which we receive from the senses as much as possible, we exert our mind as much as we can; yet we

---

[1] Vol. I. p. 161, par. 3.

[2] It seems absurd to us to talk of an 'idea' being round, but we must remember that by 'idea' Gassendi means the shape and sensible qualities of a thing as presented to us in imagination.

manage to present ourselves with nothing but mere obscurity, and as often as we wish to have a distinct thought of the Sun, the mind must return to that sensible appearance which it has received through the medium of the eye. It is sufficient for the mind not to deny that the Sun is really greater than it appears, and that if the eye approached nearer to it, it would have an idea of greater extent; but meanwhile it is to the idea in its presented magnitude that the mind attends.

4. *Next, recognising the inequality and diversity between ideas, you say:* There is no doubt that those which represent to me substances are something more, and contain so to speak more objective reality within them, than those that simply represent modes or accidents; and that idea again by which I understand a supreme God, eternal, infinite, omnipotent, the Creator of all things which are outside of Himself, has certainly more objective reality in itself than those by which finite substances are represented[1]. *Here you go at such a great pace that we must arrest your course for a little. I do not indeed have any difficulty about that which you call* objective reality. *It is enough if you in conformity with the common expression, according to which external things exist subjectively and formally in themselves, but objectively or ideally in the understanding, mean (as is evident) merely that an idea should agree with the thing of which it is the idea; and that it hence contains nothing of a representative nature which is not really in the thing itself, and represents more reality in proportion as the thing it represents contains more reality in itself. True, you immediately afterwards distinguish objective from formal reality which, as I interpret, is the idea itself, not as representative, but as an actual entity. But it is agreed that whether it be the idea or the objective reality of the idea, it must not be measured by the total formal reality of the thing, or that which the thing has in itself, but merely by that part (of the thing)[2] of which the understanding has acquired knowledge, or (what is the very same) according to the acquaintance with the thing which the understanding possesses. Thus, for example, you will be said to possess a perfect idea of a man, if you have surveyed him attentively and frequently and in many aspects; while the idea of him whom you have but seen in passing and on one occasion, and partially only, will certainly be imperfect. But if you have beheld not the man himself but a mask covering his face and his garments clothing his body completely, we must say either that you*

[1] Vol. I. p. 162, par. 1   [2] Tr.

have no idea of him, or that if you do possess one it is extremely imperfect and confused.

These are my grounds for maintaining that, though we have indeed a distinct idea of accidents and one that is true[1] of them, that of the substance which underlies them is only confused and quite fictitious. Hence, though you say that there is more objective reality in the idea of substance than in the idea of accidents, *it must first be denied that there is a true idea or representation of substance, and hence that it possesses any objective reality. Secondly, even though it should have been admitted that it does possess some, we must deny that it has more than the ideas of accidents possess, since everything that owns a reality of this sort, holds it from the ideas of those accidents, under which, or after the fashion of which we have said substance is conceived, when we declare that it could be conceived only as something extended and possessing figure and colour.*

Concerning what you add about the idea of God, I ask you how, when you are not yet sure whether a God exists, you know that God is represented by the idea of Him, as supreme, eternal, infinite, omnipotent and as creator of all things? *Do you not take this from your previously received knowledge of God, in so far as you have heard these attributes ascribed to him? If you had not heard so much before, would you describe God so? You will reply that this is brought forward merely as an example and without implying any definition as yet. So be it: but take care lest afterwards you take it as a matter already decided.*

You allege that there is more objective reality in the idea of an infinite God than in the idea of a finite thing. *But, firstly, since the human understanding is not capable of conceiving infinity, neither, consequently, does it possess or have cognisance of an idea which is representative of an infinite thing. Wherefore also he who says that a thing is infinite, attributes to a thing which he does not comprehend a name which he does not understand, since, just as the thing extends beyond his widest grasp, so the negation of limit ascribed to its extension is not understood by him, whose comprehension is always confined within some bounds.*

Next, though every highest perfection is wont to be ascribed to God, all such seem to be derived from the things which we customarily admire in ourselves, e.g. length of existence, power, knowledge, kindness, blessedness, etc.; we amplify these as much as possible, and then pronounce God to be everlasting, all-powerful, all-knowing, most

---

[1] germanam.

excellent, most blessed, etc., but the idea which represents all these attributes does not contain more objective reality on that account than the finite things taken together have, out of the ideas of which that idea is compounded, afterwards being magnified in the aforesaid way. For neither does he who says eternal, thereby embrace in his mind the total extent of the duration of that which has never begun to be and never will cease to exist; nor does he who says omnipotent envisage the whole multitude of possible effects; and so in the case of the others.

Lastly, can anyone affirm that he possesses an idea of God which is true, or which represents God as He is? How slight a thing would God be, unless He were other and had other attributes than this feeble idea of ours contains! Must we not believe that man relatively to God has a smaller proportion of perfection than that which the tiniest creature, a tick, burrowing in its skin, possesses relatively to an elephant? Hence, if the man who from observation of the perfections of the tick should construct in his mind an idea which he maintained was that of an elephant, would be held to be very silly, how can he be satisfied with himself, who out of human perfections that he beholds shapes an idea which is, he contends, that of God, and resembles Him? Tell me also how we recognise in God those perfections which in ourselves we find to be so tiny? And when we have detected them, what sort of essence must we therefore imagine is that of God? God is most certainly infinitely beyond the widest grasp, and when our mind addresses itself to the contemplation of God, it not only gets befogged but comes to a standstill. Hence it follows both that we have no reason to assert that we possess any cognate idea which represents God, and it is enough if, on the analogy of our human qualities, we derive and construct an idea of some sort or other for our use—an idea which does not transcend human comprehension, and contains no reality which we do not perceive in other things or by means of other things.

5. *You assume, next,* that it is manifest by the natural light that there must be at least as much reality in the efficient and total cause as in its effect[1]. *You do so in order that you may infer that* there must be at least as much formal reality in the cause of the idea as this idea contains of objective reality[2]. *But this is a huge stride forward and we must arrest your progress for a little.*

First, that common saying—there is nothing in the effect which is not in the cause—*seems to be understood of the material, rather*

---

[1] Vol. I. p. 162, par. 2, *ad init.*   [2] *Ibid.* p. 163, par. 1.

than of efficient causality. For the efficient cause is something external and frequently of a diverse nature from the effect. And although the effect may be said to hold its reality from the efficient cause, yet it does not acquire that which the efficient cause has necessarily in itself, but that which can be communicated from another source. The thing is quite clear in effects due to art. For although the house owes all its reality to the builder, the latter transfers to it a reality which he has derived not from himself but from some other source. So, likewise the sun acts, in variously transforming a lower material and generating animals of various kinds. Nay, even the parent from whom, we grant, his offspring derives something material, acquires that, not from an efficient, but from a material principle. Your objection, that the effect must be contained in its cause either formally or eminently, *proves nothing more than that the form which the effect possesses is sometimes similar to the form of its cause, sometimes indeed dissimilar and less perfect, to such an extent that the form of its cause towers high above it. But it does not follow that for this reason even an eminent cause gives any of its being or, in respect of what it contains formally, shares its form with its effect. For although that seems to be the case in the generation of living creatures, nevertheless you will not say that a father, in begetting a son, divides up and gives to him part of his rational soul. In a single word, an efficient cause contains its effect only in the sense that it is able to form it out of a given material and bring it into actual existence.*

Further, touching what you infer about objective reality, *I employ the example of my own image, which I can behold either in a mirror which I hold up in front of me, or in a painting. For, as I myself am the cause of my image in the mirror in so far as I dispatch from myself and convey into the mirror some semblance of myself, and as the painter is the cause of the image which appears in the picture; so, when the idea or image of me exists in you or in any other mind, it may be asked whether I myself am its cause, in so far as I transmit the semblance of myself into the eye, and by the medium of the eye into the mind itself. Or is there some other cause which delineates it in the mind as with a stile or pencil? But evidently no cause beyond myself is required; for although afterwards my understanding may amplify, diminish, compound, and handle it in other ways, I nevertheless am myself the primary cause of the whole of the reality which it contains within it. What is here said of me is to be understood also of all external objects.*

Now the reality attaching to an idea is distinguished as two-fold by you. Its formal reality cannot indeed be anything other than the fine substance which has issued out of me, and has been received into the understanding and has been fashioned into an idea. (But if you will not allow that the semblance proceeding from an object is a substantial effluence, adopt whatever theory you will, you decrease the image's reality.) But its objective reality can only be the representation of or likeness to me which the idea carries, or indeed only that proportion in the disposition of its parts in virtue of which they recall me. Whichever way you take it, there seems to be nothing real there; since all that exists is the mere relation of the parts of the idea to each other and to me, i.e. a mode of its formal existence, in respect of which it is constructed in this particular way. But this is no matter; call it, if you like, the objective reality of an idea.

Arguing from this position, it seems that you ought to compare the formal reality of an idea with my formal reality or with my substance, and the objective reality of an idea with the proportion prevailing between my members or my external figure and form. You, however, prefer to compare the objective reality of an idea with my formal reality.

Further, whatever be the explanation of the axiom discussed above, it is clear not only that as much formal reality must exist in me as there is of objective reality in the idea of me, but that even the formal reality of my idea is, as nearly as possible, nothing when compared with my formal reality and my entire substance. Hence we must indeed concede to you that there must be as much formal reality in the cause of an idea as there is of objective reality in its idea, *when the whole of the reality in the idea is practically nothing as compared with that of its cause.*

6. *You add:* that if you possessed an idea the objective reality of which was so great that you could contain it neither eminently nor formally, and thus could not yourself be the cause of it then, at length, it followed of necessity that some other being besides yourself existed in the world. For, otherwise, you would have had no sufficient argument to convince you of the existence of anything else[1]. *True, according to what you have already maintained, you are not the cause of the reality of your ideas; rather the things themselves represented by the ideas are the cause, in so far as they convey into you as into a mirror the images of themselves, even though*

[1] Vol. I. p. 163, par. 3.

you can derive from those ideas the opportunity at times of manu-facturing the notion of chimaeras. But whether you are their cause or not, is it because of this that you are uncertain about the existence of anything else besides yourself in the world? Answer sincerely, I pray, for there is no need for us, whatever the truth turn out to be about ideas, to search for arguments to decide this matter.

Next you run over the list of the ideas you possess, and besides the idea of yourself you enumerate the ideas of God, of corporeal and inanimate things, of angels, animals and men; this is in order that, since you say there is no difficulty about the idea of yourself, you may infer that the ideas of men, of animals and of angels are composed of those which you have of yourself and of God, and that the ideas of corporeal things might have proceeded from you also[1]. *But here it occurs to me to wonder how you can be said to have an idea of yourself (and one so fertile as to furnish you with such a supply of other ideas) and how it can be maintained that the matter presents no difficulties; when, nevertheless, you have really either no idea of yourself, or one which is very confused and imperfect, as we have already observed in passing judgment on the previous Meditation. In it you even inferred that nothing could be more easily and more clearly perceived by you than yourself. What if it be the case that, as you do not and cannot possess an idea of yourself, it may be said that anything else is more capable of being easily and clearly perceived by you than yourself?*

In my reflections as to the reason why it is the case that neither does sight see itself, nor the understanding understand itself, the thought presents itself to me that nothing acts on itself. Thus neither does the hand (or the tip of the finger) strike itself nor does the foot kick itself. But since in other cases, in order for us to acquire knowledge of a thing, that thing must act on the faculty that discerns it and must convey into it the semblance of itself, or inform it with its sensible appearance; it is quite clear that the faculty itself, since it is not outside itself, cannot convey a similar semblance of itself into itself, and cannot consequently acquire knowledge of itself, or, what is the same thing, perceive itself. And why, do you think, does the eye, though incapable of seeing itself in itself, yet see itself in the mirror? Why, because there is a space between the eye and the mirror, and the eye so acts on the mirror, conveying thither its sensible appearance, that the mirror re-acts on it again, conveying back to the eye that sensible appearance's own appearance. Give me

[1] Vol. I. p. 164.

*then a mirror in which you yourself may in similar fashion act;
I promise you that the result will be that this will reflect back your
semblance into yourself, and that you then will at length perceive
yourself, not indeed by a direct, but a reflected cognition. But, if
you do not give this, there is no hope of your knowing yourself.*

*I could here also press the point: how can you be said to have
an idea of God, except one such as, and acquired in the way that,
we have said? Whence comes your idea of the Angels? Unless
you had been told of them you would never have thought of them.
Of the animals? and of other things? I am practically certain
that of these you could have had no idea unless they had entered your
senses; just as you have no idea of many other things, of which
neither the appearance nor the report has reached you. But, dismissing this, I do admit that the ideas existing in the mind of diverse
things can so be compounded, as to give rise to many of the forms of
other things, although those which you enumerate do not seem to
account sufficiently for the great diversity of form you mention, and
indeed do not suffice for the distinct and determinate idea of any
definite¹ thing.*

Moreover I have doubt only *about* the ideas of corporeal things,
and this is due to the fact that there is no small difficulty in seeing
how you are able to deduce them from yourself, *and out of the*
idea of yourself alone², *as long as you pose as incorporeal and
consider yourself as such. For, if you have known only incorporeal
substance, how can you grasp the notion of corporeal substance as
well? Is there any analogy between the latter and the former? You
say that they both agree in this,—in being capable of existing; but
that agreement cannot be comprehended unless first both the two
things which agree are comprehended. What you do is to make a
common notion which implies an understanding of the particulars
before it is formed. Certainly if the mind can, out of that incorporeal substance, form the idea of corporeal substance, there is no
reason why we should doubt that a blind man, even one who has been
completely enshrouded in darkness from his birth, can form in his
own mind the ideas of light and of the colours. You say that*
consequently the ideas of extension, figure and motion, *and of other
common sensibles can be derived; but doubtless it is easy for you to
say this. What I marvel at is, why you do not deduce light, colour
and other similar things with a like facility. But we must not
linger over these matters.*

¹ certae.　　　　　² Vol. I. p. 165, par. 2.

7.   *You conclude:* Hence there remains alone the idea of God,
concerning which we must discover whether it is not something that
is capable of proceeding from me myself. By the name God I understand a substance that is infinite, independent, all-knowing, all-
powerful, and by which I myself and everything else, if anything
else does exist, have been created. Now all these characteristics
are such that the more diligently I attend to them, the less do
they appear capable of proceeding from me alone; hence, from
what has been already said, we must conclude that God necessarily
exists[1]. *This is, of course, the conclusion for which you were making.
But, as I grasp the inference, I do not see how you get this result.
You say that those characteristics* which you understand to exist in
God are of such a nature as to be incapable of proceeding from you
alone: *your intention in so doing is* to show that they must proceed
from God. *But, firstly, nothing is more true than that they have
not proceeded from you alone, so that you have had no knowledge of
them derived from yourself and merely by means of your own efforts;
for they have proceeded and are derived from objects, from parents,
from masters, from teachers, and from the society in which you have
moved. But you will say: 'I am mind alone: I admit nothing
outside of myself, not even the ears by which I hear nor the people
who converse mith me.' You may assert this: but would you assert
it, unless you heard us with your ears, and there were men from
whom you learned words. Let us talk in earnest, and tell me
sincerely: do you not derive those word-sounds which you utter in
speaking of God, from the society in which you have lived? And
since the sounds you use are due to intercourse with other men, is
it not from the same source that you derive the notions underlying
and designated by those sounds? Hence though not due to you alone,
they do not seem on that account to proceed from God, but to come
from some other quarter. Further, what is there in those things
which, on the opportunity first being furnished by the objects, you
could not henceforth derive from yourself? Do you, for that reason,
apprehend something which is beyond human grasp? It is true that
if you comprehended the nature of God there would be reason for
your thinking that it was from God you derived this knowledge.
But all those terms which you apply to God are merely certain
perfections observed to exist in human beings and other things, which
the human mind is able to understand, collect and amplify, as has
already been said several times.*

[1] Vol. i. p. 165, par. 3.

You say : that although the idea of substance might come from yourself, because you are a substance, the idea of an infinite substance could not be so derived, because you are not infinite[1]. *But you do not possess for that reason any idea of an infinite substance, except in a verbal sense, and in the way in which men are said to comprehend (which is really not to comprehend) the infinite. Hence there is no necessity in this, for such an idea to proceed from an infinite substance ; for it can be made, in the way already specified, by composition and amplification. Unless, when the early Philosophers, from the comprehension of the visible space, the single world, and limited principles which they understood, derived the ideas of those very things, and held them in such a way that by enlarging them they formed the idea of an infinite universe, of infinite worlds and of infinite principles ; you would say that those ideas had not been formed by the exertions of their own minds but had issued into the mind from the infinite universe, the infinite worlds, and infinite principles. Moreover, consider your defences :—* that you perceive the infinite by a true idea[2] : *surely if that idea were true it would reveal the nature of the infinite and consequently you would apprehend what is its leading feature, i.e. infinity. But your thought always stops short at something finite, and you talk of the infinite only because you do not perceive what is beyond your perceptions ; consequently there is not much error in saying that you perceive the infinite by negation of the finite. Nor does it suffice to say* that you perceive more reality in an infinite substance[3] than in a finite. *For you ought to perceive an infinite reality, which, nevertheless you do not do. Nay also, you do not really perceive more when you merely amplify the finite and thereupon imagine that there is more reality in that which has been enlarged than exists in it, the very same thing, while it remains within narrow bounds. Unless you also mean that those Philosophers, who conceived many worlds to exist, perceived a greater actually existing reality when doing so, than while they entertained the thought of a single world. Incidentally this suggests to me that the reason why the human mind becomes more confused in proportion to the extent to which it amplifies some form and Idea, seems to lie in the fact that the mind wrests such a form from its setting, annuls the distinctness of its parts, and so attenuates the whole, that at length it vanishes away. I might remember also that mental confusion will result from the opposite cause, as e.g. when an Idea is too much condensed.*

[1] Vol. i. p. 166, par. 1.   [2] *Ibid.* par. 2.   [3] *Ibid.*

You say : that there is no obstacle in the fact that you do not comprehend the infinite or all that is in it, and that it is sufficient for you to understand a few particulars in order to be said to have a true idea of it, and one that has the maximum clearness and distinctness[1]. *But nay, you do not have a true idea of the infinite, your idea is only of the finite, if you do not comprehend the infinite, but merely the finite. You can at most be said to know part of the infinite, but not, on that account, the infinite itself ; just as a man who had never gone outside an underground cave, might indeed be said to know part of the world but not, for that reason, the world itself. Hence, because of this, he will turn out to be foolish if he thinks that the idea of such a limited portion of the world is the true and genuine[2] idea of the whole.* But, you say, it is of the nature of the infinite not to be comprehended by you, who are finite. *I believe you ; but neither is it of the nature of a true idea of an infinite thing to represent merely a tiny part of it ; or what is rather no part of it, on account of its bearing no proportion to the whole.* You say, that it is sufficient for you to have knowledge of those few things, things you perceive clearly. *This forsooth, is as though it were sufficient to perceive the tip of a hair belonging to the man of whom you want to have an idea which resembles the reality. Would it not be a fine likeness of me if the painter were to depict a single hair of mine or the tip of it merely ? But what we may know of an infinite God is in proportion less not only by much, or by very much, but is even infinitely less than one of my hairs, or the tip of it, relatively to my whole self. In one word, these known facts prove nothing of God which they do not likewise prove of that infinite series of worlds mentioned before ; and this is all the more true in proportion as these could be more clearly understood from our clear knowledge of this one world,—than God, or an infinite entity can be derived in thought from your substance, as to the nature of which you are not yet agreed.*

8. *Elsewhere you argue thus :* For how would it be possible that I should know that I doubt and desire, that is to say, that something is lacking to me, and that I am not wholly perfect, unless I had within me some idea of a Being more perfect than myself, in comparing myself with which I recognized my deficiencies[3]? *But if you are in doubt about any matter, if you desire something and recognize that something is lacking to you, what is there wonderful in that, when you do not know everything, are not every-*

---

[1] Vol. I. p. 166, par. 3.   [2] *germanam.*   [3] *Ibid.* par. 2, *sub fin.*

thing, do not have everything ? Do you acknowledge that hence you are not wholly perfect? *Even this is certainly quite true and can be said without disparagement. Is it hence you gather that something more perfect than you exists? What? As if whatever you desire were not in some way or other more perfect than you. Thus when you desire bread the bread is not in every sense more perfect than you or than your body; it is more perfect only than that emptiness which exists in your stomach. How then do you gather that there is something more perfect than you? It is viz. in so far as you behold the totality of things which embrace both you and the bread and the rest of things; and in so doing, noticing that the separate parts of the whole have some perfection and are serviceable to one another and are able to reinforce each other, you easily come to understand that there is more perfection in the whole than in the part; and that, since you are only a part, you must acknowledge that there is something more perfect than you. It is, then, in this way that you can have the idea of a being that is more perfect than you, by comparing yourself with which you recognize your defects. I pass by the fact that other parts also may be more perfect, that you may desire what they possess and, by comparing yourself with them, acknowledge your defects. Thus you might know a man who was healthier, stronger, more handsome, more learned, calmer, and hence more perfect than yourself; and it would not be difficult for you to conceive the idea of him, and by comparing yourself with that, learn that you did not possess that degree of health, strength, and of the other perfections which existed in him.*

Shortly afterwards you propose to yourself the objection: But possibly I am something more than I suppose myself to be, and perhaps all those perfections which I attribute to God are in some way potentially in me, although they do not yet issue in action; as may be the case, if my knowledge tends more and more to grow to infinity[1]. *But you reply:* that though it were true that my knowledge gradually increased and that there were in me potentially many things which were not yet there actually, nevertheless none of these excellencies pertain to the idea of God, in which there is nothing potential, for the fact that it increases little by little is an absolutely certain token of the imperfection of my knowledge. *But though it is indeed true that what you perceive in the idea is actually in the idea, yet that is not a reason why it should exist in the thing of which you have the idea. Thus the architect constructs for himself*

[1] Vol. I. p. 167, ad init.

*the idea of a house, which idea is actually a complex of the walls,
floors, roof, and windows, etc., he has traced; nevertheless that house
and its component parts do not yet exist in actuality, but only
potentially. Thus the above idea of the Philosophers contains in
actuality an infinity of worlds; yet you cannot say that therefore
there is actually an infinity of worlds. Hence, whether something
exist in you, or whether it do not exist in you potentially, it is sufficient
that your idea or knowledge be capable of being gradually increased
and expanded; and it cannot be thence inferred that what is represented and apprehended by means of the idea does actually exist.
I gladly accept what you next recognize,* viz. that your knowledge
never will become infinite. *But you ought to acknowledge that
you will never possess a true and faithful idea of God; for there is
always more, nay infinitely more to know about God, than about that
man, the tip of whose hair merely you have seen. As a matter of
fact even if you have not seen the whole of that man, you have yet
seen another, by comparison with whom you are able to make some
conjecture about him. But nothing is ever presented to our knowledge similar to God and His immensity.*

You say that you understand God to be actually infinite, so
that He can add nothing to His perfection. *But this judgment is
about a matter of which you are in ignorance and is drawn merely
from a presumption, in the way that our Philosophers derived their
opinion about an infinity of worlds, infinite principles, and an
infinite universe, to the immensity of which nothing could be added.
But how can there be any truth in what you subjoin,* viz.: that the
objective being of an idea cannot be due to a potential but only to
an actual being, *if what we have just said about the Architect's idea
or that of the ancient Philosophers be correct? I ask you especially
how this can be so, when, as you remember, ideas of this sort are
composed of others which the mind has previously acquired, having
derived them from actually existing causes.*

9.   *You next ask*, whether, possessing now as you do the idea
of a being more perfect than yourself, you yourself could exist, if
no such being existed? *Your reply is:* 'From whom then could I
derive my existence? Perhaps from myself or from my parents, or
from some other source less perfect than God[1]?' *Then you go on to
prove* that you do not derive your existence from yourself. *But
this is not at all necessary. You also state the reason why you have
not always existed. But that also is superfluous, except in so far as*

---

[1] Vol. i. p. 167, par. 3 and par. 4.

you wish at the same time to infer that you depend upon a cause which not only produces you, but also conserves you. Thus from the fact that your lifetime falls into many parts, *you infer that you* must be created in each one of them, on account of the mutual independence that exists among them[1]. *But consider if this can be so understood. There are indeed certain effects which, in order to continue in existence and never at any moment to fail, require the continuous and efficient presence of the cause which started them. An example of such an effect is the light of the sun (though effects of this kind are not so much actually identical, but rather equivalent, as in the case of a river its water is said to be). But there are other things which we see continue, not merely when the cause which they acknowledge is no longer active, but, if you care, even when it is destroyed and reduced to nothing. Of such a sort are things which are procreated or manufactured, so many in number as to make it distasteful to recount them; but it suffices that you are one of these, whatsoever the cause of your existence turn out to be.* But, *you maintain,* the different parts of the time in which you exist do not depend on one another. *Here we may object and ask, what thing there is of which we can think, the parts of which are more inseparable from one another? What thing has parts, the order and connection of which is more inviolable? Is there anything in which there is less power of detaching the prior from the posterior of its parts, in which they cohere more closely and depend more on one another? But not to press this point, I ask what difference this dependence or independence of the parts of time, which are external, successive and non-active, makes to your production or reproduction? Certainly nothing more than the flow or passage by of the particles of water makes to the production and reproduction of a rock past which the river flows.* But, *you say,* from the fact that you existed a little while ago it does not follow that you must now exist. *I quite agree: but this is not because a cause is required to create you anew, but owing to the fact that the cause is not held to be absent which might destroy you, or because you ought not to have within you that weakness owing to which you will finally cease to exist.*

You allege that it is hence manifest by means of the light of nature, that the distinction between creation and conservation is solely a distinction of the reason[2]. *But how is it manifest, except perhaps in the case of light itself and similar effects? You add* that you do not possess a power which is capable of bringing it to pass

---

[1] Vol. I. p. 168, par. 2.   [2] *Ibid.*

that you shall exist shortly afterwards, because you are not conscious
of it, and are yet a thinking thing [1].　*But you do possess a power by
means of which you may judge that you will in future exist: though
this does not follow necessarily or indubitably, because that power of
yours, or natural constitution, does not go so far as to guard against
every destructive cause whether internal or external.　Hence also you
will exist because you have a power, not of producing yourself anew,
but one which suffices to enable you to continue to exist, unless some
destructive cause supervenes.　Moreover your conclusion,* that you
depend upon a being distinct from yourself, *is correct; but not in
the sense of your being produced anew by it, but in the sense of your
being originally produced by it.　You go on to say* that such a being
cannot be your parents or any other cause whatsoever.　*But why
not your parents, by whom you seem so manifestly produced, along
with your body?　Not to speak of the sun and the other co-operative
causes.　'Ah,'* you say, 'I am a thing which thinks, and have within
me the idea of God.'　*But were not your parents or their minds also
thinking things, also possessing the idea of God?　Hence you should
not here urge that dictum of which we have already talked, viz.* that
there must be at least as much reality in the cause as in the effect.
You say, if there be another cause besides God, we may again
enquire whether this cause derives its origin from God or from some
other thing.　For, if from itself, it will be God; if from some other
cause, we can ask the question over and over again, until we arrive
at that which is self-derived, and is God, since an infinite regress is
not permitted [2].　*But if your parents were the cause of your existence,
that cause might have been not self-derived, but dependent on something
else; and that again might have been due to something else and so on
to infinity.　Nor can you prove that that regress to infinity is absurd,
unless you at the same time show that the world has a definite
beginning in time, and that hence there was a first parent, who had
no parent.　An infinite regress seems certainly to be absurd only in
the case of causes which are so connected and subordinated to one
another, that no action on the part of the lower is possible without the
activity of the higher; e.g. in the case where something is moved by a
stone, itself impelled by a stick, which the hand moves, or when the
last link in a chain lifts a weight, while this link itself is moved by
the one above it and that by another; for in these circumstances we
must go on until we come to one thing in motion which a first moves.
But in those causes which are so arranged that, though the former is*

----

[1] Vol. i. p. 169, par. 1.　　　　　[2] *Ibid.* p. 169, par. 2.

taken away, that which depends upon it survives and may continue to act, it does not seem equally absurd. Hence when you say: that it is sufficiently manifest that here there can be no infinite regress[1], *see if it was so manifest to Aristotle, who was so strongly persuaded that there had never been a first parent.* You proceed: nor can several partial causes have concurred in your production, from which you have received the idea of the various perfections attributed to God, since they can only be found in a God who is one and single, whose unity or simplicity is a perfection of a very high order[2]. *But whether the cause of your existence is to be found in one thing or in many, it is not, therefore, necessary that such things should impress in you the idea of their perfections, which you have been able to unite. Meanwhile, however, you give us the opportunity of asking why, if there are not many causes of your existence, it has been possible at least for many things to exist, by admiring the perfections of which you have concluded that the Being must be a blessed one in which they all exist together. You know how the Poets describe Pandora. Nay, have not you, admiring in various men some outstanding knowledge, wisdom, justice, constancy, power, health, beauty, blessedness, length of existence, etc., been able to unite all these and consider how sublime he would be who possessed them all at the same time? Why can you not then increase all these perfections in various degrees until he would be all the more to be admired were it so that nothing was lacking to his knowledge, power, duration, etc., or could be added to it; for in these circumstances he would be all powerful, all knowing, eternal and so on? And when you found that such perfections could not coincide with human nature, might you not think that that would be a blissful nature, in which such a conjunction of attributes was possible? Might it not be worthy of your investigation to discover whether there is such a being in existence or no? Why might it not be possible for various arguments to induce you to believe that it was more reasonable that such a being should exist rather than not exist? Would it not be possible next to divest this of corporeity, limitation and all the remaining qualities, which imply a certain imperfection? Most people seem certainly to have proceeded in this way; although, as there are nevertheless various modes and degrees of reasoning, some have let God remain corporeal, some have allowed Him human members, and others have made Him not one but many, not to speak of other and too popular descriptions. In connection with that* perfection of unity *there is no contradiction in the conception of all*

---

*the perfections ascribed to God as being intimately joined together
and inseparable. But yet the idea by which you embrace them has
not been placed in you by Him, but has been drawn by you from the
things which you have seen, and has been amplified in the manner
described. Thus certainly do we have the description, not only of
Pandora, the goddess dowered with all gifts and perfections, but also
of the perfect State, the perfect Orator, etc. Finally,* from the fact
that you exist and possess the idea of a supremely perfect being,
you conclude, that you have a highly evident demonstration of the
existence of God. *But though your conclusion, viz.* that God exists
*is true, it is not clear from what you have said, that you have demon-
strated it in the most evident manner.*

10. *You say,* 'it remains for me to examine into the manner
in which I have acquired this idea from God; for neither have
I derived it from the senses, nor is it a fictitious idea made by me
(for it is not in my power to take from or add anything to it); and
consequently the only alternative left is that it is innate in me, just
as the idea of myself is[1].' *But I have frequently already said that
you may have partly derived it from the senses, partly made it up.
Moreover, as to your contention* that you can add nothing to and
take away nothing from it, *consider that, to begin with, it was not
equally perfect. Reflect that there may be men, or Angels, or other
natures more instructed than your own, from whom you may receive
some information about God, which you have not yet known. Reflect
that God at least could so instruct you and give you finally such a
degree of illumination, whether in this life or in another, that you
would esteem as nought anything which you now know of Him.
Whatever that knowledge finally be, consider that as the ascent can
be made from the perfections of created things to the knowledge of the
perfections of God, and that as they are not all known at a single
moment, but can be discovered in increasing numbers from day to-day,
so it will be possible for the idea of God not to be possessed in its
perfection at a single moment, but to become more perfect from day to
day. You proceed:* And one certainly ought not to find it strange
that God, in creating me, placed this idea within me, to serve as
the mark of the workman imprinted on his work. It is likewise not
essential that this mark should be something different from the
work itself. For, from the sole fact that God created me, it is most
probable that in some way He has placed His image and similitude
upon me, and that I perceive this similitude (in which the idea of

[1] Vol. I. p. 170, par. 3.

God is contained) by means of the same faculty by which I perceive myself : that is to say, when I reflect on myself, I not only know that I am something incomplete and dependent on another, something also which incessantly aspires after what is greater and better than myself; but I also know that He on whom I depend possesses in Himself all the great things to which I aspire, and that not indefinitely or potentially alone, but really, actually, and infinitely, and that thus He is God[1]. *There is indeed much appearance of truth in all this, and my objection is not that it is not true. But, I ask you, where do you get your proof ? Passing by what has been already said let us ask* : If the idea of God exists in you like the mark of the workman impriuted on his work, *what is the mode in which it is impressed ? What is the form of that mark ? How do you detect it ?* If it is not other than the work or thing itself, *are you then an idea ? Are you yourself nothing else than a mode of thought ? Are you both the mark impressed and the subject on which it is impressed ? You say* that it is to be believed that you have been fashioned after the image and similitude of God. *To religious faith this is indeed credible, but how can it be understood by the natural reason, unless you make God to have a human form ? And in what can this similitude to this Eternal Being consist ? Can you, who are dust and ashes, presume to be similar to Him, who is of an incorporeal, boundless, entirely perfect, most glorious and, what is the principal matter, an entirely invisible and incomprehensible nature ? Have you known that face to face, so as to be able, by comparing yourself with it, to affirm that you resemble it ?* You say that it is to be believed owing to the fact that He created you. *On the contrary that fact makes it incredible ; inasmuch as the work does not resemble the workman, unless when it is generated by him by a communication of his nature. But you have not been begotten by God in this way ; nor are you His offspring or a participator in His nature. You have merely been created by Him, i.e. made by Him according to an idea ; and hence you cannot say that you resemble Him more than the house resembles the workman who builds its walls. And this is true even though we grant, what you have not yet proved, your creation by God. You say* that you perceive a likeness, while at the same time you understand that you are a thing which is incomplete, dependent and aspiring towards what is better. *But is not this rather a proof of God's dissimilitude, since He on the contrary is most complete, most independent and entirely self-sufficient, being greatest and best of all ?*

[1] Vol. I. p. 170, par. 5.

I pass by the fact that when you know yourself to be dependent, you do not therefore immediately understand that that on which you depend is other than your parents; while if you do understand it to be something else, no reason offers why you should think that you resemble it. I pass by the fact also that it is strange that the rest of mankind or of minds do not understand the same thing as you do; and especially since there is no reason why we should refuse to think that God has impressed the idea of Himself on them as on you. Assuredly this one thing especially proves that there is no such idea which has been impressed on us by God; since if there had been, it would have been imprinted on all and, likewise, as one and the same, and all men would conceive God by means of a similar form and semblance, would ascribe the same qualities to him, and think the same .thing about Him. And the opposite is most notorious. These discussions, however, have now taken up too much time.

RELATIVE TO MEDITATION IV.

Of the True and the False.

1. *In the fourth Meditation you recount at the beginning what you think you have proved in the previous ones, and by means of which you presume you have opened a way for further progress. Not to interpose delay I shall cease from continually insisting that you ought to have demonstrated your results more cogently; it will be sufficient if you bear in mind what has been conceded and what has not; in order that our argument may avoid being affected with prejudice.*

You reason consequently that it is impossible that God should deceive you[1]; *and, in order to free from blame that faculty which misleads you and is exposed to error, and which you have received from Him, you conjecture that the fault resides* in non-being, of which you say you have some idea, and in which *according to your account* you participate, and between which and God you are, *according to your belief*, a mean[2]. *This is indeed a capital argument. But to pass by the contention that it cannot be explained how one can have, or what is the idea of, non-being; how we can participate in non-being, etc., I merely observe that by this distinction we do not obviate the fact that God might have given man a faculty of judgment immune from error. For without giving him an infinite capacity, He might have given him one of such a kind as not to assent to error, so that man would have had a clear perception of what he knew; and*

---

[1] Vol. I. p. 172, par. 2.   [2] *Ibid. sub fin.*

in regard to what he did not know he would not have committed himself in one direction rather than in another.

On your presenting to yourself this objection, you pronounce the opinion that you ought not to be astonished if certain things are done by God, the reason of which you do not understand[1]. *That is indeed quite correct ; but still it is surprising that you possess a true idea which represents God as all-knowing, all-powerful and wholly good, while you nevertheless see that certain of his works are not absolutely perfect and complete. So that since He at least might have made them more perfect, but yet did not do so, that seems to argue that He either did not know how, or could not, or did not wish to do so. At least it would be an imperfection in Him, if, possessing both the knowledge and the power to do so, He had refused, and had preferred imperfection to perfection.*

In refusing to employ final causes in an investigation into Physical things[2], *you act in a way which perhaps in another situation would have been quite correct. But in treating of God, it is really to be feared that you have rejected the principal argument whereby the Divine wisdom, foreknowledge, power and existence as well, may be established by our natural light. Thus, to omit the world as a whole, the heavens, and other outstanding parts of it, whence or how will you derive better arguments than from the function of the parts in plants, in animals, in men, and in your own self (or in your body) who bear the similitude of God ? It is a fact we can witness that many great men not only rise to a knowledge of God from the anatomical study of the human body, but also hymn His praises in that He has given such a conformation to all the members, and assigned to them their employment, so that He is to be extolled on account of His incomparable care and foresight.*

You will say that there are physical causes of such a form and arrangement which ought to be investigated, and that those people are foolish who have recourse to the end, rather than to the active cause or the material. But no mortal can comprehend, much less explain, what agent it is which forms and disposes in the way we observe, those valves which are constituted to serve as the orifices of the vessels in the cavities of the heart. Nor can we tell of what conformation the matter is out of which it elaborates them, or whence that matter is derived ; nor how the cause applies itself to its work, what instrument it employs, nor how it secures them ; nor what it stands in need of in order to render these valves of the proper temper, consistency, coherence, flexibility, size, figure and disposition in space. Since, then, I say, no Physical scientist is able to comprehend and declare them and other matters, what prevents him from at least admiring that most excellent contrivance and the marvellous providence which has given us valves accurately adapted to that design? Why should we not praise him, if he thereupon acknowledge that some First Cause must necessarily be admitted, which has disposed those and other matters in the wisest possible manner, and in a way most consonant with His own purposes?

You say that it is rash to investigate God's purposes. But though this may be true, if those purposes are meant which God Himself wished hidden or of which He has prohibited the investigation, it is, nevertheless, certainly not so, in the case of those which he has, as it were, placed publicly before us, which with little labour come to light, and are besides such as to procure great praise for God Himself, as for their author.

You will say perhaps that the idea of God existing in everyone, suffices to give a true and genuine[1] knowledge of God and of His providence, and apart from any reference either to the purposes of things or to anything else whatsoever. But not every one is so happily situated as you, so as to have that idea in all its perfection from birth upwards, and to behold it so clearly when offered to them. Wherefore you should not grudge those to whom God has not granted such a degree of insight, permission to acknowledge and glorify the Doer of those works from the inspection of His works. I need not recall the fact that there is no objection to using that idea which also seems to be so constructed out of our consciousness of things, that you, if you were to speak frankly, would admit you owe not indeed little but practically everything to this consciousness, for tell me, I pray, how much progress do you suppose you would have made, if from the time at which you were infused into the body, you had dwelled in it up till now with closed eyes and sealed ears, and in short had had no perception by external sense of anything outside us or of this whole universe of objects? What if meanwhile you—the whole of you—had passed the whole time in inward meditation and in revolving thoughts round and round? Tell me in good faith, and describe the ideas of God and of yourself which you think you would have acquired.

2. *The solution you next offer is,* that the creature, recognised as imperfect, should be considered not as a whole, but rather as a part of the universe, from which point of view it will be perfect[2].

---

[1] Germanam.   [2] Vol. I. p. 173, *sub fin.*

Your distinction is certainly to be commended, but at the present point we are not treating of the imperfection of a part in so far as it is a part and is compared with the integrity of the whole, but in so far as it is something complete in itself and performs a special function. And when you relate this again to the universe the difficulty always remains, whether in truth the universe would have been more perfect, if all its parts had been perfect, than as the case actually holds, when many of its parts are imperfect. Thus that State will be more perfect in which all the citizens are good, than another in which many or some are bad.

Whence, also, when a little later you say : that the perfection of the universe is in some sense greater, in that certain of its parts are not exempt from error, than if they all had been alike[1], *it is exactly as if you were to say that the perfection of a state is greater in that some of its citizens are evil than in the case when they are all good. This lets us see that just as it ought evidently to be the desire of a good prince that all his subjects should be good, so it seems it should have been the resolution of the Author of the universe to create and keep all its parts free from defect. And though you are able to allege that the perfection of those parts which are free from defect, appears greater when contrasted with those which are not exempt from it, that nevertheless is merely accidental ; just as the virtue of good men, if more striking owing to the contrast between the good and the evil, is so only by accident. Consequently, just as we should not want any of the citizens to be evil, in order that the good might thereby become more distinguished, so, it seems, it ought never to have come to pass that any part of the universe should be subject to error, in order that the parts that were free from it might thus be rendered more conspicuous.*

You say : that you have no right to complain, if God has not called upon you to play a part in the world that excels all others in distinction and perfection[2]. *But this does not remove the question why it has not been sufficient for Him to give you the smallest of perfect parts to play, and not to have given you one that was imperfect. For though, likewise, it would not be considered culpable on the part of a prince to refuse to assign offices of the highest dignity to the whole of his subjects, but to call some people to the discharge of duties of intermediate importance, others to the fulfilling of the humblest functions, nevertheless he would be blamed if over and above destining some to the execution of the most insignificant offices, he had also assigned to some a function that was base.*

[1] Vol. I. p. 178, par. 1.   [2] *Ibid.*

You declare : that you can bring no reason to show why God ought to have given you a greater faculty of knowledge than He has given you ; and however skilful a workman you represent Him to be, you should not, for all that, consider that He was bound to have placed in each and all of his works the perfections which He has been able to place in some[1]. *But the objection I only now stated remains undiminished. You must see that the difficulty is not so much, why God has not given you a greater faculty of knowing, as why He has given you one that falls into error ; no controversy is raised as to why the supreme artificer has willed not to give every thing every perfection, but why He has chosen to allot to some things imperfections as well.*

You allege : that though you cannot be free from error by means of possessing a clear knowledge of all things, you may yet avoid it by express resolve, the resolve by which you firmly make up your mind to assent to nothing which you do not clearly perceive[2]. *But however much you may be able to bear this in mind attentively, is it not an imperfection not to have clear perception of that which we need to distinguish and appraise, and to be perpetually exposed to the risk of error.*

You maintain : that error resides in the act itself, in so far as it proceeds from you and is a sort of privation, not in the faculty which you have received from God, nor even in the act in so far as it depends on Him[3]. *But, though the error does not attach directly to the faculty received from God, nevertheless it does attach to it indirectly, inasmuch as in its creation there is that imperfection which makes error possible. Wherefore,-though, as you say,* you have certainly no cause to complain of God, who in truth owes you nothing, and yet has conferred those boons upon you, for which you should render thanks to Him, *we must yet continue to wonder why He has not given us more perfect faculties, if He really knew, if He had the power, and if not inspired with malice.*

You add : that neither must you complain that God concurs with you in the act of erring ; because all these acts are true and good in so far as they depend upon God, and in a certain sense more perfection accrues to you from the fact that you can form such acts than if you could not do so ; while the privation in which alone the formal reason of falsity or error consists, does not require any concurrence on the part of God, since it is not a real

---

[1] Vol. I. p. 174, par. 2. [2] Vol. I. p. 178, par. 2.
[3] Vol. I. p. 177, par. 1.

thing nor is related to Him[1].   *But subtle though that distinction be, it is nevertheless not quite satisfactory.   If indeed God does not concur in the privation which is present in the act and is its falsity and error, He yet concurs in the act ; and unless He concurred with it there would be no privation.   Besides, He Himself is the Author of that power which is deceived or falls into error, and consequently is the source of a power which, so to speak, lacks power.   Thus the defect in the act is, it seems, to be referred not so much to that power which lacks power as to its Author who created it with this lack of power and, though he was able to do so, declined to make it effective, or more effective than it is.   It is certainly counted no fault in a workman if he does not take the trouble of making a very large key to open a little casket, but if, after making it so small, he shapes it so that it fails to open the box, or does so with difficulty.   Thus also, though God is indeed not to be blamed for giving to a mannikin a faculty of judging not so great as he thought would be necessary for either all or most or the greatest of creatures, it is still strange why he has assigned to us a faculty which is so uncertain, so confused, and so unequal to the task of deciding those few things on which He has willed that man should pass judgment.*

3.   *You next ask :* what is the cause of the existence of falsity or error in you[2].   *In the first place I do not question your right of calling* understanding only the faculty of being aware of ideas, *or of apprehending things themselves simply and without any affirmation or denial, while you make* the will and the power of free choice the faculty of judgment, *to which it belongs to affirm or deny, to assent or dissent.   The sole question I propound is why the will and liberty of choice is circumscribed by no limits in your account, while the range of the understanding is circumscribed.   The truth is that these two faculties seem to have domains of equal extent and that the understanding has at least no narrower a range than the will, since will is never directed towards anything of which the understanding has not previously had cognizance.*

I said 'at least no narrower a range' ; *for really the understanding seems to extend even further than the will.   This is so if, as a fact, will or decision, and judgment, never arise, and consequently neither do the choice of, the striving after, and aversion from a thing which we have not apprehended, nor unless the idea of that thing is perceived and set before us by the understanding.   But besides this we understand in a confused fashion many things which lead to no judgment, no striving after or avoidance of them. Likewise, the faculty of judgment is often uncertain, so that, when reasons of equal weight are present, or when no reason exists, no judgment follows, while meanwhile the understanding apprehends the matters that still continue unaffected by judgment.*

Your statement, that you can always understand more and more; to take an example, you can more and more comprehend the faculty of understanding itself, of which you can form even an infinite idea[1], *of its own self proves that your understanding is not more limited than your will, when it is able to extend even to an infinite object.* But when you take into account the fact that you *acknowledge* that your will equals the Divine will, not indeed in actual extent but formally, *consider whether the same may not be asserted of the understanding also, since you have defined the formal notion of the understanding in just the same way as you have that of the will. But tell us briefly to what the will may extend which escapes the understanding? Hence it seems* that the cause of error is not, *as you say,* due to the will extending more widely than the understanding, and going on to judge of matters of which the understanding is not aware[2]. *It is rather due to the fact that, both ranging as they do over an equally wide domain, the understanding fails to discern something well, and the will fails to judge correctly.*

Wherefore there is no reason for extending the will beyond the bounds of the intellect, *since it is not the case that it judges of things which the understanding does not perceive, and judges ill for the sole reason that the understanding perceives badly.*

In the example about your non-existence[3], *when you bring up the argument you have constructed relative to the existence of objects, you proceed correctly in so far as the reasoning refers to your own existence. But, in so far as it concerns other things, you seem to have proceeded on a false assumption; for, whatever you say, or rather pretend to say, your doubt is not genuine, and your judgment entirely allows that something else exists beyond yourself, distinct from you : it is a matter of which you are already aware that something else distinct from yourself exists. It is possible for you to suppose as you do* that there is no reason to persuade you to adopt the one belief rather than the other. *But at the same time you ought to suppose that no judgment will follow, and that your will will always be indifferent, and will not determine itself to come to a decision, until*

---

[1] Vol. I. p. 174.　　　　[2] *Ibid.*
[3] Vol. I. p. 176, par. 2.

the time that a greater probability on the one side rather than the other presents itself to the understanding.

Your next statement : that this indifference extends to those matters which are not apprehended with perfect clearness, in such a way that, however probable be the conjectures which render you disposed to form a judgment on one particular side, the simple knowledge you possess, that they are conjectures, may occasion you to judge the contrary[1] : *seems to be in no way true. For that knowledge which tells you that they are merely conjectures will indeed cause you to pass judgment in favour of that conclusion to which they point, with a certain amount of insecurity and hesitation ; but it will never make you decide for the opposite belief, unless conjectures subsequently present themselves, which are not equally but even more probable than the others.*

Though you add, that you had experience of this lately, when setting aside as false what you had formerly supposed to be absolutely true, *remember that this has not been conceded to you. For you cannot really have felt persuaded yourself that you have not seen the sun, the earth, men, and other objects, that you have not heard sounds, have not walked, eaten, or written, have not spoken (have not, i.e. used your body or its organs), and so forth.*

Finally therefore the form of error *does not seem to consist* in the incorrect use of the free will[2], *as you maintain, so much as in the dissonance between the judgment and the thing whereof we judge ; it seems to arise indeed from the fact that the understanding apprehends that thing otherwise than as it is. Whence it seems to be not so much the blame of the free will, which judges wrong, as of the understanding which does not give the correct reason. Thus the dependence of the power of choice upon the understanding seems to be such that, if the intellect indeed perceives something clearly or seems to do so, the will passes a judgment which is agreed on and determinate, whether that be really true, or whether it be thought to be true ; if, on the other hand the perception on the part of the understanding be obscure, then our will passes a judgment which is doubtful and hesitating, though taken for the time to be more true than its opposite, and this whether the matter is really true or false. The result is that it is not so much in our power to guard against error, as to refrain from persisting in error, and that the appropriate exercise of judgment is not so much the reinforcing of the strength of the will, as the application of the under-*

---

[1] Vol. I. p. 176, par. 3.   [2] *Ibid.* par. 4.

*standing to the discovery of clearer knowledge than that which our
judgment is always likely to follow.*

4. *In your conclusion you exaggerate the profit to be derived
from this Meditation; you also prescribe* how you should act in
order to arrive at a knowledge of the truth; for, *you say,* you will
arrive at this if you only devote your attention sufficiently to those
things which you perfectly understand, and if you separate them
from that which you apprehend more confusedly and obscurely[1].

*Now this is not only true but it is a truth which could be grasped
altogether apart from the previous Meditation, which thus seems to
have been superfluous. Nevertheless, my good Sir, note that the
difficulty appears not to affect the question whether, in order to avoid
error, we ought to understand a thing clearly and distinctly, but
concerns the art or method by which it is possible to discern that our
knowledge is so clear and distinct that it must be true and cannot
possibly mislead us. Nay, at the outset I made the objection that not
infrequently we are deceived even though we seem to have a knowledge
of the matter which nothing can excel in respect of clearness and
distinctness. You yourself also brought up this objection against
yourself, and nevertheless we still await the revelation of that art or
method, to the exposition of which your energies should be chiefly directed.*

RELATIVE TO MEDITATION V.

*Of the essence of material things; and, again, of God,
that He exists.*

1. *In the Fifth Meditation you first say that you distinctly
imagine* quantity, i.e. extension in length, breadth and depth;
likewise number, figure, situation, motion and duration[2]. *Out of all
these, the ideas of which you say you possess, you select figure and,
from among the figures, the triangle, of which you write as follows*:
although there may nowhere in the world be such a figure outside
my thought, or ever have been, there is nevertheless in this figure a
determinate nature, which I have not invented, and which does not
depend upon my mind, as appears from the fact that divers properties can be demonstrated of that triangle, viz. that its three
angles are equal to two right angles, that the greatest side is sub-
tended by the greatest angle, and the like, which now, whether
I wish it or do not wish it, I recognise very clearly, even though I
have never thought of them at all before when I imagined a triangle,

---

[1] Vol. I. p. 179 *ad init.*   [2] Vol. I. p. 179, par. 4.

and which therefore have not been invented by me[1]. *So much only do you have respecting the essence of material things; for the few remarks you add refer to the same matter. I have, indeed, no desire to raise difficulties here; I suggest only that it seems to be a serious matter to set up* some immutable and eternal nature *in addition to God the all-powerful.*

You will say that you merely bring forward a proposition of the schools, which states that the natures or essences of things are eternal, and that propositions can be asserted about them which have an eternal truth. But this is equally difficult, and besides, we cannot conceive how the nature of man can exist, when there is no human being, or how it can be said that the rose is a flower when not a single rose exists.

They say that it is one thing to talk of the essence, another thing to talk of the existence of things, and that though indeed things do not exist from all eternity, their essence is still eternal. But since the chief thing in objects is their essence, does God do anything of much moment when He produces existence on their part? It is clear that to Him it is no more than for a tailor to try a coat on his customer. Yet how can people maintain that the essence of man in Plato is eternal and independent of God? In virtue of being a universal, do they say? But in Plato nothing but what is individual has real existence. Though the mind, from seeing Plato, Socrates, and the resembling natures of other men, is wont to form a certain common concept in which they all agree, and which can hence be reckoned the universal nature or essence of man, in so far as it is understood to be applicable to every man; yet it can by no means be shown that the universal existed before Plato and the others existed and the mind performed the abstraction.

You will reply; is not that proposition man is animal *true even before man exists, and hence from all eternity? I say no, it seems not to be true, except in the sense that whensoever man comes into existence he will be animal. This is so, even though we allow the seeming distinction between those two statements:* man exists *and* man is animal, *owing to the fact that existence is more expressly signified by the former, essence by the latter. Nevertheless, from the former, essence is not excluded, nor existence from the latter. When we say* man exists, *we mean the man that is animal; when we assert that* man *is an animal, we mean man while he exists. But besides, since this proposition,* man is animal, *is not of greater necessity than that other*, Plato is a man, *it will therefore possess an eternal truth, and the individual essence of Plato will be not less independent of God than the universal essence of man is ; so likewise other similar results will ensue, which it would be tedious to pursue.* Yet I add *that since man is said to be of such a nature that he cannot exist without being animal, we must not therefore imagine that such a nature is anything or exists anywhere outside the mind ; but that the meaning is merely this, that if anything is a human being it must itself resemble these other objects, to which, on account of their mutual resemblance, the same appellation 'man' is given. This is a resemblance, I repeat, between individual natures, from which the understanding derives the opportunity of forming a concept or the idea or form of a common nature, from which anything that will be human ought not to deviate.*

Hence I say the same of that triangle of yours and its nature. For the triangle is indeed a sort of mental rule which you employ in discovering whether something deserves to be called a triangle. But there is no necessity for us on that account to say that such a triangle is something real and a true nature over and above the understanding, which alone, from beholding material triangles, has formed it and has elaborated it as a common notion exactly in the way we have described in the case of the nature of man.

Hence also we ought not to think that the properties demonstrated of material triangles, agree with them because they derive those properties from the ideal triangle ; they rather contain those properties themselves, and the ideal triangle does not possess them except in so far as the understanding, after observing the material ones, assigns them to it, with a view to restoring them again in the process of demonstration. This is in the same way as the properties of human nature do not exist in Plato and Socrates in the sense that they receive them from the universal nature of man, the facts being rather that the mind ascribes those properties to it after discerning them in Plato, Socrates and others, with the intention of restoring them to those individual cases, when reasoning is called for.

It is known that the understanding, after seeing Plato, Socrates and others, all of whom are rational beings, has put together this universal proposition : every man is rational; *and then when it wishes to prove that Plato is rational, it uses that as a premiss in its syllogism. Likewise, O Mind, you indeed say that you have the idea of a triangle, and would have possessed it, even though you had never seen any triangular shape among bodies, just as you have* ideas of many other figures which have never presented themselves to your senses[1].

But, if, as I have said above, you had been deprived of all sense-functions in such a way that you had never either seen or touched the various surfaces or extremities of bodies, do you think you would have been able to possess or elaborate within you the idea of a triangle or of any other figure? You have many ideas which have not entered into you by way of the senses. *So you say; but it is easy for you to have them, because you construct them out of those which have so entered and you elaborate them into various others, in the ways I above expounded.*

Besides this we should have spoken here of that false nature of the triangle, which is supposed to consist of lines which are devoid of breadth, to contain an area which has no depth, and to terminate at three points which are wholly without parts. But this would involve too wide a digression.

2. *You next attempt the proof of God's existence and the vital part of your argument lies in these words:* When I think attentively I clearly see that the existence can no more be separated from the essence of God than can there be separated from the essence of a triangle the equality in magnitude of its three angles to two right angles, or the idea of a mountain from the idea of a valley; so that there is no less incongruity in our conceiving a God (i.e. a Being who is supremely perfect) to Whom existence is lacking (i.e. in Whom a certain perfection is missing), than to think of a mountain which is not accompanied by a valley[2]. *But we must note that a comparison of this kind is not sufficiently accurate.*

For though you properly enough compare essence with essence, in your next step it is neither existence with essence, nor property with property that you compare, but existence with property. Hence it seems that you either ought to have said that God's omnipotence can no more be separated from His essence than can that equality in magnitude of the angles of a triangle from its essence; or at least, that God's existence can no more be separated from His essence than the existence from the essence of a triangle. Thus taken, each comparison would have proceeded on correct lines, and the truth would have been conceded, not only of the former but of the latter, although this would not be evidence that you had established your conclusion that God necessarily exists, because neither does the triangle necessarily exist, although its essence and its existence cannot in reality be severed,

*howsoever much the mind separates them or thinks of them apart, in
the same way as the Divine essence and existence may be thought of
separately.*

*Next we must note that you place existence among the Divine per-
fections, without, however, putting it among the perfections of a
triangle or of a mountain, though in exactly similar fashion, and in
its own way, it may be said to be a perfection of each. But, sooth to
say, existence is a perfection neither in God nor in anything else; it
is rather that in the absence of which there is no perfection.*

*This must be so if, indeed, that which does not exist has neither
perfection nor imperfection, and that which exists and has various
perfections, does not have its existence as a particular perfection and
as one of the number of its perfections, but as that by means of
which the thing itself equally with its perfections is in existence, and
without which neither can it be said to possess perfections, nor can
perfections be said to be possessed by it. Hence neither is existence
held to exist in a thing in the way that perfections do, nor if the
thing lacks existence is it said to be imperfect (or deprived of a
perfection), so much as to be nothing.*

*Wherefore, as in enumerating the perfections of a triangle you
do not mention existence, nor hence conclude that the triangle exists,
so, in enumerating the perfections of God, you ought not to have put
existence among them, in order to draw the conclusion that God
exists, unless you wanted to beg the question.*

You say: in everything else I have distinguished existence from
essence but not in God. *But how, I pray, is the existence of Plato
distinguished from the essence of Plato, unless by thought? For,
supposing now that Plato no longer exists where is his essence? Is
it not in the same way that essence and existence are distinguished by
thought in God?*

You yourself raise the objection: Perhaps, just as from my
thinking of a mountain with a valley, or of a winged horse, it
does not follow that therefore either the mountain or such a horse
exists; so from the fact that I think of God as existing it does not
follow that He exists: *but you go on to argue that a sophism is
latent here. But it would not be difficult to expose the fallacy which
you have yourself constructed, especially by assuming something
that is so manifest a contradiction as that an existing God does not
exist, and not assuming the same thing about man, or horse.*

*But if you had drawn a parallel between the mountain with its
valley, or the horse with its wings, and God as possessing knowledge,*

power and other attributes, then the difficulty would have been carried
forward and you would have had to explain how it is possible for a
sloping mountain or a winged horse to be thought of without their
existing, while a God who has knowledge and power cannot be conceived of without His existence being involved.

You say: that it is not in your power to think of God
without existence (that is of a supremely perfect Being devoid
of a supreme perfection) as it is within your power to imagine
a horse either with wings or without wings[1]. *But nothing is to be
added to this, except that, as you are free to think of a horse that
does not have wings without thinking of its existence, that existence
which, if added, will be a perfection in it due to you ; so you are free
to think of a God that has knowledge, power and the other perfections, without thinking of His existence, which, if possessed by Him
would render His perfection complete. Whence, just as from the
fact that a horse is thought of as possessing the perfection of being
winged, it is not therefore inferred that it has' existence, the chief of
perfections, through your instrumentality ; so neither from the fact
that God is considered as possessing knowledge and other perfections
is His existence deduced from that: rather it finally remains to be
proved. Although you say*: that existence quite as much as other
perfections is included in the idea of a Being of the highest perfection, *you affirm what has to be proved, and assume your conclusion
as a premiss. For I might also, on the other part, say that in the
idea of a perfect Pegasus, there was contained not only the perfection
of having wings, but also that of existing. For as God is thought
to be perfect in every kind of perfection, so is Pegasus thought to be
perfect in its own kind, and you can bring forward in criticism
nothing which cannot, if the parallel between the two be duly
observed, be taken to hold of both alike.*

You say: as in thinking of a triangle it is not necessary for
me to think that its three angles are equal to two right angles,
though that is none the less true, as is afterwards clear when we
attend to the matter; so we may indeed think of the other perfections of God without thinking of His existence, though that is
none the less true when we note that it is a perfection. *But you
see what may be said, viz. that as that property is discovered afterwards to exist in the triangle, because a demonstration proves it, so
we must employ a demonstration in order to discover existence in*

God. Otherwise it will certainly be easy for me to show that any-thing is in anything.

You say that when you attribute all perfections to God, you do not act as if you imagined that all quadrilateral figures were inscribed in the circle; since, as herein you would err,—and this is borne out by your knowledge that the rhombus cannot be in-scribed in it, you do not in the other case go astray, because you afterwards find that existence is congruent with God[1]. *But this apparently, is inevitably to act in the same way; or, if that is not so, you must show that existence is not incompatible with God, in the same way as you prove that being inscribed in a circle is incompatible with the rhombus. I pass by your remaining assertions, which are either unexplained or unproved by you, or are solved by considerations you have already adduced as, for example* : that nothing can be conceived, to the essence of which existence belongs, save God alone; that we cannot frame the thought of two or more such Gods; that such a God has from all eternity existed and will continue to all eternity; that you perceive many other things in God, which can suffer neither diminution nor change[2]. *To this is added the necessity for inspecting these matters more nearly and investigating them more diligently, in order that their truth may be revealed and that they may be acknowledged as certain, etc.*

You declare finally that the certainty and truth of all know-ledge so depends upon our apprehension of the true God alone, that, if we do not possess this, we can have no true certainty or knowledge[3]. *You bring forward the following example, saying:* When I consider the nature of a triangle, I who have some little knowledge of the principles of geometry, recognise quite clearly that the three angles are equal to two right angles; and it is not possible for me not to believe this so long as I apply my mind to its demonstration. But as soon as I divert my attention from its proof, howsoever well I recollect having clearly comprehended it, I may easily come to doubt about its truth, if I am ignorant of there being a God. For I might[4] persuade myself of having been so constituted by nature as sometimes to be deceived in those matters which I believe myself to apprehend with the greatest evidence : especially when I recollect that I have frequently judged matters to be true and certain which other reasons have afterwards impelled me to judge to be altogether false. But after I have

---

[1] Vol. i. p. 182.　　　　　　　　[2] *Ibid.*
[3] Vol. i. p. 183, par. 3.　　　　　[4] Possem, in Med. v. possum.

recognised that there is a God because at the same time I have recognised that all things depend upon Him and that He is not a deceiver, and from that I have inferred, that what I clearly and distinctly perceive cannot fail to be true: even though I no longer pay attention to the reason for which I believe that thing to be true: provided that I recollect having clearly and distinctly perceived it, no contrary reason can be brought forward which could cause me to doubt of its truth. On the contrary I have a true and certain knowledge of it. And this same knowledge extends likewise to all other things which I recollect having formerly demonstrated, such as the truths of geometry and the like[1].

In reply to this, my good Sir, since I admit that you are speaking seriously, there is nothing to say, but that it seems that you will have difficulty in getting anyone to believe that you were less certain of those geometrical proofs before the time when you established by reasoning the above conclusion about God, than after you had done so. For really those demonstrations seem to have an evidence and certainty of such a kind as by themselves to extort our assent to them, and when once recognised they do not allow the mind to have any further doubt. So true is this that the mind will as likely as not bid that evil Genius go to perdition ; just as you might have done when you (although the existence of God was not yet known) asserted with much emphasis that you could not be imposed on about that proposition and inference: I think, hence I exist. *Nay, even, however true it be, as nothing can be truer, that God exists, that He is the Author of everything, and that He is not a deceiver, since, nevertheless, these facts seem to be less evident than those geometrical proofs (of which the only proof required is that many controvert God's existence, His creation of the world, and many other truths), while no one denies the demonstrations of Geometry, is there anyone whom you can persuade that the evidence and certainty of the latter[2] is communicated to them from the former? Likewise who fancies that Diagoras, Theodorus, or any similar atheist, cannot be rendered certain of the truth of those mathematical demonstrations? Again, how often among believers do you come across one who, if asked why he is sure that in a (right angled[3]) triangle the square on its base is equal to the square on its sides, will reply: 'because I know that*

---

[1] Vol. I. p. 184.   [2] i.e. the theorems of Geometry.
[3] Added in *Disquisitio Metaphysica*.

*God exists, and that God cannot deceive, and that He is the cause
of this fact as likewise as of all others.'   Will he not rather reply:
'because I know it, and it has been shown to me by an indubitable
demonstration'?   How much the more likely is this to be the reply of
Pythagoras, Plato, Archimedes, Euclid, and other mathematicians,
none of whom seems to bring up the thought of God in order to be
quite certain of his demonstrations!   Yet, because you do not pledge
your word for others, but only for yourself, and your attitude is also
pious, there is really no reason for my objecting to it.*

Relative to Meditation VI.

*Of the existence of Material Things, and of the real distinction
between the Soul and the Body of Man.*

1.   *In the Sixth Meditation I do not object to what you say at
the beginning:* that material things may exist in so far as they
are the object of pure mathematics[1]; *since, nevertheless, material
things are the object of mixed, not of pure mathematics; and the
objects of pure mathematics, e.g. the point, the line, the superficies,
and the indivisible things consisting of these and functioning as
indivisible, are incapable of actual existence.   I have difficulty only
because here a second time you distinguish* imagination from intellection.   *Nay, O Mind, these two appear to be the action of one
and the same faculty, as we have indicated above; and, if there is
any distinction between them, it does not seem to be more than one
of greater and less.   Consider how these conclusions may thence be
now proved.*

You said above: to imagine is merely to contemplate the figure
or image of something corporeal.   *But here you do not deny that*
to understand is to contemplate the Triangle, the Pentagon, the
Chiliagon, the Myriagon, *and the other things of this kind, which
are the figures of corporeal things.   You now indeed set up the
distinction that* the imagination involves a certain application of the
cognitive faculty to a body, while intellection does not involve
any such application or effort.   *So that,* when you simply and
without trouble perceive the triangle as a figure consisting of three
angles, *you say* that that is an act of understanding.   But when,
not without some effort on your part, you have that figure, as it
were, present, and investigate it, examine it, and recognise and
discern its three angles distinctly and severally[2], then, *you say,* you

---

[1] Vol. i. p. 185, par. 3.
[2] Sigillatim is printed in A. and T.'s edition.   I emend to singillatim.   Tr.

imagine. *And hence,* since you indeed perceive without any trouble that the Chiliagon is a figure with a thousand angles, but yet cannot by application or an effort of attention, discover it, and have it, as it were, present before you and discern all its angles individually[1], but are as confused about it as about the Myriagon, or any other figure of this description, you therefore deem that you employ Intellection in the case of the Chiliagon or the Myriagon, and not Imagination.

But, nevertheless[1], there is no reason why you should not extend your imagination, as well as your intellection, to the Chiliagon, as you do to the Triangle. For you do try to some extent to imagine that figure with its host of angles in some fashion, though the number of its angles is so great that you cannot conceive it clearly. Besides, though you do perceive that a figure of a thousand angles is signified by the word Chiliagon, that is merely the force of the name; for this will not cause you to understand *a thousand angles better than you* imagine *them.*

But we must note that the loss of distinctness and increase of confusedness is gradual. For you will perceive and imagine (or understand) the quadrilateral more confusedly than the triangle, yet more distinctly than the Pentagon. Again this is more confused than the quadrilateral, but more distinct than the Hexagon, and so on in order, until you have nothing explicit to put before yourself; and because you now are not able to have an explicit conception, you make an effort in order to omit as much as possible.

Wherefore if you indeed wish to call it imagination and intellection at the same time, when you are aware of the figure distinctly and with some sensible effort, but intellection alone, when you view it confusedly merely and without or with but slight effort, you have my consent. But that will furnish no reason why you should set up more than one type of internal cognition, since it is accidental only whether you contemplate a figure in ways that differ in terms of more and less, distinct or confused, attentiveness or carelessness. Assuredly, when we wish to run over the Heptagon, the Octagon, and the other figures up to the Chiliagon, or the Myriagon, and continuously and all through attend to the greater or less degree of distinctness or remissness of attention, shall we be able to say where or in what figure imagination ceases and intellection alone remains? Does it not rather turn out to be the case that there is a continuous scale and progression in one sort of knowledge, the distinctness and

[1] Vol. I. pp. 185—6.

*toil of which decreases continuously and insensibly, while its con-
fusedness and effortlessness increases. Independently of this, note
that you depreciate intellection, while lauding imagination. For do
you not merely heap scorn on the former in allotting to it remissness
and confusion, but commend the latter, in ascribing to it diligent
care and perspicuity?*

Afterwards you assert: that the power of imagination in so far
as it is distinguished from the power of understanding is not a
necessary part of your essence[1]. *But how can that be, if they are
one and the same power, the functions of which differ merely in
respect of greater and less?*

You add: that the mind, in imagining, turns towards the body,
but, in its intellectual activity, turns towards itself or the idea it
possesses. *But what if the mind is unable to turn towards itself or
towards any idea without at the same time turning itself towards something corporeal, or represented by a corporeal idea? For indeed the
Triangle, the Pentagon, the Chiliagon, the Myriagon and the other
figures or their ideas are altogether corporeal, and the mind cannot
in its intellectual activity attend to them except as to something
corporeal or similar to the corporeal. In so far as the ideas of things
reputed to be immaterial are concerned, such as the idea of God, of
an Angel, or of the human soul or mind, it is certain also that the
ideas we do possess about these things are either corporeal or after the
fashion of the corporeal, and drawn from the human form and, at
other times, from the most subtle, the simplest and most imperceptible
objects such as air or ether, as we mentioned above. Moreover your
statement,* that it is only with probability that you conjecture that
any body exists, *cannot be uttered by you seriously, and hence need
cause us no delay.*

2. *Next you have a discussion about Sense, and first you very
rightly make an enumeration of those matters which had become
known to you by means of the senses and had been believed by you
to be true, taking nature alone as your judge and guide. Immediately
afterwards you relate the experiences, which so shook the beliefs you
had derived from your senses, as to drive you to that position at
which we found you in the First Meditation.*

*At this point I have no desire to begin a controversy about the
trustworthiness of the senses; for, if there is deception or falsity, it
is not in sense, which is merely passive and has to do only with
things that appear and must appear in the way they do owing to*

[1] Vol. i. p. 186, par. 2.

their own appropriate causes ; it resides in the judgment or in the mind, which does not act with sufficient circumspection, and does not notice that things at a distance, owing to this and that cause appear more confused and smaller than they really are when they are near at hand, and so in other cases. Nevertheless, wherever deception does occur, we must not deny that some error exists ; only the difficulty is, whether the error is always such that we can never be sure of the truth in the case of anything perceived by the senses.

But there is really no need to search for obvious examples. To take only the instances which you adduce, or rather cite as objections, I maintain that in these cases the truth of our belief seems to be amply confirmed ; when we behold a tower close at hand and touch it we are sure that it is square, though, when further off, we had occasion to pronounce it to be round, or at least were able to doubt whether it was round or square or of some other figure.

Similarly that feeling of pain, which appears still to exist in the foot or in the hand after these members have been cut off, may on occasion cause deception in those indeed who have had these limbs cut off ; and that is because the sensorial spirits have been accustomed to pass downwards into them and express sensation in them. Nevertheless those who are whole are so certain that they feel the pain in the foot or in the hand which they see pricked, that they cannot doubt about it.

Similarly also, since we wake and dream alternately as long as we are alive, deception may occur owing to a dream, because things appear in the dream to be present which are not present. Nevertheless, neither do we always dream, nor, when we are really awake, can we doubt whether we are awake or dreaming.

So too, since we can think that we are of a nature exposed to deceptions, even in things that seem most sure, we none the less think that we are naturally capable of apprehending truth. And just as we sometimes err, as when we do not detect a sophism, or when we look at a stick plunged to half its length in water, so also we sometimes apprehend the truth, as in a geometrical demonstration, or when the stick is taken out of the water, the circumstances being such that in neither of these cases can we doubt at all about the truth. And just as in other cases we may be in doubt, so at least in this case no doubt is permitted, namely that these things appear as they do ; indeed it cannot be other than absolutely true that such things appear.

Moreover as to the fact that reason counsels us not to believe much to which we are impelled by nature, it cannot at least remove the truth of that which appears—of the phenomenon[1]. *Yet there is no need for us here to discuss the question whether reason conflicts with sensuous impulsion, and opposes it merely as the right hand opposes the left when holding it up as it droops from weariness, or whether their opposition is of another sort.*

3. *You next address yourself to your purpose, but in a light and as it were skirmishing fashion. For you proceed to say:* But now that I begin to be better acquainted with myself and with the author of my being, I do not in truth think that I should rashly admit all the matters which my senses seem to teach me; neither, on the other hand, do I think that I should doubt them all[2]. *Quite right: though doubtless you had thought the very same thing already.*

The next passage is: And first of all, because I know that all the things which I apprehend clearly and distinctly can be created by God as I apprehend them, it suffices that I am able to apprehend one thing apart from another clearly and distinctly in order to be certain that the one is different from the other, since they may be made to exist in isolation by God at least; and it does not matter by what power their separation is made, in order to compel me to judge them to be different[3]. *In reply to this there is nothing to be said, save that you employ what is obscure to demonstrate something that is clear, not that I allege that there is any obscurity in the inference. I do not raise a difficulty indeed about the fact that you should previously have proved that God exists, nor, as to the matters to which His power extends, about the proof that He can effect what even you are able to comprehend. I should ask merely whether you clearly and distinctly apprehend in a triangle that property,* that the greater side subtends the greater angle, *separately from that other, according to which* the three angles taken together are held to be equal to two right angles. *Do you admit that God can therefore separate and isolate the latter property from the former, so that the triangle possesses the one and not the other, or that the latter also may be disjoined from the triangle?*

But, not to delay you here, inasmuch as this separation is but little to the point, you add: And hence from this very thing, because I know that I exist, and that meanwhile I do not remark that any other thing pertains to my nature or essence, excepting this alone, that I am a thinking thing, I rightly conclude that my essence consists solely in the fact that I am a thinking thing. *Here I*

[1] τοῦ φαινομένου.
[2] Vol. I. p. 189, *sub fin.*
[3] Vol. I. p. 190, par. 2.

should arrest your progress; but either it is enough to repeat what I said in connection with the second Meditation, or we must await your inference.

For finally you say: And although possibly (or rather certainly, as I shall say in a moment) I possess a body with which I am very intimately conjoined, yet because on the one side I have a clear and distinct idea of myself, inasmuch as I am only a thinking and not an extended thing, and on the other I possess a distinct idea of body, inasmuch as it is only an extended and not a thinking thing; it is certain that I am really distinct from my body, and can exist without it.

So this was your objective, was it? Hence, since the whole of the difficulty hinges on this, we must halt awhile, in order to see how you manage to make this position good. The principal matter here in question is the distinction between you and body. But what body do you here mean? Plainly this solid body composed of members, the body to which, without doubt, the following words refer: I possess a body connected with myself and it is certain that I am distinct from my body, etc.

But now, O Mind, there is no difficulty about this body. There would be a difficulty, if with the greater part of philosophers I were to object that you were the realisation[1]*, the perfection, the activity, the form, the appearance, or, to use a popular fashion of speech, a mode of the body. They, forsooth, do not acknowledge that you are more distinct and separable from your body than figure, or any other mode. This, too, they maintain, whether you are the entire soul, or are besides also* νοῦς δυνάμει, νοῦς παθητικός, *the potential intellect, or passive intellect, as they style it. But it pleases me to deal somewhat liberally with you and consider you as though you were the* νοῦς ποιητικός, *the active intellect, nay, even as* χωριστός, *i.e. capable of separate existence, though separable in another sense than they imagined.*

For since those philosophers assigned it to all men (if not rather to all things) as something common to them and as being the source of intellectual activity on the part of the potential intellect, exactly in the same way and with the same necessity as light supplies the eye with the opportunity of seeing (whence they were wont to compare it to the light of the sun, and hence to regard it as coming from without), I myself rather consider you (as you also are quite willing I should) as a certain special intellect exercising domination in the body.

---

[1] ἐντελέχειαν.

*Moreover I repeat that the difficulty is not as to whether you are
separable or not from this body (whence, shortly before, I hinted that
it was not necessary to recur to the power of God in order to secure
the separability of those things which you apprehend as separate), but
from the body which you yourself are: seeing that possibly you really
are a subtle body diffused within that solid one, or occupying some
seat within it.* But you have not yet convinced us that you are
anything absolutely incorporeal.   *Likewise, though in the second
Meditation you proclaimed* that you are not a wind, nor a fire, nor a
vapour, nor a breath, *do be advised of the warning I give you, that
the statement thus announced has not been proved.*

You said that you did not at that point dispute about those
matters; *but you have not subsequently discussed them, nor have you
in any way proved that you are not a body of this kind. I had hoped
that here you would make the matter good; but if you do discuss
anything, if you do prove anything, your discussion and proof merely
show that you are not the solid body, about which, as I have already
said, there is no difficulty.*

4. But, *you say,* I have on the one hand a clear and distinct
idea of myself, in so far as I am merely a thinking thing and not
extended, and on the other a distinct idea of body, in so far as it is
an extended thing, but not one that thinks. *Firstly, however, in so
far as the idea of body is concerned, there appears to be no need for
spending much pains over it. For, if you indeed make this pronouncement about the idea of body universally, we must repeat our previous
objection, namely that you have to prove that it is incompatible with
the nature of body to be capable of thinking. Thus it would be a
begging of the question when the problem was raised by you* as to
whether you are a subtle body or not, *in a way that implied that
thought is incompatible with body.*

*But since you make that assertion and certainly treat only of that
solid body, from which you maintain that you are separable and
distinct, I do not on that account so much deny that you have an idea
of yourself, as maintain that you could not possess it if you were
really an unextended thing. For, I ask you, how do you think that
you, an unextended subject, could receive into yourself the semblance
or idea of a body which is extended? For, if such a semblance
proceeds from the body, it is certainly corporeal and has parts outside
of other parts, and consequently is corporeal. Or alternatively,
whether or not its impression is due to some other source, since
necessarily it always represents an extended body, it must still have*

parts and, consequently, be extended. Otherwise, if it has no parts, how will it represent parts? If it has no extension how will it represent extension? If devoid of figure, how represent an object possessing figure? If it has no position, how can it represent a thing which has upper and lower, right and left, and intermediate[1] parts? If without variation, how represent the various colours, etc.? Therefore an idea appears not to lack extension utterly. But unless it is devoid of extension how can you, if unextended, be its subject? How will you unite it to you? How lay hold of it? How will you be able to feel it gradually fade and finally vanish away?

Next, relatively to your idea of yourself nothing is to be added to what has been already said, and especially in the second Meditation. For thence it is proved that, far from having a clear and distinct idea of yourself, you seem to be wholly without one. This is because, even though you recognise that you think, you do not know of what nature you, who think, are. Hence, since this operation alone is known to you, the chief matter is, nevertheless, hidden from you, namely, the substance which so operates. This brings up the comparison in which you may be likened to a blind man, who, on feeling heat, and being told that it proceeds from the sun, should think that he has a clear and distinct idea of the sun, inasmuch as, if anyone ask him what the sun is, he can reply: it is something which produces heat.

But, you will say, I here add not only that I am a thinking thing, *but that I am* a thing which is not extended. *But not to mention that this is asserted without proof, since it is still in question, I ask firstly: for all that have you a clear and distinct idea of yourself? You say that you are not extended; but in so doing you say what you are not, not what you are. In order to have a clear and distinct idea, or, what is the same thing, a true and genuine[2] idea of anything, is it not necessary to know the thing itself positively, and so to speak affirmatively, or does it suffice to know that it is not any other thing? Would it not then be a clear and distinct idea of Bucephalus, if one knew of him that he was not a fly?*

But, not to urge this, my question is rather: are you not an extended thing, or are you not diffused throughout the body? I cannot tell what you will reply; for, though from the outset I recognised that you existed only in the brain, I formed that belief rather by conjecture

---

[1] obliquas, i.e. inclined between, e.g. up and to the side, and hence intermediate.

[2] Germanam.

than by directly following your opinion. I derived my conjecture from the statement which ensues, in which you assert, that you are not affected by all parts of the body, but only by the brain, or even by one of its smallest parts[1]. *But I was not quite certain whether you were found therefore only in the brain or in a part of it, since you might be found in the whole body, but be acted on at only one part. Thus it would be according to the popular belief, which takes the soul to be diffused throughout the entire body, while yet it is in the eye alone that it has vision.*

Similarly the following words moved one to doubt : 'and, although the whole mind seems to be united to the whole body[2],' etc. *You indeed do not there assert that you are united with the whole of the body, but you do not deny it. Howsoever it be, with your leave let me consider you firstly as diffused throughout the whole body. Whether you are the same as the soul, or something diverse from it, I ask you, O unextended thing, what you are that are spread from head to heel, or that are coextensive with the body, that have a like number of parts corresponding to its parts ? Will you say that you are therefore unextended, because you are a whole in a whole, and are wholly in every part ? I pray you tell me, if you maintain this, how you conceive it. Can a single thing thus be at the same time wholly in several parts ? Faith assures us of this in the case of the sacred mystery (of the Eucharist)[3]. But the question here is relative to you, a natural object, and is indeed one relative to our natural light. Can we grasp how there can be a plurality of places without there being a plurality of objects located in them ? Is not a hundred more than one ? Likewise, if a thing is wholly in one place, can it be in others, unless it is itself outside itself, as place is outside place ? Say what you will, it will at least be obscure and uncertain whether you are wholly in any part and not rather in the various parts of the body by means of your several parts. And since it is much more evident that nothing can exist as a whole in different places, it will turn out to be still more clear that you are not wholly in the single parts of your body but merely in the whole as a whole, and that you are so by means of your parts diffused through the whole and consequently that you have extension.*

Secondly let us suppose that you are in the brain alone, or merely in some minute part of it. You perceive that the same thing is clearly an objection, since, however small that part be, it is nevertheless extended, and you are coextensive with it, and consequently are extended

---

[1] Vol. I. p. 196, par. 3.   [2] *Ibid.* par. 2.   [3] Tr.

*and have particular parts corresponding to its particular parts.
Will you say that you take that part of the brain to be a point?
That is surely incredible, but suppose it is a point. If it is indeed
something Physical, the same difficulty remains, because such a point
is extended and is certainly not devoid of parts. If it is a Mathematical point you know that it is given only by the imagination.
But let it be given or let rather us feign that in the brain there is
given a Mathematical point, to which you are united, and in which
you exist. Now, see how useless a fiction this will turn out to be.
For, if it is to be assumed, we must feign it to exist in such a way
that you are at the meeting place of the nerves by which all the regions
informed by the soul transmit to the brain the ideas or semblances of
the things perceived by the senses. But firstly, the nerves do not all
meet at one point, whether for the reason that, as the brain is continued
into the spinal marrow, many nerves all over the back pass into that,
or because those which extend to the middle of the head are not found
to terminate in the same part of the brain. But let us assume that
they all do meet; none the less they cannot all unite in a mathematical
point, since they are bodies, not mathematical lines, and so able to
meet in a mathematical point. And supposing we grant that they do
so unite, it will be impossible for the spirits[1] which pass through these
to pass out of the nerves or to enter them, as being bodies; since body
cannot be in or pass through what is not a place, as the mathematical
point is. But though we should allow that the animal spirits do
exist in or pass through what is not a place, nevertheless you, existing
as you do in a point, in which there are neither right hand parts nor
left hand, neither higher nor lower, nor anything similar, cannot
judge as to whence they come nor what they report.*

*Moreover I say the same thing of those spirits which you must
transmit in order to have feeling or to report tidings[2], and in order to
move. I omit that we cannot grasp how you impress a motion upon
them, you who are yourself in a point, unless you are really a body, or
unless you have a body by which you are in contact with them and at
the same time propel them. For, if you say that they are moved by
themselves, and that you only direct their motion, remember that you
somewhere else* denied that the body is moved by itself[3]; *so that we*

---

[1] The 'animal spirits' correspond to the 'nervous impulses' of modern
psychology. D. and his contemporaries believed that an actual substance
passed along the nerve when it was stimulated.

[2] of the external world? Clerselier translates this passage 'proclaim or
communicate feeling or movement.'

[3] Vol. I. p. 151, par. 1.

must thence infer that you are the cause of that movement. Next, explain to us how such a direction can take place without some effort and so some motion on your part ? How can there be effort directed towards anything, and motion on its part, without mutual contact of what moves and what is moved ? How can there be contact apart from body, when (as is so clear to the natural light)

'Apart from body, naught touches or is touched[1] ?'

Yet why do I delay here when it is on you that the onus rests of proving that you are unextended and hence incorporeal ? But neither do I think that you will find an argument in the fact that man is popularly said to consist of soul and body, inferring that if one part is said to be body, the other must be declared not to be body. For, if you did so, you would give us an opportunity of drawing the distinction in such a way that man should be held to consist of a double body, viz. the solid one and the subtle one ; and according to this scheme while the former retained the name body, the common term, the other would be given the name soul. I pass by the fact that the same thing would be said about the other animals, to which you have not granted a mind similar to your own; lucky they, if by your sanction they possess even a soul! Hence, therefore, when you conclude that you are certain that you are really distinct from your body, *you see that that would be admitted, but that it would not therefore be conceded that you were incorporeal, and not rather a species of very subtle body distinct from your grosser body.*

You add that hence you can exist apart from it[2]. *But after being conceded the point that you can exist apart from that grosser body in the same way as an odoriferous vapour does while passing out of an apple and dispersing into the air, what do you think you have gained? Something more certainly than the above mentioned Philosophers[3] wish to prove, who believe that you wholly perish at death itself ; being as it were like a figure which on the alteration of the superficies so disappears, that it may be said to be non-existent or wholly nothing. Indeed, since you were something corporeal as well, or a fine substance, you will not be said to vanish wholly at death, or wholly to pass into nothing, but to exist by means of your dispersed parts, howsoever much, on account of being thus drawn asunder, you are not likely to think any more, and will be said to be neither a*

---

[1] Tangere nec tangi sine corpore nulla potest res—a misquotation of Lucretius (*De Rerum natura* I. 305):—Tangere enim et tangi, nisi corpus nulla potest res.

[2] Vol. I. p. 190, par. 1, *sub fin.*   [3] Cf. above, p. 189.

thinking thing, nor a mind, nor a soul. Yet all these objections I
bring, not in order to cast doubt on the conclusion you intend to prove,
but merely by way of expressing my disagreement as to the cogency of
the argument set forth by you.

5. *In connection with this, you interpose several things tending*
to the same conclusion, on all of which we need not insist. One thing
I note, and that is that you say that nature teaches you by the
sensation of pain, hunger, thirst, etc., that you are not lodged in the
body as a sailor in a ship, but that you are very closely united with
it and, so to speak, intermingled with it so as to compose one whole
along with it. For if that were not the case, *you say,* "when my
body is hurt, I who am merely a thinking thing would not feel pain,
but should perceive the wound with the mere understanding, just
as the sailor perceives by sight when something is damaged in his
vessel, and when my body has need of food or drink, I should
clearly understand this fact, and not have the confused feelings of
hunger and thirst. For all these sensations of hunger, thirst, pain,
etc. are in truth none other than certain confused modes of thought
which are produced by the union and apparent intermingling of
mind and body[1]."

This is indeed quite right; but it still remains to be explained,
how that union and apparent intermingling, *or* confusion, *can be*
found in you, if you are incorporeal, unextended and indivisible. For
if you are not greater than a point, how can you be united with the
entire body, which is of such great magnitude? How, at least, can you
be united with the brain, or some minute part in it, which (as has been
said) must yet have some magnitude or extension, however small it be?
If you are wholly without parts, how can you mix or appear to mix
with its minute subdivisions? For there is no mixture unless each of
the things to be mixed has parts that can mix with one another.
Further, if you are discrete, how could you be involved with and form
one thing along with matter itself? Again since conjunction or union
exists between certain parts, ought there not to be a relation of
similarity[2] between parts of this sort? But what must the union of
the corporeal with the incorporeal be thought to be? Do we conceive
how stone and air are fused together, as in pumice stone, so as to
become a fusion of uniform character[3]? Yet the similarity between
stone and air which itself is also a body, is greater than that
between body and soul, or a wholly incorporeal mind. Further, ought

---

[1] Vol. I. p. 192, par. 3.   [2] Proportio.
[3] ut germana inde fiat compositio?

*not that union to take place by means of the closest contact? But
how, as I said before, can that take place, apart from body? How
will that which is corporeal seize upon that which is incorporeal, so to
hold it conjoined with itself, or how will the incorporeal grasp the
corporeal, so as reciprocally to keep it bound to itself, if in it, the
incorporeal, there is nothing which it can use to grasp the other, or by
which it can be grasped.*

*Hence, since you admit that you feel pain, I ask you how you
think that you, if you are incorporeal and unextended, are capable of
experiencing the sensation of pain. Thus the affection pain can only
be understood as arising from some pulling asunder of bodily parts
when something interferes and annuls their continuity. For example
a state of pain is an unnatural state, but how can that be in an
unnatural state or be affected contrary to nature, which by nature is of
one sort, simple, indivisible and immutable? Again since pain is
either alteration, or cannot occur without it, how can that be altered,
which, being more devoid of parts than a point, cannot be altered nor
can cease to be just as it is, unless it turns into nothing? I add also:
since pain comes from the foot, the arm, and from other regions at the
same time, ought there not to be in you various parts, in which you
receive it in various ways, in order not to be confused and to regard it
as being the pain of merely one part. But, in a word, the general
difficulty always remains, viz. how the corporeal can have anything
in common with the incorporeal, or what relationship may be established
between the one and the other.*

6. *I pass by the other passages in which, in a very copious and
neat argument, you strive to show that something else is in existence
besides yourself and God. For you deduce the conclusion that your
body and its corporeal faculties exist; and likewise other bodies which
despatch into your senses and into yourself the semblances of themselves,
and produce the experiences of pleasure and pain, which beget in you
desire and aversion.*

*And from this you at length derive the following conclusion, which
is, as it were, the fruit of your reasoning, in order that* since all the
sensations relative to the things which have to do with the welfare
of the body more frequently indicate to you truth than falsehood,
you may thence infer that you ought no longer to fear that falsity
may be found in matters every day represented to you by the senses[1].
You say the same, consequently, about dreams, for since they are not
connected with the whole of our actions and course of life in the

same way as what we experience when awake, *you thence establish the conclusion that real things* are presented to you, not in sleep, but when you are awake[1]. Hence, *you say next*, since God is not a deceiver, it follows that you are not deceived in such matters. *This is an extremely pious statement ; and so, too, you are assuredly quite in the right when you finally conclude :* that the life of man is subject to error, and that we must acknowledge the infirmity of our nature.

These, my good Sir, are the observations that occurred to me in connection with your Meditations. I repeat that you ought not to give yourself any thought about them, since my judgment is not of such moment as to deserve to have any weight with you. For as, when some food is pleasant to my palate, I do not defend my taste, which I see is offensive to others, as being more perfect than anyone else's ; so, when my mind welcomes an opinion which does not please others, I am far from holding that I have hit upon the truer theory. I think that the truth is rather this—that each enjoys his own opinion ; and I hold that it is almost as unjust to wish everyone to have the same belief, as to want all people to be alike in the sense of taste : I say so, in order that you may hold yourself free to dismiss everything that I have said as not worth a straw, and to omit it altogether. It will be enough if you acknowledge my strong affection for you, and do not esteem as nought my admiration for your personal worth. Perhaps some matter has been advanced somewhat inconsiderately, as is only too likely to happen when one is expressing dissent. Any such passage which may occur I wholly disavow and sacrifice ; pray blot it out, and be assured, that I have desired nothing more than to deserve well of you and to keep my friendship with you quite intact.

With kind regards[2].

Paris, 16th May, 1641.

[1] Vol. I. p. 199.   [2] vale.

THE AUTHOR'S REPLY TO THE FIFTH SET OF OBJECTIONS.

SIR[1],

    The essay in which you criticize my meditations is exceedingly well-written and carefully executed, and to me it appears that it will do much to set them in a clear light. Consequently I consider that I am greatly beholden to you for writing it, as well as to the Rev. Father Mersenne for inciting you to do so. Our friend, who is such an eager enquirer into all things, and who more especially promotes unweariedly everything that tends to the glory of God, knows that the best way of determining whether my arguments are to be treated as accurate demonstrations, is that some men of outstanding eminence in scholarship and ability, should subject them to a rigorous criticism, so as finally to make trial of my powers of giving a satisfactory answer to their objections. This is why he has challenged so many to attempt the task, and has prevailed upon some to do so, among whom I am glad to see you. For, though in order to refute my opinions you have not so much employed philosophical reasoning as made use of certain oratorical devices so as to elude my argument, this is in itself a matter of gratification to me, since I shall for this reason infer that it will not be easy to bring up in opposition to me arguments which differ from those which you have read in the preceding criticisms urged by other people. Further, if such had existed, they would not have escaped your penetration and industry, and I hold that here your only purpose has been to bring to my notice those conceptions which might be used to avoid the force of my arguments by those whose minds are so immersed in matters of sense as to shrink from all metaphysical reflections, and that you thus gave me an opportunity for meeting these. Wherefore here I shall reply to you not as a keen-eyed philosopher, but as to one of these fleshly individuals whom you impersonate.

[1] Vir praestantissime.

OF THE OBJECTIONS URGED AGAINST THE
FIRST MEDITATION.

You say that *you approve of my determination to rid my mind of prejudices,* especially since no one can pretend that there is any fault to find with this; but you would prefer me to proceed *simply and with few words*[1], i.e. to carry out my resolve only in a perfunctory manner. This is forsooth to assume that it is very easy for all to free themselves from the errors in which, since infancy, they have been steeped, and that too much care may be employed in carrying this out, a contention which no one maintains. I suppose you wished to show that many men, though verbally admitting that prejudices should be avoided, nevertheless completely fail to avoid them, because they expend no toil and pains upon the attempt, and never think that anything which they have once admitted to be true should be regarded as a prejudice. You certainly play the rôle of such people excellently here, and omit none of their possible arguments, but there is nothing in this action which seems to suggest the Philosopher. For when you say that there is no need *to imagine that God is a deceiver* or *that we are dreaming,* or anything of the kind, a Philosopher would have considered that there was some necessity for showing the reason why such matters could not be considered as doubtful, or, if he had no reason, as in truth there is none, he would not have made the said assertion. Neither would he have added that in this place *it was sufficient to plead the obscurity of the human mind* or *the feebleness of our nature.* The elimination of our errors is in no way furthered by alleging that we err owing to the dimness of our thought or the feebleness of our nature; for that is the same as merely saying that we err because we are exposed to errors, and clearly it is more useful to attend, as I have done, to all those cases in which error may chance to arise, lest we readily give the error our assent. Likewise a Philosopher would not have said *that I, in considering everything doubtful as false, did not so much dismiss an old prejudice as take up with a new one;* or he would first have tried to show that out of this supposition there arose some danger of deception. But you, on the contrary, shortly afterwards affirm *that I cannot force myself to treat as doubtful or false the things that I supposed to be false,* i.e. that I cannot adopt the prejudice which you feared I might adopt. This would cause

[1] Cf. above, p. 136.

no more surprise to a Philosopher than that at some time a stick which has been straightened out should be similarly bent back again into the opposite, i.e. crooked, shape. For he knows that falsities are often assumed instead of truths for the purpose of throwing light on the truth: for example, Astronomers imagine the existence of the equator, the zodiac, and other circles in the heaven, while Geometricians attach new lines to given figures, and Philosophers frequently act in similar fashion. But the man who describes this as *having recourse to an artifice, eagerness for verbal trickery, and seeking evasions,* and declares *that it is unworthy of philosophical candour and the love of truth,* manifests that he at least has no desire to make use of philosophical candour or to employ any argument other than rhetorical humbug.

CONCERNING THE OBJECTIONS BROUGHT AGAINST THE SECOND MEDITATION.

1.   Here you proceed to employ rhetorical wiles in place of reasoning; for you pretend that I speak in jest when I am quite serious, and take as serious, and as uttered and asserted as true, what I propounded only as a question and as arising out of common opinion for the purpose of enquiring further into it. My statement *that the entire testimony of the senses must be considered to be uncertain, nay, even false,* is quite serious and so necessary for the comprehension of my meditations, that he who will not or cannot admit that, is unfit to urge any objection to them that merits a reply. But we must note the distinction emphasized by me in various passages, between the practical activities[1] of our life and an enquiry into truth; for, when it is a case of regulating our life, it would assuredly be stupid not to trust the senses, and those sceptics were quite ridiculous who so neglected human affairs that they had to be preserved by their friends from tumbling down precipices. It was for this reason that somewhere I announced *that no one in his sound mind seriously doubted about such matters*[2]; but when we raise an enquiry into what is the surest knowledge which the human mind can obtain, it is clearly unreasonable to refuse to treat them as doubtful, nay even to reject them as false, so as to allow us to become aware that certain other things, which cannot be thus rejected, are for this very reason more certain, and in actual truth better known by us.

[1] actiones.   [2] Meditations, Synopsis, Vol. I. p. 143.

Moreover you do not accept in good faith and as seriously meant, my statement that I did not yet sufficiently understand who the thinker was, though I had explained that very assertion. You also fail to allow my statement that I did not doubt about that in which the nature of the body consisted, and had assigned no power of self-movement to it, and had imagined myself to be a soul after the fashion of wind or flame or something of the kind, assertions that I then made, deriving them from common opinion, only in order that I might show them to be false in their appropriate place.

What warrant have you for saying that *nutrition, motion, feeling etc. are referred by me to the soul*, in order that you may immediately add: *I grant this, but what becomes of the distinction you draw between the soul and the body*[1]? The fact is, that shortly before, I, in express terms, referred nutrition to the body alone, while motion and sensibility I refer for the most part also to the body, and ascribe nothing that belongs to them to the soul, save only as much as consists in thinking.

Next, what grounds have you for saying *that there was no need of such an elaborate mechanism in order to prove that I exist*[2]? Really these very words of yours give me the best grounds for believing that my labours have not yet been sufficiently great, since I have as yet failed to make you understand the matter rightly. When you say that *I could have inferred the same conclusion from any of my other actions*, you wander far from the truth, because there is none of my activities of which I am wholly certain (in the sense of having metaphysical certitude, which alone is here involved), save thinking alone. For example you have no right to make the inference : *I walk, hence I exist*, except in so far as our awareness of walking is a thought ; it is of this alone that the inference holds good, not of the motion of the body, which sometimes does not exist, as in dreams, when nevertheless I appear to walk. Hence from the fact that I think that I walk I can very well infer the existence of the mind which so thinks, but not that of the body which walks. So it is also in all other cases.

2. Next, with a not infelicitous comedy, you proceed to question me, no longer as a complete man, but as a soul in separation from the body ; and in so doing you seem to remind me that these objections proceed not from the mind of an acute

---

[1] Cf. above, p. 137, par. 4.
[2] *Ibid.* par. 2.

philosopher but from the flesh alone. I ask you therefore, O flesh, or whatever the name be by which you prefer to be known, have you so little intercourse with the mind, that you have not been able to note when I corrected that popular notion, by which it is imagined that that which thinks is like wind or some similar body? I corrected it then, surely, when I showed that it could be supposed that no wind or other body existed, and that nevertheless everything by means of which I recognize myself as a thinking being remains. Hence your subsequent questions as to *why I cannot therefore be still a wind, and why I cannot occupy space, and why I cannot be subject to many motions*[1], *etc.*, are so devoid of sense as to require no reply.

3. The next objections have no more force :—*if I am a sort of attenuated body, why can I not be nourished*[2], and the rest. I deny that I am a body. Also, once and for all, to bring the matter to completeness, since you almost always employ the same style, and do not attack my arguments but disingenuously suppress them, as if they were of no account, or quote them only imperfectly and in· a mutilated form, and thus bring together a number of difficulties which would in a popular way and by unskilled persons be urged against my conclusions, or others akin to them or even unlike them, difficulties which either are irrelevant, or have been refuted or solved by me in their appropriate places; since this is, so I declare that it is not worth while replying to each single question, for I should have to repeat a hundred times what I have already written. I shall only deal shortly with those which seem likely to cause difficulty to readers not wholly incompetent. As for those who look not so much to the force of the argument as to the multitude of the words employed, I do not value their approval so highly as to wish to become more wordy for the sake of meriting it.

Therefore I will first note, that I do not accept your statement *that the mind grows and waxes faint along* with the body, and you have no argument to prove it; for from the fact that it does not work with equal perfection in the body of an infant and in that of an adult, and that its activities are frequently impeded by wine and other corporeal bodies, this alone follows, that as long as it is united with the body, it uses it as its instrument in those operations in which it is principally engaged, but not that it is

---

[1] Cf. above, p. 138, par. 2, and p. 139, par. 1.
[2] *Ibid.* par. 2.

rendered more or less perfect by the body; your contention will
have no more force than were we to argue from the fact that a
workman does not get good results as long as he uses a bad
instrument, that he had acquired his skill in his art from the
excellence of his instrument.

It is to be noticed also that you seem wholly to fail to understand, O flesh, what it is to employ reason, when in your argument
to show that the trustworthiness of the senses ought not to be
impugned by me, you say that *although at times, when not using
the eye, I appeared to have experiences that do not occur without
the eye coming into play, yet so to err was not my universal experience*[1]. You seem to imagine that we have not a sufficient cause
for doubt if at any one time we detect an error; and again you
seem to think that we might always note the error each time that
we fall into it, when, on the contrary, the error consists in the
very fact that it is not recognized by us as an error.

Finally, since you often demand an argument from me, when
you, O flesh, possess none yourself, and since the 'onus' of the
proof presses on you, we must note that, in philosophizing correctly,
there is no need for us to prove the falsity of all those things
which we do not admit because we do not know whether they
are true. We have merely to take the greatest care not to admit
as true what we cannot prove to be true. Thus when I find that
I am a thinking substance, and form a clear and distinct concept
of that substance, in which there is none of those attributes which
belong to the concept of corporeal substance, this is quite sufficient
to let me affirm that I, in so far as I know myself, am nothing but
a thing which thinks, which statement alone I have affirmed in
the second meditation—that with which we are at present occupied.
Neither was I bound to admit that this thinking substance was
some mobile, simple, and rarified body, when I had found no reason
inducing me to believe that. But it is for you, it is your duty, to
expound the reason, if you have one; you have no right to demand
that I shall prove that false which I refused to entertain only for
the reason that I had no knowledge about it. You act as if, when
I asserted that I now lived in Holland, you were to deny that that
was to be believed, unless I proved that I was neither in China nor
in any other part of the world, because it is perchance possible that
the same body should, owing to the action of the divine power,
exist in two different places. But when you add *that I must also*

[1] Cf. above, p. 139, *sub fin.*, p. 140 *ad init.*

prove that the souls of brutes are incorporeal, and that solid matter contributes nothing to thinking[1], you not only show that you do not know on whom the onus of proof lies, but also of what should be proved by each person; for neither do I think that the souls of brutes are incorporeal, nor do I believe that solid matter contributes nothing to their thinking: I merely say that this is by no means the place for the consideration of those matters.

4. You here pursue the question of the obscurity arising out of the ambiguity of the word *soul*, an obscurity which I took such pains to remove that it is wearisome to repeat here what I have said. Therefore I shall declare only, that names have been conferred on things for the most part by the inexpert, and that for this reason they do not always fit the things with sufficient accuracy; that it is not our part to change them after custom has accepted them, but only to permit the emendation of their meanings, when we perceive that others do not understand them aright. Thus because probably men in the earliest times did not distinguish in us that principle in virtue of which we are nourished, grow, and perform all those operations which are common to us with the brutes apart from any thought, from that by which we think they called both by the single name *soul*; then, perceiving the distinction between nutrition and thinking, they called that which thinks *mind*, believing also that this was the chief part of the soul. But I, perceiving that the principle by which we are nourished is wholly distinct from that by means of which we think, have declared that the name *soul* when used for both is equivocal; and I say that, when soul is taken to mean *the primary actuality* or *chief essence of man*[2], it must be understood to apply only to the principle by which we think, and I have called it by the name *mind* as often as possible in order to avoid ambiguity; for I consider the mind not as part of the soul but as the whole of that soul which thinks.

You have a difficulty, however, you say, *as to whether I think that the soul always thinks*[3]. But why should it not always think, when it is a thinking substance? Why is it strange that we do not remember the thoughts it has had when in the womb or in a stupor, when we do not even remember the most of those we know we have had when grown up, in good health, and awake? For the

---

[1] Cf. above, p. 140, par. 2.   [2] actu primo sive praecipua hominis forma.
[3] Cf. above, p. 141, par. 2.

recollection of the thoughts which the mind has had during the period of its union with the body, it is necessary for certain traces of them to be impressed on the brain; and turning and applying itself to these the mind remembers. Is it remarkable if the brain of an infant or of one in a stupor is unfit to receive these residual impressions?

Finally when I said *perhaps it is the case that what I have not yet known* (to wit, my body) *is not diverse from that which I do know* (my mind), *I do not know, I do not discuss this matter*, etc.; you object: *if you are ignorant, if you do not dispute the matter, why do you assume that you are none of those things*[1]? But here it is false that I have assumed something of which I was ignorant; for plainly, on the contrary, because I did not know whether body was the same as mind or not, I made no assumption about the matter, but treated of the mind alone, until afterwards in the sixth meditation, not assuming but demonstrating the matter, I showed that mind was really distinct from the body. But you, O flesh, are to the highest degree involved in error, since though you have no reason or the very slightest by which to show that mind is not distinct from body, you none the less assume it.

5. To one who gives close attention to my words what I have said of the imagination is sufficiently clear; but there is no reason for wonder if to the unreflective it is quite obscure. Moreover I warn those people that my statements as to what I have asserted to be no part of the knowledge which I have of myself do not conflict with what I said before about those matters, as to which I was ignorant whether or not they appertained to me; for it is plainly one thing to appertain to me, another to belong to the knowledge which I have of myself.

6. What you say here, my admired flesh, seems to me not to consist of objections so much as of carpings that require no answer.

7. Here also you find much to carp at, but your complaints seem to require a reply no more than the preceding ones. For your queries about the brutes are not relevant here, since the mind when communing with itself can experience the fact that it thinks, but has no evidence of this kind as to whether or not the brutes think; it can only come to a conclusion afterwards about this matter by reasoning *a posteriori* from their actions. I have no difficulty in disowning those inept statements which you put into my mouth, for it is enough for me to have pointed out once that

[1] Cf. above, p. 142, *ad init.*

you do not reproduce faithfully everything I have said. But I have often adduced the criterion by which the difference between mind and body is detected; viz. that the whole nature of the mind consists in thinking, while the whole nature of the body consists in being an extended thing, and that there is nothing at all common to thought and extension. I have often also shown distinctly that mind can act independently of the brain; for certainly the brain can be of no use in pure thought: its only use is for imagining and perceiving. And although, when imagination or sensation is intense (as occurs when the brain is troubled or disturbed), the mind does not readily find room for thinking of other matters, yet we experience the fact that, when imagination is not so strong, we often understand something entirely diverse from it: for example, when we sleep we perceive that we are dreaming, while in having the dream we must employ the imagination; yet our awareness of the fact that we are dreaming is an act of the intellect alone.

8. Here, as frequently elsewhere, you merely show that you do not properly understand what you attempt to criticize. For, neither have I abstracted the concept of wax from that of its accidents; rather have I tried to show how its substance was manifested by means of accidents, and how the reflective[1] and distinct perception of it, one such as you, O flesh, seem never to have had, differs from the vulgar and confused idea. Nor can I see what argument you rely on to prove your confident affirmation that a dog can discriminate in the same way as we do, unless that, since you see that it is made of flesh, you believe that everything which exists in you is also in it. But I, failing to detect mind in it, think that nothing similar to that which I recognize in mind is found in it.

9. I am surprised that while here you confess that all those matters which I am aware of in wax, *show indeed that I distinctly know that I exist*, you maintain *that they do not demonstrate what I am*[2], since the one thing cannot be proved without the other. Nor do I see what else you expect the matter to yield, unless it be some revelation about the colour, odour or taste of the human mind, or the nature of the salt, sulphur, or mercury that go to its composition; for you wish us to examine it, as though it were a wine, *by a sort of chemical analysis*[3]. That is really worthy of you,

---

[1] Reflexa.   Clerselier's F. V. has ' clear and distinct.'
[2] Cf. above, p. 149, *ad init.*   [3] p 151, l. 5.

O flesh, and of all those who, conceiving nothing except what is wholly confused, are ignorant of the proper object of investigation in each inquiry. As for me, my belief has always been that nothing else is required in order to manifest the nature of substance except its various attributes, so that our comprehension of its nature is more perfect in proportion to the number of its attributes which we discern. Just as in wax we are able to distinguish many attributes, one that it is white, another that it is hard, a third that it can be liquefied, etc., so also in mind we can recognize as many—one that it has the power of being aware of the whiteness of wax, another that it possess the power of recognizing its hardness, a third of knowing that it can be liquefied, i.e. that it can lose its hardness, etc. ; for he can perceive its hardness who is not aware of its whiteness, viz. a man born blind; and so in the other cases. Whence it can be clearly inferred that nothing yields the knowledge of so many attributes as our mind, because as many can be enumerated in its case as there are attributes in everything else, owing to the fact that it knows these ; and hence its nature is best known of all. Finally, you here incidentally urge the objection that, *while not admitting the existence in myself of anything save mind, I none the less speak of the wax that I see and touch, which I could not do except by using my hands and eyes*[1]. But you ought to have noticed that I had carefully pointed out that I did not then deal with the sight and touch which are effected by means of organs, but solely with the thought of seeing and touching ; and that this does not imply the use of these organs is testified to us every recurring night in dreams. True you have not really failed to note this ; you have only wished to show how absurd and unjust are the cavillings of those whose design is not so much to understand as to raise objections.

CONCERNING THE OBJECTIONS TO THE THIRD MEDITATION.

1. Splendid ! Here at length you do bring up an argument against me, a feat which, so far as I can make out, you have hitherto failed to accomplish. In order to prove *that it is not a sure rule that what we very clearly and distinctly perceive is true*, you allege that to great intellects, which it appears ought to have had the most numerous clear and distinct perceptions, it has seemed nevertheless that the truth of things was hidden either in

[1] Cf. above, p. 149, par. 1.

God or at the bottom of a well. Here I admit that your argument
as drawn from authority is quite right. But, O flesh, you should
have remembered that you here were addressing a mind so far
withdrawn from corporeal things that it does not even know that
anyone has existed before it, and hence cannot be influenced by
the authority of others. Your passage referring to the sceptics
is a good enough commonplace, but proves nothing, as neither
does your point about people facing death on behalf of false
opinions, because it can never be proved that they clearly and
distinctly perceive what they pertinaciously affirm. I do not
question what you next say, viz. that it is not so much a question
of taking pains to establish the truth of the rule, as of finding a
method for deciding whether we err or not when we think that
we perceive something clearly. But I contend that this has been
carefully attended to in its proper place where I first laid aside all
prejudices, and afterwards enumerated all the chief ideas, distinguishing the clear from the obscure and confused.

2. I marvel indeed at the train of reasoning by which you
try to prove that all our ideas are adventitious and none of them
constructed by us, saying—*because the mind has the power not only
of perceiving these very adventitious ideas, but, besides this, of
bringing together, dividing, reducing, enlarging, arranging, and
everything similar to this*[1]: whence you conclude that the ideas of
chimaeras which the mind makes by uniting, dividing, etc., are
not made by it itself but are adventitious. In the same way you
will be able to prove that Praxiteles never made any statues,
because he did not produce from himself the marble used in their
sculpture ; and again that you cannot have made these objections,
because to their composition have gone words which have not been
invented by you but have been communicated to you from others.
But, as a matter of fact, the form of a chimaera does not reside in
the parts of goat or lion, nor does the form of your objections lie
in the single words which you have used but consists solely in the
putting of them together.

I am also surprised that you maintain the thesis that the idea
of *Thing* cannot exist in the mind *unless at the same time the ideas
of animal, plant, stone, and of all universals are found there*[2]. This
is as though, in order to acknowledge that I am a thinking thing,
I ought to acknowledge animals and plants, since I ought to
acknowledge *Thing*, i.e. what *Thing* is. You have nothing truer

1 Above, p. 153, par. 1.   2 Above, p. 154, par. 1.

than this to urge here when dealing with *the truth*; and finally, since you attack only matters about which I have made no assertion, you merely wage warfare with the winds.

3. Here, in order to break down the reasons on account of which I thought that we must doubt the existence of material things, you ask *why I walk about on the earth etc.*[1] But this manifestly involves a begging of the question; for you assume what has to be proved, viz. that it is so certain that I walk on the earth that I can have no doubt on the matter.

In adding to my own objections—those I urged against myself and myself refuted—the following one, viz. *why one born blind has no idea of colour, or one born deaf, of sound*[2], you quite clearly show that you have not a single criticism of moment to make. How do you know that one born blind has no idea of colour, when often enough in our case even when the eyes are closed the sense of light and colour is stimulated? And, though your contention be conceded, has not the man who denies the existence of material things as much ground for saying that one congenitally blind is destitute of ideas of colour because his mind lacks the faculty of forming them, as you have for asserting that their absence is due to his being without eyes to see?

Your next point regarding the twofold idea of the sun proves nothing; but, in taking both ideas as one because they refer to the single thing, the sun, your action amounts to saying that the true and the false do not differ when affirmed of the same subject. Further, in denying that the notion derived from astronomical reasoning is an idea, you restrict the term idea to the images alone which are depicted in the imagination, contrary to my express assumption.

4. You do exactly the same thing when you deny that substance is a true idea, because, forsooth, substance is perceived not by the imagination but by the intellect alone. Yet you know that long ago, O flesh, I protested that I had nothing to do with those whose wish it is to employ their imagination only and not the intellect.

Really when you say that the *idea of substance has no more reality than it holds from the ideas of those accidents under which, or after the fashion of which, it is conceived*[3], you show that you have in truth no distinct idea of it at all; for substance can never

---

[1] p. 155, par. 1. [2] *Ibid.* par. 2.
[3] Cf. above, p. 158, par. 2.

be conceived after the fashion of accidents, nor can it derive its reality from them. On the contrary accidents are commonly conceived by Philosophers after the fashion of substance, viz. as often as they are said to be real accidents; for no reality (i.e. no kind of being[1] other than modal) can be ascribed to them, which is not taken from the idea of substance.

Nay, when you say that the idea of God possesses reality only *owing to the fact that we have heard certain attributes predicated of Him*[2], I should like you to tell us whence men at the beginning, the men from whom we have learned them, drew this very idea of God. If it was from themselves, why may we not derive this same idea from ourselves? If from a revelation by God, this proves that God exists.

Moreover in your next statement, *that he who says that anything is infinite attributes to a thing which he does not comprehend a name which he does not understand*[3], you fail to distinguish an exercise of intellect conformable to the scale of our understanding, such as each one of us experiences himself to employ in thinking about the infinite, with a concept adequate to the things, such as no one possesses not only in the matter of the infinite but perhaps not even in connection with any thing else however small. Neither is it true that the infinite is apprehended by a negation of boundary or limitation, since on the contrary all limitation contains a negation of the infinite.

Further it is not the case that *the idea which represents all those perfections which we ascribe to God contains no more objective reality than finite things have*[4]. You yourself confess that these perfections are amplified by our understanding in order to be ascribed to God. Do you, then, not think that the things which are so augmented are not greater than those that have not been so dealt with? Again, what can account for the power of amplifying all created perfections, i.e. of conceiving something greater or more ample than they, unless the fact that the idea of something greater, viz. of God, exists in us? Finally, neither is it true that *God will mean something very little, unless He be greater than as conceived by us;* for He is conceived as infinite and nothing can be greater than the infinite. You, however, confuse intellectual activity with imagination, and feign that we imagine God after the fashion of some huge man, in the same way as if one who had never seen an elephant

---

[1] entitas.
[2] Cf. above, p. 158, par. 3.
[3] *Ibid.* par. 4.
[4] Above, p. 159, par. 1.

were to imagine that it was like a very huge insect, e.g. a tick; which, I agree with you, would be excessively foolish.

5. Here, though you make a great display so as to appear to contradict me, yet you do not conflict with me at all, since clearly you come to the same conclusion as I do. Nevertheless you intersperse a number of statements drawn from here and there, from which I strongly dissent, as e.g. that the axiom, *nothing exists in the effect which has not previously existed in the cause*, is to be understood of the material rather than of the efficient cause[1]; for the perfection of the form can never be understood to pre-exist in the material but only in the efficient cause. So too with your doctrine *that the formal reality of an idea is a substance*, and so forth.

6. If you had anything to say in proof of the existence of material things, without doubt you would have advanced it here. But when you only ask *whether my mind is uncertain as to whether anything else besides itself exists in the world*[2], and feign that there is no need to search for arguments to decide this, thus making an appeal merely to prejudiced beliefs, you show much more clearly that you can give no reason for what you affirm, than if you had refrained from saying anything.

No point that you raise here in disputing about ideas requires any reply, since you restrict the term idea solely to the images depicted in the fancy, while I extend it to whatever is thought.

But by the way I should like to ask what the argument is by which you prove *that nothing acts on itself*[3]. It is, forsooth, not your wont to employ argument. But here you have used as an illustration the finger which does not strike itself and the eye which does not see itself in itself but in a mirror, to prove your case. To this we have an easy reply; it is not the eye which sees the mirror rather than itself, but the mind which alone recognizes both mirror, and eye, and itself as well. Likewise other examples can be given in the domain of corporeal things: e.g. when a top draws itself round in a circle, is not that rotation an action which it exerts on itself?

Finally it must be noted that I did not assert *that I deduced the ideas of material things from the mind*[4], as you rather insincerely here pretend I do. For afterwards I showed in express terms that they often come from bodies, and that it was owing to this that

---

[1] Above, p. 15), par. 1, *sub fin.*   [2] Above, p. 162, *ad init.*
[3] *Ibid.* par. 3, *ad init.*   [4] Above, p. 163, par. 3, *ad init.*

the existence of corporeal things was demonstrated. But in this passage I only explained that no such reality was found in them as to make us conclude, from the fact that nothing exists in the effect which has not formally or eminently pre-existed in the cause, that they cannot have originated solely from the mind; and this contention you do not attack at all.

7. In this passage you have nothing to say which you have not mentioned already and which has not been refuted by me. I shall make one observation about the idea of the infinite, *which,* you say, *cannot be true, unless I comprehend the infinite;* your opinion is *that at most I could be said to know part of the infinite, but indeed a very small part of it, which bears no more proportion to the infinite than the representation of a tiny hair does to the entirety of the man to whom the hair belongs*[1]. I announce, I say, that it is a manifest contradiction that, when I comprehend anything, that thing should be infinite; for the idea of the infinite, in order to be true, cannot by any means be comprehended, since this very incomprehensibility is comprised within the formal concept[2] of the infinite. Likewise it is none the less manifest that the idea we possess of the infinite does not represent merely a part of it, but really the whole infinite, in that fashion in which it has to be represented through the instrumentality of a human idea, although doubtless another much more perfect, i.e. more accurate and more distinct idea, can be framed by God, or by any other intelligent nature more perfect than a human being. This is parallel to the case of one ignorant of geometry who, we do not doubt, has the idea of a complete triangle when he understands that it is a figure comprised within three lines, although Geometricians can learn many other things about the said triangle and discover them in its idea, of which the beginner is unaware. Thus, just as it suffices to understand a figure bounded by three lines in order to have an idea of a complete triangle, so also it is enough to understand a thing bounded by no limits in order to have a true and complete idea of the whole of infinity.

8. Here you repeat the same error when you deny that we can have a true idea of God. For, although we are not aware of everything which is in God, yet everything we do cognize in Him is truly there. The remarks you interpose here and there, such as, *that bread is not more perfect than him who desires it*[3]; *that though I perceive something actually to exist in idea, that is no reason why*

---

[1] Cf. above, p. 166.   [2] ratione.   [3] Above, p. 167, *ad init.*

it should exist actually in the thing of which it is the idea[1] *; that I pass judgment on matters of which I am ignorant*[2], and the like, show only that you, O flesh, wish rashly to attack matters which in many cases you have failed to understand. For it is not *to be inferred from the fact that a man desires bread, that the bread is more perfect than the man*, but only that he who is in want of bread is less perfect than he himself is when he has no lack. Again *from the fact that something exists in idea, I do not infer that it exists in the actual world*, except when no other cause for that idea can be given but the thing which it represents as actually existing; and this I have shown to be true not of many worlds, nor of any other thing, save God alone. Nor, once more, do I *pass judgment on matters of which I am ignorant*, for I have adduced reasons for my judgment, reasons so convincing that none of them has been at all impugned by you.

9. When you deny *that we continually require the activity*[3] *of the primal cause in order that we may continue to exist*, you dispute a matter which all Metaphysicians affirm to be manifest, but one about which the unlearned often do not reflect, attending as they do only to causes *of coming* into being, but not to those *of being*[4]. Thus an architect is the cause of a house and a father of his son *in respect of coming into being* merely, and for this reason, when it is an absolute production, an effect can remain in existence without any cause of this kind; but the sun is the cause of the light proceeding from it, and God is the cause of created things, not only *in respect of their coming into existence*, but also *in respect of their continuing to exist*, and must always expend His activity on the effect in the same way in order to make it stay the same thing.

This can be plainly demonstrated from what I explained about the independence of the parts of time, which you in vain attempt to elude by propounding *the necessary character of the connection between the parts of time* considered in the abstract[5]. Here it is not a question of abstract time, but of the time or duration of something which endures; and you will not deny that the single moments of this time can be separated from their neighbours, i.e. that a thing which endures through individual moments may cease to exist.

---

[1] Above, p. 167, par. 2.   [2] Above, p. 168, par. 2.   influxu.
[4] causas *secundum fieri*, non autem *secundum* esse.
[5] Cf. above, p. 169, par. 1.

When you allege *that we possess a power which suffices to guarantee our preservation, unless some destructive cause supervene*[1], you do not notice that you ascribe to the creature a perfection of the Creator, if the creature is to be able to continue in existence in independence of anything else; while you assign to the Creator the imperfection of a creature, because He must aim at non-existence[2] by means of a positive act, whenever he wishes to cause a cessation of our existence.

Your subsequent statement—that *the possibility of a regress to the infinite is not absurd*, is invalidated by what you yourself afterwards say. For you allow *that it is absurd in the case of causes which are so connected with one another that no action on the part of the lower is possible without the higher*[3]; now it is with such a cause alone that we are concerned here, viz. with causes *in being*, not with causes *in bringing into existence*, like parents. Hence I am not in conflict with the authority of Aristotle; nor does your argument about Pandora bear against me. You allow that all the perfections I see in man can be in varying degrees so augmented that afterwards I behold them to be such as cannot fall within human nature; but this is all I want in order to prove the existence of God. For it is that very power of amplifying all human perfections to such an extent that they are apprehended as more than human; and this, I maintain, could not have come about unless we had been created by God. Yet I am by no means surprised that the evidence of my demonstration of this position is not clear to you, for I have not up to this point noticed that you have correctly grasped any of my arguments.

10. In attacking my statement, *that nothing can be added, nothing taken away from the idea of God*[4], you appear not to have attended to that common saying among Philosophers—that the essences of things are indivisible. For the idea represents the essence of the thing, and if something is added to it or subtracted from it, it is forthwith the idea of something else: it is thus that Pandora, thus that all false gods are portrayed by people who do not conceive the true God aright. But after the idea of the true God is once conceived, although new perfections can be detected in it which had not previously been noticed, this does not cause any increase in that idea, but merely renders it more distinct and explicit, because they must all have been contained in the very same idea, since it is

---

[1] Cf. above, p. 169, par. 2.
[2] tendere in non ens.
[3] Above, p. 170.
[4] Above, p. 172.

assumed to have been true. The idea of the triangle is similarly not
increased when we have remarked in it certain properties previously
ignored. Further I should inform you that *the idea of God is not
formed by us seriatim by amplifying the perfections of created
beings*, but is constituted as a whole at one time by the fact that
mentally we apprehend an infinite being that is incapable of any
amplification.

When you ask *whence I get my proof that the idea of God is, as
it were, the mark of a workman imprinted on his work, and what is
the mode in which it is impressed, what is the form of that mark*[1], it
is very much as if I, coming across a picture which showed a
technique that pointed to Apelles alone as the painter, were to say
that that inimitable technique was, so to speak, a mark impressed
by Apelles on all his pictures in order to distinguish them from
others, but you replied with the questions: 'what is the form of
that mark?' and 'what is its mode of impression?' Such an
enquiry would seem to merit laughter rather than any reply.

What answer do you deserve when you go on to say : *if it is not
other than the work or thing itself, you yourself then are an idea,
you are nothing but a mode of thought, you are yourself both the mark
impressed and the subject on which it is impressed*[2] ? Would it not
be an equally clever thing to urge, when I said that the technique
of Apelles was that by which his pictures were distinguished from
others, that it was nothing other than the pictures themselves :
that therefore those pictures were nothing but the technique, and
did not consist of matter at all, and that hence they were merely a
mode of painting, etc. ?

When, in order to disprove *that we are made after the image of
God*, you state its consequence, that *God will therefore have a human
form*, and go on to recount all the particulars in which human
nature differs from the divine, is there anything cleverer in this
than if, in order to show that certain pictures by Apelles were not
made after the likeness of Alexander, you were to allege that this
implied that Alexander was like a picture, whereas pictures were
composed of wood and paint, not of bones and flesh as Alexander is?
Now the nature of an image is not such that it is identical with
that of which it is an image in all particulars, but only that it
copies it in certain respects ; and it is clear that that perfect power
of thought which we understand to be in God, is represented by
that less perfect faculty which we possess.

[1] Above, p. 172.   [2] Above, p. 173.

In preferring to compare God's act of creation to the operation of a workman rather than to generation by a parent, your action has no warrant. For, although these three modes of action are wholly distinct, yet there is less distance to traverse in arguing from natural production to the divine, than in proceeding from artificial production. But, neither did I say that there was as much resemblance between us and God as prevails between children and parent; nor likewise is there never any likeness between the work of a workman and himself: take for example the sculptor who chisels a likeness of himself.

With how bad faith do you report my words when you pretend that I said that *I perceived a likeness to God in the fact that I am an incomplete and dependent being,* when on the contrary I brought that into the argument to prove our dissimilarity from God, lest it should be thought that I wished to make men equal with God. For I said that not only did I perceive that I was inferior to God in these very matters though nevertheless I aspired to greater things, but that also those very qualities were greater in God—those qualities to which, though they were so great, I found something comparable in myself; and this was shown by the fact that I dared to aspire to them.

Finally when you say how strange it is *that other men do not think about God in the same way as I do, when He has impressed the idea of Himself on them exactly as on me,* it is precisely as if you were to marvel that since all are acquainted with the idea of a triangle, they do not all perceive an equal number of truths about it, and some probably reason about this very figure incorrectly.

CONCERNING THE OBJECTIONS TO THE FOURTH MEDITATION.

I have sufficiently explained our idea of *nothing,* and the way in which we participate in *non-existence,* by calling it a negative idea and saying that it means merely that we are not the supreme Being, and that we lack many things. But you are always discovering imaginary difficulties.

When you say *that I see that certain of God's works are not absolutely perfect and complete*[1] you openly invent something which I have neither stated there nor thought; all that I said being that if certain things were considered not in the light of being but part

[1] Above, p. 175, par. 2.

of the world, as they really are, but as complete wholes, then they might seem to be imperfect.

The arguments you adduce on behalf of final causality are to be referred to the efficient cause; thus it is open to us, from beholding the uses of the various parts in plants and animals to regard with admiration the God who brings these into existence, and from a survey of His works to learn to know and glorify the author of these works, but that does not imply that we can divine the purpose for which He made each thing. And although in Ethics, where it is often allowable to employ conjecture, it is at times pious to consider the end which we may conjecture God set before Himself in ruling the universe, certainly in Physics, where everything should rest upon the securest arguments, it is futile to do so. We cannot pretend that certain of God's purposes rather than others are openly displayed; all seems to be equally hidden in the abyss of His inscrutable wisdom. Likewise you ought not to pretend that mortals can understand no other sort of cause; for there is nothing else which is not much easier to comprehend than one of God's purposes, while, as to those which you have brought forward in illustrating the difficulty in question, there is no one who does not think that he is acquainted with them.

Finally, as you here ask me in such a straightforward manner, *what sort of an idea I think my mind would have possessed either of God or of myself, if, from the time at which it was infused into the body, it had remained there with closed eyes and without employing any of the other senses*[1], I shall give you my answer ingenuously and candidly. I do not doubt that the mind under such circumstances (provided only that we suppose that it is not impeded by the body in its thinking, as equally at the same time that it is not aided by it) would have exactly the same idea of God and of itself as it now possesses, save only that these ideas would be much purer and clearer. For the senses hamper the mind in many things and in nowise aid the perception of these ideas, and there is nothing to prevent all men noticing equally well that they have these ideas, except the fact that they are too much occupied with the perception of the images of corporeal things.

2. Here you are everywhere guilty of a false assumption in taking as a positive imperfection *the fact that we are liable to err*, since this is really (except with respect to God) the negation of a greater perfection. Again the comparison between the citizens of a

---

[1] Above, p. 176, par. 3.

State and the parts of the universe is not strictly accurate; for a bad disposition on the part of citizens is, relatively to the State, something positive, but this does not apply to a man's being liable to err, or not possessing all perfections, when that is taken relatively to the good of the universe. A better comparison could be drawn between the man who would like to have the whole of the human body covered with eyes, in order that it might appear more beautiful, because no bodily part is more beautiful than the eye, and him who thinks that no existing creatures ought to be liable to err, i.e. should not be wholly perfect.

It is plainly a false supposition on your part *that God has assigned to some a function which is base*[1], *and has allotted imperfections to us*, and so forth. Plainly likewise it is false *that God has assigned to man a faculty of judgment which is so uncertain, so confused, and so unequal to the task of deciding those few things on which He has willed that man should pass judgment*[2].

3. You desire me here *briefly to state to what the will may extend, which escapes the understanding*[3]. Precisely to everything in which we happen to err. Thus when you judge that the mind is a certain attenuated body, you are indeed able to understand that the mind is itself, i.e. a thinking thing, and likewise that an attenuated body is an extended thing; but assuredly you do not understand that the thing which thinks and the extended thing are one and the same thing, you only wish to believe it because you have already believed it and do not willingly change your mind. Thus when you judge that an apple which has been poisoned will suit you as food, you indeed understand that its odour, colour, and similar qualities are pleasant, but not that the apple is therefore good for you as food; it is because you wish to believe it that you pass that judgment. So while I confess that there is nothing that we wish about which we do not understand something, I deny that what we understand equals what we will; for we may wish many things about the same matter of which we understand very little. Moreover when we judge wrongly, we do not therefore will wrongly, but perchance something wrong; neither do we understand anything wrongly, we are only said to understand awrong when we judge that we understand something better than we really understand it.

You next deny certain truths about the indeterminateness of the will; and although they are in themselves quite evident,

[1] Above, p. 177, par. 3. [2] Above, p. 178, par. 1.
[3] Above, p. 180, par. 2.

I refuse to undertake to prove them before your eyes. For these matters are such that anyone ought to experience them in himself, rather than be convinced of them by ratiocination; but you, O flesh, appear not to pay heed to what the mind transacts within itself. Refuse then to be free, if freedom does not please you; I at least shall rejoice in my liberty, since I experience it in myself, and you have assailed it not with proof but with bare negations merely. Perchance I shall receive more credence from others, because I affirm that which I have experienced and anyone may experience in himself, than you who make your denial merely because you chance not to have experienced it.

Yet it can be shown conclusively from your words that you yourself have had that experience. For in denying *that we can guard against error*, because you will not have it that the will can be borne towards anything to which it is not determined by the understanding, you at the same time allow that *we can refrain from persisting in error*[1]. But to do so is wholly impossible unless the will has the power of directing itself towards one side or the other apart from any determination by the understanding, the fact which you denied. For, if the understanding has once determined the will to propound some false judgment, I ask you: when first it (the will) begins to take heed lest it continue in error, what is it that determines it to do so? If that determination is due to itself then it can be moved in a certain direction without impulsion by the understanding, which you denied, and about which alone the dispute has been raised. If, on the other hand, it is the understanding which is responsible, it is not the will itself which takes heed; and what happens is merely that, just as it was formerly impelled towards the falsity which the understanding set before it, so now it accidentally happens to be directed towards the truth, because the understanding has set the truth before it. But besides this I should like to know what conception you have of the nature of falsity, and how you think that it can be an object of the understanding. I, who by falsity understand only the privation of truth, am convinced that it is an absolute contradiction that the understanding should apprehend the false under the guise of the truth; but this would be a necessary consequence if understanding could determine the will to embrace the false.

4. As to the profit to be derived from these Meditations I have given sufficient warning in the brief preface, which I think you have

[1] Above, p. 181, *sub fin.*

read, that those will not gain much *who, not taking care to comprehend the sequence and connection of my arguments, devote themselves
only to controverting isolated passages*[1]. Further, as to the method
by which we are able to distinguish those thing which we really
perceive clearly, from that which we only think we so perceive,
although I believe that I have expounded it with sufficient care, as
has been already said, I nevertheless am by no means confident
that people who make too little effort to divest themselves of their
prejudices, and so complain that I have not spoken of these *simply
and in few words*, will easily grasp this method.

CONCERNING THE OBJECTIONS TO THE FIFTH MEDITATION.

1. Here, after quoting one or two of my words, you add that
they are all that I have to say about the question in hand[2]; and this
compels me to warn you that you have not paid enough attention
to the mutual connection between my statements. For I believe it
to be such that, to the proof of any one matter, everything which
has gone before contributes, as well as much of what follows. Hence
it is impossible for you in good faith to report what I have to say
about any one topic, unless you take into account the whole of
what I have said about the others.

You say *that it seems to you to be a serious matter to set up some
immutable and eternal being in addition to God*; and you would be
quite right if it were a question of existence, or merely if I had set
up something with an immutability not dependent on God. But in
the same way as the poets feign that, while the fates were indeed
established by Jove, yet once established, he was restricted in his
action by his maintenance of them; similarly I do not think that
the essence of things, and those mathematical truths which may be
known about them, are independent of God; yet I think that
because God so wished it and brought it to pass, they *are* immutable
and eternal. Now whether you think this to have serious consequences or the reverse, to me it is sufficient if it is true.

Your attack upon the universals of the dialecticians, which you
next undertake, does not touch me, since I do not conceive of
universals in the same way as they do. But as to the essences
which are clearly and distinctly conceived, such as that of the
triangle or of any other geometrical figure, I shall easily compel you

[1] Vol. I. p. 139, par. 2.   [2] Above, p. 183, par. 1.

to acknowledge that the ideas existing in us of those things, are not derived from particulars ; for here you say that they are false, evidently because they do not agree with your preconceived notions about the nature of things.

Shortly afterwards also you say *that the objects of pure mathematics, e.g. the point, the line, the superficies, and the indivisible things consisting of these, and functioning as indivisibles, are incapable of actual existence*[1] : whence it follows that no triangle and none at all of the things which are understood to belong to the essence of the triangle or any of the other geometrical figures, has existed at any time ; hence it follows that these essences are not derived from any existing things. But, say you, they are false. That is forsooth in your opinion, because you suppose the nature of things to be such that these essences cannot be conformable to it. But, unless you also maintain that the whole of geometry is a fiction, you cannot deny that many truths are demonstrated of them, which, being always the same, are rightly styled immutable and eternal. But though they happen not to be conformable to the nature of things as it exists in your conception, as they likewise fail to agree with the atomic theory constructed by Democritus and Epicurus, this is merely an external attribute relatively to them and makes no difference to them ; they are, nevertheless, conformable certainly with the real nature of things which has been established by the true God. But this does not imply that there are substances in existence which possess length without breadth, or breadth without depth, but merely that the figures of geometry are considered not as substances but as the boundaries within which substance is contained.

Meanwhile, moreover, I do not admit *that the ideas of these figures have at any time entered our minds through the senses*[2], as is the common persuasion. For though, doubtless, figures such as the Geometers consider can exist in reality, I deny that any can be presented to us except such minute ones that they fail altogether to affect our senses. For, let us suppose that these figures consist as far as possible of straight lines ; yet it will be quite impossible for any really straight part of the line to affect our senses, because when we examine with a magnifying glass those lines that appear to us to be most straight, we find them to be irregular and bending everywhere in an undulating manner. Hence when first in infancy we see a triangular figure depicted on paper, this figure cannot show

[1] Cf. above, p. 190, par. 2.   [2] Cf. above, p. 185, par. 2.

us how a real triangle ought to be conceived, in the way in which geometricians consider it, because the true triangle is contained in this figure, just as the statue of Mercury is contained in a rough block of wood. But because we already possess within us the idea of a true triangle, and it can be more easily conceived by our mind than the more complex figure of the triangle drawn on paper, we, therefore, when we see that composite figure, apprehend not it itself, but rather the authentic triangle. This is exactly the same as when we look at a piece of paper on which little strokes have been drawn with ink to represent a man's face; for the idea produced in us in this way is not so much that of the lines of the sketch as of the man. But this could not have happened unless the human face had been known to us by other means, and we had been more accustomed to think of it than of those minute lines, which indeed we often fail to distinguish from each other when they are moved to a slightly greater distance away from us. So certainly we should not be able to recognize the Geometrical triangle by looking at that which is drawn on paper, unless our mind possessed an idea of it derived from other sources.

2. Here I do not see to what class of reality you wish to assign existence, nor do I see why it may not be said to be a property as well as omnipotence, taking the word property as equivalent to any attribute or anything which can be predicated of a thing, as in the present case it should be by all means regarded. Nay, necessary existence in the case of God is also a true property in the strictest sense of the word, because it belongs to Him and forms part of His essence alone. Hence the existence of a triangle cannot be compared with the existence of God, because existence manifestly has a different relation to essence in the case of God and in the case of a triangle.

Nor is it more a begging of the question[1], *to enumerate existence among the things belonging to the essence of God*, than to reckon the equality of the three angles of a triangle to two right angles among the properties of the triangle.

Nor is it true *that essence and existence can be thought, the one apart from the other in God*[2], as in a triangle, because God *is* His existence, while a triangle is not its own existence. I do not, nevertheless, deny that existence is a possible perfection in the idea of a triangle, as it is a necessary one in the idea of God; for this fact makes the idea of the triangle one of higher rank than the

[1] Cf. above, p. 186, par. 4.   [2] Cf. above, p. 186, par. 5.

ideas of those chimerical things whose existence can never be supposed. Hence you have not diminished the force of this argument of mine in the slightest, and you still remain deluded *by that fallacy, which you say I could have exposed so easily*[1].

I have elsewhere given a sufficient answer to your next objections. You are plainly in error when you say *that existence is not demonstrated of God, as it is demonstrated of the triangle that its three angles are equal to two right angles*[2]; for the way in which both are proved is alike, except that the demonstration proving existence in God is much simpler and clearer. I pass over the rest, because, though saying *that I explain nothing*, you yourself explain nothing and prove nothing, save only that you are able to prove nothing.

3. Against these criticisms in which you point to Diogenes, Theodorus, Pythagoras and others, and adduce the case of the Sceptics, who had doubts about these very geometrical demonstrations, I affirm that they would not have done so, if, as they might have done, they had known God. Further, one thing is not proved to be better known than another, because it appears to be true to more people, but only because to those who know both, as they may, it appears to be prior in knowledge, and more evident and certain.

CONCERNING THE OBJECTIONS TO THE SIXTH MEDITATION.

1. I have already dealt with the objection *that material things as the objects of pure mathematics do not exist*.

Moreover it is false that the thinking of a Chiliagon is confused; for many deductions can be drawn from it most clearly and distinctly, which would not occur if it were perceived only in a confused manner or, as you say, merely *in respect of the force of the name*. But as a matter of fact we perceive the whole figure at the same time clearly although we are not able to imagine it as a whole at the same time; which proves that the two powers of understanding and imagining differ, not so much in respect of more and less, but as two wholly diverse modes of operation. Thus, in thinking, the mind employs itself alone, but in imagining it contemplates a corporeal form. And though geometrical figures are wholly corporeal, nevertheless the ideas by which they are understood, when they do not fall under the imagination, are not on that account to be reckoned corporeal.

[1] Cf. above, p. 186, par. 6.   [2] Cf. above, p. 187, *sub fin.*

Finally it is worthy of you alone, O flesh, to think *that the idea of God, of an Angel, and of the human mind, are corporeal, or after the fashion of the corporeal, derived forsooth from the human form, and from other very subtle, simple, and imperceptible objects, such as air or aether*[1]. For whosoever thus represents God or the mind to himself, tries to imagine a thing which is not imageable, and constructs nothing but a corporeal idea to which he falsely assigns the name God or mind. For, in the true idea of mind, nothing is contained but thought and its attributes, of which none is corporeal.

2. In this passage you show very clearly that you rely on prejudices merely and never divest yourself of them, when you wish to make out that we suspect no falsity in matters in which we have never detected falsity ; it is thus that, *when we behold a tower close at hand and touch it, we are sure that it is square*[2], if it appear to be square ; so too when we are really awake *we cannot doubt whether we are awake or dreaming*[3] ; and so forth. Now you have no reason to think that all the things in which error can reside have been noticed by you, and it could easily be proved that you sometimes are wrong about those things which you accept as certain. But when you come round to the position at which you state, *that at least we cannot doubt that things appear as they do*[4], you have returned to the true path ; your statement is one that I have myself made in the second Meditation. But here the question raised concerned the reality[5] of external objects, and in what you have contributed to this there is nothing correct.

3. I shall not here delay to notice your tedious and frequent repetitions of such statements as, e.g. *that I have failed to prove certain matters*, which nevertheless I have demonstrated ; *that I have treated only of the solid body*, though I have dealt with every kind of matter, even of the subtlest ; etc. What opposition other than a plain denial is merited by affirmations of this kind, which are not supported by reasons ? Yet incidentally I should like to discover what argument you use to prove that I have treated of solid matter rather than of that which is subtle. Have I not said : ' *I possess (a body) united with myself, and it is certain that I am distinct from my body* '? And I cannot see why these words are not equally applicable to an impalpable and to a solid body ; nor do I think that anyone but you could fail to see this. Apart from this, in the second Meditation I made it evident that mind could

be understood as an existing substance, though we did not understand anything to exist that was wind, or fire, or vapour, or breath,
or anything else of a bodily nature however impalpable and refined.
I said however that at that point[1] I did not discuss whether it was
in truth distinct from every kind of body; but in the present
passage[2] I did discuss the matter and proved my assertion. But
you show that you have wholly failed to comprehend the controversy
by your confusion of the issue as to what may be known of the soul
with the question as to that which the soul really is.

4. Here you ask, *how I think that I, an unextended subject, can
receive into myself the resemblance or idea of a thing which is
extended*[3]. I reply that no corporeal resemblance can be received in
the mind, but that what occurs there is the pure thinking of a
thing, whether it be corporeal or equally whether it be one that is
incorporeal and lacking any corporeal semblance. But as to
imagination, which can only be exercised in reference to corporeal
things, my opinion is that it requires the presence of a semblance
which is truly corporeal, and to which the mind applies itself,
without, however, its being received in the mind.

Your statement *about the idea of the sun, which a blind man
can derive merely from the sun's warmth*[4], is easily refuted. For
the blind man can have a clear and distinct idea of the sun as a
source of heat although he does not possess the idea of it as a
source of light. Nor is your comparison of me to that blind man
just: firstly, because the act of knowledge which apprehends a
thing that thinks is much more extensive than our apprehension
of a thing which warms, as it is much more than that of anything
else, as was shown in its proper place; secondly, because no one
can prove that that idea of the sun which the blind man forms,
does not contain everything which can be learned of the sun, save
those who, being endowed with sight, are aware in addition of its
light and figure. You, however, not only know nothing more than
I do of mind, but do not even have knowledge of the very thing
I recognize in it; so that in this comparison it is rather you who
play the part of blind man, while I, along with the whole human
race, could at most be said to be one-eyed.

In adding that *the mind is not extended*[5], my intention was
not thereby to explain what mind is, but merely to proclaim that
those people are wrong who think that it is extended. In the

[1] Med. II. Vol. I. p. 152.   [2] Med. VI. Vol. I. p. 190.
[3] Above, p. 196, par. 4.   [4] p. 197, par. 2.   [5] Above, p. 197, par. 3.

same way if any people affirmed *that Bucephalus was Music*[1], it would not be idle of others to deny the statement. In good truth your subsequent attempts to prove that mind is extended because it makes use of a body which is extended, seem to employ no better reasoning than if you were to argue that because Bucephalus neighs and whinnies, and so utters sounds that are comparable with Music, it followed that Bucephalus is Music. For, though mind is united with the whole body, it does not follow that it itself is extended throughout the body, because it is not part of its notion to be extended, but merely to think. Neither does it apprehend extension by means of an extended semblance existing in it, although it images it by applying itself to[2] a corporeal semblance which is extended, as has already been said. Finally there is no necessity for it itself to be a body although it has the power of moving body.

5. What you say at this point *relatively to the union of mind and body*[3] is similar to what precedes. At no place do you bring an objection to my arguments; you only set forth the doubts which you think follow from my conclusions, though they arise merely from your wishing to subject to the scrutiny of the imagination matters which, by their own nature, do not fall under it. Thus when you wish to compare the union of mind and body with the mixture of two bodies, it is enough for me to reply that no such comparison ought to be set up, because the two things are wholly diverse, and we must not imagine that there are parts in mind because it is aware of parts in body. Whence do you derive the conclusion that everything which mind knows must exist in mind? If that were so, then, when it was aware of the magnitude of the earth, it would be obliged to have that object within it, and consequently would not only be extended but greater in extent than the whole world.

6. Here though you do not contradict me at all, you have nevertheless much to say; and hence, the reader may discover that the number of your arguments is not to be inferred from any proportion between them and the prolixity of your words.

---

[1] Descartes misread Gassendi's *musca* (fly) as musica. Cf. above, p. 197, par. 3. The mistake must have occurred when he saw Gassendi's work in MS. But in spite of the fact that *musca* appeared in the printed version when the work was published, so that Descartes had the opportunity of rectifying his error, he refrained from doing so. This provoked an attack by an opponent, Revius, in *Statera Philosophiae Cartesianae*, a pamphlet published at Amsterdam in 1650.

[2] convertendo se.　　　　[3] Cf. above, p. 201, par. 3.

Up to this point we have had a discussion between mind and flesh, and, as was but natural, in many things they disagreed. But now, at the end, I catch sight of the real Gassendi, and look up to him as a man of great philosophical eminence. I salute him as a man noted for his intellectual candour and integrity of life, and shall endeavour, by employing all the courtesies which I can muster, to merit his friendship at all times. I therefore ask him not to take it amiss if, in replying to his objections, I have used a Philosophical freedom, since their entire contents caused me very great pleasure. Among other things I rejoiced that such a long and carefully composed dissertation contained nothing in opposition to my reasoning, nothing opposed even to my conclusions, to which I was not able very easily to reply.

THE SIXTH SET OF OBJECTIONS[1].

Though we have read through your Meditations with very great attention, as well as your previous replies to objections, there are still some slight difficulties left, which it is right you should remove.

The first *is that it does not appear altogether certain that we exist, from the fact that we think*[2]. *For in order to be sure that you think, you ought to know what to think, or what thinking, is, and what your existence is; but since you do not yet know what these things are, how can you know that you think or exist? Since, then, in saying* I think, *you do not know what you are saying, and since in adding* therefore I exist, *you are equally ignorant of the meaning of what you say, and indeed do not know that you are saying or thinking anything, since in order to do so it seems to be necessary for you to know that you know what you are saying, and once more to know that you know that you know what you say, and so on to infinity, it is clear that you cannot know whether you exist, or even whether you think.*

But to point out a second difficulty, when you say that you think and exist[3], *someone will maintain that you deceive yourself, and that you do not think, but are only moved, and that you are nothing other than a corporeal motion, since no one meanwhile has been able to grasp the demonstration by means of which you think that you have proved that no corporeal motion can be what you call thought. Have you, then, by means of that Analysis which you employ, so subdivided all the motions of your subtle matter, that you are sure that you can show us, who give our utmost attention and are, we think, sufficiently clear sighted, that the reduction of our thoughts to those corporeal motions is self-contradictory?*

---

[1] urged by divers Theologians and Philosophers, F. V.
[2] Cf. Med. II. Vol. I. p. 150, par. 1.
[3] Cf. Med. VI. Vol. I. p. 190, par. 2.

Our third *difficulty is very much of the same kind. For though some of the Church Fathers have, along with the Platonists, believed that the Angels are corporeal (which led to the Lateran Council's conclusion that they could be depicted), and entertained the same belief with regard to the rational soul, which some of them indeed thought was conveyed to each man from his progenitor; they nevertheless maintained that Angels and the soul alike thought; hence they seem to have believed that this could be effected by corporeal motions, or even was identical with those very corporeal motions, from which they in no way distinguished thinking. The thinking of monkeys, dogs, and other animals seems to confirm this; for dogs bark in their sleep, as if they were chasing hares or rushing at robbers; and they are aware when awake that they run, and when dreaming, that they bark: though, with you, we recognize that there is nothing in them distinct from their bodies. But if you deny that the dog knows that it is running or thinking, besides the fact that this is an unproved assertion, the dog himself might perhaps pass a similar judgment with respect to us, that we forsooth are unaware that we run and think, when we run or when we think. For firstly you do not behold the dog's internal mode of operation, just as he is not directly aware of yours, and secondly there is no lack of men of great attainments who at the present day concede reason to the animals or have in previous ages done so. So far are we from believing that all these operations can be satisfactorily explained by mechanism, without imputing to them sensation, life, and soul, that we are ready to stake anything in proving that that is both an impossibility and an absurdity. Finally there are not lacking those who are likely to assert that man himself also is without sensation and understanding, and that all his actions can be effected by means of dynamical mechanisms and do not imply mind at all, if apes, dogs, and elephants can discharge all their functions in virtue of this mechanism; since, if the limited reasoning power of the brutes differs from human reason, it does so only in degree, and this implies no difference in essence.*

Our fourth *difficulty tenders the knowledge of the Atheist*[2], *which he asserts to be absolutely certain and, judged according to your canon, most evident, when he makes the statements:* if equals be taken from equals, the remainders are equal; the three angles of a rectilinear triangle are equal to two right angles, *and thousands similar; for he cannot frame those statements mentally without*

---

[1] ἀδύνατον, L. V.   [2] Cf. Reply to Objj. II. above, p. 29, *ad init.*

*believing them to be absolutely certain. The Atheist contends that
this is so true that even if God does not exist and is not even
possible, as he believes, he is no less certain of these matters than if
God did really exist. He denies that any reason for doubting can
be advanced, to disturb him in the slightest or make him hesitate.
For, what will you advance? That God, if He exists, can deceive
him? The Atheist will reply that he could not be deceived in these
matters even though God were to put forth all the force of His
omnipotence in the attempt.*

Hence arises the fifth *difficulty whose root is found in that
deception which you wholly deny of God Himself*[1]*. For, since many
Theologians believe that the damned, both angels and men, are
continuously deceived by God's having implanted in them the idea
of a fire that is torturing them, so that they firmly believe and think
that they clearly see and perceive that they are really being tortured
by the fire, though no such fire exists, is it not possible that God
deceives us with similar ideas and continually makes sport of us by
despatching similar phantasms or ideas into our minds? Hence we
should imagine that we clearly saw, and perceived by each of our
senses things that nevertheless are not outside us, so that sky and
earth are not real and we do not really possess arms and feet and
eyes etc. This can happen without any wrongfulness or injustice,
since the Lord is supreme over everything and has the absolute power
of disposing what belongs to him; especially since such action avails
to repress the pride of men, and punish their sins, whether the punish-
ment inflicted be on account of original sin or of other causes obscure
to us. These contentions seem to be confirmed by those passages of
Scripture which show that we can know nothing, e.g. the words of
Paul in 1st Corinthians, chapter 8, verse 2 :* If any man thinketh,
he says, that he knoweth anything, he knows not yet as he ought
to know ; *and the passage in Ecclesiastes, c. 8, v. 17 :* I beheld that
of all the works of God man can find out no reason of those that
are done under the sun ; and so much the more as a man labours
to seek it out, the less shall he discover ; nay even though a wise
man says that he knows, he shall not be able to find it out. *And
that the wise man in saying this, has employed deliberate reason, and
not spoken in haste, or thoughtlessly and violently, the whole of his
book makes clear, especially when the question of the mind comes up,
which, you contend, is immortal. For in verse 19, c. 3, he says that*
the death of man is as the death of beasts. *And lest you should*

[1] Cf. Med. III. Vol. I. p. 171, par. 1, and Med. IV. p. 172, par. 2.

reply that this is to be understood of the body alone, he adds that man has no preeminence over the beasts. *Further, speaking of the spirit of man itself, he denies* that there is anyone who knoweth whether it goeth upward, *i.e. whether it is immortal,* or whether it goeth downwards with the spirits of the beasts, *i.e. perishes. Neither may you allege that these words are said in the character of an unbeliever; in such a case the writer ought to have made that quite clear and provided a refutation of these statements. Again you must not contend that no reply on your part is called for, since Scripture is a matter for the Theologians; for since you are a Christian it is proper for you to be ready to reply to everything that can be objected to the faith, especially against the positions you desire to establish, and to use all your powers to make your results satisfactory.*

The sixth *difficulty arises from the indifference of the judgment*[1] *or liberty which you refuse to allow to the perfection of choice, but ascribe to an imperfect will alone, thus removing the indifference as often as the mind clearly perceives what ought to be believed or performed or left undone. But do you not see that by positing this you destroy the liberty of God, from Whom you remove that indifference as to whether He will create this world rather than another or any world at all? Though yet it belongs to the faith to believe that God has from eternity been indifferent as to whether He would create one, or many, worlds, or no world. But who doubts that God has at all times had the clearest vision of all things that were to be done or left undone? Therefore the clearest vision and perception of things does not annul the indifference of choice; and if it cannot harmonize with human liberty, neither will it be compatible with the divine, since the essences of things are, like numbers, indivisible and unchanging. Wherefore indifference is included no less in the divine than in human freedom of choice.*

The seventh *difficulty will affect the superficies*[2] *in which or by means of which you say that all sensations take place. For we do not understand how it can happen that it is neither part of the sentient bodies, nor part of the air itself and its vapours, of which you say that it is no part, not even the exterior*[3]*. Nor at the same time do we comprehend that no body whatsoever nor substance, as you assert, possesses real accidents which by the divine power may exist apart from any subject and, as a matter of fact, do exist, in the*

---

[1] Cf. Med. IV. Vol. I. p. 175.
[2] Cf. Reply to Objj. IV. above, p. 119, par. 2.   [3] extremum.

Sacrament of the Altar. There is however no reason for our Doctors to be perturbed until they have seen whether you are going to prove that in your Physics, for which you make us hope, and which they scarcely believe will propound the matter so clearly that your conclusions will be capable of acceptance, or will merit acceptance, to the exclusion of the former doctrine.

The eighth *difficulty arises out of your reply to the fifth set of objections. How can the truths of Geometry or Metaphysics such as you mention be immutable and eternal, and yet not be independent of God*[1]*? What is the species of causality by which they are related to Him or dependent on Him? What possible action of God's could annul the nature of the triangle? And how could He from all eternity bring it to pass that it was untrue that twice four was eight? or that a triangle had not three angles? Hence either these truths depend upon the understanding alone while it thinks them*[2]*, or upon existing things, or they are independent, since God evidently could not have brought it to pass that any of these essences or verities was not from all eternity.*

Finally the ninth *difficulty seems to us very important, when you say that we ought to distrust the operation of the senses, and that the certitude of the understanding far exceeds that of the senses*[3]*. But what if the understanding can enjoy no certitude, which it has not first received from a good disposition of the senses? Or again if it cannot correct the error of any sense, unless another sense first correct the said error? Refraction makes a stick thrust into the water appear broken, though nevertheless it is straight; what corrects the error? The understanding? Not at all; it is the sense of touch. So, too, in other cases. Hence if you bring in all the senses properly disposed, which always give the same report, you will obtain the greatest possible certainty of which man is capable; but this certitude will often escape you if you trust to the operations of your mind, which often goes astray in matters about which it believed there was no possibility of doubt.*

These are the principal matters which caused us trouble. And we pray you to add some sure rule and certain infallible tokens by which we may be quite sure, when we apprehend one thing thus perfectly apart from another, that it is certain that the one is so distinct from the other, that the two can, by the divine power at least, exist apart; i.e. we wish to know surely, clearly, and distinctly

---

[1] Cf. Reply to Objj. v. above, p. 226, par. 3.   [2] haec. No objection, F. V.
[3] Cf. Medd. I. and VI. Vol. I. pp. 145 and 189.

that that distinction of the understanding is not due to the under-standing itself but proceeds from the very things distinguished. For when we contemplate the immensity of God, not thinking of His justice; or when we view His immensity, not thinking of the Son or of the Holy Spirit; do we have a complete perception of that immensity, or of God as existing, apart from those other Persons, whose existence an infidel could deny with as much right as you deny mind or thought of the body? Therefore just as it will be a false conclusion for anyone to argue that the Son and the Holy Spirit are in essence distinct from God the Father, or can be separated from Him, so neither will anyone grant that thought or the human mind can be distinguished from the body, though you may conceive the one apart from the other, and deny the one of the other; nor may you think that this can be proved by means of any mental abstraction on your part. If you can manage to reply to these objections, there seems to be certainly nothing at all left to which our Theologians can take exception.

Appendix.

A few questions derived from other people will here be added in order that your reply to them may be conjoined to your answer to the previous objections, since they belong to the same argument. Certain very learned and clear-sighted men wish to have a careful explanation of the three following points.

1. *How I know with certainty that I have a clear idea of my soul.*

2. *How I know with certainty that that idea is wholly diverse from anything else.*

3. *How I know with certainty that that contains no element of corporeity.*

Certain others have propounded the following argument.

CERTAIN PHILOSOPHERS AND GEOMETRICIANS TO MONSIEUR DESCARTES.

With howsoever great an effort we bethink ourselves as to whether the idea[1] *of our mind or that of a human being, i.e. our knowledge and perception of it, contains anything corporeal, we do not venture to assert that what we call thought can in no wise attach to*[2] *any*

---

[1] Idola. A. and T. suspect the correctness of the word, as Clerselier's F. V. leads us to suppose that *Idea* is intended.
[2] convenire.

body, whatsoever be the motions[1] *which characterize it.   For since
we discern that while there are certain bodies which do not think,
there are others, e.g. human bodies and perchance those of the brutes
which do think, will you not regard us as being guilty of sophistry
and undue boldness, if we therefore conclude that there are no bodies
which think?   We can scarce refrain from believing that we
would deserve to be for all time derided by you, if we had first
forged that argument derived from ideas on behalf of the mind as well
as of God, and you had then by your analytical method*[2] *condemned
it.   But you seem to be so much preoccupied and prepossessed by
this method that you have apparently now so obscured*[3] *your
mental vision that you are no longer free to see that the several
mental properties or operations which you discover within you depend
upon corporeal motions.*

*If not, unloose the bond which, you say, confines us with adaman-
tine chains and prevents our minds from raising their flight above
the body.   The bond consists in this—We perceive very well* that
two and three make five, that if equals be taken from equals the
remainders are equal ; *we are convinced of the truth of these and
a thousand other propositions, just as you find you also are.   Why
are we not similarly convinced by your ideas or our own, that the
human soul is distinct from the body and that God exists?   You
will say that you are not able to put this truth into our minds
unless we think along with you.   But lo! we have read what you
have written seven times and have, so far as in us lay, given an
attention to it equal to that of the Angels, and have nevertheless not
yet been convinced.   We do not, however, think that you will prefer
to say that our minds are all steeped in brutish ignorance and
wholly unfit for Metaphysical investigation, though for thirty years
accustomed to deal with that science ; we believe that you will not
rather do this than confess that your arguments derived from the
idea of the mind and that of God are not of such weight and power
as to be able to master and in due right bring into subjection the
intelligence of men of learning who have tried with all their power
to detach themselves from solid matter.   On the contrary we think
that you will make that confession if you re-read your Meditations
in the spirit of critical analysis with which you would treat them
if they had been brought forward by an opponent.*

---

[1] agitated by some secret motions, F. V.
[2] Analysi.   [3] tuae menti callum obduxisse.

Finally, as long as we do not know what can be achieved by bodies and their motions, and since you admit that no one can know everything which God has implanted in any body and can implant, apart from a revelation by God Himself, how can you be sure that God has not implanted in certain bodies a power and property of such a kind that they can doubt, think, etc. ?

These are our arguments or, if you so prefer it, our prejudices. If you can cure us of them, we call God to witness that great will be the thanks with which all of us will reward you for freeing us from the tangle of thorns which is suffocating in us the truth you have sown. May the all-good God bring this to pass, the God towards whose glory alone we know all your efforts have been directed.

REPLY TO THE SIXTH SET OF OBJECTIONS.

1. It is indeed true that *no one can be sure that he knows or that he exists, unless he knows what thought is and what existence*[1]. Not that this requires a cognition formed by reflection or one acquired by demonstration ; much less does it require a cognition of a reflective cognition, by which we know that we know, and again know that we know that we know and so *ad infinitum*. Such knowledge could never be obtained about anything. It is altogether euough for one to know it by means of that internal cognition which always precedes reflective knowledge, and which, when the object is thought and existence, is innate in all men ; so that, however overwhelmed by prejudice and attentive to the words rather than their signification, though we may feign that we do not possess that knowledge, we cannot nevertheless really be without it. When, therefore, anyone perceives that he thinks and that it thence follows that he exists, although he chance never previously to have asked what thought is, nor what existence, he cannot nevertheless fail to have a knowledge of each sufficient to give him assurance on this score.

2. Nor can it occur that, when one perceives that he thinks, understanding at the same time what it is to move, he should think *that he is deceived, and that he does not think but only moves*[2]. For since plainly the idea or notion he has of thought is quite different from that of corporeal movement, he must necessarily understánd the one as quite different from the other. Yet on account of his habit of ascribing many diverse properties, between

---

[1] Cf. above, p. 233, par. 2.   [2] Cf. *ibid.* par. 3.

which he discerns no connection, to one and the same subject, he may doubt, he may even affirm that he is one and the same thing which thinks and moves in space. But it must be noted that there are two ways in which things of which we have diverse ideas can be taken to be one and the same thing; to wit, either in respect of unity and identity of nature, or merely by unity of composition. Thus, for example, our ideas of figure and motion are not the same, neither those of understanding and willing, nor of bones and flesh, nor of thought and of an extended thing. Nevertheless we clearly perceive that to the same substance to which the possibility of having figure belongs, the possibility of moving also belongs, so that what is figured and mobile is one by unity of nature ; similarly we see that a thing which is intelligent and wills is one and the same by unity of nature. But we do not perceive the same in the case of the thing which we regard under the form of bone, and of that which we view as flesh ; hence we cannot take these to be one and the same thing by unity of nature, but only by unity of composition, viz. in so far as the animal possessing bone and flesh is one and the same. But now the question is, whether we perceive a thinking thing and an extended thing to be one and the same by unity of nature, a unity such that we find that between thought and extension there is the same affinity and connection as we notice to prevail between figure and motion, or between understanding and willing. Or whether shall we rather say that they are one and the same only by unity of composition, in so far as they are found in the same man, in the way in which bones and flesh exist in the same animal. Now this latter alternative is that which I affirm, because I find a total diversity between the nature of an extended and that of a thinking thing, a diversity not less than that between bones and flesh.

But since at this point an appeal to authority enters into the dispute, I am compelled, lest this should imperil the truth, to reply to what you add, viz. *that no one hitherto has been able mentally to grasp my demonstration*, by saying that though not many people have as yet examined my argument, quite a number affirm that they understand it. And just as the witness of one man who, having made a voyage to America, declares that he has seen the Antipodes, merits more credence than that of a thousand others who deny their existence merely because they have no knowledge of them ; so likewise in the case of those who properly examine the validity of arguments, greater weight attaches to the authority of one man who says that he understands a certain argument aright, than of a thousand others who, without appending any reason, maintain that it cannot be understood. For though they do not understand it, that does not prevent its being understood by others; and, since, in inferring this conclusion, they show that they do not have an accurate apprehension of what it is to reason, very little faith should be reposed in them.

Lastly to the question:—*whether by my Analysis I have sub-divided all the motions of my subtle matter so as to be sure that I can show men who have given their best attention and are, as they think, sufficiently clear-sighted, that the reduction of our thoughts to corporeal motions*, i.e. as I interpret, that thoughts and corporeal motions are one and the same, *is self-contradictory*, I reply that, though to me it is very certain, I do not promise that others can be convinced of the same truth however attentive they are and, in their own judg-ment, clear-sighted. At least I cannot promise it so long as they fasten their attention not on the objects of pure intelligence but on those of the imagination, as apparently those have done, who have pretended that the dissection of some subtle matter will give us the distinction between thought and motion. For the distinction can only be grasped by observing that the motions of a thing that thinks and that of a thing that is extended or mobile are wholly diverse and mutually independent of each other, and that it is self-contradictory[1] that those things which are clearly understood by us to be diverse and independent, cannot be sundered, at least by God. So that however often we find them in one and the same subject as, e.g., thought and corporeal motions in the same man, we ought not on that account to believe that they are one and the same thing by unity of nature but only in virtue of unity of composition.

3. What is here advanced about the Platonists and their partisans, has now been rejected by the whole Catholic Church and commonly by all Philosophers. Moreover the Lateran Council, though concluding that Angels could be depicted, did not at the same time agree that they were corporeal. But even though they were in truth believed to be corporeal we should certainly not even in their case have reason to believe that their minds are more inseparable from their bodies than men's are, neither also, though it were imagined that the human soul were derived from the pro-creator, could it be concluded that the soul is corporeal, but only that as the body arises from the body of the parents so the soul

---

[1] repugnet.

itself proceeded from the parents' soul.   As for dogs and apes, even
though I were to grant that thought existed in them, it would in
nowise follow that the human mind was not to be distinguished
from the body, but on the contrary rather that in other animals
also there was a mind distinct from their body.   This is a doctrine
that these very Platonists, whose authority you lately lauded, held,
following the Pythagoreans in this, as is clear from their belief in
Metempsychosis.   However, not only have I asserted that plainly
the brutes do not possess thought, as is here assumed, but I have
given a most stringent proof of this, a proof which no one has
hitherto refuted.   Yet the people who affirm that *dogs when awake
know that they run, and even when dreaming, that they are barking*[1],
as if they could take up their station in the animals' hearts, really
assert this merely and do not prove it.   For although they add *that
they do not believe that the operations of the beasts can be explained
by mechanism, apart from sensation, life, and soul* (i.e. as I interpret,
without thought; for I have neither denied to the brutes what is
vulgarly called life, nor a corporeal soul, nor organic sense), *and
that they are ready to stake anything in proving that that is both an
impossibility and an absurdity*, this should not be taken to be a
reason.   The like can be asserted about any other proposition however true; nay people are not wont to offer pledges, except where
their proof lacks reasons; and since once upon a time men scouted
the existence of the Antipodes in almost exactly the same way,
I fancy that a matter should not be straightway held to be false
because certain people scout it.

   You conclude by adding that *those are not lacking who are likely
to assert that man himself also is without sensation and understanding,
and that all his actions can be effected by means of dynamical
mechanisms and do not imply mind at all, if apes, dogs, and elephants
can discharge all their functions in virtue of this mechanism.*   But
this argument surely proves nothing at all except that there are
some men who conceive all things so confusedly, and who stick so
tenaciously to the opinions that they have taken up in a prejudiced
manner and understand only in a verbal way, that, rather than
change them, they deny of themselves facts that they can at no
moment fail to experience within them.   For surely we cannot help
at every moment experiencing within us that we think; nor can
anyone infer from the fact that it has been shown that the animate
brutes can discharge all these operations entirely without thought,

[1] Cf. p. 235.

that he therefore does not think; unless it be that having previously persuaded himself that his actions are entirely like those of the brutes, just because he has ascribed thought to them, he were to adhere so pertinaciously to these very words, '*men and brutes operate in the same way*,' that when it was shown to him that the brutes did not think, he preferred to divest himself of that thought of his of which he could not fail to have an inner consciousness, rather than to alter his opinion that he acted in the same way as the brutes. But I cannot easily persuade myself that there are many people of this kind. Far more will be found who, if it is conceded *that thought is not to be distinguished from bodily motion*, will with much better reason conclude that it is the same thing in us and in them, since they notice in them all corporeal movements as in us : they will add *that a difference merely of greater and less makes no difference to the essence*, and will infer that, though perchance they think that there is less reason in the beasts than in us, our minds are exactly of the same species ; and such a conclusion will be justly drawn.

4. As to the Atheist's knowledge, it is easy to prove that it is not immutable and certain. For, as I have already in a former place said, in proportion to the impotence assigned to the author of his being, the greater will be his reason for doubting whether he may not be of such an imperfect nature as to be deceived in matters which appear most evident to him ; and he cannot be set free from that doubt unless he first acknowledges that he has been created by the true God, a God who has no intention to deceive[1].

5. Moreover that it is self-contradictory that men should be deceived by God is clearly demonstrated from the fact that the form of deception is non-existence, towards which the supreme existent cannot incline. In this all theologians are agreed, and all the certainty of the Christian faith depends upon this doctrine. For why should we trust God's revelations, if we thought that we were sometimes deceived by Him ? And though Theologians commonly affirm that the damned are tortured by hell fire, they do not therefore believe that they *are deceived by a false idea of a tormenting fire which God has implanted in them*, but rather that they are tortured by real fire, for the reason that, *just as the incorporeal spirit of the living man is naturally confined in the body, so by the divine power it is easily after death confined in corporeal fire.* Cf. *The Master of the Sentences*[2], Book IV, Distinction 44.

---

[1] a vero et nescio fallere Deo.   F. V. principe de toute vérité.
[2] L. V. Mag. lib.

As to the passages of Scripture, I do not think that it is my part to reply to them, unless when they appear to contradict some opinion that is peculiar to me. For when my doctrine merely contains things that are common to all Christians, such as are the object of attack here, e.g. that something can be known and that human souls are not like those of animals, I should stand in dread of the charge of arrogance, if I did not prefer to content myself with the replies that have already been discovered by others, rather than devise new arguments ; for I have never intermeddled with theological studies, except in so far as they contributed to my private instruction, nor do I find within me so much of the divine grace as to feel called to this sacred occupation. But I shall not on the present occasion avail myself of this resource, for fear that I may give some people an opportunity of thinking that I keep silence because I cannot give a satisfactory explanation of the passages adduced.

Firstly therefore I maintain that the passage from St Paul, I Corinth. chap. 8. ver. 2[1], ought only to be understood of the knowledge which is not conjoined with love, i.e. of the knowledge of the Atheists, because whoever knows God as he ought, cannot avoid loving Him or fail to have love. And this is confirmed by the preceding words : '*Knowledge puffeth up, but love edifieth*,' and those which immediately follow : '*Moreover if anyone love God, He (i.e. God) is known by him.*' Thus the Apostle does not mean that we can possess no knowledge at all, because he admits that those who love God know him, i.e. have knowledge about him. He says merely that those who have not love and hence do not know God sufficiently, although they imagine that in other matters they know something, nevertheless do not know as they ought to know, just because they ought to begin with the knowledge of God, and subsequently range the knowledge of all other things under this single cognition, as I have explained in my Meditations. Thus this very passage, which was adduced against me, so openly confirms my opinion about this matter, that I disbelieve that it can be properly explained by those who differ from me. But if anyone contends that the pronoun '*He*' does not refer to God[2] but to the man who is known of God and approved by Him, another Apostle, to wit St John in his first Epistle, chap. 2, wholly favours my explanation.

---

[1] Above, p. 236.
[2] Cf. the interpretation in the English authorised and revised versions.

For in verse 2[1] he says as follows : *and hereby we know that we know Him, if we keep His commandments* ; in chap. 4. verse 7, *everyone that loveth is begotten of God and knoweth God.*

The same conclusion must be derived from the passages in Ecclesiastes. For it has to be noted that Solomon in that book, while indeed not acting the part of an unbeliever but in his own character, in so far as he was previously a sinner and had turned away from God, there repenting of his sins says that, in so far as he employed human wisdom and did not relate that wisdom to God, he could find nothing which wholly satisfied or in which there was not vanity. Hence on this account he says in many places that we ought to turn towards God, as expressly in chap. 11. verse 9 : *And know thou that for all these things God will call thee into judgment,* and in what follows up to the end of the book. Specially also those words in chap 8. verse 17 :—'*And I understood that of all the works of God man can find out no reason of those that are done under the sun' etc.*—should not be understood to hold good of any man, but of him whom he has described in the previous verse : *There is that neither by day nor night seeth sleep with his eyes.* It appears that thus the Prophet meant to announce there that those who are too assiduous in their studies are not fitted to lay hold of the truth ; and certainly those who know me will not readily say that this saying applies to me. But we should attend especially to those words : '*the things which are done under the sun.*' For the words recur frequently in the book, and always refer to natural things to the exclusion of their subordination to God, just because God, being above all things cannot be comprised among those which are under the sun. Hence the sense of the words cited is, that man cannot know natural objects properly, so long as he does not know God, which is just my own contention. Finally in chap. 3.[2] verse 19, it is clearly not said that '*the death of man is as the death of beasts*' nor that '*man has no preeminence over the beasts,*' except in so far as this refers to the body, for in the passage there is mention only of those things that pertain to the body. Immediately afterwards also he adds something separately about the soul : *who knoweth if the spirit of the sons of Adam ascends upwards and if the spirit of the beasts descends downwards?* That means, if human spirits are to enjoy celestial bliss, what man knows this by human reasonings and as long as he does not turn himself toward God? Certainly I have

---

[1] Verse 3 in the English N. T.
[2] 5 in F. V., a typographical error.

tried to prove by natural reason that the soul is not corporeal; but I admit that it can only be known through faith whether it is to ascend above.

6. As to the freedom of the will, a very different account must be given of it as it exists in God and as it exists in us. For it is self-contradictory that the will of God should not have been from eternity indifferent to all that has come to pass or that ever will occur, because we can form no conception of anything good or true, of anything to be believed or to be performed or to be omitted, the idea of which existed in the divine understanding before God's will determined Him so to act as to bring it to pass. Nor do I here speak of priority of time; I mean that it was not even prior in order, or in nature, or in reasoned relation[1], as they say [in the schools], so that that idea of good impelled God to choose one thing rather than another. Thus, to illustrate, God did not will to create the world in time because he saw that it would be better thus than if he created it from all eternity; nor did he will the three angles of a triangle to be equal to two right angles because he knew that they could not be otherwise. On the contrary, because he worked to create the world in time it is for that reason better than if he had created it from all eternity; and it is because he willed the three angles of a triangle to be necessarily equal to two right angles that this is true and cannot be otherwise; and so in other cases. And though it may be said that it is the merit of the saints which is the cause of their obtaining eternal life, this causes no difficulty; for their merits are not causes of their obtaining this in the sense that they determine God to will anything; they are merely the cause of an effect of which God wished them from all eternity to be the cause. Thus that supreme indifference in God is the supreme proof of his omnipotence. But as to man, since he finds the nature of all goodness and truth already determined by God, and his will cannot bear upon anything else, it is evident that he embraces the true and the good the more willingly and hence the more freely in proportion as he sees the true and the good the more clearly, and that he is never indifferent save when he does not know what is the more true or the better, or at least when he does not see clearly enough to prevent him from doubting about it. Thus the indifference which attaches to human liberty is very different from that which belongs to the divine. Neither does it here matter that the essences of things are said to be indivisible:

[1] ratione ratiocinata.

for firstly no essence can belong in a univocal sense both to God and His creature; and finally indifference does not belong to the essence of human liberty, since we are free not only when our ignorance of the right renders us indifferent, but also, and chiefly, when a clear perception impels us to prosecute some definite course.

7. My conception of the superficies by which I believe our senses are affected, is not different from that employed (or which ought to be employed) by all mathematicians and philosophers; they distinguish it from body and assume it to be wholly devoid of depth. But the term superficies is taken in two ways by mathematicians: viz. in the sense of a body, to the length and breadth of which they attend and which is viewed altogether apart from its depth, although depth be not denied of it; or only as a mode of body, when straightway all depth is denied of it. Consequently for the sake of avoiding ambiguity I said that I spoke of that superficies which, being only a mode, can be no part of body; for a body is a substance, and a mode cannot be a part of substance. Yet I did not deny that it was the extremity of a body; nay, on the contrary, I said that it could with the greatest propriety be called the extremity of the contained body as much as of the containing, in the sense in which one says that bodies are contiguous when their extremities are together. For certainly when two bodies touch each other, the extremity of each is one and the same, and this is part of neither but the same mode of both, and can even remain although these bodies are removed, provided only that others of accurately the same size and figure succeed to their place. Nay that space which the Aristotelians call the superficies of the surrounding body can be understood to be no other superficies than that which is no substance but a mode. For neither is the place of a town changed, although the surrounding air be changed or some other substance be substituted for it, nor consequently does the superficies which is here taken for a place form any part of the surrounding air or of the town.

In order to refute the doctrine of the reality of accidents it seems to me that there is no need to produce other arguments than those which I have already employed. For firstly, since all sensation is effected through contact, it is of a corporeal superficies alone that we can have sensation; and yet if there are real accidents they must be different from that superficies, which is merely a mode; therefore if there are any such, we cannot have sensation of them. But who ever believed that they existed unless he thought he experienced them by sensation ? Secondly it is contradictory that real accidents should exist, because whatever is real can exist separately apart from any other subject ; but whatever can exist separately is substance not accident. And it makes no difference whether it be said that real accidents can be disjoined from their subject, not naturally, but merely by the divine power ; for coming to pass naturally is nowise different from coming to pass by the ordinary power of God, which does not differ at all from his extraordinary power, and does not make any further contribution to things, so that if everything which can exist naturally apart from a subject is substance, so whatever by the power of God, however extraordinary it may be, is capable of existing without a subject, must likewise be termed substance. I do indeed admit that one substance can be the accident of another : but yet when this happens it is not the substance itself which has the form of an accident, but only the mode in which it is accidental. For example when his clothing is an accident of a man, it is not the clothing itself but merely his *being clothed* which is an accident. But because the principal reason which moved Philosophers to posit real accidents was that they thought that the perceptions of the senses could not be explained without assuming them, I have promised that I will explain these facts minutely with reference to each sense in my Physics. Not that I wish that any of my opinions should be taken on trust, but that I thought that those who have judged correctly in the matter of those accidents which I have already explained in the case of vision in my Dioptrics, will easily guess what I am able to make good in the case of the others.

8. To one who pays attention to God's immensity, it is clear that nothing at all can exist which does not depend on Him. This is true not only of everything that subsists, but of all order, of every law, and of every reason of truth and goodness ; for otherwise God, as has been said just before, would not have been wholly indifferent to the creation of what he has created. For if any reason for what is good had preceded His preordination, it would have determined Him towards that which it was best to bring about ; but on the contrary because He determined Himself towards those things which ought to be accomplished, for that reason, as it stands in Genesis, *they are very good* ; that is to say, the reason for their goodness is the fact that He wished to create them so. Nor is it worth while asking in what class of cause fall that goodness or those other truths, mathematical as well as metaphysical, which

depend upon God; for since those who enumerated the classes of cause did not pay sufficient attention to causality of this type, it would have been by no means strange if they had given it no name. Nevertheless they did give it a name; for it can be styled efficient causality in the same sense as the king is the efficient cause of the laws, although a law is not a thing which exists physically, but is merely as they say [in the Schools] a moral entity. Again it is useless to inquire how God could from all eternity bring it about that it should be untrue that twice four is eight, etc.; for I admit that that cannot be understood by us. Yet since on the other hand I correctly understand that nothing in any category of causation can exist which does not depend upon God, and that it would have been easy for Him so to appoint that we human beings should not understand how these very things could be otherwise than they are, it would be irrational to doubt concerning that which we correctly understand, because of that which we do not understand and perceive no need to understand. Hence neither should we think *that eternal truths depend upon the human understanding or on other existing things*; they must depend on God alone, who, as the supreme legislator, ordained them from all eternity.

9. In order rightly to see what amount of certainty belongs to sense we must distinguish three grades as falling within it. To the first belongs the immediate affection of the bodily organ by external objects; and this can be nothing else than the motion of the particles of the sensory organs and the change of figure and position due to that motion. The second comprises the immediate mental result, due to the mind's union with the corporeal organ affected; such are the perceptions of pain, of pleasurable stimulation, of thirst, of hunger, of colours, of sound, savour, odour, cold, heat, and the like, which in the Sixth Meditation are stated to arise from the union and, as it were, the intermixture of mind and body. Finally the third contains all those judgments which, on the occasion of motions occurring in the corporeal organ, we have from our earliest years been accustomed to pass about things external to us.

For example, when I see a staff, it is not to be thought that *intentional species*[1] fly off from it and reach the eye, but merely that rays of light reflected from the staff excite certain motions in the optic nerve and, by its mediation, in the brain as well, as I have explained at sufficient length in the Dioptrics. It is in this cerebral

---

[1] F. V. minute images flying through the air commonly called intentional species.

motion, which is common to us and to the brutes, that the first grade of perception consists. But from this the second grade of perception results ; and that merely extends to the perception of the colour or light reflected from the stick, and is due to the fact that the mind is so intimately conjoined with the brain as to be affected by the motions arising in it. Nothing more than this should be assigned to sense, if we wish to distinguish it accurately from the intellect. For though my judgment that there is a staff situated without me, which judgment results from the sensation of colour by which I am affected, and likewise my reasoning from the extension of that colour, its boundaries, and its position relatively to the parts of my brain, to the size, the shape, and the distance of the said staff, are vulgarly assigned to sense, and are consequently here referred to the third grade of sensation, they clearly depend upon the understanding alone. That magnitude, distance and figure can be perceived by reasoning alone, which deduces them one from another, I have proved in the Dioptrics. The difference lies in this alone, that those judgments which now for the first time arise on account of some new apprehension, are assigned to the under-standing ; but those which have been made from our earliest years in exactly the same manner as at present, about the things that have been wont to affect our senses, as similarly the conclusions of our reasonings, are referred by us to sense. And the reason for this is just that in these matters custom makes us reason and judge so quickly, or rather we recall the judgments previously made about similar things ; and thus we fail to distinguish the difference between these operations and a simple sense perception.

From this it is clear that when we say that *the certitude obtain-able by the understanding is much greater than that attaching to the senses* the meaning of those words is, that those judgments which when we are in full maturity new observations have led us to make, are surer than those we have formed in early infancy and apart from all reflection ; and this is certainly true. For it is clear that here there is no question of the first or second grade of sense-perception[1], because in them no falsity can reside. When, there-fore, it is alleged that refraction makes a staff appear broken in the water, it is the same as if it were said that it appears to us in the same way as it would to an infant who judged that it was broken, and as it does even to us who, owing to the prejudices to which we from our earliest years have grown accustomed, judge in

[1] sentiendi.

the same way. But I cannot grant what you here add, viz. that that error is corrected *not by the understanding but by the touch.* For, although it is owing to touch that we judge that the staff is straight, and that by the mode of judging to which from infancy we are accustomed, and which is hence called *sense*, this, nevertheless, does not suffice to correct the error. Over and above this we need to have some reason to show us why in this matter we ought to believe the tactual judgment rather than that derived from vision; and this reason, not having been possessed by us from the times of infancy, must be attributed not to sense but to the understanding. Hence in this instance it is the understanding solely which corrects the error of sense; and no case can ever be adduced in which error results from our trusting the operation of the mind more than sense.

10. Since the remainder of what you bring forward consists of doubts rather than of objections, I do not take so much upon me as to dare to promise that I shall be able to give a satisfactory account of matters concerning which I see that so many learned and clever men have hitherto had difficulties. Nevertheless, in order to do my best and not prove wanting in my cause, I shall relate in good faith the means by which I had the fortune to free myself wholly from these same doubts. For thus, if they chance to be of use to others, I shall be highly pleased; if not, I shall feel guilty of no rashness.

When first the reasons expounded in these Meditations had led me to infer that the human mind was really distinct from the body and was more easily known[1] than it, and so on, what compelled me to assent to this was that I found nothing in these arguments which was not coherent nor derived from highly evident principles according to the rules of Logic. But I confess that I was not thereby wholly persuaded, and that I had almost the same experience as the Astronomers, who, after many proofs had convinced them that the Sun was many times larger than the Earth, could not prevail upon themselves to forego judging that it was smaller than the Earth when they viewed it with their eyes. But when I proceeded farther, and, relying on the same fundamental principles, paused in the consideration of Physical things, first of all by attending to the ideas or notions of each separate thing which I found within me, and by distinguishing the one carefully from the other, in order that all my judgments might harmonize with them, I observed that nothing at all belonged to the nature or essence[2] of body, except

[1] F. V. notiorem, L. V.   [2] F. V. rationem, L. V.

that it was a thing with length, breadth, and depth, admitting of various shapes and various motions. I found also that its shapes and motions were only modes, which no power could make to exist apart from it; and on the other hand that colours, odours, savours, and the rest of such things, were merely sensations existing in my thought, and differing no less from bodies than pain differs from the shape and motion of the instrument which inflicts it. Finally I saw that gravity, hardness, the power of heating, of attracting, and of purging, and all other qualities which we experience in bodies, consisted solely in motion or its absence, and in the configuration and situation of their parts.

But since these opinions differed very greatly from the beliefs which I had previously possessed respecting the same things, I began to reflect as to what had caused me to believe otherwise before; and the chief reason I noticed to be that from infancy I had passed various judgments about physical things, for example, judgments[1] which contributed much to the preservation of the life which I was then entering; and I had afterwards retained the same opinions which I had before conceived touching these things. But since at that age the mind did not employ the corporeal organs properly and, remaining firmly attached to these, had no thoughts apart from them, it perceived things only confusedly; and although it was conscious of its own proper nature, and possessed an idea of thought as well as of extension, nevertheless, having no intellectual knowledge, though at the same time it had an imagination of something, it took them both to be one and the same, and referred all its notions of intellectual matters to the body. Finally, since during the rest of my life I had never freed myself from these prejudices, there was nothing which I knew with sufficient distinctness, and nothing which I did not assume to be corporeal; even though the ideas of those things which I supposed to be corporeal were formed and conceived in such a way as to refer to minds rather than to bodies.

For since I conceived gravity, for example, in the fashion of a real quality of a certain order, which inhered in solid bodies, although I called it *a quality*, in so far as I referred it to the bodies in which it inhered, yet because I added the epithet *real*, I thought in truth that it was a substance; just as clothing regarded by itself is a substance, although when referred to the man whom it clothes it is a quality. Similarly the mind, though as a matter of fact a

[1] *Or* 'about things,' so F. V.

substance, can be styled the quality of the body to which it is conjoined. And although I imagined that gravity was diffused throughout the whole of the body possessing weight, nevertheless I did not ascribe to it that very extension which constituted the nature of the body; for true bodily extension is of such a nature as to prevent any interpenetration of parts. At the same time I believed that there was as much gravity in a man of gold or of some other metal a foot long, as in a piece of wood ten feet long; nay I believed that it was all contracted within a mathematical point. In fact I also saw that while it remained coextensive with the heavy body, it could exercise its force at any point of the body, because whatever the part might be to which a rope was attached, it pulled the rope with all its weight, exactly as if the gravity resided in the part alone which the rope touched and was not diffused through the others. Indeed it is in no other way that I now understand mind to be coextensive with the body, the whole in the whole, and the whole in any of its parts. But the chief sign that my idea of gravity was derived from that which I had of the mind, is that I thought that gravity carried bodies toward the centre of the earth as if it contained some knowledge of this centre within it. For it could not act as it did without knowledge, nor can there be any knowledge except in the mind. At the same time I attributed also to gravity certain things which cannot be understood to apply to mind in the same sense; as e.g. that it was divisible, measurable, etc.

But after I had noted these things with sufficient care, and had accurately distinguished the idea of mind from the ideas of body and corporeal movement, and had discovered that all my previous ideas of real qualities or substantial forms had been composed or manufactured by me out of the former set of ideas, I easily released myself from all the doubts that are here advanced. For firstly I had no doubt that I possessed *a clear idea of my own mind*[1], of which naturally I had the most intimate knowledge[2], nor could I doubt that *that idea was wholly diverse from the idea of other things, and contained within it no element of corporeity.* For since I had sought to find out the true ideas of all other things as well and seemed to have a general acquaintance with all of them, I found nothing in them which was not wholly different from the idea of the mind. And I saw that there was a much greater

---

[1] *Soul* in Appendix (1), above, p. 239.
[2] F. V. adds 'since it was constantly present to and bound up with me.

distinction between those which, though I thought of each atten-tively[1], appeared none the less distinct on that account, such as mind and body, than between those, in the case of which, though we can understand the one without thinking of the other, we do not see that the one can exist without the other, when we think of each. Thus certainly God's immensity can be understood, though we do not attend to His justice ; but it is wholly contradictory that when we attend to either we should think that God is great without being just. It is possible also rightly to apprehend God's existence, without having knowledge of the persons of the holy Trinity, which indeed a mind illumined by faith can alone perceive; yet when they are once recognized, I deny that there can be discerned between them a real distinction in respect of the divine essence, whatever be admitted to prevail in respect of their relation to one another.

Finally I had no fear lest, preoccupied with my Analysis, I might perhaps have been led astray when, seeing that *there are certain bodies which do not think*[2], or rather clearly understanding that certain bodies can exist without thought, I preferred to conclude that thought did not belong to the nature of the body, rather than to infer from my observing that *certain other bodies, e.g. human bodies, do think*, that thought was a mode of body. For, in truth, I have never seen or perceived that human bodies think, but only that they are the same men who possess both thought and a body. And I clearly saw that this fact must be due to the compounding of a thinking with a corporeal thing, because when I examined the thinking thing separately I found nothing in it belonging to the body, just as neither could I discover anything of the nature of thought in corporeal nature separately considered. But, on the other hand, when I examined all the modes of body and of mind alike, I perceived none at all the concept of which did not depend on the concept of the thing of which it was a mode. Likewise, from the fact that we often perceive two things conjoined, it is not permissible to conclude that they are one and the same thing ; but from the fact that we sometimes notice one of them apart from the other, it is highly proper to infer that they are diverse. Neither should the power of God deter us from drawing this conclusion, because it is not less conceptually repugnant that those things which we clearly perceive to be twain and diverse should be intrinsically and apart from all

[1] 'at the same time,' F. V.   [2] p. 240, *ad init.*

composition one and the same, than that those which are in no way distinct should be dissevered. Consequently if God has implanted in certain bodies the power of thinking (as He really has in the case of human bodies), this very power can be separated from them, and thus it is none the less really distinct from them.

Neither do I marvel that formerly, before I had liberated myself from the prejudices of the senses, I rightly perceived *that two and three make five, that if equals be taken from equals the remainders are equal*[1], and many similar things, when nevertheless I did not think *that the soul of man was distinct from his body*. For it is easy to see that the reason why, when a mere infant, I made no mistake respecting these propositions which all equally admit, was that I, like all other children, was not accustomed to count two and three, before the capacity for judging that they make five had developed. On the other hand from my earliest years I conceived mind and body as a sort of unity (noticing in a confused way that I was compounded out of them); and this occurs practically in all imperfect knowledge, viz. that many things are apprehended as a unity, which afterwards a more careful scrutiny shows to be distinct.

But I do marvel greatly that learned men, *accustomed to the study of Metaphysics for thirty years*[2], after reading my Meditations *seven times over*, should think *that if I re-read them in the same spirit of critical analysis with which I should treat them if they had been brought forward by an opponent, I should not believe that the arguments therein contained were of such weight and power, as to compel assent on the part of all*, though meanwhile they themselves can point to no flaw in my reasonings. Indeed they do me more honour than I deserve or than should be paid to any man, in thinking that I employ an Analysis by the aid of which either true demonstrations are overthrown, or false ones so cloaked and embellished as to be incapable of refutation by anyone. On the contrary I announce that I have only sought to discover a method for detecting the certitude of true and the error of false arguments. Hence it is not the fact that men of learning do not yet assent to my conclusions which moves me, so much as that after attentive and frequent reading of my arguments, they can point to nothing in them that is either wrongly assumed or incorrectly reasoned. For their difficulty in admitting the conclusions can be ascribed to their inveterate habit of thinking otherwise about these matters;

---

[1] Above, p. 240, par. 2.　　　[2] *Ibid.*

thus their case would be similar to that of the Astronomers above mentioned, who had a difficulty in imagining that the Sun was greater than the Earth, although that fact was proved by the strictest reasoning. But I do not see that there can be any reason why neither they nor any others, to my knowledge, have up to this time found no error in my reasonings, except that these are wholly true and certain; especially since they are derived from no obscure or unknown principles, but are deduced step by step from, to begin with, a complete doubt as to all things, and next from those truths which, to a mind set free from prejudice, seem most evident and most certain of all. For hence it follows that no flaws at all can exist in them that would not be easily noticed by anyone of average ability. Hence I think that I have a right to conclude not so much that my doctrines are invalidated by the authority of these men of great learning, though after a repeated perusal of my writings they have not yet succeeded in gaining their assent, as that on the contrary, their authority strengthens my position, since after so much accurate scrutiny they have noted no errors or fallacies in my proofs.

THE END.

THE SEVENTH SET OF OBJECTIONS WITH THE AUTHOR'S ANNOTATIONS THEREON, OTHERWISE A DISSERTATION CONCERNING FIRST PHILOSOPHY.

My dear Sir[1],

You set me many questions concerning the new method of investigating the truth, and you not only require me to answer but insistently urge me to reply. Nevertheless I shall keep my own counsel and decline to do you this favour, unless you first concede me something. In this dissertation let me wholly leave out of sight those who have written or said aught about this subject. To this I join the request that you would so construct your interrogations as not to seem to ask about what others have thought and with what mind and what issue they conceived their opinions, or whether these were true or not. Let us imagine that no one has had anything to say, write, or think about those matters, and investigate only the things that your meditations and inquiry into a new method of philosophizing, will show you to be subjects of difficulty. This will enable us both to discuss the truth and to discuss it in a way that will allow us to observe the laws of that friendship and respect which ought to be shown towards learned men. Since you consent and promise to observe this, I also shall respond to your compliance. Therefore

ANNOTATIONS.

You set me many questions. Since I received this dissertation from its author after I had imperatively demanded that the comments I heard he had written on my *Meditations concerning First Philosophy* 'should either be openly published or at least sent to me, in order that I might put them along with the remaining

[1] vir clarissime.

objections to the same Meditations that others had made,' I could not do otherwise than put it along with them here. Nor also could I doubt that I am the person whom he here addresses, though really I do not remember of ever having asked him what he thought *of my method of investigating the truth.* On the contrary, having a year and a half ago seen a certain Attack of his upon me, wherein I judged there was no attempt to discover the truth, while things which I had neither written nor thought were fathered upon me, I made no concealment of the fact that in future I should regard anything that came from him alone as unworthy of a reply. But because this writer is a member of a Society[1] famous on account of its learning and piety, and all who belong to it are in such close union with one another that it is unusual for one member to do anything of which all the others do not approve, I admit that I not only demanded but urgently insisted, that some members of that Society should examine my writings and should think fit to point out to me whatever in them was alien to the truth. I appended many reasons on account of which I hoped that they would not refuse me this request. I said that, hoping for this, 'I should value very highly anything written in future either by this author or by any other member of the same Society, concerning my opinions. I likewise should not doubt that, whatsoever was the name of the man credited with its composition, this work would come from the hands not of that one man alone, but of several of the most learned and most sagacious members of the Society, and that consequently it would contain no cavilling, no sophistry, no abuse, and no empty verbiage, but only the strongest and most irrefutable reasoning. I doubted not that no argument which could legitimately be brought against me would be omitted; so that thus their efforts alone would, I trusted, free me from all my errors, and if anything I had published was not refuted in their reply, I should believe that it was incapable of being refuted by anyone, but was wholly true and certain.' Therefore I should hold the above opinions about the present dissertation, and should believe that it was written by order of the whole Society, if I was sure that it contained no cavilling, no sophistry, no abuse, and no empty verbiage. But if the opposite is the case, I certainly believe it to be a crime to attribute it to men of such sanctity. And since I do not trust my own judgment in this matter I shall state my opinion here with frankness and candour,

[1] The Jesuits.

not expecting the reader by any means to believe what I say, but merely to give him an opportunity of investigating the truth.

Nevertheless I shall keep my own counsel etc. Here my critic declares that he will assail no one's writing, but will merely reply to my questions. But the truth is that I have never asked him any question; indeed I have never spoken to the man nor even seen him. The questions which he pretends I asked, he has constructed for the most part out of expressions which occur in my Meditations; and thus it is quite evident that it is precisely those Meditations which he attacks. Now it is possible that he has reputable and pious motives for pretending that the opposite is the case; but if that is not so I cannot help suspecting that he hopes by this means to be freer to impute things to me, because nothing in what I have written can convict him of falsehood if he professes that it is not these he attacks. Besides it looks as if he wishes to avoid giving his readers an opportunity of reading my work; for to talk of my book would be to put them in the way of reading it. Again it appears that he wishes to describe me as being so futile and ignorant that the reader will turn away from anything which at any time comes from my pen. He thus tries to make a mask for me clumsily pieced together out of fragments of my Meditations, not for the purpose of hiding my features but of rendering them uncomely. I, however, now strip it off and cast it from me, both because I am not accustomed to dramatic acting with its masks[1], and because the methods of the play-house are hardly in keeping here, where I am engaged on discussing a very serious question with a man who follows the religious life.

QUESTION FIRST.

WHETHER AND HOW DOUBTFUL MATTERS ARE TO BE TREATED AS THOUGH THEY WERE FALSE.

You ask me first whether that law for investigating the truth is valid[2]; that everything in which there is the minimum of dubiety is to be treated as though it were false.

If I am to reply, I must first put several questions to you:

1. *What is that* minimum of dubiety *you mention?*
2. *What is* to treat a thing as though it were false?
3. *In what respect is it* to be treated as though it were false?

---

[1] Histrioniae. D. refers to the classical drama.

[2] legitima.

§1. What is the Minimum of Doubt?

In respect of doubt, what is that Minimum *you mention? You say, 'I will not detain you long. That is to some extent doubtful, about which I may doubt whether it is so or otherwise, not rashly indeed, but for valid reasons. Besides that is to some extent doubtful, concerning which, in spite of its seeming clear to me, I may be deceived by some evil Spirit[1], who wishes to make sport of me, employing his devices and sleight of hand to make that which is really false appear to be true and clear. The degree of doubtfulness in the first class of dubious matters is not slight; while the second does contain some dubiety, and though it is the minimum of doubt, it is enough not only to allow us to call the matter doubtful but to make it really so. Do you wish for an illustration? That earth, sky, and colour exist; that you have head, or eyes, or body or mind, are matters of dubiety falling within the first class of the doubtful. To the second belong such statements as: 2 and 3 make 5; the whole is greater than its part; and the like.'*

All very well. But if this is the case, tell me, pray, what there is wholly exempt from doubt? What is immune from the fear with which that subtle rascally Spirit threatens us? 'Nothing,' *you say,* 'absolutely nothing, until we have proved with certainty and from the most impregnable metaphysical principles that God exists and cannot deceive us. Consequently we get this unique law:* if I do not know whether God exists, and, if he exists, whether he may be a deceiver, I clearly am incapable of ever being sure about anything else. *But, to show you thoroughly what I mean, I should point out that unless I have first known that God exists, and is a veracious God who will restrain that evil spirit, I shall have occasion and indeed will be bound always to fear that it is making sport of me and is imposing the false upon me, in the guise of the truth, as clear and certain. But when I thoroughly understand that God exists and can neither be deceived nor deceive, and so must of necessity prevent that Spirit imposing on me in matters that I understand clearly and distinctly, then if there are any such, if I perceive anything clearly and distinctly, I shall say that these are true, are certain, so that then the following will be the law of truth and certainty:* Everything is true which I perceive very clearly and distinctly.' *I have no further question to ask here, but pass to the second point, viz.*

[1] malo Genio.

§ 2. What is meant by Treating a Thing as though it were False?

Now since it is doubtful whether you possess eyes, head, or body, and consequently must treat those beliefs as though they were false, I should like to know what you mean by that. Does it consist in saying and believing 'it is false that I have eyes, head, or body,' or in believing and with a general reversal of all my opinions, *saying, 'I do not have either eyes or head or body?' To be succinct, does it consist in believing, saying, and affirming the opposite of what is doubtful? 'Exactly so' you reply. All very well. But kindly reply further. It is not certain that 2 and 3 make 5. Shall I then believe and affirm '2 and 3 do not make 5?' 'Believe it and affirm it,' you reply. I go further. It is not certain that while I speak I am waking and not dreaming. Shall I then believe and affirm: 'thus while I speak I am not awake but am dreaming?' 'Believe it and say it,' is your response. Not to weary you, I shall conclude by bringing up the following question. It is not certain that what appears clear and certain to the man who doubts whether he is waking or dreaming, is really clear and certain. Shall I therefore believe and say: 'that which appears clear and certain to a man who doubts whether he is waking or dreaming, is not clear and certain but obscure and false?' Why do you hesitate? You* cannot indulge your diffidence more than is fair. *Have you never had the experience which many have had, viz. of seeming to see many things while asleep that appeared clear and certain, but which afterwards are discovered to be doubtful, nay false?* It is indeed prudent never at all to trust those who have even once deceived you. *But you say, 'it is altogether different with matters of the highest certainty. They are such that they cannot appear doubtful either to one who dreams or to a madman.' But, my dear sir, are you speaking seriously when you give out that matters of the highest certainty cannot appear doubtful even to dreamers or to madmen? What sort of things can they be? If people when asleep, or the insane sometimes think things to be certain which are ridiculous and extravagant, may they not believe matters of certainty, even of the highest certainty, to be false and doubtful? I knew a man who once, when falling asleep, heard the clock strike four, and counted the strokes thus—one, one, one, one. Then because he fancied in his mind that this was absurd he shouted out 'Ho! Ho! the clock is going mad. It has struck one o'clock four times!' Really is there anything too absurd and irrational to come into the mind of one who is dreaming or in a delirium? What will a dreamer not believe? Of what will he not approve, and plume himself about it as though it were a magnificent discovery of his own? But not to carry our conflict into other matters, let us take your statement:* What appears certain to a man who is in doubt whether he is dreaming or awake, is certain, and so certain that it can be laid down as the basis of a science and a metaphysic of the highest certainty and accuracy. *Now you have certainly failed to persuade me that this dictum is as certain as that other:* '2 and 3 make 5,' *and at least not so certain that no one can doubt it at all, nor can be deceived in it by some evil Spirit; nor do I fear that if I persist in thinking so, anyone will think my conduct obstinate. Therefore one of two alternative conclusions results. Either in accordance with your principle it is not certain that what appears to be certain to a man who doubts whether he is awake or dreaming, is certain; and consequently what appears to be certain to a man who doubts whether he is awake or dreaming, may and ought to be considered as false and as wholly false. Or else, if you have any other principle peculiar to yourself you will communicate it to me. I now come to my third question, and*

§ 3.　To what Extent is a Thing to be treated as False?

I ask, since it seems not to be certain that 2 and 3 make 5, and since the principle previously quoted obliges us to believe and say 2 and 3 do not make 5, ought I to believe this continuously to the extent of persuading myself that it cannot be otherwise than so, and that that is certain? You are astonished at my question. It does not seem strange to me, since I myself am astonished. Yet reply you must, if you are to get an answer from me. Do you wish to have it a certainty that 2 and 3 do not make 5? Nay do you wish that to be, and to seem to all, so certain as to be safe from the wiles of an evil spirit?

You laugh, and say: 'How did that ever come into a sane man's head?'

What then? Is it to be doubtful and uncertain, just in the same way as the statement—2 and 3 make 5? If this is so, and the statement—2 and 3 do not make 5, is doubtful, I shall believe, and in accordance with your principle assert, that it is false. Consequently I shall affirm the opposite and assert:—2 and 3 do make 5. I shall accord the same treatment to the remaining objects of doubt and, since it does not seem to be certain that any body exists, I shall say: no body exists. *Then because that statement,* no body exists, *is not certain, I shall state, my attitude being completely reversed,* some body does exist. *Thus body will at the same time exist and not exist.*

That is so, you say. This is what it is to doubt, viz. to move in a circle, to advance and retire, to affirm a thing and to deny it, to screw up and unscrew the peg.

That is quite splendid. But what am I to do in the matter of using those statements that are dubious? Take the case, 2 and 3 make 5; *or that other,* some body exists. *Shall I affirm them or deny them?*

You say you will neither affirm them nor deny them. You will employ neither, and will regard both their affirmation and their denial as false; you will look for nothing from those who so assent, except an assent to this also as a matter of doubt and uncertainty.

Since there is nothing more for me to ask, I shall reply in my turn, employing however a short epitome of your doctrine, which is as follows.

1. *It is possible for us to be in doubt about all things, and especially about material things, so long as we have no other foundation for the sciences than those on which we have hitherto relied.*

2. *To treat anything as false is to withhold your assent from it as though it were openly false and, altering our attitude to its direct opposite, to assume an opinion which represents it as false and imaginary.*

3. *That which is doubtful is to be treated as though it were false in such a way that its opposite also is doubtful, and we have to consider it too as false.*

ANNOTATIONS.

I should be ashamed to be too diligent and spend many words in commenting on all the things which, though here expressed in words almost identical with mine, I nevertheless do not recognize as mine. I merely ask my readers to recall what I said in Meditation I, and at the beginning of II and III, and in the synopsis of these Meditations. For they will acknowledge that almost everything here set down, though drawn from these sources, is so perverted, distorted and wrongly interpreted that, although in their right place they contain nothing that is not highly rational, here, nevertheless they seem to be extremely absurd.

For valid reasons[1]. I said at the end of Meditation I that
everything which I had not yet comprehended with sufficient clearness could be doubted by us, provided we did so for 'reasons that
were very powerful and maturely considered.' But I did so because
there the question was about only that supreme kind of doubt which,
I have insisted, is metaphysical, hyperbolical and not to be transferred to the sphere of the practical needs of life by any means. It
was of this doubt also that I said the very least ground of suspicion
was a sufficient reason for causing it. But my critic in his friendly
and frank way brings forward as an example of the things of which I
said we might doubt 'for valid reasons' the questions whether the
earth exists, or whether I have a body, in order that the readers,
who know nothing of this metaphysical doubt, referring it to the
practical life, may think that I am out of my mind.

Nothing, you say, absolutely nothing[2]. I have sufficiently explained in various places the sense in which that *nothing* ought to
be understood. So, for example, that as long as we attend to some
truth which we perceive very clearly, we cannot indeed doubt it.
But when, as often happens, we do not attend to any truth in this
way, although we remember that we have often known such truths
quite well, there is none, nevertheless, of which we may not rightly
doubt if we are unaware of the fact that everything we perceive
clearly is true. Here, however, my friend with great accuracy
interprets my *nothing* in such a way that, from the fact that once,
to wit in Meditation I, I said there was nothing of which we might
not doubt, assuming there that I was not attending to anything
which I clearly perceived, he infers that in the following Meditations
also I can be sure of nothing. This is to imply that the arguments
which for a time cause us to doubt any matter, have no legitimacy
or validity unless they prove that the matter must always be in
doubt.

To believe, to say, to affirm the opposite of what is doubtful[3].
When I said that doubtful matters should sometimes be treated as
though they were false, or rejected as if they were false, I clearly
explained that I merely meant that, for the purpose of investigating
the truths that are metaphysically certain, we should pay no more
credence to doubtful matters than to what is plainly false. Thus
surely no sane man can interpret my words otherwise, or attribute
to me the opinion of wishing to believe the opposite of what is
doubtful, especially, as the matter is subsequently put, *of believing*

[1] Cf. above, p. 262, l. 4.　　　[2] Cf. p. 262, par. 2.　　　[3] Cp. p. 263, l. 8.

it to the extent of persuading myself that it cannot be otherwise than thus, and that that is certain[1]. At least only a man who is not ashamed of being a caviller could do such a thing. And although my critic does not actually affirm this interpretation of my words, but merely puts it forward tentatively, I am surprised that a man of his holiness should in this respect copy the basest detractors, who often take this method of giving utterance to the opinion which they wish to be entertained about others, adding that they themselves do not believe it, so that, having stated the calumny, they may get off scot free.

It is altogether different with matters of the highest certainty. They are such that they cannot appear doubtful either to one who dreams or to a madman[2]. I cannot tell by what Analysis my subtlest of critics is able to extract this from my words. It would indeed have been possible to infer from what I have said that everything which anyone clearly and distinctly perceives is true, although that person in the meantime may doubt whether he is dreaming or awake, nay, if you want it so, even though he is really dreaming or is delirious. This is for the reason that nothing whatsoever can be clearly and distinctly perceived, whoever be the person perceiving it, that it is not perceived to be such as it is, i.e. which is not true. But because it is the wise[3] alone who know how to distinguish rightly between what is so perceived, and what merely seems or appears to be clear and distinct, I am not surprised that our good friend mistakes the one for the other.

This is what it is to doubt, viz. to move in a circle etc.[4] I said that we ought to pay no more credence to things that are doubtful than if they were false, in order that we may wholly dismiss them from mind and not in order to affirm now one thing, now its opposite. My critic, however, leaves no opportunity for cavilling untried. But meanwhile it is worth noting that he himself at the end, where he says he makes a brief epitome of my doctrine, attributes to me none of those opinions which either previously or in the sequel he attacks and holds up to scorn. Doubtless this is to let us know that he was only jesting when he concocted them and ascribed them to me, and did not seriously believe that I entertained them.

---

[1] Cf. p. 264, par. 2.   [2] Cf. p. 263.
[3] prudentes.   [4] Cf. p. 265, par. 2.

REPLY.

Reply 1. *Assume the meaning of the law, ' in the investigation of the truth that which is to the slightest extent doubtful is to be treated as though it were false,' to be : ' when we are investigating matters that are certain, we ought not to rely on anything which is not certain or is to the slightest extent doubtful.' In this case your law is quite sound, is of established usage, and one of the best known truths common to all Philosophers.*

Reply 2. *If the said law is understood to mean the following : ' when we investigate matters that are certain, we ought to reject everything that is not certain, or is in any way doubtful, and make no use of such matters at all, to the extent of treating them as though they were non-existent, or rather not taking them into account at all, but rather dismissing them wholly from mind' : in this case again your law is quite sound, valid and a common place with beginners. It is, in fact, so like the preceding version of it as to be hardly distinguishable from it.*

Reply 3. *Suppose the law next to be taken in the following way : ' when we investigate matters that are certain, we ought to reject everything that is doubtful and affirm that the asserted fact does not exist, but that its opposite really holds ; and we ought to take this latter statement as a secure foundation for our argument, or to put it otherwise, make use of the assumption that the matters doubted do not exist, or base our argument upon their non-existence.' Now in this case the law is invalid, fallacious, and in conflict with sound Philosophy. For it assumes something doubtful and uncertain for the purpose of investigating what is true and certain. To express the matter differently, it assumes as certain something that may be wholly otherwise than as we suppose it to be ; to wit, we treat doubtful things as though they did not exist, whereas it is quite possible that they do exist.*

Reply 4. *If a man were to understand that law as last expressed and employ it in his investigation of matters that are true and certain, he would expend all his toil and trouble and labour to no profit since, like anyone else who did so, he would achieve the opposite of his quest quite as much as his object itself. Do you want an illustration ? Suppose a man were to enquire whether he were a body or were corporeal, and to that intent made use of the following statements :—* ' *it is not certain that any body exists ; therefore in accordance with the law just approved, I shall affirm and say—no body exists.*' *Then he will resume: 'no body exists; but I am, and exist, as I have quite properly ascertained from other sources: therefore I cannot be a body.' Very fine indeed; but look and see how the same beginning will lead to the opposite conclusion. 'It is not certain,' he says, 'that any body exists; therefore, in accordance with the law, I shall affirm and assert that no body exists.' But what sort of a statement is that? No body exists? That is certainly doubtful and uncertain. Who can make it good? Whence will he draw his proof? His proof is merely fictitious. 'No body exists' is really a doubtful statement; therefore in accordance with your law I shall say: 'some body does exist.' But I am and exist; therefore possibly I am a body, if there is no reason for believing otherwise. Look at our result:—possibly I am body and it is impossible for me to be a body. Is that enough for you? But I fear that I have done quite as much as I obtain in the following questions. Therefore*[1]

ANNOTATIONS.

Here in his first two replies my critic has approved of everything which I laid down concerning the subject under discussion, or that can be elicited from my writings. But he adds that it is *quite common property, a common place of philosophers.* Yet in his two latter replies he censures the opinion which he wishes people to believe held, though that is so absurd as to be incapable of entering the mind of a sane man. But it is very astute of him to do so, meaning as he does to influence by his authority those who have not read my Meditations or have not read them attentively enough to understand properly what is in them. Thus they will think that my opinions are ridiculous, while others who do not believe this will at least be persuaded that I have adduced nothing that is not *quite common property and a common place of beginners.* True I do not dispute this last statement. I have never sought to derive any praise from the novelty of my opinions. For, on the contrary, I believe them to be the most ancient of all beliefs, as being the truest. Further, it is my habit to study nothing so much as the scrutiny of certain very simple truths, which, being innate in our minds, are such that, when they are laid before anyone else, he believes that he has never been ignorant of them. But certainly it may easily be understood that my critic impugns my theories merely because he thinks them good and new. For if he believed them to be so absurd as he makes them out to be, he would surely

[1] Cf. Second Question, p. 271.

judge them worthy of contempt and silence, rather than of a long and factitious refutation.

Therefore in accordance with the law just approved, I shall affirm and say the opposite[1]. I should like to know where he has ever found this law promulgated. He has already laid quite enough stress upon it, but in the same passage I have already given a sufficient denial to my authorship of it, viz. in my annotations on the words : *To believe, say, and affirm the opposite of what is doubtful.* Nor do I believe that he will go on maintaining that it is mine if he is questioned about the matter. He introduced me above in paragraph 3, as speaking about doubtful matters in the following terms : *You will neither affirm nor deny them, you will employ neither, and will regard both their affirmation and denial as false.* Shortly afterwards in his epitome of my doctrine his version is that we ought *to withhold our assent from the doubtful as though it were openly false, and, altering our attitude to its direct opposite, assume an opinion which represents it as being false and imaginary*[2]. Now this is plainly something quite different from *affirming and saying the opposite*, in such a way as to treat that opposite as true in the way he here supposes I do. Further when I, in Meditation I, said that I sometimes tried to convince myself of the opposite of the belief that I had formerly rashly held, I immediately added that I wished to do so in order to balance the weight of my prejudices equally on both sides and not be inclined towards one rather than the other. But I made it clear that it was not my intention to regard either as true or to set that up as the foundation of our most certain knowledge, as is unfairly represented elsewhere by my critic. Therefore I should like to know what his intention was in bringing up this law of his framing. If it is for the purpose of ascribing it fictitiously to me, I mark a lack of candour on his part; for it is clear from what he has said that he knows well enough that it is not any law of mine, because no one could believe that both alternatives ought to be considered false, as he said was my opinion, and at the same time affirm and allege that the opposite of one of them was true, as his version of the law has it. But if he adduced this law merely to show animus, in order that he might have some means of attacking me, I nevertheless wonder at the acumen of his intellect, that has been able to excogitate nothing more plausible or subtle. I marvel that he has had leisure to expend so many words in refuting an opinion of an absurdity that would hardly impose even on a

[1] Cf. p. 268, *sub fin.*   [2] Cf. p. 265, par. 8.

child of seven years of age. For we must observe that up to the present time he has attacked nothing at all but this perfectly inept law of his own framing. Finally I marvel at the strength of his imagination, seeing that, waging war as he does merely upon that most unreal of chimaeras which he has evolved from his own brain, he has nevertheless adopted the same attitude and employed the same words, as if he had really had me as his opponent, and been face to face with me in the conflict.

SECOND QUESTION.

WHETHER IT IS A GOOD METHOD OF PHILOSOPHIZING TO SET ASIDE EVERYTHING THAT IS DOUBTFUL.

You ask, 2: whether it is a good method of philosophizing to set aside all matters that involve any doubt. Unless you disclose this method in some detail you need not expect an answer from me. However, you do this.

'*In order to philosophize,*' *you say,* '*in order to discover whether there be anything certain, and of the highest certainty, and what that is, this is my procedure. Since all is doubtful and uncertain, I treat everything which I have ever believed, or which I have previously known, as false, and I set all such things aside completely, and convince myself that neither earth nor sky nor any of the things I previously believed to be in the world exist; nay, not even the world itself, nor my body, nor mind, in a word nothing, I affirm, exists. Then having made this general renunciation, and having protested that nothing exists, I plunge into my own philosophy and, led by its counsels I track out the true and certain cautiously and prudently, just as if there existed some very powerful and cunning Spirit who wanted to lead me into error. Wherefore, not to be deceived, I look around attentively and have quite determined on the plan of admitting nothing that is not of such a nature that, however much that scoundrelly Spirit strives to deceive me, he is quite unable to do so in this case, and even I myself cannot compel myself to conceal my knowledge of the fact or deny it. I reflect therefore, I revolve and revolve things in my thought until something of the kind sought may arrive, and when I have struck upon it, I use it (as Archimedes used his fulcrum) for eliciting other facts, and in this wise I derive one fact from another in a way that shows them to be wholly certain and well attested.*'

*That is very fine indeed, and so far as appearances go, I should
have no difficulty in replying that this method appears to me to be
both brilliant and distinguished. But because you expect a careful
reply, and I cannot give you that without first employing and
practising your method and so testing it, let us enter that well beaten
and safe road, and ourselves find out where it really leads to ; and
knowing as you do its meanderings, its defiles, and detours, and
having long exercised yourself in tracing them, I beg you to conduct
me through them yourself. Come, express your mind ; you have either
a comrade or a pupil with you to whom to show the way. What do
you bid me do ? Though it is new to me and, since I am not
accustomed to its obscurity, to be dreaded, I am quite willing to enter
that route, such a powerful attraction does the appearance of the
truth exercise over me. I hear your reply; you bid me do what I
see you do, plant my steps where you put yours. That is certainly
an excellent way of commanding and leading me ! How well you let
me think of you ! I am ready.*

§ 1.   The Disclosing of the Entry into the Method.

'*Firstly,*' you say, '*as I revolved previous truths in my mind,*
I feel constrained to confess that there is nothing in all that I
formerly believed to be true of which I cannot in some measure
doubt, and that, not just through want of thought or through levity,
but for reasons which are very powerful and maturely considered ;
so that henceforth I ought not the less carefully to refrain from
giving credence to these opinions than to that which is manifestly
false, if I desire to arrive at any certainty[1]. *Wherefore,* I shall not be
acting amiss, if, taking of set purpose a contrary belief, I outwit my
own self and pretend for a time that all those old opinions are entirely
false and imaginary, until at last, having thus balanced my former
prejudices with my latter, my judgment will no longer be dominated
by bad usage or turned away from the right knowledge of the truth[2].
Therefore let me suppose that some evil genius not less powerful
than deceitful has employed his whole energies in deceiving me.
I shall consider that the heavens, the earth, colours, figures, sounds
and all other material things are nothing but the illusions and
dreams of which this genius has availed himself in order to lay
traps for my credulity[3]. *I shall persuade myself that nothing at all
exists in the world, that there is no sky, no earth, that there are no*

---

[1] Cf. Med. pp. 147, *sub fin.*, 148, *ad init.*   [2] Cf. Med. p. 148, par. 2.
[3] Cf. Med. p. 148, par. 3.

minds, no bodies; (remember I say no minds, no bodies). This is the goal, and the principal goal. I shall consider myself as having no hands, no eyes, no flesh, no blood, nor any sense, yet as falsely believing myself to possess all these things. I shall remain obstinately attached to this idea[1].'

Here kindly pause a little, in order that we may collect a fresh supply of energy. The novelty of your proposal has not failed to move me somewhat. Do you bid me renounce every old belief?

You say, ' I bid you set aside everything.'

Everything? He who says ' everything,' leaves no room for exceptions.

You repeat, ' everything.'

Really I can with difficulty bring myself to do so, yet I shall obey. But it is exceedingly hard and, to speak frankly, I have a scruple in complying, a scruple which, if you do not relieve me from it, will I fear prevent our entry into the method from being so successful as we wish. You confess that you doubt all your old beliefs and, as you say, you are compelled to confess this. Why not permit the same force to bear on me that I also may be forced to admit it? Tell me what it is that compels you. True you have just now said that the reasons influencing you were valid and well considered. But what are they then? If they are valid, why set them aside? Why not retain them? If they are doubtful and replete with suspicion how can they have brought any force to bear upon you?

But you say, ' they are a mere preliminary; look and see. It is my wont to send them in front, like slingers, to begin the battle. For example, our senses sometimes deceive us; we sometimes dream; sometimes people go delirious and believe they see things which they do not see, and which exist nowhere.'

Have you finished speaking? When you promised me valid and well-considered reasons, I expected them to be certain and free from all doubt, such as are demanded by your tract which we are now employing, and rising to such a pitch of accuracy as to dispel the least suspicion of dubiety. But are the reasons you allege of this nature? Not mere doubts and nought but suspicious surmises? ' Our senses sometimes deceive us.' ' We sometimes dream.' ' People sometimes go delirious.' But whence do you derive all that with certainty and complete infallibility, and in accordance with that rule of yours which you have always in evidence?—' We must take the

[1] Cf. Med. p. 148, par. 3.

utmost pains not to admit anything as true which we cannot prove to be true?' *Has there been any time when you said to yourself with certainty: 'Now without doubt my senses are deceiving me, and of this I am quite aware'; 'Now I am dreaming'; 'I was dreaming a little time ago'; 'This man is suffering from a frenzy, and believes he sees things which he does not see, but yet is not lying'? If you say there ever was such a time, be sure you prove that; nay, satisfy yourself lest that evil Spirit you spoke of may perhaps have given you an illusion. It is greatly to be feared that when you now make the statement as something valid and well-considered, that rascal is making a mock of you, and is winking at the man he has hoodwinked. But, if you say that there was no such time, why so confidently assert: 'Sometimes we dream'? Why not in accordance with your first law determine to say: 'It is not quite certain that our senses sometimes deceive us, that we have sometimes dreamed, that men have sometimes gone delirious; therefore I shall assert and resolve upon the following: "Our senses never deceive us, we never dream, people never go delirious"'?*

But, you say, 'I suspect it.' Now this is my scruple. So far as I have proceeded I have found your arguments to be feeble, and like fleeting suspicions. Consequently I fear to press on. It is I now who am suspicious.

You reply: 'Suspect away. It is enough if you are suspicious. It is enough if you say: "I don't know whether I am awake or dreaming. I don't know whether my senses deceive me, or do not."'

I beg your pardon, but for me it is not enough. Nor do I at all see how you make the following inference: 'I don't know whether I am awake or dreaming': 'therefore I sometimes dream.' What if I never do? What if always? What if you cannot even dream, and that Spirit is convulsed with laughter because he has at length persuaded you that you sometimes dream and are deceived, while that is far from being the case? Trust me, from the time when you brought that Spirit on the stage, from the time when you subjected your valid and well-considered reasons to that 'perhaps,' you have raised an evil that has brought you no advantage. What if the sly fellow presents all these matters as doubtful and unstable, when they really are quite reliable, meaning thereby, after you have turned aside from them all, to lead you into the abyss? Would it not be more prudent, before you turn aside from them all, to propound some reliable law which will enable you to set aside what you do set aside without fear of error? The matter is certainly important, nay of

*the highest moment, that general renunciation of our old opinions
which you propose; and if you comply with my suggestions, you will
call your thoughts into council and seriously deliberate them.*

Nay, you say, 'I cannot yield too much to distrust,' *and*
'I know that there can be neither peril nor error in this course[1].'
What? 'I know'? *Is that certain and beyond all doubt?
And has our great shipwreck of truth left at least this driftwood
floating? Or is it the case that because you are opening a new
Philosophy and are thinking of the whole school, this has to be written
in golden letters on your portal:* 'I cannot indulge my incredulity
too much.' *Is it the consequence that the entrants into your temple
are bidden to lay aside their ancient belief that* '2 and 3 make 5,'
but to retain this, 'I cannot indulge my incredulity too much'? *But
what will you say if a disciple chance to murmur at this; if he
cannot swallow the fact that he is bidden abandon the old belief
which everyone accepts, that* '2 and 3 make 5' *because an evil
Spirit may deceive him, while he is instructed to retain that doubtful
principle, full of flaws—*'I cannot indulge my incredulity too much'—
*as if in this case the evil Spirit could not impose upon him? But
will you substantiate this for me, so that I shall not be in fear, shall
have no apprehensions about that evil Spirit? Certainly though you
may try to strengthen my confidence in any way you please, it is not
without extreme fear of too great incredulity that I renounce all my
ancient and practically innate beliefs, and forswear as false—*'an
argument in* Barbara *has a valid conclusion.' And to judge by your
demeanour, not even you who offer yourself as a guide to others are
free from fear. Be frank and ingenuous as is your wont; do you
feel no scruple in giving up that ancient belief—*'I have a clear and
distinct idea of God'? *Do you readily renounce—*'Everything which
I perceive very clearly and distinctly is true'—*or—*'To think, to
grow, to feel, do not appertain at all to the body but to the mind'?
*But why should I go through the whole series of such statements?
My question regarding them is serious and I ask you kindly to reply.
Can you in thus parting with the old Philosophy and entering the
new, reject, divest yourself of, forswear these as false. I mean from
the heart? Do you assert and affirm the opposite:* 'now I do not
have a clear and distinct idea of God'; 'up to the present I have
been mistaken in believing that growth, thought and sensation did
not appertain to the body at all, but to the mind'? *But what have
I done? I have been forgetful of what I promised to do. I had*

---

[1] Cf. Med. i. p. 148, par. 2.

committed myself entirely to you at the beginning, had vowed myself your ally and disciple, and here I am hesitating at the very outset, timid and obstinate.   Pray forgive me !   I have sinned greatly and have merely shown the smallness of my intellectual capacity.   It was my duty to have laid aside all fear and to plunge boldly into the fog of renunciation ; but I have been unwilling and have resisted. If you spare me I shall make amends and quite wipe out my ill- deeds by a full and generous enfranchisement and remission of all my old beliefs.   I renounce, I forswear everything which I once held true.   Do not mind though I do not protest my belief in that sky or earth which you wish to do away with.   Nothing exists, absolutely nothing.   Go on and lead the way ; I shall follow.   You are certainly easy to follow !   So don't refuse to lead on.

ANNOTATIONS.

And it is all doubtful, everything I have previously known[1]. Here my critic has written *known* for *thought I knew.*   For there is an opposition between the words *I knew* and *is doubtful* which doubtless he has nevertheless failed to perceive.   Nor must we set his action down as malicious.   If that were so he would not have treated the matter so cursorily but would have pretended that the contradiction was one of my creating and would have made a long story of it.

Remember I say no minds, no bodies[2].   This is advanced in order to give an opportunity for much pettifogging argument afterwards, because at the outset, since I assumed that I did not yet fully comprehend the nature of the mind, I put it in the list of dubious matters.   But afterwards perceiving that the thing which thinks cannot fail to exist, and applying to that thinking thing the term mind, I said that mind exists.   Now this looks as though I had forgotten that I had first denied the same, when I took the mind to be something unknown to me.   It looks too as if I had thought that we must always deny the things which I then denied because they seemed to me doubtful, and that it was impossible I should ever compass the restoration of their certainty and evidence.   We must note too that throughout he treats doubtfulness and certainty not as relations of our thought to objects, but as properties of the objects and as inhering in them eternally.   The consequence is that nothing we have once learned to be doubtful can ever be rendered

[1] Cf. above, p. 271, par. 3.   [2] Cf. above, p. 273, *ad init.*

certain. But this must be attributed merely to his goodness of heart, not to spite.

Everything[1] *?* Here he is making play with the meaning of the word *everything* just as above he did with the word *nothing.* The argument is quite futile.

You are compelled to confess this[2]. Here again is an empty trifling with the word *compelled.* For we may well enough be compelled to doubt by arguments that are in themselves doubtful, and not to be afterwards retained, as we above noted. They are indeed valid so long as we do not possess any others to remove our doubt and introduce certainty. It was because I found none such during the course of Meditation I, however much I looked around and reflected, that I therefore said that my reasons for doubting were valid and well considered. But this exceeds my critic's comprehension. For he adds : *When you promised valid reasons I expected them to be certain and free from all doubt, such as are demanded by your tract*[3], as if the imaginary brochure which he has invented would be referred to the statements of the first Meditation. Shortly afterwards he says : *Has there been any time when you said to yourself with certainty:* '*Now without doubt my senses are deceiving me, and of this I am quite aware,' etc.*[4]*?* But he does not see that here again there is a contradiction, because something is held to be true without doubt, and at the same time the very same thing is doubted. What a man he is !

Why so confidently assert, 'sometimes we dream'? Here again he errs, but without evil intent. For I asserted nothing at all confidently in the first Meditation, which is full of doubt, and from which alone all these statements are drawn. He could in it find equally well : 'we never dream,' and 'we sometimes dream.' When shortly afterwards he adds : *Nor do I at all see how you make the following inference.* '*I don't know whether I am awake or dreaming; therefore I sometimes dream*[5]'; he ascribes to me a style of reasoning worthy only of himself, because he is so good-natured.

What if that sly fellow (the evil Spirit) *presents all these matters as doubtful and unstable when they really are quite reliable*[6]*?* Here it is clear, as I pointed out above, that he treats doubt and certainty as though they existed in the objects, not in our thought. Otherwise how could he pretend that I propounded something as

---

[1] Cf. p. 273. [2] Cf. p. 273, middle. [3] Cf. *ibid.* last par.
[4] Cf. p. 274, *ad init.* [5] Cf. p. 274, par. 3. [6] Cf. *ibid. sub fin.*

dubious which was not dubious but certain? Seeing that the only cause that makes a thing dubious is that it is propounded as dubious. But perhaps it was the evil Spirit that prevented him from seeing the contradiction in his words. It is to be regretted that this Spirit so often causes difficulties in our critic's thinking.

The matter is certainly important, nay of the highest moment, that general renunciation of our old opinions which you propose[1]. I pointed this out with quite enough emphasis at the end of my reply to the fourth set of objections, and in my preface to these Meditations, which I therefore presented only to those of robuster mental powers to read[2]. I already pointed the same thing out also in very express terms in my discourse on Method which appeared in French in 1637, pp. 16 and 17. Since I there described two kinds of mind, by both of which such a renunciation is to be strenuously avoided, my critic ought not to father his own errors on me if he chance to be included in either of these two classes.

What? '*I know*' etc.[3] When I said that I knew that I ran no risk in making that renunciation, I added: *because then, on that occasion, I was not considering the question of action, but only of knowledge*[4]. From this it is clearly evident that when I said ' I know ' I spoke only of the moral mode of knowing, which suffices for the regulation of life, and which I have often insisted is so vastly different from that Metaphysical mode of knowing which is here in question, that apparently no one but our critic could fail to recognize that.

That doubtful principle, full of flaws—I cannot indulge my incredulity too far[5]. Here again there is a contradiction in his words. For no one fails to recognize that a person who is incredulous and hence neither affirms nor denies anything, cannot be led into error even by any evil Spirit. But the example my critic adduces above, about the man who counted one o'clock four times, shows that a person adding 2 and 3 together can be deceived.

But it is not without extreme fear of too great incredulity that I renounce these old beliefs[6]. Though he is at great pains to prove that we ought not to distrust ourselves too much, it is nevertheless worthy of note that he does not bring the least scrap of argument to prove that, except that he fears or distrusts our need of distrusting ourselves. Here again then is a contradiction. For because he is fearful, but does not know for certainty that he

---

[1] Cf. p. 275, *ad init.*   [2] Med. vol. I. p. 139.   [3] Cf. above, p. 275.
[4] Cf. Med. p. 149.   [5] Cf. p. 275, middle.   [6] Cf. *ibid.*

ought not to distrust himself, it follows that he ought to distrust himself.

Do you feel no scruple in giving up that ancient belief, 'I have a clear and distinct idea of God'? Do you readily renounce, 'Everything which I very clearly perceive is true[1]*'?* He calls these ancient beliefs because he fears lest they may be regarded as new and as first perceived by me. But so far as I am concerned he may do so. He also wishes to suggest a scruple concerning God, though he does so only casually; perchance lest those who know how studiously I have excepted everything which pertains to piety and generally to morals from this renunciation, may think he is calumniating me. Finally he does not see that the renunciation affects only those who do not yet perceive anything clearly and distinctly. Thus for example the Sceptics with whom he is familiar, have never, in so far as they are Sceptics, perceived anything clearly. For owing to the mere fact of having perceived anything clearly they would have ceased to doubt and to be Sceptics. Further, because before making this renunciation scarcely any others perceive anything clearly, at least with that clearness required for metaphysical certainty, the renunciation is therefore very advantageous for those who are capable of such clear knowledge and who do not yet possess that. But as things show, it would not be thus beneficial to our author; indeed I believe that he ought carefully to refrain from it.

Whether 'To think, to grow, to feel do not belong to the body but to the mind[2] *is not to be set aside without hesitation'?* My critic reports these words as though they were mine, and at the same time as though they were so certain as to be incapable of being doubted by anyone. But nothing is more noteworthy than that in my Meditations I ascribe nutrition wholly to the body, not to the mind or that part of man which thinks. Thus it is proved by this fact alone, firstly that he wholly fails to understand my Meditations though he has undertaken to refute them, and that he falsifies matters, because it was when I was quoting popular opinion that I referred growth and nutrition to the soul. Next he shows that he himself holds many beliefs as indubitable which are not to be admitted without examination. But finally he comes to the complete truth of the matter, when he concludes that in these things *he has merely shown the smallness of his intellectual capacity*[3].

---

[1] Cf. p. 275.   [2] Cf. *ibid. sub fin.*   [3] Cf. p. 276.

THE ACTUAL ENTRY INTO THE METHOD.

You say, 'after setting aside everything old I begin to philoso-
phize thus. I am, I think ; I am, as long as I think. This
assertion, " I exist," is necessarily true each time that I pronounce
it, or that I mentally conceive it[1].'

Splendid, my good friend! You have found the point which
Archimedes wanted to discover ; there is no doubt that, if you so
please, you will be able to move the world ; look, now it all begins
to sway and tremble. But I beg you (for I have no doubt you wish
to prune things down, so that there shall be nothing in your Method
which is not apt, coherent and necessary) say why you have
mentioned the mind, when you say it is mentally conceived[2]? *Did*
you not order the banishment of mind and body? But perhaps it
was by chance that you let this pass: it is so difficult even for an
expert to forget altogether the things to which we have been
accustomed since childhood, that it may be easily thought that a
slip on the part of a raw hand like me if it chance to occur, is
hardly likely to be thought ill of. But go on, I entreat you.

You say, 'I shall consider what I am, and what I formerly
believed myself to be, before I embarked upon these last reflections.
I shall withdraw all that might even in the slightest extent be
invalidated by the reasons which I have just brought forward, in
order that there may be nothing at all left beyond what is absolutely
certain and indubitable[3].

Shall I dare, before you push inwards, to ask why you, the man
who has abandoned with such solemn declarations all your old beliefs
as dubious and false, want to inspect them again, as if you hoped to
get something good out of these rags and tatters. What if once you
thought ill of yourself? Nay, since everything you forswore a little
time ago was dubious and uncertain (otherwise why did you set it
aside?), how does it come about that the same things are now not
dubious and uncertain? Unless, perchance, that renunciation you
made was like Circe's drug, to call a potion of forgetfulness by
another name. Yet it is an evil thing both to suspect your counsel
and to regard it as sound. It is often the case that people who
bring their friends into palaces and public halls to show them the
sights enter by a private side-door not by the official and public
entrance. I shall follow even by subterranean passages if I have
hopes of arriving some time at the truth.

[1] Cf. Med. II. vol. I. p. 150, par. 1.   [2] *Ibid.*   [3] Cf. *ibid.* par. 2.

You say, 'What then did I formerly believe myself to be?
A man undoubtedly[1].'

*Here again suffer me to admire the devices you employ, you who,
in order to investigate the certain, employ the doubtful; who in order
to bring us into that light bid us plunge into darkness. Do you
want me to take heed of what I formerly believed myself to be? Do
you wish me to pick up again that clouted coat, old and worn as it
is and long since set aside,* 'I am a man'? *Suppose that we were
to have among us here Pythagoras or one of his disciples. He might
tell you that he had been a barn-door fowl. I don't need to accentuate
this objection by instancing madmen, fanatics, or delirious and
frenzied people. But you are experienced, an expert guide. You
know all the twists and turnings of the argument and I shall keep
up heart.*

Your next words are, 'What is man?'

*If you want me to reply, permit me first to ask: which man is
it about whom you are enquiring? What do you enquire about
when you ask what is man? Do you mean that man which once
I falsely fancied I was, which I believed myself to be, and whom,
ever since, thanks to you, I made my renunciation, I have affirmed
I am not? If it is this man, the man of whom I formed such an
erroneous conception, he is a certain compound of soul and body.
Have I done enough? I believe so, because you continue as follows.*

ANNOTATIONS.

*I thus begin philosophizing: I am, I think. I am, so long as
I think.* Note that my critic here admits that the beginning of
philosophizing or of the firm establishment of any proposition has
been based by me on my knowledge of my own existence. This
lets us see that, when in other places he has pretended that I based
it on the positive or affirmative renunciation of all doubtful beliefs,
he has asserted the contrary of what he really believed. I need
not mention further how subtly he introduces me at the commencement of my philosophical labours, with 'I am, I think' etc.
For even though I say nothing his candour will be in all cases
quite apparent.

Why did you mention the mind, when saying 'is mentally
conceived'? *Did you not order the banishment of mind and body?*
I have already said that it is the word *mind* which supplies him
with this puzzle. But *is mentally conceived* means merely *is thought;*

[1] Cf. Med. p. 150, par. 3.

hence he is quite wrong in assuming that *mind* is mentioned in so far as it is part of man. Besides, though I had already rejected body and mind with all other things, as being doubtful or not yet clearly perceived by me, this does not prevent me from picking them up again, if I chance to perceive them clearly. But of course my critic cannot grasp this because he thinks that doubt is something inseparable from the objects doubted. For shortly afterwards he asks: *How does it come about that the same things are now not dubious and uncertain?* (meaning the things which formerly were doubtful). He wants me likewise to forswear them with every solemnity, and wonders at my devices, saying I employ the doubtful in order to investigate what is certain; as if I had taken as the foundation of my Philosophy the principle that everything doubtful must be taken to be falsehood.

Do you want me to take heed of what I formerly believed myself to be? Do you wish me to pick up again that clouted coat etc.[1]? Here I shall make use of a very homely example for the purpose of explaining to him the rationale of my procedure, in order that in future he may not misunderstand it or dare to pretend that he does not understand it. Supposing he had a basket of apples and, fearing that some of them were rotten, wanted to take those out lest they might make the rest go wrong, how could he do that? Would he not first turn the whole of the apples out of the basket and look them over one by one, and then having selected those which he saw not to be rotten, place them again in the basket and leave out the others? It is therefore just in the same way that those who have never rightly philosophized have in their mind a variety of opinions some of which they justly fear not to be true, seeing that it was in their earliest years that they began to amass those beliefs. They then try to separate the false from the true lest the presence of the former should produce a general uncertainty about all. Now there is no better way of doing this than to reject all at once together as uncertain or false, and then having inspected each singly and in order, to reinstate only those which they know to be true and indubitable. Thus it was no bad course to reject everything at the outset, and then, noticing that I knew nothing more certainly and evidently than that in virtue of my thinking I existed, it was not wrong to assert this first. Finally it was not wrong for me afterwards to ask, who was the person I formerly believed myself to be, not meaning now to adopt exactly

[1] Cf. above, p. 281.

the same beliefs, but in order to reinstate any among them that were true, and reject those that were false and reserve such as were doubtful for examination at a future time. Whence it is evident that it is quite silly of our critic to call this the *art of eliciting certainties out of uncertainties* or, as below, *a method of dreaming*[1]. Again all his trivialities here about Pythagoras's barn-door fowls, and what follows in the next two paragraphs about the opinion of others is quite irrelevant. For there was no need, nor was it my wish to recount all the opinions that others have held, but merely to set forth what had naturally and spontaneously occurred to myself or what the popular opinion had been, whether that were true or false, since my purpose in repeating those beliefs was not directed towards securing belief in them but merely concerned their examination.

§ 2. WHAT IS BODY?

You say, 'what is body?' 'what did' I formerly understand by body?'

Do not be vexed if I keep a sharp look-out, if everywhere I am fearful of falling into a snare. Wherefore pray tell me, what body is it about which you ask? That which I once represented in my mind, consisting of definite properties, but of which, I am forced by the law of renunciation to suppose, my conception was erroneous? Or do you have some other sort of body in view, supposing that any other such can exist? How do I know? I am in doubt as to which it is. But if you mean the former kind it is easy for me to reply: By body I understood all that which can be defined by a certain figure, something which can be confined in a certain place, which can fill a given space in such a way that every other body will be excluded from it; which can be perceived by sense, and moved by any other body that comes in contact with it[2]. *This was my belief about body of the former kind. Consequently I gave the name of body to everything possessing the properties I have recounted in this list. Nevertheless I did not go on to believe that nothing different from that could either be or be called body, especially since it is one thing to say, 'I understood by body, this or that,' and quite another 'I understood nothing but this or that to be body.' If it is the second kind of body about which you are enquiring, I shall quote in my reply the opinion of more recent philosophers (since it is not so*

---

[1] Cf. above, p. 281, l. 4, and below, p. 285, l. 10, also p. 293.
[2] Cf. Med. p. 151.

much my individual opinion you seek to discover as what anyone may chance to believe). By body I understand everything admitting of being circumscribed by a place like a stone. Another property is the capacity of being defined by its place in such a way that the whole of it is in the whole of the place, and the whole is in every part, as is the case of the indivisible parts of quantity, or of a stone, or of similar things, which some of our more recent writers introduce and pourtray as being indivisible after the fashion of the Angels or of indivisible souls, securing in this a certain amount of applause at least among themselves, as we may see in Oviedo[1]. A further quality is to be extended actually, like a stone, or virtually like the above-mentioned indivisibles. Another is to be divisible into a number of parts, like the stone, or to be incapable of such partition, like the said indivisibles. Yet again a body may be moved by another, as a stone that is forced upwards, or by itself, like a stone falling downwards. Once more it can feel, as a dog does, think, as monkeys can, or imagine, like a mule. Anything that I have formerly come across, which was moved either by something else or by itself, which felt, imagined or thought, I have called a body, unless there was some reason for not doing so, and such things I even now call body.

But this, you say, was wrong and quite erroneous. For I judged that to have the power of self-movement, as also of feeling or thinking, by no means pertained to the nature of body[2].

You judged? Since you say so, I believe it; thought is free. But while you so thought, you allowed each individual to retain his own opinion freely; and I shall not believe you to be, as you would like, the arbiter of all thoughts, rejecting some and approving others, unless you possess some canon that is certain and handy. But since you have made no mention of this, when you bade us renounce all our former beliefs, I shall take advantage of the liberty that nature has granted us. You formerly judged, and I formerly judged. I judged one thing, you another, and perhaps both of us were wrong. Certainly our judging was not free from doubt, if both of us had at the very outset to divest ourselves of those previous opinions. Wherefore, not to prolong the strife too far, if you wish to define body in your own peculiar way, as in the way first given, I have no objections. I go so far as to admit, as long as I remember your definition, that you have defined not body universally but a certain kind of body

---

[1] Oviedo was a Catholic writer on philosophy who published his works in France. The work here referred to appears to be that termed *Integer Cursus Philosophicus* by R. P. Franciscus de Oviedo, 1640.

[2] Cf. Med. p. 151.

which you have grasped in a single conception.   But I contend that you have omitted the rest of the things known as body, which according to the opinion of the learned are subject to dispute, or about which nothing certain, at least nothing so certain as you require has been determined, so as to enable us to say whether they are bodies or not. Thus it is doubtful and uncertain whether up to the present we have secured a correct definition of all body.   I ask you therefore kindly to proceed and I shall follow with a gladness that is gladness itself; such a power over me does the new and unwonted hope of deriving the certain from the uncertain exercise.

ANNOTATIONS.

Feel as a dog does; think as monkeys can; or imagine like a mule. This is designed to introduce a verbal dispute. Desiring to be able to show that I have been wrong in assigning as the differentia between mind and body the fact that the former thought, while the other did not, but is extended, he says that everything which feels, imagines and thinks receives from him the title body. Well, let him call such objects mules or monkeys if he likes. If he ever succeeds in establishing their acceptation in this sense I shall not refuse to employ the terms. But meanwhile he has no reason for blaming me for using the recognized expressions.

§ 4.   WHAT SOUL IS.

You say, ' What is soul?'   ' What did I understand by the soul?'   And here is your reply. Either I did not perceive what this was or I imagined it to be something extremely rare like a wind, a flame, or an ether, which was spread through my grosser parts. To it, however, I referred nutrition, locomotion, feeling and thought[1].

That is quite enough.   But you will surely allow me to put a question here.   When you enquire about the soul[2], do you ask us to produce our old opinions, the beliefs we formerly held?

You say, ' Yes.'

But do you think that our opinions were correct, so that this would render your method of no use?   Do you think that no one has wandered so very far in the dark?   The truth is that the beliefs of Philosophers about the soul have been so various and so discordant, that I cannot sufficiently admire the skill by which you hope so confidently to extract a wholesome drug of assured use out of such a

---

[1] Cf. Med. p. 151.   [2] de animo.

*worthless sediment.   Yet we know that the poison of adders will
yield us a medicine.   Do you then wish me to add to your beliefs
about the mind the opinions actual or possible that certain other
people may have?   You don't want to enquire of me whether these
opinions are right or wrong; it is enough if an opinion is such as to
entail the holders' thinking that it can be driven out of their mind
by no force of reasoning.   Now certain of them will say that the
soul is a certain kind of body so-called.   Why be astonished?   This
is their opinion and, as they believe, it does not lack some colour of
truth.   Thus they call it body; but that consists in whatever is
extended, has three dimensions, is divisible into determinate parts.
Again, to take a particular illustration, they find in, say, a horse,
something extended, and divisible, such as flesh, bones, and all that
external bodily structure that invades our senses: they therefore
conclude, constrained to do so by weight of reasoning, that besides
that external structure there is something internal, and that that is
indeed of a fine texture, dissolved and extended throughout the bodily
frame, tri-dimensional and divisible, so that when the foot is cut off
some part of that internal thing also is lost.   They believe that the
horse is a compound of two extended things, which are tri-dimensional,
and divisible.   Thus it is a union of two bodies which, as differing
from one another, receive distinct names, the one—the external
structure—retaining the name of Body, while the other—the internal—is called Soul.   Further as regarding sense, imagination,
and thought, they think that the capacity for exercising these
functions resides in the soul, or internal body, though they involve
a certain relation to the external frame, apart from which there is no
sensation.   The account varies from writer to writer; so why should
I go over them one by one?   Among them will be found some who
think that all souls are as we have just described them.*

You reply—' what impiety! no more of that!'

*Yes, it is impious.   But why do you ask about it?   What do
you make of atheists?   Of fleshly minded men whose thoughts are
always riveted on the dregs of creation, so that they are aware of
nothing but body and flesh?   Nay, since you wish by your method to
establish and demonstrate the incorporeal and spiritual nature of
man's soul*[1], *you should by no means take that as granted, but rather
persuade yourself that you will have opponents who will deny this, or
who at least for purposes of disputation will maintain the opinions
which I have expounded to you.   Wherefore, pretend that one of these*

---

[1] animus.

*people is present, ready to reply to your question 'what is the soul[1] ? '
as you yourself replied before : The soul is something corporeal, of a
fine structure and subtle, spread throughout the external body, and
the principle of all sensation, imagination, and thought.   Thus there
are three grades of being, Body, the Corporeal or soul[1], and Mind or
spirit, as to the nature of which we are enquiring.   Wherefore let us
henceforth express these three grades by the three terms Body, Soul,
and Mind.   I repeat, let there be some one to make this reply to your
question. Has he given a sufficient answer ? However, I don't want
to anticipate anything belonging to your method ; I shall rather
follow.   Then you go on to say—*

ANNOTATIONS.

You say, 'yes[2].' Here and almost everywhere else my opponent
introduces me as making replies which are quite different from my
real beliefs.   But it would be too tedious to recount all his fabrications.

*Nay, since you wish by your method to establish and demonstrate
the incorporeal and spiritual nature of man's soul, you should by no
means take that as granted[3].* This is false—to pretend that I took
for granted what I ought to have proved. To such fabrications,
which are so freely spread abroad and have absolutely nothing to
rest on, there is nothing to be replied save that they are false.
Nothing at all about what is to be called body, or soul, or mind
appeared in my discussion. What I did on the other hand was to
explain two things, viz. that which thinks and that which is
extended, to which two I proved that everything else could be
referred. I established also by reasoning the fact that these two
things are substances really distinct from one another. One of
these substances I called mind, the other body ; and if my critic
doesn't like these names he can invent others, and I shall not
mind.

§ 5.   A Test applied to our Entry into the Method.

*You say, 'all is well ; the foundations have been auspiciously
laid ; I am, so long as I think.   This is certain, this is unshaken.
But next I must erect something upon this and take great care lest the
evil Spirit impose upon me. I am. But what am I? Doubtless some
one of the opinions I previously held about myself is true.   I believed
myself to be a man, and that man possesses body and soul. Am I*

---

[1] animus.   [2] Cf. p. 285.   [3] Cf. p. 286, *sub fin.*

then a body? Or am I a mind? Body is extended, bounded in place, impenetrable and capable of being seen. Have I any of these qualities? Extension? How could it exist in me, seeing there is no such thing to be found? I dismissed it at the outset. Shall I ascribe to myself the capacity for being touched or being seen? But the facts are that though I believe I am visible or can be touched by myself, I am not really seen, not really touched. This was fixed for me from the time when I made my renunciation. What then? I attend, I think, I turn my thoughts round and round, but nothing turns up. I am tired of going over the same old round. I find within myself none of the attributes that attach to body. I am not a body. I am nevertheless and know that I am; and, while I know that I am, I know nothing belonging to the body. Am I then a mind? What did I formerly believe to belong to the mind? Is any attribute of that kind to be found in me? I thought that it belonged to the mind to think. But after all, after all I think. Eureka! Eureka! I have found it. I am, I think. I am, so long as I think; I am a thinking thing; I am mind, understanding, reason. This is my method, which has enabled me happily to proceed. Follow comrade!'

O lucky man! to emerge from such darkness practically at one bound into the light. But, I beg you, give me your hand and steady my tottering steps, while I stumble along in your footprints. I should like to follow them exactly but, in proportion to my capacity, rather more slowly. I am, I think. But what am I? Any of the things that I formerly believed myself to be? But were my opinions true? That is not certain. I have abandoned all my old beliefs and treat them as false. I was wrong to trust them.

'Nay, but,' you exclaim, 'plant yourself firmly here!' Plant myself firmly? Everything totters! What if I am something else? 'You are too captious,' you say; 'you are either a body or a mind.'

Be it so, thus! Though, as a fact, I waver. Kindly take my hand, I scarcely dare to go on. What, pray, if I am a soul[1]? What if something else? I cannot tell.

But, you reply, 'exactly; either body or mind.'

Be it so, then. I am either a body or a mind. Am I not rather a body? Certainly I must be a body, if I find anything in myself which I formerly believed to belong to body. Yet I fear I was wrong to hold that belief.

'Come on,' you reply, 'fear nothing!'

[1] animus.

I shall venture, therefore, since you so raise my spirits. I had formerly believed that to think was something pertaining to body. But after all, after all, I think. Eureka! Eureka! I have found it! I am, I think, I am a thinking thing, I am something corporeal, I am extension, something divisible, terms previously devoid of meaning for me. What! do you get angry and let me go on ahead and spurn me with your hand? I have gained the bank and stand on the same shore as you, thanks to you and the renunciation you made.

'But you have no business to be here,' you reply.

Why? what have I done wrong?

'It is quite wrong of you to bring up the assertion that you had formerly believed yourself to be something corporeal. What you ought to have believed was that you were something mental.'

But why had you not given me warning about this principle? Why, when you saw me all braced up and ready for the complete renunciation of my old beliefs, did you not bid me retain this at least, nay take it from you as a sort of fare, viz. 'to think is something mental'? But to me is wholly due the credit of getting you to emphasize this declaration in future for your beginners, and carefully to instruct them not to forswear that along with their other principles, with e.g. 'Two and three make five.' Yet I cannot be at all confident that they will manage to follow you. Each man has his own notions and you will find few people to agree with you in that 'ipse dixit' of yours, as his silent disciples bowed to Pythagoras's opinion. What if some are unwilling? What if some people refuse? if they are recalcitrant? if they remain obstinately attached to their old opinions? what will you do? But not to invoke the aid of your other disciples, I want you to do one thing. When you promise that you will establish by weight of argument that the human soul is not corporeal but wholly spiritual, and if you have proposed as the foundation of your demonstrations, 'to think is a property of the mind, or of a thing that is wholly spiritual and incorporeal,' will it not look as if your postulate expressed in new words the very statement which was originally the subject of enquiry? As if any person were so stupid, that, believing that 'to think is a property of a thing that is spiritual and incorporeal,' and knowing at the same time and being conscious that he thought, he could doubt of the existence in him of something spiritual and quite immaterial. (Is there really anyone who needs some person to prompt him to discover that rich vein of thought within himself?) Now, that you may not think that all this is idle

assertion on my part, how many people are there, and those serious
philosophers, who hold that brutes think and who therefore suppose
that thought, while not being an attribute common to all bodies, is an
attribute common to extended soul, such as belongs ' *brutes, and con-*
sequently that it is not a property (in the fourth sense[1]*) of mind or what*
is spiritual. What will such philosophers say, pray tell me, when they
are asked to set aside this opinion of theirs in order so lightly to
assume yours? You yourself, in craving this from us as a postulate,
do you ask us to oblige you by conceding this or do you wish us to
make a fresh start again? But what is the need for my going on
with this discussion? If I have done wrong in going on so far, do
you wish me to retrace my steps?

ANNOTATIONS.

But what am I? Doubtless some one of the opinions I previously
held about myself is true[2]. Here as in countless other places he
ascribes a certain opinion to me without the slightest shadow of
excuse for doing so.

This was fixed for me from the time when I made my renunciation[3].
Here again he falsely assigns an opinion to me which I do not hold.
For I never drew any conclusion from the fact that I had renounced
my former belief. On the other hand I expressed exactly the
contrary when I said, 'But perhaps it is true that these same
things which I supposed were non-existent because they are unknown
to me, are really not different from the self which I know[4].'

Am I then a mind[5]*?* It is likewise false that I asked whether
I was a mind. For I had not yet explained what I understood by
mind. But I enquired whether there existed in me any of the
features I was in the practice of attributing to the soul as I had
formerly described it. And since I did not find in myself everything
which I had referred to it, but thought alone, on that account I did
not say that I was a soul, but merely a thinking thing. To this
thinking thing I gave the name of mind, or understanding, or
reason, and in doing this I had no intention of signifying by the
term mind anything more than by the term thinking thing. It was
not with that purpose that I exclaimed 'Eureka! Eureka! I have
found it'; as he so unfairly and sophistically represents. On the

---

[1] The Schoolmen distinguished four senses of the term property: in the
fourth it means *id quod pertinet omni et soli et semper* (what belongs to the
whole of a species, to it alone, and at all times).
[2] Cf. p. 287, *sub fin.*   [3] Cf. p. 288, l. 7.
[4] Cf. Med. II. p. 152, par. 2.   [5] Cf. p. 288, l. 13.

contrary I added 'that the significance of these terms was formerly unknown to me[1].' Thus it cannot be doubted that I meant precisely the same thing by these terms and by the expression 'thinking thing.'

I was wrong to trust my old beliefs. '*Nay*,' *you exclaim.* This again is absolutely false. For there I never assumed that my previous beliefs were true. I merely examined them to see if they were true.

I am either body or mind. It is false once more that I ever affirmed this.

It is quite wrong of you to bring up the assertion that you had formerly believed yourself to be something corporeal. What you ought to have believed was that you were something mental. It is false that I bring forward this assertion. My critic may say if he cares that the thing which thinks is better termed body than mind; I shan't gainsay him. But that is a question which he must discuss not with me but with students of language. If however he pretends that I have used the term mind to imply anything more than is meant by the term thinking thing, I have my denial ready. As I have again where shortly afterwards he adds: *If you have presupposed the assertion 'to think is a property of the mind or of a thing that is wholly spiritual' etc. do you wish me to oblige you by conceding this, or do you wish me to make a fresh start again?* Now I deny that I ever presupposed in any way that the mind was incorporeal. I finally proved this in the sixth Meditation.

But it is very wearisome for me to have to convict my opponent so often of falsification. In future I shall pass it over without notice and shall be a silent spectator right up to the end, while he plays his little game. But surely it is shameful to see a reverend Father so given to the love of quibbling as to make a buffoon of himself, and present himself as captious, dull and small-witted. Here it is not the Epidicus or Parmeno, the clowns of the ancient comedy, that he tries to imitate, but their modern representative, that very cheap fool who affects to produce laughter by his own *bêtises*.

§ 6. THE ENTRY ATTEMPTED ANEW.

'*All right*,' *you say*, '*so long as you follow closely in my steps.*'

Resume then, I implore you; my feet shall not deviate from your tracks a hair's breadth.

[1] Med. p. 147.

' I think,' you say.

So do I.

' I am,' you add, *' so long as I think.'*

So it is equally with me.

Your next question is, ' But what am I ? '

Sagely uttered! For this is what I want to know, and gladly do I say along with you : ' But what am I ?'

You go on : ' Am I what I formerly believed myself to be ? What was my previous belief about myself ? '

Now don't go on repeating the same words. I have heard them often enough. But, I entreat you, help me. When there is much darkness round my feet I cannot see where to set them.

' Say the words along with me,' you reply ; ' put your footsteps alongside of mine. What did I formerly believe myself to be ? '

Formerly ? Was there ever a former time ? Did I formerly believe ?

' Wrong ! ' you reply.

But you, yourself, kindly excuse me, have gone wrong in talking away about ' formerly.' I renounced all my former beliefs. Even ' formerly ' has become nothing, is nothing. But what a kind guide you are ! You take my hand and lead me !

You say, ' I think, I am.'

Just so! I think, I am. I have got hold of this securely and this alone. Beyond this one fact there is nothing, has been nothing.

But hurrah ! you add ; ' what did you formerly believe yourself to be ? '

You want me, I think, to make certain whether I have allotted a fortnight or a whole month to this apprenticeship in renunciation. Really I have given only this brief hour of discussion with you, and with such contention of spirit that the shortness of the time is counterbalanced by the effort required. But I give you a month, a year, if you wish it. Just so! I think, I am. There is nought besides this. I have renounced all.

But you urge me to recollect, to remember.

What is this ' recollection' ?

True, I now think that formerly I thought. But does the fact that now I think, that formerly I thought, imply that formerly all the time I did think ?

Your answer is ' Faint heart ! you are afraid of a shadow. Pluck up courage. I think.'

Poor luckless creature that I am ! The darkness gathers round

*me, and now I am not certain of that ' I think,' which previously was
so clear. I dream I think, I don't think it.*

' Nay,' you reply, ' he who dreams thinks.'

I see light. To dream is to think, and to think is to dream.

*' Not at all,' you say. ' To think extends more widely than to
dream. He who dreams thinks; but he who thinks, does not therefore
dream, but thinks in the waking state.'*

*But is that so? Do you dream that or do you think it? What!
if you are dreaming when you say that thought is a wider term than
dreaming, will it therefore be wider? If you care I shall have no
trouble in dreaming that dreaming is wider than thinking. Whence
do you have your knowledge that thought is the wider term, if thought
does not exist but only dreaming? What will happen if, so often as
you thought that you were awake and thinking, you were not awake
and thinking, but you dreamed that you were awake and thinking,
and consequently the operation is merely the single one of dreaming,
which you employ on the one occasion when dreaming that you dream,
and on the other, in dreaming that you are awake and thinking.
What will you do now? You are silent. Do you want to take my
advice? Let us find another ford. This is doubtful and untrust-
worthy; so much so that I am really surprised that you tried to
show me the way across without having made trial of it before.
Don't therefore ask me who it was I formerly believed myself to be,
but whom I now dream that I formerly dreamed myself to be. This
done, I shall reply to you. But lest our discourse be impeded by
the use of words proper to people who dream, I shall employ the language of our waking state, provided you remember that ' to think '
means henceforth merely ' to dream ' and that nothing more is
affirmed in your thoughts than by a dreamer in his dreams. Nay
you must designate your method a* Method of Dreaming, *and this
must be the culmination of your art, viz.:* He who reasons well
dreams. *I think this doctrine will go down well, because you proceed
as follows.*

' What therefore did I formerly believe myself to be?'

*Now here is the stone on which I previously stumbled. We must
both take care. Wherefore suffer me to ask why you did not premise
the statement ' I am one of the things that I formerly had believed
myself to be,' or ' I am that which I formerly believed myself to be.'*

You say there is no need to do so.

*Nay, pardon me, there is the greatest need. Otherwise your
labour is all in vain in discovering what you formerly believed*

yourself to be. Indeed suppose it possible for you not to be what you form rly believed yourself to be, as in Pythagoras's case, but something else. Will it then not be useless for you to ask what you believed yourself formerly to be?

But you say the above statement is one of my old beliefs and has been set aside.

Very true, if indeed everything has been set aside. But what can you do? You must either come to a halt here or make use of it.

'*Nay,' you say, 'we must try again and take another way. So! I am either body or mind. Am I body?'*

Pardon me, that is going too far. Whence do you derive that statement 'I am either body or mind,' now that you have set aside your belief in both body and mind? Nay, what happens if you are neither body nor mind, but soul[1], or something else? What do I know about it? This is the very question we are investigating, and if I knew the answer, if I were acquainted with it, I should not distress myself so much. Again I should not like you to think that it was merely the love of trudging around this land of renunciation that brought me here into the midst of its gloom and peril. It is the hope of attaining certainty that alone either attracts me or compels me.

'*Let us resume then,' you answer. 'I am either a body, or something not a body, i.e. incorporeal.'*

Now you are on another, quite a new track. But are you sure that it is going to lead you aright?

You say it is most trustworthy and entirely necessary.

Why then did you set it aside? Did I not rightly fear that something ought to be retained, and that it was possible you did indulge your incredulity too far? However, so be it. Let this be certain. What next?

'*Am I a body?' you go on. 'Do I find within myself any of that which I formerly judged to belong to the body?'*

But here is another rock of offence. Without any doubt we shall hit against it unless you first grant as a premiss this paragon of beliefs 'I was right in my former judgment about what pertains to the body'; or 'nothing belongs to the body save what I formerly understood to belong to it.'

'*Wherefore so?' you say.*

Precisely because if you omitted anything in your former list of

---

[1] animus.

attributes, if your judgment was wrong and, 'being human, you repudiate nothing that may well happen to human nature[1],' all your trouble will be superfluous, and you will inevitably be exposed to the dread of being left in the plight of the rustic in the story. For he, on seeing a wolf for the first time and at a great distance, stopped and thus addressed his master, a raw youth whom he was accompanying. 'What do I see?' he said. 'Without doubt it is an animal; it moves and runs forward. But what sort of animal? Surely one of those that I have seen already. Now what are they? The ox, the horse, the goat and the ass. Is it an ox? No; it doesn't have horns. A horse? No; you could hardly say it has a horse's tail. A goat? But the goat has a beard, this beast none; it isn't a goat. Therefore it must be an ass, since it is neither ox, horse, nor goat.' Now don't laugh, but wait for the end of the story. 'But come,' said his young master, 'why don't you make out that it is a horse with as much reason as that it is an ass? See! Is it an ox? No; it doesn't have horns. An ass? Not a bit; I don't see the ears. A goat? No; it has no beard. Then it is a horse.' The rustic, somewhat perturbed by this novel analysis, exclaimed: 'But it is not an animal at all. Here are the animals I know, the ox, the horse, the goat and the ass. It is not an ox, nor a horse, nor a goat, nor an ass. Therefore' (with great triumph) 'it is not an animal, and hence it is non-animal.' Here is a stout Philosopher for you, bred not in the Lyceum but in the cow-house! Do you want to err in his company?

'Enough,' you say, 'I see your point. But the rustic's error lay in thinking (though he did not openly mention it) that he had seen all the animals, or that there was no animal besides those he knew. But what has this to do with the matter we have in hand?'

Well the two cases are as similar as a couple of glasses of milk. Don't pretend. You too keep something suppressed in your mind. Is it not this: 'I know everything which has anything to do with or can possibly have anything to do with the body.' Or this: 'Nothing belongs to the body except what I understood belonged to it formerly'? But if you did not know everything, if you have omitted even one thing; if you have ascribed to the mind anything that really belongs to the body or to something corporeal, e.g. the soul[2]; if you were wrong in separating thought, sense, and imagination from the body or the corporeal soul; if you suspect, I add, that you have erred in

---

[1] Cf. Terence, *Heautontimoroumenos*, Act I, Scene 1, *v.* 25.
[2] animae.

*one of these points, ought you not to fear the same issue to your
argument, and that any conclusion you get may be wrong? Certainly
though you drag me, I shall stick here obstinately and shan't stir a
step farther, unless you remove this obstacle.*

*'Let us go back,' you answer, 'and try a third avenue of approach.
Let us attempt all the entrances, paths, twists and turnings of the
method.'*

*Very good, but on the understanding that you will not merely
brush by, but remove any doubtful matter that may occur. Come,
lead away. I am for complete precision in everything. Proceed.*

§ 7. Third Attempt to Effect an Entrance.

You say, 'I think.'

I deny it. You dream that you are thinking.

But you say that this is what you call thinking.

*But you are wrong to do so. I call a fig a fig. You are
dreaming. This is all you'll get. Go on.*

'I am, so long as I think,' is your next word.

All right. Since you want to put it so, I shan't object.

But you say this is certain and evident.

I deny it. You merely dream that it is certain and evident.

*But you persist, saying that it is at least certain and evident to
one who dreams.*

*I deny it. It merely seems, or appears to be so, it is not really
certain.*

*Against this you urge: 'But I don't doubt it. I am conscious of
it in myself, and an evil Spirit. can't deceive me here even though he
tries hard.'*

*I deny this. You dream that you are conscious in yourself of
it, that you don't doubt, and that this is evident. Those two things
are very different; viz. 'to a dreamer' (and you may add 'to one
awake' also) 'something appears certain and evident,' and 'to a
dreamer' (just as to one who is awake) 'something is certain and
evident.' This is the end of the matter; there is no going beyond it.
Hence let us try another approach, so that we may not waste our
lives here dreaming. Though something must be granted; to reap
you must sow. But you are quite confident. Proceed. You are
getting on.*

What you say is: 'Whom did I formerly believe myself to be?'

*Have you done with that 'formerly.' There is no road that way.
How often have I told you that you were shut off from all your old*

possessions?   You are, so long as you think, and you are certain that you are so long as you think.   I enforce the point 'so long as you think'; all the past is doubtful and uncertain, the present alone is left you.   Yet you persevere.   I admire a man whom ill-fortune cannot break.

'There is nothing,' you say, 'in me who think, who am a thinking thing, nothing, I repeat, belonging to the body or to anything corporeal.'

I deny this.   Prove it.

You answer: 'From the time that I renounced everything, no body, no soul[1], no mind, in a word, nothing exists.   Therefore if I am, as I am certain that I am, I am not a body nor anything corporeal.'

How I admire your warmth and the way you syllogize, referring at each step in the argument to our form of reasoning!   Come here, I will show you a quicker way out of these labyrinths, and seeing that you are generous I shall be more so.   I deny both your antecedent, your consequent and the necessary connection between the two.   Do not be annoyed, pray!   My notion is not without warrant.   Here are my grounds.   I deny the necessary connection, because you might as well prove the opposite, thus 'Since I renounced all, neither mind, nor soul, nor body, in a word, nothing exists.   Therefore if I am, as I am, I am not a mind.'   Now here is the flaw, which the sequel will show you plainly.   Meanwhile, bethink yourself as to whether it is better to derive the following conclusion henceforth from your antecedent: 'Therefore if I am, as I am, I am nothing.'   Certainly, either the assertion of the antecedent was wrong, or, if it is asserted, it is annulled by the condition brought forward, viz. 'If I am.'   Wherefore I deny that antecedent; 'From the time that I renounced all, no body exists, nor soul[1], nor mind, nor anything else'; and I am quite right in doing so.   For while renouncing everything you are either wrong in doing so, or you do not wholly renounce everything; nor can you do the latter, since you yourself who make the renunciation necessarily are.   Therefore to make an accurate reply I must say: when you assert Nothing is, no body, no soul, no mind, etc., the alternatives are (1) that you either exclude yourself from that proposition Nothing is, etc., and really mean: Nothing is except myself; which you must necessarily do, in order that your proposition may come into existence and may remain in existence. This is just what the ordinary Logic teaches about such propositions

[1] animus.

as : ' *Every proposition written in this book is false' ; ' I am not
telling the truth,' with a crowd of similar judgments which always
except themselves from the condemnation they pass.   Or again*
(2) *according to the other alternative, you include yourself also,
and desire to be non-existent while you renounce your old possessions
and say :* Nothing exists etc.   *On the former alternative it is
impossible to maintain the proposition: 'Since I renounced everything,
nothing exists etc.'   For you exist and are something; and necessarily
you are either body, or soul*[1], *or mind or something else ; and so either
body or soul or mind or something else exists.   On the second alternative you are wrong, and indeed commit a double error.   To begin
with you attempt the impossible and, though existing, want to cancel
your existence ; and next you upset that assertion in the consequent
when you add : ' Therefore if I am, as I am, etc.'   For how can it
come about that you are, if nothing is ?   And so long as you affirm
that nothing is, how can you affirm that you are ?   Again if you
affirm that you are, don't you destroy the proposition asserted shortly
before, viz. ' Nothing is etc. ' ?   Therefore the antecedent is false, and
false also the consequent.   But now you renew the conflict.*

' *While I maintain,' you say, ' that nothing exists, I am not
certain that I am body, soul*[1], *mind, or anything else.   Nay I am
not sure that any other body, soul or mind exists.   Therefore by the
law of renunciation which relegates the doubtful to the realm of the
false, I shall say and affirm that there is no body, nor soul, nor
mind, nor anything else.   Therefore if I am, as I am, I am not
a body.'*

*That is splendid.   But, pray, suffer me to straighten out your
statements singly, to weigh them, and balance them.   In saying
' Nothing is, etc., I am not certain that I am body, soul, mind or
anything else.'   I distinguish the antecedent: ' You are not certain
that you are determinately a body, determinately a mind, or anything else determinately.'   Let this antecedent be granted, for it
is about this question that you are enquiring.   But again we may
say you are not certain that you are indeterminately either body,
soul, or mind, or anything else ; now I deny this antecedent.   For
you are, and are something and are necessarily either body, or soul,
or mind or something else ; and you cannot seriously place this in the
realm of the doubtful, however much an evil Spirit tempt you to do
so.   I come now to the consequent : ' Therefore by the law of renunciation I shall say that there is no body, no soul, no mind, nor*

------

[1] animus.

anything else.' I make a distinction as to the consequent thus.
I shall say: 'No body, soul, or mind, or anything else exists determinately.' Let the connection between antecedent and consequent
be granted. But I may also say: 'Neither body, nor soul, nor
mind, nor anything else exists indeterminately.' Now I deny this
consequent. In the same way I draw a distinction as to your
ultimate consequent: 'Therefore if I am, as I am, I am not a body.'
Determinately I concede it; indeterminately I deny it. Behold my
generosity! I have augmented your statements by adding this
triumph of reasoning to their number. But don't despond! Array
your line of battle anew! You delight me!

Your next words are: 'I know I exist. I ask who that "I" is
whom I know. It is quite certain that the knowledge of this, taken
precisely so, does not depend on those things which I do not yet know
to exist.'

What more? Have you said all you intend to say? I expected
you to state a consequence, as shortly before. Perhaps you feared
you would get no better results. This is highly prudent, according
to your way of doing things; but I take up the separate points
again. You know that you exist. All right. You ask who the
you is whom you know. Just so, and I ask the same question along
with you, and we have been asking this question for a long time.
Knowledge of that which you seek does not depend on those things
which you have not yet known to exist. What am I to say? The
answer is not yet sufficiently clear; and I don't see quite well where
your old dictum comes in. As a matter of fact, if you ask who that
you is whom you know, I shall raise the same question too. But why
do you ask, if you already know?

You reply: 'But I knew that I existed; I don't know who
I am.'

Excellent! But whence will you discover who that you which
exists is, save from what you either knew formerly or some time will
know? You will not discover the answer from what you formerly
knew. That is teeming with obscurity and has been given up.
Therefore your knowledge will come from what you don't yet know,
but will know afterwards; and I can't see why you are here so much
perturbed.

'I do not yet know,' you reply, 'that what you mention exists.'

Keep up hope; some day you will find out.

But you ask next what you are to do meanwhile.

You will await its discovery, though I shall not allow you to *remain long in doubt. I make a distinction as formerly. You do not know who you are determinately and clearly: this I deny. For you know that you are something and necessarily either body or soul or mind or something else. But what then? You will know yourself afterwards clearly and determinately. What will you do now? That single dilemma,* Determinately or Indeterminately, *will keep you at a stand-still a whole century long. Cry for another way, if there is any left. But be daring and don't yet give up the contest. Great and novel enterprises are beset by great and novel difficulties.*

You reply that there is one way left, but that if it is blocked by any obstacle or stone of stumbling, your cause is lost. You will retrace your steps and these shores of renunciation will see you wandering thereon no more. You want to know if I wish to explore this route also.

Right, but on the understanding that, since it is the farthest, you may be very sure that it is my last attempt. Go on ahead.

§ 8. The Fourth Attempt to Effect an Entrance— the Problem given up in Despair.

You say, 'I am.'
I deny it.
You proceed: 'I think.'
I deny it.
You add: What do you deny?
I deny that you exist, that you think. Well do I know what I did, when I said: 'nothing is.' It is quite a notable exploit; at one blow I have cut myself adrift from everything. Nothing exists; you do not exist, you do not think.

'But my good sir,' you say, 'I am certain, I am conscious in myself, this is my consciousness, that I am, that I think.'

Even though you put your hand upon your heart, even though you swear and protest, I shall deny it. Nothing is, you are not, you do not think, you are not conscious in yourself. Here is the obstacle; and I set it before your eyes that you may know it and avoid it. If the proposition, 'nothing is,' is true, the following also, 'you do not exist, you do not think,' is necessary. But, as you wish, 'Nothing is,' is true. Therefore the other, 'You do not exist, you do not think,' is also true.

'That is being too strict,' you contend, you must relax somewhat. Since you request me to do so, I shall grant your petition, and with great good-will. You are: I allow it. You think: I grant

*it. You are a thinking thing, you add, 'a thinking substance,' so
much are you given to grandiloquent language. I rejoice, I congratulate you; but no further. Yet you want to go on and you
summon up your spirits for the last time.*

* 'I am,' you say, 'a thinking substance, and know that I, a
thinking substance exist, and I have a clear and distinct conception
of this thinking substance. Yet I do not know that body exists, nor
any of those things which pertain to the concept of corporeal substance.
Nay, body does not exist, nor any corporeal thing. I have renounced
all that. Therefore the knowledge of the existence of a thinking thing
or of an existing thinking thing, does not depend on the knowledge of
the existence of body, or of an existing body. Therefore since I exist,
and exist as a thinking body, and body does not exist, I am not a
body. Therefore I am a mind. These are the things that compel
my assent, since there is nothing in them that is not coherent
and reasoned to form evident principles according to the laws of
Logic.'*

* O swan-like strain! But why didn't you talk like this before?
Why did you not clearly and intelligibly remove afar off that former
renunciation of yours? I have reason to complain of you, seeing you
allowed us to wander long here, nay you led me by pathless and
impassable places, when you could have brought me to the goal with
a single step. I have reason to be wroth and, unless you were my
friend, to vent all my spleen upon you, for you have not been so
candid and handsome as you used to be; nay you are keeping something entirely to yourself and not going shares in it with me. You
are amazed? I shan't detain you long. Here is the source of my
complaint. Shortly before, just a few steps back, you asked who that
you was whom you knew. Now not only do you know who you are
but you have a clear and distinct concept of that. Either you were
concealing something, and were pretending ignorance, because you
were very cunning; or you have some subterranean code of truth
and certainty which you are keeping out of view. Though I prefer,
if you point to this hidden source, to be curious rather than cross.
Whence, pray tell me, comes that clear and distinct concept of
thinking substance? If it is owing to the words employed, to the
facts themselves, that it is so clear and evident, I shall ask you again
and again to show me that concept, so clear and distinct as it is, if
only once, in order that I may fashion myself anew from one glimpse
of it, especially since it is practically from it alone that we expect to
find out the truth, which is costing us such toil to discover.*

'*Look,*' you say, '*I knew with certainty that I am, that I think, and that I exist as a thinking substance.*'

Kindly wait a little till I get myself ready to frame such a difficult concept. I also know and am quite well aware that I exist, that I think and that I, a thinking substance, exist. Proceed now at last, if you please.

'*Nay,*' you say, '*the matter is finished. When I thought that I, a thinking substance, existed, I formed a clear and distinct concept of thinking substance.*'

Goodness, gracious! What a subtle and acute fellow you are! How in a moment you penetrate and traverse everything which is, and everything which is not, which can, and which cannot be! You form a clear and distinct conception of thinking substance, while conceiving clearly and distinctly the existence of thinking substance. Therefore if you know it clearly, as you know it at once (so happy is your talent), that no mountain exists without its valley, will you straightway possess a clear and distinct concept of a mountain without a valley? But, because I am not acquainted with the device by which you achieve this, the new achievement itself does not impress me. Disclose your method, I beg you, and show how it is possible for that concept to be clear and distinct.

Without hesitation you say:—'*I clearly and distinctly conceive a thinking substance to exist, and I conceive nothing corporeal, nothing spiritual*[1], *nothing else besides, but merely a thinking substance. Therefore that concept of mine of a thinking substance is clear and distinct.*'

At last I have your answer, and I believe I understand it. That concept of yours is clear because you are quite certain in your knowledge; it is distinct, because you are aware of nothing else. Have I hit the nail on the head? I believe so, for you add:

'*That wholly suffices to let me affirm that I, in so far as I know myself, am nothing other than a thinking thing.*'

Indeed it is quite sufficient; and if I have grasped your meaning clearly, the clear and distinct concept of a thinking substance which you form is due to the fact that it represents to you that a thinking substance exists, no attention being paid to the body, the soul, the mind, or to anything else, but merely to the fact that it exists. Thus you say that you, in so far as you know yourself, are nothing but a thinking substance, but not a body, not a soul, not a mind, nor anything else. Consequently if you existed precisely to the extent to which you have knowledge of yourself, you would be merely a thinking

[1] spirituale.

*substance and nothing besides. I fancy you are chuckling and con-
gratulating yourself, and think this unusually long spun out argument
of mine is meant to secure delay, to postpone the issue and let me
off without attempting to pierce your yet unbroken array. But really
I mean something quite different. Do you want me with a single
word to shatter all your massed battalions and rend even your
reserves, dense and serried as may be their formation? I shall employ
not one word but three, and conquer so completely that no survivor
will be left to tell the tale.*

*Here is my first. The argument which reasons from knowledge
to existence is not valid. Reflect on this for a fortnight at least, and
it will bear fruit. You will have no reason to regret it if you thus
cast your eyes on the following table. Thinking substance is that
which either understands, or wills, or doubts, or dreams, or imagines,
or feels. Thus cognitive acts, like understanding, willing, imagining
and feeling, all come under the common notion of thought or perception, or consciousness, and we say that the substance in which they
inhere is a thinking thing.*

Thinking substance

corporeal, or having a body and using it		incorporeal, or not possessing a body, nor using it	
extended and divisible	inextended and indivisible	God	angel
soul[1] of horse · soul of dog	mind of Socrates · mind of Plato		

*Now for the second. Take those terms—determinately, inde-
terminately; distinctly, confusedly; explicitly, implicitly. Revolve
those too in your mind for a few days. It will be worth your
while to apply them one by one, as is proper, to your various pro-
nouncements, to separate and distinguish those opposites from one
another. I should not shirk doing this now unless I feared it would
prove wearisome. Here is my third objection. The argument that
wants too much in its conclusion gets nothing at all. Here then is
no time left for meditation. The emergency presses. Come, bethink
yourself of your words and see if I come on in the same way. I
am a thinking thing, I know that I am a thinking substance, that
thinking substance exists and that, nevertheless, I do not yet know
that mind exists, nay, no mind exists. Nothing exists, everything
has been set aside. Therefore knowledge of the existence of, or of
existing thinking substance does not depend on the knowledge of the*

[1] anima.

*existence of, or of an existing mind. Therefore since I exist, and
exist as a thinking thing, and the mind does not exist, I am not
mind; therefore I am body. Well why do you say nothing? Why
do you retreat? I have not yet given up all hope. Follow me now.
Hurrah! Courage! I bring forward the old formula and method
for regulating the reason familiar to all the ancients and (shall I
venture?), thoroughly well known to all mankind. Pray bear with
me and do not be vexed; I have borne with you. Perhaps that will
open a way, as is usual in a situation that is intricate and of which
we have despaired. Or certainly, if that does not come off we shall
at least, in extricating ourselves, have pointed out the error of your
method, if such exists. Here, then, is your matter put in form.*

§ 9.　The Matter Safely Recast in the Old Form.

*Nothing which is such that I can doubt whether it exists, actually
exists.*

Every body is such that I can doubt whether it exists.

Therefore no body actually exists.

*Not to raise old issues again, I ask if you do not acknowledge
the major premiss as your own proposition. The minor must also
be yours, if you are to get the conclusion. I resume therefore—*

No body actually exists.

Therefore nothing actually existing is a body.

I proceed: Nothing actually existing is a body.

I (I a thinking substance) actually exist.

Therefore I (I a thinking substance) am not a body.

*Now your face beams! A new springtime of hope opens in it.
My formula favours you, and so does the result which the formula
creates. But note my sardonic laughter. Put mind in the place of
body and then draw the conclusion with formal correctness, viz.
Therefore I (I a thinking substance) am not a mind. Thus—*

*Nothing which is such that I can doubt whether it actually exists
does actually exist.*

All mind is such that I can doubt whether it actually exists.

Therefore no mind actually exists.

Nothing actually existing is mind.

I (I a thinking substance) actually exist.

Therefore I (I a thinking substance) am not mind.

*What then? The form is correct and valid; it never errs, it
never brings a false conclusion unless the premiss chance to be false.
Therefore, of necessity, any flaw that we judge to exist in the*

consequent, is not due to the form but to something erroneously stated in the premises. Now really do you think that the assertion to which are due all your subsequent wanderings is properly stated, viz. ' Nothing which is such that I can doubt whether it exists or not or is true, actually exists or is true.' Is that certain? Are you so familiar with it as to be able to insist upon it confidently and with unembarrassed mind? Tell me, pray, why you deny the statement ' I have a body'? Doubtless because it seems to you doubtful. But is this also not doubtful, viz. ' I do not have a body'? Is there anyone likely to take as the foundation of his whole science and doctrine and especially of a doctrine which he wishes to impose on others as the controlling power of their thought, a statement which he would be prudent to deem false? But enough. This is the end at last, the term of our wanderings; I hope for nothing in the future. Therefore to your question ' Whether the renunciation of everything doubtful is a good method of philosophizing,' I reply as you expect, frankly and openly, and without mincing matters.

ANNOTATIONS.

Up to the present our Reverend Father has been jesting. And because in the sequel he seems to be in earnest and to want to assume a quite different character, I shall in the meantime briefly jot down anything among his jests that has struck me.

These words of his : *Formerly? Was there ever a former time? I dream I think, I don't think it*[1], and the like are humorous sallies worthy of the character he has assumed. So too with the serious question : *Can to think extend more widely than to dream*[2]*?* and the said argument *About the method of dreaming,* and the consequence that, *He who reasons well dreams*[3]. But I don't think that I ever gave the least provocation for these jibes, because I expressly pointed out when talking of the things I renounced, that I did not affirm that they existed, but that they seemed. Consequently in asking what I had thought myself formerly to be, my question was directed to discover merely what it then seemed to me I had formerly thought. And when I said that I thought, I did not inquire whether I was awake or asleep when I thought. I am surprised that he calls my method a Method of Dreaming when it seems to have roused him into a sufficiently wide awake condition.

Likewise the reasoning suits his assumed character well enough when, in order that I may discover what I previously thought I was,

[1] Cf. p. 292.   [2] Cf. p. 293.   [3] *Ibid.*

he wishes me to state the following premiss : *I am some one of the things which I formerly believed myself to be,* or : *I am that which I formerly believed myself to be*[1]. Shortly afterwards, for the purpose of inquiring whether I am a body, he wants me to premise this wonderful proposition : *I was right formerly in my judgment about what pertains to the body,* or : *Nothing belongs to the body save what I formerly understood to belong to it*[2]. For statements which are manifestly contrary to reason, are designed to provoke laughter. It is manifest that I could have asked with quite useful results what I had formerly believed myself to be, and whether I was a body, although I did not know whether I was any of the things that I had formerly believed myself to be, and although my opinion had not been correct, in order that I might examine that very question by the help of what I was then going to perceive for the first time ; and, if nothing else, I should at least discover that in that direction no further progress was possible.

My critic again plays his part excellently in his tale about the rustic. But in this there is nothing more ridiculous than the fact that, when he thinks that it is an application of my words, it applies only to his own position. For directly afterwards he finds fault with me for not presupposing this dictum : *I was right formerly in my judgment about what pertains to the body,* or : *Nothing pertains to the body save what I formerly understood to belong to it.* But now he takes this very statement about the omission of which by me he complains, and which is wholly evolved from his own imagination, and criticizes it as though it were mine, likening it to the absurd reasoning of the rustic in his fable. But nowhere, because I presuppose that my former judgment about the nature of body was correct, have I denied that the thing which thinks is a body ; it was because I used the term body to signify only a thing of which I had sufficient knowledge, to wit, extended substance, and I recognised that what thinks is distinct from this.

The *jeux d'esprit* which have already appeared rather often and are found here, e.g. *you say, 'I think.' I deny it, you are dreaming*[3], etc. *'It is certain,' you add, 'and evident.' I deny it, you are dreaming ; it merely seems, or appears to be so, it is not really certain*[4], etc., are in this respect at least funny, that if the arguments were intended to be serious, they would be so silly. But lest beginners should chance to go wrong here, and think that to one who doubts whether he is awake or dreaming nothing else can be certain and

[1] Cf. p. 294.   [2] *Ibid.*   [3] Cf. p. 296.   [4] *Ibid.*

evident, but that everything must only seem or appear to be,
I should like them to recall what was above remarked (at F)[1], viz.
that what is clearly perceived, no matter by whom it is perceived,
is true and does not merely seem or appear to be true. Yet there
are very few who rightly distinguish between that which is really
perceived and that which they fancy they perceive, because but few
are accustomed to clear and distinct perceptions.

Up to this point our Actor has displayed to us no memorable
spectacle of battle; he has merely interposed some slight barriers
and after brandishing his weapons there for a time he speedily
sounds the retreat and betakes himself to some other part of the
field. But here[2] for the first time he begins a mighty conflict
with an enemy quite worthy of his stage, viz. with a shade of me,
visible indeed to none else, but educed from his own brain. Lest it
should not appear sufficiently unreal, he has actually gone to the
fountain head of the Non-existent[3] itself in order to derive matter
for its composition. But he takes the combat seriously; he argues,
gets warm, makes truce, calls in Logic to his help, renews the fight,
scrutinizes my statements one by one, weighs them, balances them.
But fearing to take the blows of his valiant assailant on his
shield, he shuns them also with his body. Soon he begins
to make distinctions and, creating a diversion by means of his
Determinately and Indeterminately[4], he escapes by flight. Really
that makes a most entertaining spectacle; especially if the cause
of such a mighty quarrel is known. Well, here it is :—He chanced
to read in my writings that any true opinions we have before we
philosophize seriously are mixed up with so many others that are
either false or at least doubtful, that hence in order to separate
them from the rest it is best to reject all alike to begin with, or to
refuse not to renounce them all, so that it may be possible afterwards more conveniently to distinguish those that were true all the
time, or to discover new truths, and to admit nothing but what is
true. Now this is just the same as if I had said that in order to
prevent there being any rotten apples among those of which our
tub or basket is full, we should begin by turning them all out, and
then fill up once more either by putting back again those in which
there is no flaw or getting similarly sound ones from elsewhere.
But my critic, not grasping such a profound speculation, or at any
rate pretending that he does not grasp it, expresses astonishment

[1] Cf. p. 267. F is a section mark in the Latin edition not reproduc
this translation. [2] Cf. p. 297. [3] ex ipso Nihilo. [4] Cf.

especially because I said ' Nothing is not to be renounced ' ; and after meditating long and deeply on that *Nothing* he has so got it on the brain that, though now his arguments tell against himself, he cannot easily shake himself free of the notion.

After this successful combat, elated with his belief in his victory he assails a new enemy, and once more believes that this is some shade of me, for what he opposes is always of that self-same phantasy. Now however he constructs it out of new materials, viz. out of the words : *I know that I exist ; I ask who I am, etc.*[1] And because he is not so familiar with this semblance of me as with the preceding, he attacks more cautiously and merely skirmishes. The first missile he directs against me is : *Why do you ask, if you already know*[2] ? But because he imagines that his opponent will ward it off with the reply, *I know that I am, not who I am*[3], he immediately hurls this more potent weapon : *Whence do you derive the knowledge who you are unless from what you either formerly knew, or some time will know ? But not from what you formerly knew ; that is teeming with obscurity and has been given up. There- fore your knowledge will come from what you don't yet know but will know afterwards*[4]. Believing that the luckless shade is much put out and almost brought to earth by this blow, he imagines he hears it exclaim : *I do not yet know that what you mention exists.* Then, changing his wrath to pity he consoles it with these words : *Keep up hope ; some day you will find out*[5]. Next he makes the shade reply to this in a querulous and supplicating tone with : *What shall I do meanwhile ?* But in an imperious voice as becomes a conqueror he cries, ' *You will await its discovery.*' Howsoever, being pitiful, he does not allow me to be long in doubt, but flying once more to the side issue : *Determinately, Indeterminately ; clearly, confusedly*, and seeing no one following him there secures a lonely triumph. Now certainly all these jests are excellent examples of that fooling which depends upon the unlooked for simulation of stupidity on the part of a man whose looks and garb gave promise of wisdom and seriousness. But, to let this appear more clearly, we ought to consider our Actor friend as a serious and learned man, who, in order to attack our Method of investigating truth, which bids us reject everything as uncertain and, beginning with the knowledge of our own existence, thence proceeds to the exami- nation of our nature, i.e. of that thing which· we already know to

---

[1] Cf. p. 299, par. 2.　　　[2] Cf. *Ibid.* par. 3.　　　[3] Cf. *Ibid.* par. 4.
[4] Cf. *Ibid.* par. 5.　　　[5] Cf. *Ibid. sub fin.*

exist, tries to prove that there is no approach this way to that further knowledge, and employs the following argument : *Since you know only that you exist, but not who you are, you cannot learn this from what you formerly knew, since you have renounced everything ; then what you learn must come from what you do not yet know.* But to this even a three years' child could reply that nothing prevents him learning from what he once knew, because though he has set that aside on account of its being doubtful, he may afterwards adopt it again, when he has had proof of its truth ; and besides, though it were conceded that nothing can be learned from former knowledge, yet at least another way lies perfectly open, viz. that with which he is not yet familiar, but which study and observation will make plain. But here my friend constructs for himself a pretended opponent, who not only admits that the former road is closed, but himself shuts the second with the dictum : *I do not know that the things you mention exist.* This is as if no new knowledge of existence could be acquired and the absence of this precluded all acquaintance with the essential nature of things. But this is surely the stupidest notion possible. Still it contains an allusion to my words. for I wrote that the knowledge I have of a thing which I know to exist cannot depend on the knowledge of what I do not yet know to exist[1]. He, however, ridiculously transfers this, which I enunciated merely about the present, to the future, in the same way as if he were to conclude that because we cannot yet behold those who are not yet born, but will be born this year, we shall never be able to see them. For surely it is highly evident that the knowledge we now possess of a thing which is known as existing, does not depend upon the knowledge of that which is not yet known as existing. For the very reason that if anything is perceived as belonging to something that exists, of necessity it also is perceived to exist. But with the future the case is quite different, because nothing prevents my knowledge of a thing which I know to exist being increased by other facts which I do not yet know to exist, but shall finally learn just when I perceive them to pertain to that thing. My critic however proceeds to say, *Keep up hope ; some day you will find out ;* and next, *I shan't allow you to remain long in doubt.* Now by these words he bids us expect either that by the way proposed it is impossible to arrive at any further knowledge ; or certainly, if he suppose that his opponent has closed that route against him (which, however, would be

[1] Cf. Med. ii, vol. i, p. 152.

foolish), that he will open another. But all that he adds is : *You know who you are indeterminately and confusedly, not determinately and clearly.* Now the most natural inference to draw from these words is that there is a way to further knowledge open to us, because by meditation and observation we are able to bring about a change from mere indeterminateness and confusedness in our knowledge to clearness and determinateness. Nevertheless he thus concludes, the words *Determinately, Indeterminately furnish a dilemma that will keep us at a standstill a whole century long*[1], and consequently we must look out for some new route. To me it seems that he could have devised nothing better calculated to simulate an appearance of foolishness and weakness on the part of his own understanding.

You say, 'I am,'—I deny it. You proceed: 'I think.' I deny it, etc. Here he returns once more to do battle with the former shade, and thinking that he has felled it to the ground at the first assault, he boastfully exclaims : *It is quite a notable exploit, at one blow I have cut myself adrift from everything.* But seeing that this shadow takes its origin from his own brain and cannot perish unless he die along with it, even though felled to the ground, it revives. It puts its hand to its heart, and swears that it is, that it exists. My critic, softened by this new style of entreaty, graciously permits it to live, to collect its spirits for the last time and give vent to much futile babble. This he does not refute, but on the contrary gets on friendly terms with it and passes on to other pleasantries.

He begins by scolding it in the following words : *Shortly before, just a few steps back, you asked what you were: Now not only do you know who you are, but you have a clear and distinct concept of that*[2]. Next he asks *to be shown that concept, so clear and distinct as it is, in order that he may fashion himself anew from one glimpse of it.* Then he pretends that it is disclosed to him in the following words : *I certainly know that I am, that I think, that I exist as a thinking substance. The matter is finished*[3]. That this is not adequate he proves by the following example : *you know also that no mountain exists without a valley, therefore you have a clear and distinct concept of a mountain without a valley*[4]. He interprets this in the following way : *That concept of yours is clear because you are quite certain in your knowledge; it is distinct because you are aware of nothing else.—And thus the clear and distinct concept that you form is due to the fact that it represents to you that a*

[1] Cf. p. 300.   [2] Cf. p. 301, par. 3.   [3] Cf. p. 302, par. 1.   [4] Cf. *Ibid.* par. 4.

thinking substance exists, no attention being paid to the body, the soul, the mind, or to anything else, but merely to the fact that it exists. Finally he resumes the military frame of mind and imagines he sees these *massed battalions and reserves in dense and serried formation,* which our new Alexander will shatter with a breath,

As the winds scatter the leaves or tufts of thatch[1],

and so *no survivor will be left to tell the tale.* With his first breath he utters the following words : *The argument which reasons from knowledge to existence is not valid*[2]. At the same time he flourishes like a standard a table in which he has given a description of thinking substance according to his own pleasure. With his second breath the following comes out : *Determinately, indeterminately. Distinctly, confusedly. Explicitly, implicitly.* In the third place we have : *The argument that wants too much in its conclusion gets nothing at all.* Finally here in his last deliverance : *I know that I exist as a thinking substance, and nevertheless I do not yet know that the mind exists. Therefore the knowledge of my existence does not depend upon my knowledge of existing mind. Therefore since I am, and the mind does not exist, I am not a mind. Therefore I am a body*[3]. On hearing this the shade keeps silence, retreats, gives up hope and allows him to lead it captive in triumph. Here I could point out much that is worthy of undying laughter, but I prefer to spare my Actor-friend's cloth ; indeed I believe that it hardly becomes me myself to keep up mirth long about such trifles. Wherefore here I shall note only such matters as perhaps some people might believe I admitted (though they are remote from the truth), if I said nothing at all about them.

First of all I deny that he has any right to complain, alleging that I said I had a clear and distinct concept of myself before I had sufficiently explained how that is attained, seeing that, to use his words, *I had asked who I was just a few steps back.* For between these two points I recounted all the properties of a thing which thinks, viz. intelligence, will, imagination, memory, and feeling, etc., as well as all the other properties popularly remarked which do not belong to its concept, in order that I might distinguish the one set from the other. Now this could not be hoped for except upon the removal of our prejudices. Yet I admit that people who do not divest themselves of their prejudices can with difficulty ever

---

[1] Cf. Plautus, *Mil.* I. 1, 17, Quasi ventus folia, aut paniculam tectoriam. But D. reads panicula tectoria.
[2] Cf. p. 303, par. 2.   [3] Cf. p. 304, *ad init.*

attain to a clear and distinct idea of anything. For it is manifest that those concepts which we possessed in childhood were not clear and distinct; and that hence, unless they are deposed from their place, they will render obscure and confused any that we subsequently acquire. Therefore when he wishes to be shown *that clear and distinct concept in order that he may fashion himself anew by seeing it*[1], he is trifling; as also when he introduces me as revealing it to him in the words: *I certainly know that I am*, etc. But when he wishes to refute that trifling account of the matter by the following example: *You also know with certainty that no mountain exists without a valley; therefore you have a clear and distinct concept of a mountain without a valley*, he deceives himself with a fallacy. For from the preceding words he can only conclude: *Therefore you clearly and distinctly perceive that no mountain exists without a valley*, but not: *you have a concept of a mountain without a valley*. For since no such concept exists we do not need to possess it, in order to perceive that there is no mountain without a valley. But, forsooth; he *has such a happy talent*, that he is unable to refute the very futilities he has constructed without employing fresh ones.

When afterwards he says that *I conceive thinking substance, but conceive nothing corporeal, nothing spiritual, etc.* I admit this so far as corporeal substance is concerned, because I had previously explained what I meant by the term body or corporeal; viz. what is extended, or in the concept of which extension is contained. But it is most stupid of him to say what he does in the next words about spiritual substance; and so it is in many other places, where he represents me as saying: *I am a thinking thing, but not body, not soul, not mind*[2], etc. For I can deny of a thinking thing only those matters in whose concept I find no thought contained; but that this holds with the soul[3] or with the mind I have never maintained in my writings or thought.

Again when afterwards he says that *he understands my meaning, and that I think my concept is clear because I am quite certain in my knowledge, and that it is distinct because I am aware of nothing else*, he pretends to be very slow of apprehension. For to perceive clearly is one thing, to know with certainty another; for we now know many things with certainty not only by means of faith which is the gift of God, but also because we have perceived them clearly before, and yet we do not at the present clearly perceive them.

[1] Cf. p. 301, par. 3.   [2] Cf. p. 302 *sub fin.*   [3] de animo.

Moreover, the knowledge of other things by no means prevents our cognition of any particular thing from being distinct. I have never given the least occasion in my writings for such absurd inferences.

Besides, his dictum : *The argument which reasons from knowledge to existence is not valid*[1], is plainly false. For although from the fact that we know the essence of any particular thing, it does not follow that it exists ; nor from the fact that we think that we know a thing does it follow that that is, if there is a possibility of our being deceived : nevertheless the argument from knowledge to existence is quite valid, because it is impossible to know anything, unless it really is as we know it. We either know it as existent if we perceive it to exist, or as of this or that nature, if only its nature is known to us.

It is likewise false, or at least affirmed by him without the least reason, *that some thinking substance is divisible*[2], as he has it in that table in which he brings forward the diverse species of thinking substance, as though instructed by an oracle. For we cannot at all understand extension or divisibility on the part of thought, and it is quite absurd to affirm as true with a single word what has neither been revealed by God, nor is grasped by the intellect. Here I cannot conceal my opinion that his doctrine of the divisibility of thinking substance seems to me very dangerous and quite opposed to the Christian religion. For as long as anyone admits it, he will never by force of reasoning acknowledge the real distinctness between the human soul and the body.

The words *Determinately, indeterminately; Distinctly, confusedly; Explicitly, implicitly*, standing alone, as they do here, have no meaning at all. They seem to be merely pretences employed by my Critic when he wishes to persuade his pupils, though he has nothing valuable to say, that he has, nevertheless, much that is valuable in his thought.

Likewise his other dictum : *The argument which wants too much in its conclusion gets nothing at all*, ought not to be admitted without drawing a distinction. For if by the expression *too much* is meant only something in excess of what was sought, as when beneath[3] he objects to the arguments by which I have demonstrated the existence of God, because he thinks that their conclusion contains more than the laws of prudence require, or any mortal demands, his contention is false and absurd ; because the more

[1] Cf. p. 303, par. 2.   [2] Cf. *Ibid.*   [3] Cf. Reply 4, p. 320.

there is in the conclusion, so long as it is rightly inferred, the better is it, and no laws of prudence can ever be opposed to this. But if by the expression *too much* he means not simply something more than was sought, but something incontrovertibly false, then indeed what he says is true. But the Reverend Father makes a great mistake in attempting to foist anything like this on me. For when I wrote : ' The knowledge of the things which I know to exist, does not depend on the knowledge of the things which I do not yet know to exist; and yet I know that a thing which thinks exists, and do not as yet know that body exists; therefore the knowledge of a thing which thinks does not depend on the knowledge of the body[1],' I inferred nothing excessive and nothing incorrect. But when he assumes the statement : *I know that a thinking thing exists, and I do not yet know that mind exists; nay, no mind exists, nothing exists, everything has been renounced*, he assumes something quite nonsensical and false. For I cannot affirm or deny anything of mind, unless I know what I understand by the term *mind*; and I can understand none of the things which that term customarily signifies in which thought is not contained. Thus it is a contradiction for anyone to know that a thinking thing exists and not to know that mind or some part at least of what is signified by the term mind, exists. The words that my critic puts at the end : *Nay, no mind exists, nothing exists, everything has been renounced*, is so absurd as not to deserve any answer. For since subsequently to our renunciation we have acknowledged the existence of a thing which thinks, the acknowledgment of the existence of mind goes along with that (at least in so far as this is the term that stands for a thing which thinks); consequently we have no longer renounced it.

Finally when he commences his application of formal syllogism to the argument and lauds that as *a method of regulating the reason*[2] opposed to mine, he apparently wishes to prove that I do not favour the syllogistic forms, and that hence the Method I possess is highly irrational. But this is false, as is clear enough from my writings, in which I have nowhere refused to employ syllogisms when the situation demanded such treatment.

Here he brings forward a syllogism constructed out of false premises, which he asserts to be mine but which I deny time and again. For as to the major: *nothing which is such that we can doubt whether it exists, actually exists*, it is so absurd that I have no

---

[1] Cf. Med. II. p. 152.   [2] Cf. p. 304, par. 1.

fear of his being able to persuade others that I am its author, unless
he finds people whom he can at the same time persuade that I am
not of sound mind. Nor can I sufficiently admire the sage counsel,
the faith, the hope and the confidence with which he has undertaken
this. Thus in the first Meditation, in which I was concerned not with
the establishment of any truth, but only with the removal of prejudices, after showing that those opinions in which I had been
accustomed to place the highest confidence could be considered as
doubtful, and that hence I must withhold assent from them no
less than from what was openly false, lest I might meet with any
impediment in my search for truth, I added these words: 'But it
is not yet sufficient to have noticed this; I must take care to bear
it in mind. For our customary *opinions* keep continually coming
back and, almost against my will, seize on my credulity, which is, as
it were, enslaved to them by long usage and the law of familiarity.
Nor shall I ever get out of the habit of assenting to and trusting
them, so long as I assume them to be such as they really are, viz.
in some sense indeed *doubtful*, as has already been shown, but none
the less very probable, and such that it is much more reasonable to
believe them than to deny them. Wherefore I imagine I shall not
act amiss if *I change my attitude to its complete contrary* and,
deceiving myself, *pretend* for a time that *they are altogether false
and imaginary*, until at length I shall as it were equally balance the
weight of my respective prejudices, and my judgment will no longer
be dominated by bad usage or turned away from the right knowledge
of the truth[1].' Out of this passage our Author has chosen the
following words, neglecting the others: '*opinions in some sense
doubtful,*' '*change my attitude to its complete contrary,*' and
'*pretend that they are in some sense doubtful.*' Besides, in place
of the word *pretend* he has substituted *affirm, believe, and shall so
believe as to affirm as true the contrary of that which is doubtful.*
He has tried to make out that this is as it were a dictum or an
absolute rule which I always used, not for the purpose of getting rid
of prejudices, but for laying the foundation of the most certain and
accurate metaphysics. Firstly, nevertheless, he has brought this
forward only with hesitation and surreptitiously, viz. in pars. 2 and
3 of his first Question[2]. Nay, in that third paragraph, after assuming
that according to my rule he ought to believe that 2 and 3 do not
make 5 he asks *whether he should therefore so believe that, as to
persuade himself that it cannot be otherwise*[3]. After several feints

[1] Cf. Med. I, vol. I, p. 148.   [2] Cf. pp. 263—5.   [3] Cf. p. 264, par. 2.

and some superfluous talk he introduces me as thus finally replying
to this absurdest of all questions: *you will neither affirm nor deny;
you will employ neither, and will treat both as false*[1]. Now these
words, attributed to me by himself, show clearly that he knew quite
well that I did not believe as true the contrary of what is doubtful,
and that according to my opinion no one could use that as the
major premise of a syllogism from which a certain conclusion is to
be expected. For the two things are contradictory, viz. neither to
affirm nor deny, *i.e.* to employ neither, and the affirmation and use
of one of them as true. But gradually he forgets those things that
he had related as being my assertions, and not only affirms the
opposite but insists upon it so often, that this forms practically the
unique object of his attack throughout the whole of his dissertation;
all the twelve errors which, from this point onwards to the end he
makes out to have been committed by me, are constructed by him
out of this alone.

This forces me to the conclusion that both here where he affirms
as my belief this major premise: *nothing which is such that I can
doubt whether it exists actually exists*, and in all other passages where
he attributes to me anything of the kind, it is clearly proved that,
unless I am quite ignorant of the meaning of the verb *to lie*, he is
lying without excuse or speaking contrary to his mind and conscience.
And although I am very unwilling to use such a discourteous word,
yet the defence of the truth which I have undertaken requires this
of me, and thus I shall not refuse to call by its proper name what
he does not blush to do so openly. And since in the whole of this
treatise he does little else than try and persuade the reader of, and
enforce upon him, this identical foolish falsehood expressed in an
immense variety of ways, I fail to see any other excuse for him than
that perhaps he has so often repeated the same thing, that gradually
he has persuaded himself that it is true and no longer recognizes it
as a fabrication of his own. Next as to the minor premise: *Every
body is such that I can doubt whether it exists*[2], or: *Every mind is
such that I can doubt whether it exists*[3]; if this is understood to
apply to any time whatsoever indefinitely, as it must be understood
if it is to yield him his conclusion, it is also false and I decline to
own it. For immediately after the beginning of the second Meditation, when I said with certainty that there existed a thinking
thing, which in popular usage is called *mind*, I could no longer
doubt that mind existed. Similarly after the sixth Meditation, in

[1] Cf. p. 265, par. 4.   [2] Cf. p. 304 § 9.   [3] Cf. *Ibid.*

which I ascertained that the body existed, I could no longer doubt
its existence. What a colossal intellect our author has! He has
with supreme art devised two false premises such that a false
conclusion follows from them in good form! But I don't understand
why he here ascribes *sardonic laughter* to me, since in his Dissertation I found merely a source of pleasure, not indeed of an intense
kind, but quite real and genuine. The reason is that, in criticizing
so many things for which I am not responsible but which are
fictitiously ascribed to me, he clearly shows that he has left no
stone unturned, in order to find something meriting censure in my
writings and has found nothing at all.

But certainly it is made sufficiently clear that the humour he has
shown up to this time has not been heartfelt, both by the serious
onslaught with which he concludes this section, and especially by the
succeeding replies, in which he is not only gloomy and severe, but
even quite cruel. To account for this we must note various things.
To begin with he has no cause for hatred and has found nothing to
censure except that single absurdity which with such prudence and
insight he foisted on me, and which a little before I could only
characterize as being a lie. Yet he thinks that he has now completely
convinced the reader that I believe that. (True this cannot be by
force of reasoning, since reasons he has none. But in the first place
he relies on his admirable assurance in affirmation, which, in a man
who makes a peculiar profession of piety and Christian charity, is
never deemed capable of being exercised in support of a falsehood to
so colossal, so shameless an extent. Secondly, he employs a pertinacious and reiterated repetition of the same assertion, and this often
brings it about that the custom of hearing what we know to be false,
produces the habit of believing those things to be true. These two
devices then are wont to have more influence than all the weight of
argument among the vulgar and all who do not examine things
carefully.) So now he haughtily insults the man he has vanquished
and scolds me as a solemn pedagogue might lecture his pupil, and
in the following heated replies holds me guilty of sins more in
number than the ten commandments. But we must excuse the
Reverend Father, as he seems to be no longer master of himself.
Just as people who have drunk too much are wont to see two
objects instead of one, so he in excess of charitable zeal, finds in a
single statement of his own fashioned contrary to his mind and
conscience, twelve charges to make against me. These I ought to
style nothing but abuse and calumny were I not ashamed here to

speak openly and without disguising my words. But, believing
that now it is my turn to jest, I shall call them hallucinations
merely, and beg the Reader to remember that there is not the least
word in his criticisms of me which follow in which he has not been
suffering from delusion.

REPLY[1].

Reply 1. *The Method is faulty in its principles. They are
both non-existent and infinite. Other systems, in order to evolve
the certain from the certain, do indeed posit, clear, evident and
innate principles,* e.g. The whole is greater than its part; out of
nothing, nothing comes, *and a great variety of this type, on which
they rely when mounting upwards and pressing onwards safely to the
truth. But this method proceeds on other lines and in its attempt to
get something, not out of something else but out of nothing, cuts off,
renounces and forswears its principles one and all; it changes our
attitude towards them completely, but lest in its flight it should seem
to have no wings to propel it, it assumes new ones, which like Icarus
it fixes on with wax, and posits novel principles wholly contrary to
our old beliefs. It drops its old prejudices only to adopt new ones; it
lays aside certainties in order to assume what is doubtful. Wings it
has, but waxen; it soars aloft only to fall. It labours to construct
something out of nothing and ends in achieving nothing at all.*

Reply 2. *The Method is faulty in respect of the means it employs.
It has none, forsooth, though at the same time it takes away our
previous instruments; nor does it bring any to occupy their place.
Other systems have logical formulae and syllogisms and sure methods
of reasoning, by following which, like Ariadne's clue, they find
their way out of labyrinths and easily and safely unravel matters
that are intricate. But this new method on the contrary disfigures
the old formula, while at the same time it grows pale at a new danger,
threatened by an evil Spirit of its invention, dreads that it is dreaming,
doubts whether it is in a delirium. Offer it a syllogism; it is scared,
at the major, whatsoever that may be. 'Perhaps,' it says, 'that Spirit
deceives me.' The minor ? It will grow alarmed and say it is
doubtful. 'What if I dream ? How often have not things appeared
certain and clear to a dreamer which, after the dream is over, have
turned out to be false ?' What finally will the method say as to the
conclusion ? It will shun all alike as though they were traps and
snares. 'Do not delirious people, children, and madmen believe that*

---

[1] Reply to the second Question, cf. p. 271.

*they reason excellently, though wanting anything like sense and judg-
ment? What if the same thing has happened to me? What if that
evil Spirit casts dust into my eyes? He is evil, and I do not yet
know that God exists and is able to restrain that deceiver.'* What
will you do here? What is to be done, when that method will declare,
and obstinately maintain, that the necessity of the conclusion is doubtful,
unless you first know with certainty that you are neither dreaming
nor crazy, but that God exists, is truthful, and has put that evil
Spirit under restraint? What is to be done when the method will
repudiate both the matter and the form of this syllogism?—'*It is the
same thing to say that something is contained in the concept or nature
of some matter and to say that it is true of that matter. Yet
existence, etc.'* What about other things of this kind? If you urge
them, he will say: '*Wait until I know that God exists and till I see
that evil Spirit in bonds.'* But you will reply: '*This has at least
the advantage that, though it brings forward no syllogisms, it safely
avoids all fallacies.'* That is capital; to prevent the child from
having catarrh we shall remove its nose! Could other mothers have a
better way of wiping their children's noses? This leaves me therefore
just one thing to say, viz. '*If you take away all form nothing remains
but the formless, the hideous.'*

Reply 3. *The Method has a flaw at the finish, for it attains no
certainty. But certainty it cannot attain, while it itself closes
against itself all the avenues to truth. You yourself have seen and
experienced this in those Ulyssean wanderings in which you have
wearied both yourself and me your comrade. You contended that
you were a mind, and possessed a mind. But you were not able to
prove that at all, and stuck in quagmires and thickets, and indeed
did so so often that I can scarcely recall the number of times. Yet
it will be advantageous to tell them over again in order to give its
proper strength and substance to this reply of mine. Here then are
the chief heads of the suicidal procedure of the Method, of the way in
which it cuts itself off from all hope of attaining to the light of truth.
1. You know not whether you are dreaming or waking, and ought
not to give more credence to your thoughts and reasonings (if you
really possess any, and do not merely dream that you possess them)
than a dreamer puts in his. Hence everything is doubtful and uncertain and your very conclusions are insecure. I shall not adduce
examples; go yourself and review the treasures of your memory and
produce anything which is not infected with that taint. I shall
congratulate you if you do so. 2. Before I know that God exists to*

*restrain the evil Spirit, I ought to doubt everything and hold everything
as altogether suspect.   Or certainly, to follow the common philosophy
and old method of reasoning, before everything it must be determined
whether there are and what are these really safe propositions, and we
must instruct beginners to keep them in mind.   Hence just as in the
former case, all are doubtful and wholly useless for the purpose of
investigating the truth.   3. If there is anything that has the least
doubt, change completely your attitude towards it and believe it to be
false.   Nay, believe the opposite and employ it as a principle.   Hence
I have shut up all avenues to the truth.   For what do you hope from
this: 'I have not a head; there is no body, no mind,' and a thousand
other such statements ?   Do not say that your renunciation has not
been made in perpetuity, but is like a public vacation which has been
instituted for a particular time, a month, or a fortnight, in order that
everyone may give the more heed to its observance.   For let it be so,
let the renunciation be only temporary; yet it is at that time that you
are in quest of the truth, it is then that you use, nay misuse, what
you renounce, just as though the whole truth depended on that, and
consisted in that as in something fixed and stable.   'But,' you say,
'I employ this renunciation in order to make steady pedestal and
column, as architects are wont to do.   Do they not construct a
temporary scaffolding and use it to hoist the column and establish
it finally in its place, and then after this has discharged its function
admirably break it up and take it away ?   Why not imitate them?'
Imitate away, so far as I am concerned, but look out lest your
pedestal and column lean so much upon your temporary scaffolding
that they will fall if you remove it.   It is this that seems to merit
censure in your method.   It reposes on false foundations, and it leans
upon them so much that if they are removed it itself falls to the
ground.*

Reply 4.   *The Method errs by going too far.   That is to say it
contrives to accomplish more than the laws of prudence require of it,
more than any mortal demands.   Some people indeed seek for a demonstration of the existence of God and of the immortality of the human
mind.   But certainly no one has hitherto been found who has not thought
that it is enough, if he knows that God exists, and that the world is
governed by him, and that the souls of men are spiritual and immortal,
with as much certainty as the statement that 2 and 3 make 5, or
'I have a head,' 'I have a body'; and so have made anxiety about
seeking for a higher truth superfluous.   Besides, just as in the
practical life there are assured limits of certainty which quite suffice*

to allow everyone to conduct himself with prudence and in safety; so in thought and speculation there are definite boundaries, such that he who attains to them is certain. Nay, so certain is he that rightly, when anything else in which others wish to attempt to push farther is either in a desperate case or wholly lost, he prudently and safely falls in with the maxim: 'No further, nothing too much.' But you say, 'the glory is not a common one, viz. that of moving forward the boundaries of knowledge and forcing a passage which no one in the centuries behind us has attempted.' Certainly no praise would be too high for you, but to secure it you must effect your journey without coming to grief. Wherefore:

Reply 5. There is an error of defect. That is to say, in straining too far it fails altogether. I wish to take you alone as witness, you alone as judge. What have you accomplished with all your magnificent appliances? Of what avail has been that pompous renunciation, so universal and so liberal, that you have not spared yourself anything indeed except the well-worn maxim I think, I am, I am a thinking thing? I call it well worn, nay so familiar even to the common herd, that no one since the beginning of the world has been found to doubt it even in the least degree, much less to demand seriously of himself a proof that he is, exists, thinks, and is a thinking thing. Consequently no one will give you any thanks, and quite rightly too, unless perhaps we take into account what I do in virtue of my friendship and singular good-will towards you, in approving of your sustained effort to confer a benefit on the human race, and praising your attempt.

Reply 6. Your Method commits the common error of which it convicts remaining systems. Thus it is astonished that all mortals affirm and assert with such unimpaired confidence: 'I have a head, I possess eyes,' etc. Yet it is not astonished at itself saying with equal confidence: 'I have not a head,' etc.

Reply 7. It has a vice peculiar to itself. Thus to the belief held with a certain amount of assurance (a sufficient amount) by other men: 'I have a head, body exists, mind exists,' it with a design peculiar to itself opposes the contrary: 'I have not a head, there is no body, no mind,' not only as certain but as so certain that it can be taken as the foundation of an accurate Metaphysic. In fact it rests its weight on this so much that if you remove this prop it falls to the ground.

Reply 8. Imprudence is one of its errors. Thus it does not notice that 'doubtful' is like a two-edged sword; while avoiding *the one edge it is wounded by the other. It is doubtful, according to the method, 'whether any body exists'; and since this is doubtful it does away with it and posits the opposite: 'there is no body.' But imprudently leaning on this, which is itself doubtful, it comes by a wound.*

Reply 9. *It errs also wittingly; for with full consciousness and deliberation and though adequately warned, it blinds itself and voluntarily abandons things that are necessary for an investigation of the truth. It finishes by deluding itself by its own Analysis, not only achieving what it does not intend, but even what it most fears.*

Reply 10. *Sins of commission must be ascribed to it; it returns to its ancient opinions, though that has been forbidden by solemn edict; and contrary to the laws of renunciation, it resumes what it has renounced. It is enough for you to use your memory to be convinced of this.*

Reply 11. *Sins of omission also are to be found in it. For it is not once merely that it transgresses that principle which it lays down as the basis of our thinking:* The greatest care must be taken not to admit anything which we cannot prove to be true. *It barefacedly assumes as quite certain and gives no proof of the statements:* Our senses sometimes deceive us; we all dream; some people go delirious, *and other similar assertions.*

Reply 12. *The Method contains either nothing sound, or nothing new; at most it contains what is superfluous.*

For if it alleges that by its renunciation of the doubtful it means what is called that Metaphysical abstraction by which what is doubtful is considered only as doubtful and our mind is to that extent bidden shun that, (where anything certain is under investigation,) and no more credence is given to the doubtful on that occasion than to what is false; in that case what it says will be sound, *but not at all* new, *nor will that abstraction be new, but old and common to all philosophers up to the last single one.*

If by that renunciation of what is doubtful it is meant that it must be set aside in the sense of being supposed and alleged to be false, and if the method treats the doubtful as false and its opposite as true; what is said will be something new *but not at all* good, *and though that renunciation will be novel, it will be erroneous.*

If it alleges that by force and weight of reasoning it achieves the following result with certainty and clearness: 'I am a thinking thing and, in so far as a thinking thing, neither mind, soul[1], nor

---

[1] animus.

body, but a thing so much withdrawn from these that I can be com-
prehended, though these have not yet been grasped, exactly as animal
or sentient thing can be grasped, without our knowing what neighs,
lows, etc., this will be something sound *but not* new *at all.   For this*
is a dictum preached everywhere from all the chairs of philosophy ;
it is taught in express words by everyone who thinks that certain
animated creatures think ; and, if thought comprise sense as well,
so that everything which feels, sees and hears also thinks, all who
believe that the brutes feel, i.e. all to the last man, are in agreement.

But if the method declare that it has proved by valid and well-
considered reasons that a thinking thing and substance[1] *really exists,*
but that at the time of its existence the mind, the body, and the soul
do not really exist; in this case what it says will be new, *but by no*
means sound, *just as if it said that animals could exist without there*
being lions, foxes, etc.

Another way to interpret this method is to suggest that the author
says he thinks, i.e. understands, wills, imagines and feels, and thinks
in such a way that he beholds and reviews his own thought by a
reflex act.   This will imply also that he thinks, or knows, or considers
that he thinks (which truly is to be conscious and have consciousness
of any activity).   And if it is maintained that this is a property
of a faculty or thing which has a position superior to matter, and
is wholly spiritual, and that it is on this condition that we are mind
and spirit ; in this case the doctrine will be something not hitherto
stated but which ought to have been stated before.   I was waiting for
this to appear, and when I saw the efforts, futile as they were to
produce it, I wanted time and time again to suggest it.   To say this
would be to say something sound, *but nothing* new, *for we have been*
told it by our teachers and they by theirs, and one generation by the
preceding, in my opinion, beginning with the creation of the race.

If, then, this is the upshot, with what a superfluity of matter
will we not be left ?   What redundancy !   What vain repetition !
What about those devices for securing glory and prestige ?   To what
purpose this talk about the deception of the senses, the illusion of
dreamers, and the freaks of delirium ?   What an ending for that
renunciation which was to be of such austerity that we were to be
allowed to retain nothing but a mere scrap ?   Why those journeys so
long and continuous to distant shores, afar from the senses, amidst
shades and spectres ?   Finally; what will they do towards establishing

---

[1] Se revera existere rem et substantiam cogitantem. But it is impossible in
English to personify the 'Method' to this extent.

the existence of God, claiming as they do that it cannot stand unless everything in the universe is turned upside down? But what is the reason for interpolating new opinions so often and to such an extent in order to lay aside the old, and then, after dismissing the new, assuming the old once more? Perhaps just as the Good Goddess[1] and Consus[2] and others each had their own peculiar rites, so those new mysteries require new ceremonies! But why has not the method, dropping all circumlocutions, expressed the truth neatly, clearly and briefly in a few words then?—'I think, I have consciousness of thought, therefore I am a mind'?

Finally there is the interpretation that the method alleges that understanding, willing, imagining, feeling, i.e. thinking, are properties of the mind, in such a way that there are no animals at all except man, that think, imagine, feel, see, and hear etc. This doctrine will be new, *but not* sound. *It will be indeed gratuitous, and thanklessly will it be received unless some chance preserve and rescue it (that is its last refuge), appearing at its own time, like the god in the machine, a marvel for the gaping crowd. But how long have we given up any hope of that happening?*

Last reply. *Here I think you are fearful for your method, which you love so and which you cherish and treat as your own child. You fear lest, now that I have charged it with many sins, now that it shows flaws and threatens everywhere to collapse, I should deem that it ought to be thrown into the rubbish-heap. But don't be frightened. I am your friend. I shall overcome your apprehension, for I am not mistaken; I shall keep silence and await events. I know you and your keen and clear-sighted mental vision. When you have got some time for meditation, and especially when you have thought over your faithful Analysis in a secret retreat, you will shake off the dust from it, cleanse it anew, and place before our sight a well trimmed and refined Method. Meanwhile take this, and listen to me while I proceed to reply to your questions. I shall embrace in them many things which in my zeal for brevity I have lightly drawn together, such as, what concerns the mind, the true, the false, and similar topics. But you yourself repeat what had escaped the prudent, and*

---

[1] *Bonae Deae* the goddess of Chastity and Fertility.

[2] Descartes' critic has *Conscii*, which must be a mistake for *Consi*. Consus was another ancient Italian divinity.

THIRD QUESTION.

WHETHER A METHOD CAN BE DEVISED ANEW.

You ask, 3, *whether* * * *, (The Reverend Father sent nothing more than this. When the rest were asked for, he replied that he had now no leisure for writing. But we made it a matter of scrupulous observance not to omit the least syllable of what he wrote).

ANNOTATIONS.

Whatever may be the nature of my Method of inquiry into truth, I should have deemed it sufficient to have reported this wonderful pronouncement upon it in order to expose its falsity and absurdity, if it had proceeded from an unknown individual. But the person who makes this attack holds a position of such eminence that it will be difficult for anyone to believe that he is either not in his right mind, or is extremely untruthful and slanderous and impudent. Consequently, in order to prevent his excessive authority prevailing against the manifest truth, I ask my readers to remember that above, in what preceded these replies, he has proved nothing or next to nothing against me, but has employed only silly quibbles in order to make out that my opinions were so ridiculous as not to need a reply. I want people to be quite clear about the fact that in these replies he does not indeed try to prove anything, but falsely assumes that everything which he fictitiously ascribes to me has already been proved by him. In order to appreciate the better the equity of his judgment they should remember that previously in his indictment he put things only in a jesting way, but now in his subsequent judgment he is at the extreme of seriousness and severity. Again in the first eleven replies he condemns me without hesitation and with a high hand, but finally in the twelfth he deliberates and distinguishes : *If this is the interpretation, the method contains nothing new ; if that, nothing sound etc.* Whereas, nevertheless, in every one of them he is treating merely of one and the same thing viewed in different ways ; and that is nothing but his own fabrication, a fabrication the absurdity and dullness of which I shall here set out by means of a simile.

Everywhere in my writings I made it clear that my procedure was like that of Architects planning houses. In order to construct stable houses where the ground is sandy, and stone or clay or any other durable earthy matter is employed in building, they first dig ditches and throw out of them the sand and whatever else rests on or is mixed with the sand, so that they may rest the foundations on firm soil. For so I, also, at first rejected everything doubtful, as they throw out the sand; then perceiving that it is indubitable that a substance which doubted, *i.e.* which thought, existed, I used this as the rock on which I rested the foundations of my philosophy. But our critic is like a common mason who, wishing to be taken in his town for an expert craftsman, and on that account being very jealous of an Architect who was constructing a chapel there, eagerly sought for opportunities of criticising his art; but who being so poorly educated as not to be able to understand what it was to which the Architect trusted, ventured to assail nothing but the first and most obvious beginnings. Thus he noted that the first step was to dig a trench and remove not only the sand and loose earth, but any timber, stones etc. mixed up with the sand, in order to arrive at a hard stratum and there lay the foundation of the chapel. Besides, he has heard that the Architect, replying to questions about the reason for digging trenches, has said that the surface earth on which we stand is not stable enough for bearing the weight of large edifices; that sand is particularly unstable, because not only does it yield when a heavy weight presses on it, but also because a flow of water often bears it away, thus producing an unexpected collapse of anything resting on it. Finally the Architect has related how when such subsidences occur, as they do from time to time, in mines, the miners are in the habit of ascribing their cause to spectres or evil spirits inhabiting the subterranean places. Our Workman then makes this an opportunity for pretending that the Architect takes their trenching operations to be equivalent to the construction of the chapel. He alleges that the Architect takes either the ditch or the rock uncovered at its base, or if anything is reared above this trench, that at least only if the trench itself meanwhile remain empty, to be all that requires to be done in the construction of the chapel; and he says that the Architect himself is so foolish as to fear lest the earth on which he stands will give way under his feet or that ghosts will make it subside. Perhaps he manages to persuade a few children of this, or others so ignorant of the art of building that it seems to them novel and strange to dig trenches in order to lay the foundations of houses; and who readily believe a man whom they know and whom they believe to be well enough skilled in his trade and honest, touching an Architect whom they do not know and of whom they have heard that he has as yet constructed nothing, but has merely dug trenches. Then he becomes so well pleased with this figment of his that he becomes hopeful of persuading the whole world of its truth. And although the Architect has now had all the trenches previously excavated filled with stones, and has erected his chapel on the top, and employed the hardest building material, and has built most securely and called on everyone to look and see, our Workman nevertheless sticks to his old idea and still hopes to get people one and all to believe his nonsense. To this end he stands daily in the public streets making sport of the Architect to the passing throng. And this is the style of his argument :—

Firstly he introduces his opponent ordering the digging of trenches and the removing from them not only of sand but also of everything lying among or resting upon the sand, even though it were unhewn boulders, even squared stones ; in a word it appears that *everything* must be removed, *nothing* whatsoever left. He lays great stress upon those words, *nothing, everything, even unhewn boulders, even stones.* At the same time he feigns that he wants to learn that art of building from the Architect, and that he would like to descend with him into those trenches. *I beg you to conduct me through them yourself,* he says. *Come express your mind ; you have either a comrade or a pupil to whom to show the way. What do you bid me do ? Though it is new to me and, since I am not accustomed to its obscurity, to be dreaded, I am quite willing to enter that route....I hear you reply ; you bid me do what I see you do, to plant my steps where you put yours. That is certainly an excellent way of commanding and leading me ! How well you let me think of you. I am ready*[1].

Next pretending that he is in dread of the spectres that lurk in these underground excavations, he tries to provoke the mirth of the spectators by the following words : *But will you substantiate this for me, so that I shall not be in fear, shall have no apprehensions about that evil spirit ? Certainly though you may try to strengthen me in any way you please, it is not without extreme fear that I descend into this darkness*[2]. Again, shortly afterwards, he exclaims : *But what have I done ? I have been forgetful of what I promised to do. I had committed myself entirely to you at the beginning, had vowed myself your ally and disciple, and here I am hesitating at the very outset, timid and obstinate. Pray forgive me ! I have sinned*

---

[1] Cf. p. 272.
[2] A paraphrase of p. 275, middle.

greatly and have merely shown the smallness of my intellectual capacity. It was my duty to have laid aside all fear and to plunge boldly into that subterranean gloom ; but I have been unwilling and have resisted[1].

In the third place he represents the Architect as showing him the stone or rock in the bottom of the ditch on which he wishes his whole edifice to repose. He greets them with jeers : *Splendid, my good friend ! You have found the point that Archimedes wanted to discover : there is no doubt that if you so please you will be able to move the world ; look now, it all begins to sway and tremble. But, I beg you (for I have no doubt you wish to prune things down so that there shall be nothing in your science which is not apt, coherent and necessary), why have you let this stone remain ? Did you not order the removal of all stones along with the sand ? But perhaps it was by chance that you let this pass : it is so difficult even for an expert to forget altogether the things to which we have been accustomed since childhood, that a slip on the part of a raw hand like me if it chance to occur is hardly likely to be thought ill of*[2], *etc.* Further, the Architect having collected some broken stones along with the sand that had been thrown out of the trenches in order to use these materials for building, his critic thus assails him with derision : *Shall I dare, before you push onwards, to ask why you, the man who with such solemn declarations, rejected all broken stones as not being sufficiently stable, want to inspect them again as if you hoped to get something good out of that rubble*[3]? *etc. Nay, since everything you rejected a little time ago was weak and threatening to collapse (otherwise why did you set it aside ?) how does it come about that the same things are now not weak and on the point of collapse*[4]? Again shortly afterwards he says : *Here again suffer me to admire the devices you employ, you who, in order to establish the certain, employ the uncertain : who, in order to bring us into the light, bid us plunge into darkness*[5], *etc.* At this point he talks away in a very silly fashion about the designations and duties of Architect and Workman respectively and he contributes nothing to the discussion, except that, by confusing the meaning of the terms, he is less able to distinguish the one from the other.

The fourth episode finds both standing in the bottom of the

---

[1] An almost literal reproduction of p. 275 *sub fin.* and p. 276, l. 6.
[2] A paraphrase of p. 280, ll. 5—17.
[3] Cf. *ibid.* par. 4.   [4] *Ibid. infra.*
[5] A variant of p. 281, ll. 3—6.

trench. The Architect thereupon attempts to begin the construction
of his wall. But in vain ; for at the very outset when he wants to
lay a squared stone there at the base, the Workman at once reminds
him that he had ordered the removal of all stones, and that it was
hence inconsistent with the rules of his art to lay down this one.
This reminder, then, prevailing with him like an Archimedian
demonstration forces him to desist from work. And next when he
begins to use rough stones or bricks, or slaked lime mixed with
sand, or any other material, the Workman keeps on inveighing :
' You have rejected everything ; you have retained nothing,' and
repeating the words Nothing, Everything etc. as though they were
incantations, he succeeds in destroying all the Architect's handi-
work. The harangue he made was so like what we find above in
paragraphs 5 and 9, that there is no need to report his words here.

The final and fifth scene shows him, when he sees a large enough
crowd collected round him, adopting a new tone, and changing his
comic jocosity for the severity of tragedy ; he wipes the plaster from
his face and, with a serious countenance and a censorious voice,
enumerates and condemns all the Architect's errors (those forsooth
which he supposes he has shown in the previous acts). I shall
recount the whole of this judgment of his just as he stated it at
the final incident where he acted his pretty play before the
crowd ; and this I shall do in order to show how my critic has
imitated his workman prototype. The latter pretends that the
Architect has asked him to pronounce judgment on his art, and
he replies in the following way.

In the first place, your Art makes a mistake about the founda-
tions. They are both non-existent and infinite. Other methods
indeed of constructing houses lay very stable foundations, e.g. of
squared stones, bricks, rough rock, and countless similar substances,
reposing on which the walls mount upwards. But your method
proceeds quite otherwise and, in its attempt to get something, not
out of something but out of nothing, it tears down, digs up, and
casts away every scrap of the old foundations. It changes its
attitude completely but, lest in its flight it should seem to have
no wings to propel it, like Icarus it assumes new ones and fixes
them on with wax. It lays down new foundations entirely the
opposite of the old ones ; but in so doing it avoids the instability of
the previous basis only by incurring a new weakness. It upsets what
is firm in order to rely on what is weak ; it employs wings, but
waxen ones. It rears a mansion to the skies, but only to have it

fall. Finally it labours to construct something out of nothing and ends by achieving nothing at all[1].

Now the very church alone which the Architect has already built proves that all this is the silliest of nonsense. For it is quite clear that in it the foundations have been most firmly laid, and that the Architect has destroyed nothing which was not worthy of destruction; and that he has never departed from the precepts of others unless he had some better plan; that the building soars to a great height without threatening to fall; finally that he has constructed not out of nothing, but out of the most durable material, not nothing, but a stable and well-built church to the glory of God. But all this together with the other matters in which my critic has suffered from delusions, can be seen clearly enough from the Meditations alone which I published. But there is no reason to impugn the writer's historical knowledge (from whom I took the Workman's words) because he introduced his popular critic as attributing wings to Architecture, as well as much else that seems hardly to be in harmony therewith. For probably this was intentional and it was meant thereby to show how agitated he was when he uttered such things. And certainly all such similes are equally out of place when talking of the Method of inquiring into truth, though my critic nevertheless employs them.

The second reply was: *The* Architect's procedure *is wrong in respect of the means it employs. It is forsooth possessed of none, though at the same time it removes our previous instruments; and it brings none to occupy their place. Other arts of this kind employ a rule, a level and a plumb line; and employing these to extricate themselves from a labyrinth of difficulties, they manage with ease and exactitude to build together masses of rock however shapeless. But this, on the contrary, disfigures the old shape of buildings, though at the same time it grows pale with a new fear, pretending that subterranean ghosts threaten it, and in terror lest the earth subside and the sands disperse. Set up your column; whatever that be, your art will be apprehensive at the laying of the pedestal and base. 'Perhaps,' it says, 'the ghosts will cast the column down.' It will be anxious and say the pillar is weak. What if it is only gypsum and not marble? How often have other things appeared to us to be strong and firm which afterwards, when we came to try them, were found to be easily broken? What then will happen when we come to the crown of the column? Your new method will avoid everything*

[1] Cf. p. 318.

at all times like snares and traps. Have not bad Architects often constructed other buildings which, though they thought them strong, came down of their own accord? What if this style is subject to the same contingency? Suppose the spectres disturb the soil? They are evil. Nor have I known any foundation laid on so firm a rock that the spectres are unable to do anything to overturn it. What will you do here? What, when your art will declare and obstinately maintain that the durability of the crown of the column is doubtful, unless you previously know with certainty, that the column neither consists of fragile material nor rests on the sand, but is based on solid rock, rock which the underground spirits are unable ever to overturn? What, when it will repudiate both the matter and the form of this column? (Here with a jocular audacity he produced a representation of one of these very columns which the Architect had set up in his chapel.) *What about other things of this kind? If you urge them he will say, ‘Wait till I know that there is a rock beneath me and that no ghosts can ever overturn it.’ But you will reply, ‘This has at least the advantage that, though it sets up no new pillars, it safely avoids constructing any wrongly.’ That is a capital preventive of the child’s catarrh etc.,* as above[1]. I will not continue, as the rest is too coarse for repetition. So I ask the reader to compare the present replies with the similar versions of which my critic is the author.

Now this reply like the preceding is convicted of the most impudent falsehood by the existence itself of the chapel in question, since there were in it many strong columns, among them that very one, the picture of which the Workman displayed, making out that the Architect had repudiated it. In the same way my writings definitely settle the fact that I do not cast aspersions on the syllogism and deface its ancient form; I have used it in my writings wherever there was need. Among other syllogistic arguments he has extracted from my works that very one of which he here pretends that I reject both the matter and the form. For it will be found at the end of the reply to the First set of Objections, in Proposition 1, where I prove the existence of God. Moreover I cannot see what is his purpose in making this fabrication, unless perhaps he wishes to hint that everything which I have propounded as true and certain is in conflict with that renunciation of doubtful beliefs with which alone he wishes to identify my Method. Now this is just the same as, and not less childish and silly than, if the

---

[1] Cf. pp. 318, 319.

Workman were to pretend that the digging out of the trench for the purpose of laying the foundation of houses was the whole of the architect's art, and if he complained that anything the Architect constructed was in disagreement with that excavation.

The third reply was : *Your art has a flaw at the finish, for it ends by constructing nothing stable. But stability it cannot secure, since it itself closes against itself all avenues towards that end. You yourself have seen and experienced this in these Ulyssean wanderings in which you have wearied both yourself and me your companion. You contended that you were an Architect or were possessed of the Architect's art. But you were unable to prove that at all, and stuck in quagmires and thickets, and indeed did so so often that I can scarcely recall the number of times. Yet it will be advantageous to tell them over again now in order to give its proper substance and strength to this reply of mine. Here then are the chief heads of the suicidal procedure of your art, of the way in which it cuts itself off from all hope of securing its end. 1. You know not whether beneath the surface there is sand or rock and therefore you ought not to trust to rock more than to sand (if in spite of all you do some time come to have rock beneath you). Hence everything is doubtful and uncertain. I shall not adduce examples. Go yourself and review the treasures of your memory and produce anything which is not infected with that taint. I shall congratulate you if you do so. 2. Before I have found firm soil beneath which I know there is no sand and with no underground spirits troubling it, I ought to reject everything and treat all materials in every way with suspicion. Or certainly to follow the old and common style of building, it must be determined whether there are and what are those materials which really ought not to be rejected, and the diggers ought to be instructed to leave those in the trench. Hence, just as in the former cases, everything is lacking in strength, and quite useless for the construction of buildings. 3. If there is anything in the least liable to be upset, change completely your attitude towards it and believe it to have already fallen, nay believe it ought to be flung out of the trench, and use the empty trench alone as a foundation. Hence I have shut up all the avenues leading to the completion of the building. For what do you hope from this : ' There is no earth here, no sand, no stone,' and a thousand other such statements ? Do not say that this excavation is not to go on for ever but, like a public vacation which has been instituted for a set time, so this also is for a definite period and goes on until the trench is a certain depth corresponding to the depth of the sand at the spot: Let it be so, let the excavation go on for a time only ; yet it occurs at the time during which you imagine that you are building, at the time when you employ, nay misemploy the emptiness of the trench in your scheme, just as though the whole of the building art depended on that art and consisted in that as its stable foundation. 'But,' you say, ' I employ it in order to make steady pedestal and column as other Architects are wont to do. Do they not construct a temporary scaffolding and use it to hoist the column ?*[1]'

Now in this none of the Workman's statements are more ridiculous than what is to be found in our Author's thought. What I have subsequently demonstrated proves that my rejection of doubtful beliefs no more precludes an attainment of knowledge of the truth, than the excavations which the Architect prescribes prevents him from constructing his chapel. Surely otherwise he ought to have noted something false or uncertain in my conclusions. But since he neither does this nor is able to do so, it must be confessed that he is suffering from a quite inexcusable delusion. I have not laboured more to prove that I, or a thinking thing was mind, than my opponent to prove that he *was* an Architect. But our Author with all his toil and effort has certainly not here proved anything except that he has no mind, or at least that his mind is not of good quality. Neither from the fact that metaphysical doubt proceeds so far as to suppose that a man does not know whether he is dreaming or awake, does it follow that he can discover no certainty, any more than that because an Architect, when he begins digging operations, does not yet know whether he is to find rock or clay or sand or anything else beneath the surface, it follows that he will not be able to discover rock there, or that when he has found it he ought not to trust it. Nor from the fact that, before a man knows that God exists, he has an opportunity of doubting everything (viz. everything of which he does not have a clear perception present in his mind, as I have a number of times set forth) does it follow that nothing is of avail in the pursuit of truth, more than it was a consequence of the Architect's getting everything turned out of the trench before firm soil was reached, that there was no rubble or anything else in the trench which he might afterwards deem of use in laying the foundations. It was no stupider a mistake on the part of the Workman to say that the common and ancient style of Architecture forbade their being thrown out

[1] Cf. pp. 319, 320.

of the trench and instructed the diggers to retain them, than it is for our Author both to say that *before everything it must be determined whether there are and what are those really safe propositions that are free from doubt* (for how could they be determined by one whom we suppose as yet to know none?), and in the same breath to assert that this is a precept of the common and ancient Philosophy (in which no such precept is found). Nor was it more crass stupidity on the part of the Workman to pretend that the Architect wanted to take an empty ditch as his foundation and that all this building depended upon doing so, than it was manifest raving on the part of my Critic to say that *I employ the opposite of what is doubtful as a principle, that I abuse what I renounce; just as though the whole truth depended on that, and consisted in that as in its stable foundation,* unmindful of the words which he had above reported as mine; *you will neither affirm nor deny, you will treat both as false.* Finally, in comparing the digging of a trench in order to lay a foundation to the setting up of a scaffolding, the Workman did not show his lack of knowledge to any greater extent than our author did in likening the renunciation of doubtful beliefs to this also.

The fourth reply was: *Your art errs by going too far. That is to say, it strives to accomplish more than the laws of prudence require of it, more than any mortal demands. Some people indeed seek to construct durable houses for themselves. But certainly no one has hitherto been found who has not thought it enough for him, if the house in which he lived were as firm as the earth which supports us, so that anxiety about seeking for a still greater strength is superfluous. Besides, just as in walking there are certain conditions relative to the stability of the ground we tread on, which quite suffice to allow everyone to walk on it in safety, so in the building of houses there are certain limiting conditions, such that he who attains to them is certain, etc.,*[1] as above.

Now though here it is unjust of the Workman to blame the architect, it is with still greater injustice that my critic blames me in the corresponding case. For it is true that in the construction of houses there are certain conditions implying less than absolute firmness of the ground, beyond which it is not worth our while proceeding, and these vary in proportion to the size and mass of the building we are constructing. For it is safe to build the lowlier class of cottages upon sand, the stability of which relative to their burden is as great as that of rock relative to high towers. But it

[1] Cf. pp. 320, 321.

is utterly false that in laying the foundations of a philosophy there are any such limits not reaching so far as full certainty, in which we may prudently and safely acquiesce. For since truth consists in what is indivisible, it is possible that a matter whose complete certainty we do not recognize, however probable it appear, is wholly false. Certainly it would not be prudent philosophising on the part of a man who took as the foundation of his science statements which he knew to be possibly false. Indeed what answer will he make to the sceptics who overpass all the boundaries of doubt? How will he refute them? Oh, he will reckon them among the desperate or the lost! Very fine indeed; but meanwhile to what class will they assign him? Neither must we think that the sect of the sceptics is long extinct. It flourishes to-day as much as ever, and nearly all who think that they have some ability beyond that of the rest of mankind, finding nothing that satisfies them in the common Philosophy, and seeing no other truth, take refuge in Scepticism. Those people are especially such as demand a proof to be given them of the existence of God and the immortality of the soul. Hence what our author here states constitutes a very bad example, especially as he has a name for great learning. It shows that he thinks there is no possibility of refuting the errors of the Sceptical Atheists; and thus all his efforts result in strengthening and confirming them. Nay it is true that though no contemporary Sceptics have any doubt when it comes to the practical life about possessing a head and about 2 and 3 making 5, and the like; they say they only employ those statements as truths because they have an appearance of being true, but that they do not believe them with certainty because there are no convincing arguments impelling them to do so. And because to them the existence of God and the immortality of the human mind do not have the same appearance of truth, they think that therefore they ought not to make use of these beliefs even in practical life, unless a proof is first given them with sounder reasoning than any which secures adherence to beliefs that have an appearance of being true. Now since it was those beliefs the truth of which I proved and, at least to my knowledge, no one before me, I think that no greater slander could be devised than that for which our author is responsible when throughout the whole of his Dissertation he continually assigns to me, reiterating the imputation a countless number of times, that single error which constitutes the speciality of Scepticism, viz. excessive doubt. Very liberal is my Critic in recounting the list of my sins. For although he says that *the glory is not a common one, that of moving forward the boundaries of knowledge and forcing a passage which no one in the centuries behind us has attempted,* and though he has no reason for suspecting that I have not done this in the very matter of which he is treating, as I shall show directly, yet he reckons this against me as a sin, saying, *certainly no praise would be too high for you, but to secure it you must effect your journey without coming to grief.* Evidently he wishes his readers to believe that I have come to grief then, or committed some error ; yet he does not believe so himself, nor indeed has he any reason to suspect it. For surely if he had been able to devise the least reason for suspecting some straying from the path on my part at any point in the whole of the route by which I conducted the mind from the knowledge of its own existence to the knowledge of the existence of God, and its distinctness from the body, doubtless in a dissertation of such length, such verbosity and such poverty of topics, he would not have failed to mention it. He would have far preferred to do this, rather than change the question, as he always has done whenever the argument required him to treat of that subject, or in such a silly fashion represent me as discussing whether a thinking thing was Mind. Therefore he had no reason for suspecting that I had made any error in what I asserted, and in the Arguments by which I, first of all men, upset the doubt of the Sceptics. He confesses that this is worthy of the highest praise. Yet he has sufficient audacity to censure me on the very same count, and fictitiously ascribes to me that doubt which he might with better right have imputed to any of the rest of mankind who have never refuted that doubt, rather than to me alone. But in his commentary we find

The fifth reply. *There is an error of defect. That is to say, in expending too much effort it completes nothing. I wish to take you alone as witness, you alone as judge. What have you accomplished with all your magnificent appliances? Of what avail has been that pretentious excavation, so universal and so liberal, that you have not spared yourself even the most durable of stones, except this one, this one as to the retention of which you quote the painfully common statement: 'The rock which is discovered lower than any sand, is strong and durable.' This is a truth, I repeat, so familiar to the common herd*[1], *etc.* as above.

Now here I expected to find both the Workman in question and

---

[1] Cf. p. 321.

my Critic to prove something.   But just as the former's only object
was to ask what was the result of the Architect's excavations,
except that he had laid bare some rock, and to dissimulate the fact
that he had reared his chapel upon this rock; so my Critic asks
me merely what I have effected by my rejection of doubtful beliefs
other than that I have found this commonplace: *I think I am,*
seeing he holds it of no account that from this I have demonstrated
the existence of God and many other truths.   And he wants to
take me alone as witness, witness I suppose of his glaring audacity;
just as elsewhere also and in the matter of other fabrications he
says *that all to the last man believe them, and that they are doctrines
taught from every chair of philosophy*[1] *; that we have been told it by
our teachers and they by theirs and so on right up to the creation of
the race,* and the like.   But we should no more trust these assertions
than the oaths of certain men, who are wont to use the more
protestations the greater they believe to be the incredibility and
falsity of what they want us to believe.

The Workman's next reply, No. 6.   *Your art commits the
common error of which it convicts remaining systems.   Thus it is
astonished that all mortals affirm and assert with such unimpaired
confidence: 'The sand is strong enough on which we stand.   This
ground we tread on does not move, etc.,' yet it is not astonished at
itself saying with equal confidence: ' We must clear away the sand,
etc*[2].*'*

Now this is no sillier than what our Author in similar circumstances affirms.

Reply 7.   *It has a vice peculiar to itself.   Thus to the belief
held with a certain amount of assurance (a sufficient assurance) by
other men, to the effect that the earth on which we stand, sand, stones,
etc. are firm enough, it, with a design peculiar to itself, opposes the
contrary statement, and takes the trench, forsooth, out of which sand,
stones, and the rest have been cast, not only as something strong, but
so strong that it can found upon it the solid structure of a chapel.
In fact it rests its weight on this so much that if you remove these
props the whole falls to the ground*[3].

Here the illusion is no greater than that which besets our
Author, so long as he is forgetful of the words: *You will neither
affirm nor deny, etc.*

Reply 8.   *Imprudence is one of its errors.   Thus it does not
notice that the instability of the ground is like a two-edged sword;*

---

[1] Cf. p. 323, par. 1.   [2] Cf. p. 321.   [3] Cf. *ibid.*

while avoiding the one edge it is wounded by the other. Sand is not a stable enough soil for it; because[1] *it does away with this and posits the opposite, viz. a ditch empty of sand, and imprudently relying on this empty ditch as though it were something firm it comes by a wound*[2].

Here again we have only to remember the words : *You will neither affirm nor deny.* All this talk about a double-edged sword is more worthy of the sagacity of our Workman than of my Critic.

Reply 9. *It errs also wittingly, for with full consciousness and deliberation, and though adequately warned, it blinds itself and voluntarily abandons those things that are necessary for the building of houses. It finishes by deluding itself with its own rule, not only achieving what it does not intend but even what it most fears*[3].

But the Architect's success in building his chapel, and the truths I have succeeded in demonstrating, show how much truth there is in the charge against each of us respectively.

Reply 10. *Sins of commission must be ascribed to it. It returns to its ancient opinions, though that has been forbidden by solemn edict and, contrary to its laws about excavation, it resumes what it has renounced. It is enough for you to use your memory to be convinced of this*[4].

In his similar accusation our Author is forgetful of the words : *You will neither affirm nor deny.* Otherwise how could he keep countenance in pretending that that had been forbidden by solemn edict which he previously said had not even been denied ?

Reply 11. *Sins of omission also are to be found in it, for it is not once merely that it transgresses that principle which it lays down as a basis: ' The greatest care must be taken not to admit anything which we cannot prove to be true.' It barefacedly assumes as quite certain and gives no proof of the statements: 'Sandy soil is not firm enough on which to build houses,' and other similar assertions*[5].

Here it is clear that our Author[6], like my Critic in the case of the rejection of doubtful beliefs, was under a delusion, applying to the excavation of a foundation what belongs only to the construction alike of buildings and of a philosophy. For it is absolutely true

---

[1] Quia. It ought to be quapropter = wherefore (cf. p. 322 *ad init.*) in order to make the construction safe; but in that case the accuracy of the quotation would not be exact.

[2] Cf. p. 322. [3] *Ibid.*

[4] *Ibid.* [5] *Ibid.*

[6] It ought to be Caementarius—the mason or workman.

that nothing is to be admitted as true, which we cannot prove to be true when it is a question of setting it up or affirming it. But when it is only a case of casting a thing out of a trench or setting aside a belief, it is sufficient to have suspicions about it.

The twelfth reply was: *Your art contains nothing sound or nothing new; at most what is superfluous.*

For (1) *if it alleges that by its excavation of the sand it means that excavation which other architects employ, when they throw out the sand only if they think it not strong enough to bear the weight of buildings; in that case what it says is* sound, *but not at all* new*; nor will that method of excavation be new, but old, and common to all architects up to the last single one*[1].

(2) *If by that digging out of the sand it is meant that the whole of the sand must be thrown away, all removed and none retained, and none of it or its opposite, viz. the vacuity of the place which it formerly filled, must be employed as something firm and stable; that will be something* new *but not at all* good, *and though your method of excavation will be novel, it will be spurious*[2].

(3) *If it alleges that by force and weight of reasoning it achieves the following result with certainty and clearness: 'I am an expert in Architecture, and practise it; nevertheless, in so far as I am this, I am neither architect, mason, nor hodman, but something so much withdrawn from these that I can be comprehended though these have not yet been grasped, exactly as animal or sentient thing can be grasped without our knowing what neighs, lows etc.*[3]*': this will be something* sound *but not* new *at all. For every cross-road resounds with this tale, and it is taught in express words by everyone who thinks that there are experts in architecture; and if architecture likewise embraces the construction of walls, so that those also are versed in Architecture, who mix lime and sand, who hew stone, and carry up the material in hods, all who think that labourers practice this craft, i.e. all to the last man are in agreement*[3].

(4) *If it declare that it has proved by valid and well considered reasons that its professor really exists and is a man skilled in Architecture, but that at the time of his existence, no architect really exists, nor any mason, nor hodman; in this case what it says will be* new, *but by no means* sound, *just as if it said that animal could exist without there being lions, foxes, etc*[4].

(5) *Another way to interpret this art is to suggest that the*

[1] Cf. p. 322.   [2] *Ibid.*
[3] Cf. p. 323.   [4] *Ibid.*

architect builds, i.e. employs the science of architecture in constructing buildings and builds in such a way that he beholds and reviews his own action by a reflex act. This will imply also that he knows or considers that he builds (which truly is to be conscious and to have consciousness of any activity). And if it is maintained that this is a property of architecture, i.e. of an art which holds a place superior to the science of hodmen, and that it is on this condition that he is an architect; in this case the doctrine will be something not hitherto stated, but which ought to have been stated before. I was waiting for this to appear, and when I saw the efforts, futile as they were, to produce it, I wanted time and time again to suggest it. To say this would be to say something sound, but nothing new, for we have been told it by our teachers and they by theirs and, in my opinion, one generation by another beginning with the creation of the race[1].

If, then, this is the upshot, with what a superfluity of matter will we not be left? What redundancy! What vain repetition! What about those devices for securing glory and prestige? To what purpose this talk about the instability of the sand, and disturbance of the earth, and spectres, empty figments to terrify us? What an ending for that excavation which was to be so profound that we were to be allowed to retain nothing but a mere scrap! Why those journeys so long and continuous to distant shores, afar from the senses, amidst shades and spectres? Finally what will they do towards securing the stability of your chapel, claiming as they do that it cannot stand unless every thing is turned upside down? But what is the reason for interpolating new materials so often and to such an extent in order to lay aside the old, and then after dismissing the new, resume the old once more? Perhaps just as while we are in a temple or in the presence of sovereign spirits we ought to behave ourselves otherwise than when in taverns or hovels, *so these new mysteries require new ceremonies. But why has not your art, dropping all circumlocutions, expressed the truth neatly, clearly, and briefly in a few words thus: ' I build, I have consciousness of this building, therefore I am an Architect'?*

(6)   *Finally there is the interpretation that your art alleges that it constructs houses, that it plans their bedrooms, apartments, porches, doors, windows, pillars and the rest, in the mind beforehand, and arranges them, and next, in order to get them constructed, gives instructions to those who supply the material, to the quarrymen, masons,*

[1] Cf. p. 323.

roof-makers, hodmen and other workmen, and directs their work, and that this is the peculiar function of the Architect in the sense that no other workmen can effect that function. This doctrine will be new but not sound. *It will indeed be gratuitous and thanklessly will it be received, unless some chance preserve and rescue it (that is its last refuge), appearing at its own time, like the god in the machine, a marvel for the gaping crowd.* But how long have we given up any hope of that happening?

Last reply. *Here I think you are fearful for your art, which you love so and which you cherish and treat, pardon me, as your own child. You fear lest, now that I have charged it with so many sins, now that it shows flaws and threatens everywhere to collapse, I should deem that it ought to be thrown into the rubbish-heap.* But don't be frightened. I am your friend. *I shall overcome your apprehensions, if I am not mistaken; I shall keep silence and await events. I know you and your clear and keen-sighted mental vision.* When you have got some time for meditation and especially when you have thought over your faithful rule in a secret retreat, you will shake off the dust from it, cleanse it anew, and place before our sight a well balanced and polished Architecture. *Meanwhile take this and listen to me while I proceed to reply to your questions. I shall embrace in them many things which, in my zeal for brevity I have lightly drawn together, such as, what concerns the arches, the openings for windows, the columns, the porches, and the like*[1]. But here we get the programme of a new comedy.

Whether Architecture can be Established Anew.

You ask thirdly. When this point was reached, some of his friends seeing that the excessive jealousy and hatred by which he was agitated, had now become quite a disease, prevented him from going about declaiming in the streets any longer, and forthwith carried him to a doctor.

Now I should certainly not venture to imagine any such similar fate for my Critic. I shall here go only so far as to note how accurately he has imitated that Workman in all his actions. It is quite in the same way that he acts the judge, the upright judge forsooth, who takes great and scrupulous care lest he pronounce any rash decision. After condemning me eleven times over on the one count of rejecting the doubtful in order to establish the certain,

[1] Cf. p. 324.

and as it were digging trenches in order to lay the foundations of my building, he at length on the twelfth occasion comes to the examination of the point to be discussed and says,

1. If I have understood it, as he in reality knows I have understood it, and as is clear from the words, *You will neither affirm nor deny*, etc., which he himself attributed to me : then indeed my doctrine contains something *sound*, but nothing *new*.

2. But if I have understood it in that other way, from which he has extracted the eleven preceding errors, and which he yet knows is quite remote from my meaning, seeing that above in paragraph 3 of his first question he has introduced me as taking an attitude of wonder and mockery towards it and saying : *How could that come into the mind of any sane man?* Then my doctrine, forsooth, contains some *novelty*, but nothing that is *sound*. Now in the history of abuse has there ever been any person, I don't say so impudent, so mendacious, so contemptuous of all truth and verisimilitude, but so impudent and of such short memory, that in an elaborate dissertation to which much thought has been given, he has charged some one with holding an opinion, which in the beginning of the same dissertation, he admitted was held in abhorrence by the very man whom he charged with holding it, to such an extent that he believed that no sane man could entertain it?

As to the questions which follow (numbers 3, 4, and 5), both in my Critic's and in the Workman's list of charges, they are quite irrelevant, and were never set forward either by me or by the Architect. It seems very likely that the Workman first devised them, in order that, since he dared not undertake any of the things the architect performed, for fear of showing too evidently his lack of skill, he might nevertheless appear to attack something else besides his policy of excavation. And it appears that my Critic has in this respect followed his methods.

3. For when he says that a thinking thing can be understood, though the mind is not known, nor the soul, nor the body, his philosophy is no better than that of the Workman, when he says that to be skilled in Architecture belongs no more to an architect than to a mason or hodman, and that one so skilled can be understood apart from any of these.

4. Just as, also, it is equally inept to say that a thinking thing exists though the mind does not exist, as to assert that one skilled in architecture can exist though no architect exists (at least if the word mind is taken in the sense in which I, following established

usage, announced I understood it). And it is no more contradictory that a thinking thing should exist without a body than a man skilled in architecture should exist without there being masons or hodmen.

5. Likewise when my Critic says that it is not sufficient that a substance be a thinking one, for it to have a higher position than matter, and be wholly spiritual, such as alone he wishes to call mind, but that in addition it requires by a reflex act to think it thinks or have a consciousness of its own thought, his delusion is as great as that of the Workman when he says that one who is skilled in architecture ought to consider by a reflex act that he possesses that skill before he can be an architect. For although no one as a matter of fact is an architect who has not often reflected or at least been able to reflect that he possesses the skill required in building, yet manifestly he does not require to make that reflection in order to become an architect. Nor is there any more need for that consideration or reflection in order that thinking substance be placed above matter. For the first thought, whatever it be, by which we become aware of anything does not differ more from the second by which we become aware that we have become aware of that, than this second differs from the third by which we become aware that we have become aware that we have become aware. Again if it be allowed that the first function belongs to a corporeal thing, there is not the least reason why the second should not be so attributed also. Wherefore we must note that our Critic commits a much more dangerous error here than the workman. For he removes the true and highly intelligible differentia between corporeal and incorporeal things, viz. that the former think but the latter do not, and substitutes in its place another which can in no wise be thought essential, viz. that the former reflect that they think, while the latter do not. Thus he does all that he can towards preventing a true understanding of the distinction between the human mind and the body.

6. He is less to be excused in favouring the cause of the brutes and wishing to ascribe thought to them not less than to men, than the Workman in attempting to arrogate to himself and his like a skill in architecture no less than that possessed by the Architect.

Finally it is in everything sufficiently apparent that both have been alike in thinking not of objections that had any truth or verisimilitude, but merely of such as might be trumped up for the purpose of casting aspersions on an enemy and representing him as quite unskilled and a fool, to those who did not know him or do not take pains to inquire more curiously into the truth of the matter. Indeed he who reports about the Workman, in order to express his mad hatred, relates how he extolled the Architect's excavations as a magnificent contrivance, but scorned the uncovering of the stone which that excavation revealed and the chapel built upon it as matters of no moment. Yet nevertheless out of his friendship and singular good will to him he rendered thanks etc. Likewise at the end he introduces himself as making these wonderful declarations : *If, then, this is the upshot, with what a superfluity of matter will we not be left ?　What redundancy !　What vain repetitions !　What about those devices for securing glory and prestige*[1]*?* etc. And shortly after : *Here I think you are fearful for your art, which you love and cherish so,* etc. Likewise : *But don't be frightened, I am your friend.* All this describes the Workman's malady so graphically that no poet could draw a more living picture. But it is surprising that our Author should imitate all the same peculiarities with such enthusiasm that he does not notice what he himself is doing, and does not employ that reflex act of thought by which, according to his recent statement, men are distinguished from the brutes. For he surely would not say that there was too great a display of words in my writings if he considered how many more he employs himself. In what I cannot call his attack since he uses no arguments to further it, but (to use a somewhat bitter expression since there is none other that so well expresses the truth of the matter) in his revilings, he attacks at large length merely the subject of the doubt of which I treated. Neither would he have talked of *vain repetition* if he had seen how prolix, how redundant, how full of empty loquacity is the whole of his Dissertation, in the end of which, he nevertheless says, he has studied brevity. But since he there says that he is friendly to me, in order that I may deal with him in the friendliest fashion, I shall do as the Workman's friends did who carried him off to the doctor and shall commend him to his Superior[2].

---

[1] Cf. p. 323.
[2] These words seem to foreshadow the ' Letter to Father Dinet ' which follows this work and followed it in the original edition.

LETTER TO DINET.

PREFATORY NOTE

Dinet, who became Confessor to the King of France, was Descartes' instructor as a boy at the Jesuit College of La Flêche, and Descartes ever bore for him the profoundest regard, as is shown by the tone in which he writes.

In the second edition of the 'Meditations, Objections and Replies' this Letter is appended. The Seventh Objections are by Père Bourdin, the Jesuit whose superior was Père Dinet, and Descartes explains to the latter his grievance against Bourdin, as also against Gisbert Voët, a Protestant Minister of Utrecht. This letter is therefore closely connected with the 'Objections,' and is printed at the end of these in the edition of MM. Adam and Tannery.

E. S. H.

TO THE MOST REVEREND FATHER DINET OF THE SOCIETY OF JESUS, HEAD OF THE PROVINCE OF FRANCE. FROM RENATUS DES CARTES.

When recently I indicated to the Reverend Father Mersenne by the letter which I wrote to him, that I would have greatly desired that the Dissertation which I learned the Reverend Father[1] had written concerning me should have been published by him, or else that it should have been sent to me in order that I might have it published with the rest of the Objections that others had sent me; and when I asked that he should try to obtain this either from him, or else, because I judged it a most just request, at least from your Reverence, he replied that he had placed my letter in your Reverence's hands, and that not alone had you favourably received it, but that you had even given many indications of singular sagacity, kindness, and good-will towards me. And this I have very clearly recognised even from the fact that the Dissertation in question was sent me. This not only makes me deeply grateful to you, but it also impels me here to say freely what I think of that Dissertation, and at the same time to ask your advice concerning the plan of my studies.

To tell the truth I no sooner held this Dissertation in my hands, than I rejoiced as though I had in my possession a great treasure ; since there is nothing more to be desired than either to protest the certainty of my opinions, as it may haply be if, after distinguished men have examined them, no error is discovered in them, or else that I should be shown my errors in order that I may correct them. And just as in well constituted bodies there is a union and inter-connection of parts so great that no single part employs merely its own strength, but, especially, a sort of common strength

---

[1] i.e. the Rev. Father Bourdin.

belonging to the whole supplements the agency of each member; so, being aware of the intimate connection that ordinarily exists between the various members of your Society, I did not judge, when I received the Dissertation of the Reverend Father[1], that I received the communication of one individual, but I believed that it was an exact and accurate judgment on my opinions formed by the whole body of your Society.

Nevertheless, after having read it, I was very much taken aback, and I then began to see that I must judge of it in quite another way than I had at first done. For without doubt had the work come from one who was imbued with the same spirit as that which pervades all your Society, more, or certainly not less, kindness, gentleness, and modesty would be observed in it than in the case of those private individuals who have written to me on the same subject; but far from that being so, if you could compare it with their objections to my Meditations, you will not fail to believe that it is the latter which have been composed by men who lead the religious life, convinced that the former is conceived in terms so bitter as to shame any private person and certainly one bound by special vows to practise virtue more than other men. There should also be observed in it a love of God and an ardent zeal for the advancement of His glory; but on the contrary it appears as though the writer impugned all reason and truth, and, by ill-founded authorities and fictions, the principles of which I availed myself in proving the existence of God and the real distinction between the soul of man and the body. There should in addition be observed knowledge, reason and good sense, but short of desiring to place in the category of knowledge an acquaintance with the Latin tongue such as the riff-raff of Rome had in olden days, I have not observed in his writings any trace of these, any more than I have observed any reasoning which was not either illegitimate or false, nor finally any token of ingenuity of mind, which was not more worthy of an artizan than of a Father of the Society. I do not speak of prudence, or of other virtues which are so pre-eminent in your Society, and which yet do not appear in this Dissertation, nor is there in it the slightest trace of such shown. But one might at least expect to remark in it a reverence for truth, probity and candour; on the contrary it is very manifestly seen by the notes I have written[2], that nothing can be imagined more removed from every appearance

[1] Bourdin.
[2] Cf. Obj. vii. Vol. ii. p. 257.

of truth than all that he imputes to me in this writing. And further, just as when one portion of our body is so disposed that it is impossible for it to follow the law that is common to the whole body, we infer that it is suffering from some disease peculiar to it, so the Dissertation of the Reverend Father clearly demonstrates to us that he does not enjoy that health which is found in the rest of the body of your Society. As however we do not the less esteem the head of a man, or the man in his entirety, because there may possibly be certain evil humours that have flowed against his will and in spite of himself, either into his foot or finger, but rather praise the constancy and virtue with which he does not fail to endure the pains inflicted by his cure : and as no one has ventured to condemn Caius Marius for having varicose veins, and as on the contrary he is often more praised by writers for having courageously suffered one of his legs to be cut, than for having obtained the consulate on seven different occasions and having obtained many victories over his enemies ; so, not being ignorant of the pious and paternal affection that you cherish for all that pertains to yourselves, the more unsatisfactory the Dissertation seems to me, the more do I esteem your integrity and prudence in having desired it to be sent to me, and the more do I honour and reverence your whole Society. But inasmuch as the Reverend Father has consented to send me his Dissertation, in case it may seem rash in me to judge that he did not do it of himself, I will explain why I feel impelled to believe this, and so I shall narrate all that has hitherto passed between him and me.

As early as the year 1640 he wrote against me other treatises on Optics which I hear that he read out to his pupils, and he even gave copies to these pupils for purposes of transcription—not perhaps to all, as to that I am ignorant, but certainly to some, and it may be credited that it was to those who were the most cherished and faithful, for on making request of one of them, in whose hands it had been, for a copy, he could not be persuaded to give it. Subsequently he published theses upon that subject, which were for three days sustained in your College of Paris with great display and extraordinary publicity ; while it is true that on this occasion he touched on some other matters, he was chiefly engaged in disputing about my opinions, and obtained many successes at my expense— successes not difficult to achieve over an absentee. I further saw the Attack on me which served as Preface to these Disputations which were read at the beginning, and which the Reverend Father had composed with much toil and study. Here the object was clearly none other than to impugn my opinions ; nevertheless the words objected to and laid to my charge were none that I had ever written and thought, and they were all so nonsensical that it was impossible that they should occur to any sane man, any more than those which he attributed to me in his Dissertation. This I explained at the time in the Notes upon it which I sent privately to the author, whom I did not then know as belonging to the Society.

And in the theses it is not only that he condemned my opinions as false, which would be open to any one to do, especially if he had reasons ready to prove his point ; but also, with his usual candour, he altered the signification of certain terms. Thus, for example, the angle which in optics is called the refractive[1], he calls the angle of refraction[2]. The subtlety is much the same as when in his Dissertation he says he understands by body[3] that which thinks[4], and by soul[5], that which is extended[6], and by this artifice certain of my discoveries were expressed in very different language, and brought forward as his own, while me he convicted of having a different and quite foolish opinion about them.

Being warned of this, I at once wrote to the Reverend Rector of the College, and begged that ' since my opinions had been judged worthy of public refutation, he would not also judge me unworthy —I who might still be counted amongst his disciples—to see the arguments which had been used to refute them.' And I added many other reasons which seemed to me to suffice to cause him to grant me what I asked for, such as, amongst others, that ' I much preferred being instructed by those of your Company than by any others whatever, because I excessively honour and respect them both as my masters and as the only instructors of my youth ; I have further in the Discourse on Method[7], p. 75, asked all those who may read my writings to take the trouble of making me acquainted with any errors into which they may have seen me slide, telling them that they will ever find me ready to correct them, and that I do not think that any one will be found, above all amongst those who profess a religious life, who would prefer to convict me of error in the presence of others, and in my absence, rather than to show me my faults, and that at least I could not doubt that

---

[1] refractus.   [2] dabat nomen anguli refractionis.   [3] corpus.
[4] id quod cogitat.   [5] animam.   [6] id quod est extensum.
[7] In this edition, Vol. i. p. 126.

love to his neighbour would be shown by a person such as I describe.'

To this the Reverend Rector made no reply, but the Reverend Father[1] wrote to me that he would send me his treatises in a week, that is, the reasons which he made use of in order to impugn my opinions. A short time thereafter I received letters from certain other Fathers of the Society which promised me in his name the same thing in about six months, perhaps because, as they did not approve of these treatises (for they did not expressly avow that they were aware of anything which he had done against me), they demanded this time in order to correct them. And finally the Reverend Father sent me letters, not only written by his own hand, but also sealed with the seal of the Society, which showed me that it was by the order of his superiors that he wrote; what he said was (1) *That the Reverend Rector, seeing that the communications I had addressed to him concerned him alone, had ordered him to reply to them himself, and to give me his reasons for his action.* (2) *That he had never undertaken, nor would he ever undertake any special attack on my opinions.* (3) *That if he had never responded to the request made in the Method, p. 75, this must be attributed to his ignorance, since he had never read the Method through.* (4) *As regards the Notes which I had made on his opening discourse he had nothing to add to what he had already replied, and would have written if his friends had not counselled him to do otherwise*; that is to say, he had nothing whatever to say on my notes because he had indicated nothing but that he would send me the reasons he had for combating my opinions; and by these words he simply declared that he would never send them to me, because his friends had dissuaded him from doing so.

From all these things it was easy to see that he had burned with the desire of denouncing me and had undertaken that enterprise on his own account and without the consent of the other Fathers of the Society; and consequently that he was actuated by another spirit than that of your Society; and finally that there was nothing he desired less than that I should see what he had written against me. Although it seemed to me to be quite unworthy to see a man of his sacred profession, with whom I had never had any controversy, and who was quite unknown to me, so publicly, so openly, and so extraordinarily biassed against me, giving as his

---

[1] Bourdin.

excuse simply that he had never read my Discourse on Method, the untruth of which clearly appeared from the fact that he had frequently censured my Analysis, both in his Theses and in that opening discourse, although I nowhere else treated of it at all or even spoke of it under the name Analysis, excepting in that Discourse on Method which he declared he had never read. Yet at the same time, since he promised in the future to abstain from annoying me, I freely overlooked the past.

And I do not wonder in the least that the Reverend Rector had on the first occasion ordered nothing more severe than that he himself should give me his reasons for his proceeding, and thus confess openly that he could not maintain in my presence one of those things that he had arrogantly advanced against me, whether in his Theses or during his Disputations, or in his Treatises ; and that he had likewise nothing to reply to the notes I had written on his Attack. But I am certainly much astonished that the Reverend Father has had so great a desire to attack me, that after having seen the little success that this first Attack had happily had, and that, after the time during which he had promised me *to carry on no particular warfare against my opinions*, nothing that was new passed between him and me, or even between me and any one of your members, he yet wrote his Dissertation. For if he does not carry on a *particular warfare* against my opinions, I am altogether ignorant of what combating the opinions of others means, if perchance he does not excuse himself by saying that as a matter of fact he does not impugn my opinions, but those of other insane ones, which calumniously he has ascribed to me ; or else that he never thought that his Dissertation would fall into my hands. For it is easy to judge by the style in which it is written, that it has never been purposely designed to be placed in the number of the Objections made against my Meditations ; for this is sufficiently clear from the fact that he did not wish me to see his other Treatises (for what could they contain worse than what it contains ?) ; it is finally very manifest by the wonderfully full licence which he gives himself to attribute to me opinions quite different from my own, for he would have shown himself a little more restrained than he is, had he thought that I should have reproached him publicly. For that reason I feel and express my deepest thanks for receiving the Dissertation, certainly not to him, but to the Society and to you.

I should have liked that this opportunity, such as it is, now offered me of thanking you, could be conjoined with concealment of the injuries which he has done me, rather than with some desire to avenge myself, lest I should seem to do this for my own sake ; and in fact I should not do so did I not think that it would conduce to your honour and that of your Society, and lead to the discovery of very useful truths. But, as the Reverend Father teaches mathematics in your College of Paris, which may be called one of the most celebrated in the whole world, and as the mathematical is the faculty in which I am said principally to be engaged, so, just as there is no person in all your Society whose authority can more efficaciously impugn my opinions than his, there is similarly no one whose errors in this matter could more easily be attributed to you all, were I to pass them over in silence. For many people would persuade themselves that he alone from out of all your Body, had been selected to judge of my opinions, and thus that on the above question as much regard ought to be paid to him alone as to you all, and in this matter that the same judgment should be passed on you as on him.

And further, though the advice which he has followed in this matter is very well suited to impede, or temporarily retard, the knowledge of the truth, it is not sufficient to suppress it altogether, and you would certainly receive no honour if it came to be discovered. For he made no effort to refute my opinions by reasoning, but contented himself with setting forth as mine, other opinions of a very inappropriate and pointless description, conceived in terms sufficiently like mine, and simply mocking them as unworthy of being refuted. By this artifice he would easily have turned away all those who do not know me, or who have never seen my writings, from reading them ; and he would perhaps by this means have prevented a yet further examination by those who having seen them do not sufficiently understand them as yet, that is to say, the most part of those who have seen them : for, as a matter of fact, they would never have doubted that a man of his profession, and especially one belonging to your Society, would have dared confidently to set forth opinions as mine, which were not mine, and to mock at them.

And to this end it would have helped greatly that his Dissertation had not been seen by all, but had merely been communicated privately to certain of his friends ; for by this means it would have been easy for him to arrange that it would be seen by none of those who could have recognized his fictions ; and the others would have placed so much the more credence in him, inasmuch as they would be persuaded that he would not have desired to bring it to light in case of its prejudicing my reputation, and that he was rendering to me the service of a friend. And yet there would have been no danger of its not being read by a sufficient numbr of persons; for if he had only been able to persuade the friends of your Society, in your College of Paris, as he hoped to do, this their opinion would have easily passed on to all the other members of your Society who are scattered over the world; and from them it would have passed to almost all other men, who had placed their trust in the authority of your Society. And if that had happened, I should not have been much surprised, for since each of you is incessantly occupied with his own particular studies, it is impossible that all can examine all the new books which are every day in great numbers published; I fancy however that you would refer a book to the judgment of whoever of your Society was the first to read it, and follow his judgment in deciding whether the others would read the work, or abstain from so doing. It seems to me that this has already been proved in respect of the Treatise which I published on Meteors; for seeing it treats of a section of philosophy which is therein explained more accurately, if I am not mistaken, and more probably, than it is by any of the authors who have written upon it before me, I do not see that there is any reason why these philosophers who year by year teach Meteors in your College, should not deal with it, if it be not that possibly by believing the wrongful judgments made upon me by the Reverend Father, they have never read it.

But as long as he never did anything but attack those writings of mine which deal with physics or mathematics, I did not concern myself greatly. But seeing that in this Dissertation he undertook to destroy, not by reasoning, but by abuse, the principles of Metaphysics of which I availed myself in demonstrating the existence of God and the real distinction between the soul of man and the body, I judged the knowledge of these truths to be so important, that I believed no sensible man could object if I undertook to defend what I have written with all my strength. And it will not be difficult to accomplish this, for, since he has not objected to anything in me but that I carried doubt much too far, it is not necessary in order to show how unjust he is in blaming me for this, that I should here mention all the places in my Meditations in which I have diligently, and, if I mistake not, more accurately than any other who has written on the subject, successfully refuted that doubt; but it is sufficient that I should here make known to you

what I have expressly written in the beginning of my reply to the
third Objection; for I set forth no reasons for doubt with the object
of persuading others thereto, but on the contrary for the purpose
of refuting them; in this matter I clearly followed the example of
doctors who 'describe the illness in regard to which they wish to
teach the cure.' And tell me, pray, who has been so audacious and
impudent as to blame Hippocrates or Galen for having shown the
causes which engender illness, and who has concluded therefrom that
they neither of them taught anything but the Method of falling ill?

Certainly those who know that the Reverend Father has had
this audacity, would have difficulty in persuading themselves that
in this matter he acted on his own account and following his own
counsel, if I did not myself bear witness and make known, how it
came about that his previous writings against me had not been
approved by your Society, and his last Dissertation has been sent
to me at your request. And as this could not be more conveniently
done than in this letter, I think that it is not out of place that
I cause it to be printed with the Annotations which I have made
on his Dissertation[1].

And in order that I might myself derive some profit therefrom,
I would like here to say something to you of the Philosophy on
which I am engaged, and which, if nothing prevents me, I mean to
bring to light in one or two years[2]. Having in the year 1637
published some specimens of this Philosophy, I did all in my power to
protect myself from the ill-will which I well saw, unworthy as I was,
would be drawn upon me; this was the reason why I did not wish to
put my name to them; not as perhaps has appeared to some, because
I had not confidence in the truth of the reasons contained in them,
and was in any degree ashamed of having written them; it was for
the same reason that I declared expressly in my Discourse on
Method that it appeared to me that I should in nowise consent to
my philosophy being published during my life. And I should still
be of the same mind if, as I hoped, as reason seemed to promise me,
this had freed me from at least some measure of ill-will. But the
result was quite otherwise. For such has been the lot of my
writings, that although they could not have been understood by
many, yet because they were comprehended by some, and indeed
by persons who were very intellectual and learned, who deigned to

---

[1] The *Notae* of Descartes, interpolated in the *Dissertatio* of Father Bourdin,
appeared, as a matter of fact, under the title of *Objectiones septimae* etc. in the
same volume as this Letter to Father Dinet.

[2] i.e. *The Principles of Philosophy*, published in 1644.

examine them with more care than others, many truths which had
not hitherto been discovered were there recognised as being present,
and the fame of this becoming bruited abroad, made many persons
likewise believe that I knew somewhat as certain and incontro-
vertible in philosophy, which was not subject to dispute. This
finally caused the greater part not only of those who, being outside
the Schools, were at liberty to philosophize as they liked, but even
the greater part of those who teach, more especially of the younger
teachers, who place their trust more on strength of intellect than on
a false reputation for knowledge, and, in a word, all those who love
truth, to beg me to bring my philosophy to the light of day. But
as to the others, that is to say those who prefer to appear learned
rather than to be such, and who already imagine themselves to have
acquired some renown amongst the learned just because they are
able to dispute with acrimony in all the controversies of the Schools,
since they feared that if the truth came to be discovered all these
controversies would cease, and by the same means all their teaching
would come into contempt; and further having some idea that if
I published my philosophy the truth might be discovered; they
have not indeed dared to declare openly that they did not desire
that it should be published, but they have betrayed a great animosity
towards me. And it has been very easy for me to distinguish the
one from the others. For those who wish to see my philosophy
published, recollected very well that I had intended not to publish it
during my life, and many even complained of me that I preferred to
leave it to our successors rather than to give it to my contemporaries;
however all men of intelligence who knew the reason of it, and who
saw that it was not due to want of will on my part to serve the
public, did not for all that like me the less. But as for those who
apprehended that it might never see the light, they have never
recollected the facts of the case, or at least they have not wished to
believe them, but on the contrary they supposed that I had merely
promised its publication : hence according to these I was called *the
famous promiser* and compared to those who for many years boasted
that they were going to publish books, to which they had never
even put pen. This likewise causes the Reverend Father to say
that *I had been expected to publish for so long that now we must
despair of publication altogether*; this is truly absurd, as if one
could expect something of a man not yet old, which no one has
been able to accomplish during centuries. And it not also bears
evidence of imprudence, since in thinking to blame me, he yet

confesses that I am such that a few years have sufficed to make the delay of a work on my part seem long which I should not expect him to finish within a thousand years supposing we both could live so long. Men of this type in the full belief that I had resolved to publish this philosophy which gave them so much apprehension, as soon as it was in a state of readiness, commenced to decry by calumnies, concealed as well as open and public, not only the opinions expounded in the writings which I had already published, but principally also this to them still unknown philosophy, with the idea either of preventing me from printing it, or of destroying it so soon as it came to light and so to speak strangling it in its cradle. At first I did nothing but laugh at the vanity of all their efforts, and the more vehemently I found them attacking my writings, the higher in my opinion did they rate me. But when I saw that their number increased from day to day, and, as generally happens, that there were many more who lost no occasion of seeking to injure me than there were of those who were desirous of giving me their support, I dreaded that they might by their secret practices acquire some power, and more disturb my leisure, if I remained constant in my design of not printing my philosophy, than were I to oppose them openly ; and by producing the whole of that which they do fear I shall see to it that they have nothing to fear. I have resolved to give to the public all the small amount of my meditations on philosophy, and to work to the utmost of my power to bring it to pass that if they are found to be true, my opinions may be generally accepted. This will cause their not being prepared in the same order and style as I have formerly adopted with the greater part of them in the Treatise whose argument I expounded in the Discourse on Method, but I shall make use of a mode of writing more suited to the usages of the Schools, in treating each question in short articles, so that each one may depend for its proof only on those that precede, and thus all may together form but one single body. And by this means I hope that the truth of all things as to which there is disputation in philosophy will be so clearly seen that all those who desire to seek it will find it very easily in my writings.

In fact all young people seek truth when first they apply themselves to the study of philosophy. All others also, of whatever age, seek it when they meditate alone by themselves on the matters of Philosophy, and examine them for their own use. Even the princes and magistrates and all those who establish academies or colleges, and who furnish great sums for the teaching of Philosophy in them, are quite unanimous in desiring that as far as possible, only true philosophy shall be taught. And if it be permitted by princes that dubious and controversial questions shall be agitated, it is not in order that those who are their subjects shall by this custom of disputation and controversy learn to become more contentious, more refractory, and more opinionative, and thus less obedient to their superiors and more likely to become seditious, but merely in order that, by such disputes, they may be convinced of the truth ; or if a long experience has persuaded them that it is rarely discovered by such means, they are yet so jealous of it, that they believe that the small amount of hope there is of finding it should not be neglected. For there has never been a people so savage or barbarous, or one which shrinks so much from the right use of the reason which pertains to man alone, as to desire opinions to be taught in its midst contrary to the known truth. And there is no doubt that we ought to prefer truth to all the opinions opposed to it, however deep-rooted and common they may be ; and that all those who teach others should be obliged to seek it with all their might and when they have found it to teach it.

But perhaps it may not be thought that it will be found in the new philosophy which I promise. For it is not likely that I alone should have seen more clearly than thousands of the most intelligent of men who have accepted the opinions commonly received in the Schools ; and roads frequently followed and known are always more reliable than new and unknown ones, and this is particularly true of our theology, as to which the experience of many years has shown us that it agrees with the old and ordinary philosophy very well, and this is uncertain with regard to a new one. And it is for that reason that some maintain that we must early prevent its publication and demolish it, in case, by attracting to itself by the charm of novelty a multitude of ignorant persons, it may gradually increase, and strengthen itself through time, or else trouble the peace and quietude of the Schools or Academies, or even bring new heresies into the Church.

I reply to this that in truth I make claim to nothing, nor do I profess to see more than other men ; but this perhaps has been of use to me, namely, that, not trusting very much to my own genius, I followed only the simplest and easiest roads. For we must not be astonished if anyone makes more progress in following these paths than others, endowed with much greater talent, make over the rough and impenetrable roads which they follow.

I further add that I do not desire that my simple word should be accepted regarding the truth of what I promise, but that judgment should be made on the writings which I have already published. For I did not there make trial of one question or two, but explained more than a thousand which had not so far been expounded by any one before; and although hitherto many had looked at my writings askance, and endeavoured in all sorts of ways to refute them, no one that I know of has as yet been able to find them not true. If an enumeration is made of all the questions that have during all the centuries through which the other philosophies have flourished, been through their means solved, we shall find them neither so numerous nor so celebrated as those˙ of mine. But further, I state boldly that the solution of no one question has ever been given by the aid of the principles of the philosophy of the Peripatetics, that I myself cannot demonstrate to be false and illegitimate. And to prove this, let any one set before me, not all, for I do not consider that they are worth the trouble of employing much time upon, but some of the most striking questions, and I promise that I shall stand by what I have said. I simply make it known here in order to remove all matter of dispute, that in speaking of the particular principles of the Peripatetic philosophy, I do not except questions the solution of which are derived either entirely from the experience common to all men, or from the consideration of figures and movements proper to mathematicians, or finally from the notions of metaphysics which are commonly received, and which seem to have been admitted by me just as much as are the preceding, as appears from my Meditations.

I go further and say what may seem to be a paradox, viz. that there is nothing in all this philosophy in so far as it is termed Peripatetic and different from others, that is not new; and that on the other hand there is nothing in mine that is not old. For, as regards principles, I accept those alone which have been generally accepted by all philosophers, and which for that reason are the most ancient of all; and that which I finally deduce from them appears to be, as I clearly show, so contained and implied in these principles, that it would seem that it is likewise very ancient, since nature herself has engraved it upon our minds. But, on the other hand, the principles of the ordinary philosophy, at least at the time at which they were invented by Aristotle or by others, were new, nor should they be esteemed to be better now than they then were; and nothing has been as yet deduced from them which is not contested, and which, according to the custom of the Schools, is not subject to change at the hands of individual philosophers, and hence which is not entirely new, since it is every day made afresh.

As to theology, as one truth can never be contrary to another truth, it would be a kind of impiety to fear that the truths discovered in philosophy were contrary to those of the true Faith. And I even assert that our religion teaches us nothing which could not be as easily, or even more easily, explained in accordance with my principles, than with those commonly received. And it seems to me that I have already given a sufficiently full proof of that at the end of my Reply to the Fourth Objections, in respect of a question in which we usually have the greatest trouble in making philosophy accord with theology. And I am still ready to do the same in regard to other questions, were there need ; and even likewise to show that there are many things in the ordinary philosophy which are not really in accordance with these that in theology are certain, although this is usually dissimulated by those who support that philosophy, or through long habit of acceptance of them, the fact is not perceived.

We must not likewise fear that my opinions may increase too much by attracting to them a multitude ignorant and greedy for novelty. On the contrary, since experience shows that those who approve of them are the more cultivated, whom not novelty but truth attracts, they cannot make headway too quickly.

We must not either apprehend that it may disturb the peace of the Schools; but on the other hand, since all the philosophers embroil themselves in so many controversies that they can never be in a greater warfare than they now are, there is no better method for establishing peace amongst them, and refuting the heresies which day by day revive their controversies, than by obliging them to receive the opinions which, like mine, are proved to be true. For the clear conception that we have of them, will remove all matter of doubt and disputation.

And from all this we see clearly that there is in truth no reason why some men should be so anxious to turn away others from a knowledge of my opinions, except that holding them to be evident and certain, they are afraid that they should stand in the way of that reputation for learning that they themselves have acquired through the knowledge of other less probable reasoning. So that this very envy that they bear, is no small proof of the truth and certainty of my philosophy. But lest perhaps I may seem to be boasting falsely of the envy in which I am held, with nothing to call in evidence but the Dissertation of the Reverend Father, I shall tell you here what has happened not long since in one of the most recent Academies of these Provinces.

A certain Doctor of Medicine[1]—a man of most subtle and perceptive mind, and of the number of those who, although they are well taught in the philosophy of the Schools, yet because they disbelieve it and are open minded, are not on that account very proud, nor imagine themselves to be wise in the way in which others do, who are so to speak drunken with knowledge—read my Dioptric and Meteors so soon as they saw the light, and at once judged that they contained within them the principles of a Philosophy more true than any other. And having diligently collated them and deduced others from them, he was so skilful and diligent as in a few months to compose an entire treatise on Physiology which, when shown to a few of his own friends, gave them such pleasure that they made application to the magistracy and obtained for him a professoriate of medicine which was then vacant, and which he had hitherto not tried to procure. In this way, having become professor, he judged that it was his duty to make it his business mainly to teach those things which had procured him the office; and that so much the more that he believed them to be true, and held the contrary to be false. But as it came to pass that by this means he attracted to himself a large number of auditors who deserted the other classes, certain of his colleagues, seeing that he was preferred to them, commenced to be envious and frequently brought complaints against him to the magistracy, requesting that he should be forbidden to teach the new doctrine. And yet for three years they could obtain nothing against him excepting that he was exhorted to teach the elements of the ordinary philosophy and medicine along with his own principles, so that by this means he should put it in the power of his audience to read the works of others. For the magistracy being prudent, saw very clearly that if these new opinions were true, it should not prevent their being published; if, on the other hand, they were false, there was no need to prohibit them, because in a short while they would collapse of themselves. But seeing that on the contrary they grew from day to day, and that they were followed out for the most part by men of highest merit and distinction, rather than by the more humble and

[1] Henricus Regius or Henry de Roy, of Utrecht, at one time an ardent adherent of Descartes.

youthful who were more easily turned aside by the authority or advice of the envious, the magistrates gave a new employment to this doctor, which was indeed to explain on certain days of the week certain extra lessons on Problems of Physics[1]—both those suggested by Aristotle and by others—thus giving to him a better occasion for the treatment of all portions of Physics than he could have had in merely dealing with his own subject of Medicine. And his other colleagues would have thereafter remained quiet and given place to the truth, if it had not been that one, the Rector of the Academy[2], resolved to use all the machinery in his power to oust him. And in order that you may know something of these my adversaries I shall in a few words sketch his character.

This one is termed a theologian, an orator, and a controversialist; and he has acquired great repute amongst the populace from the fact that declaring now against the Roman church, now against others which are different from his own, and now against the powers that be, he betrays an ardent and indomitable zeal for religion, and occasionally also mingles in his discourse words of a scurrilous kind which gains the ears of the commonalty; but since every day he brings out many little books which, however, deserve to be read by none, and further cites various authors who yet more frequently tell against him than in his favour, and whom he probably knows only by their table of contents; and as he speaks very boldly, but also with very little skill, of all the sciences, as though he were very learned in them, he passes for being very wise before the ignorant. But those persons who have greater understanding who know how he has always shown himself ready to quarrel with anybody, and how frequently in disputes he has brought forward abuse rather than reasons, and basely retreated after being vanquished, if they are of a religion different from his, openly jeer at and disdain him; and some have even so controverted him publicly that it would seem that nothing further remained to be said against him; and if they are of the same religion, although they excuse and support him as much as they can, they yet do not in their hearts approve of him.

After this individual had been Rector for some time, it came to pass that when my medical friend was presiding at the defence of certain theses by some of his pupils, they were not given an opportunity to reply to the arguments brought before them, but were

---

[1] Regius was made Professor Extraordinary of Physics on Sept. 6, 1638, and an Ordinary Professor on March 18, 1639.

[2] Gisbertus Voetius, Rector of the University of Utrecht 1641-1642.

disturbed all the time by students stamping their feet. I do not say that this stamping was instigated by this theologian through his friends, for as to this I have no knowledge, but certainly it was not done previously; and I heard afterwards from some who are worthy of credence, and who were present, that it could not have been excited through the fault of the President or his respondents, since these noises always began before they had explained their views. And yet the report was spread abroad that the new philosophy was badly defended, in order to make everyone conclude that it was not worthy of being publicly taught.

It happened also that as there were frequently disputes under the presidency of this physician, and as the theses were filled with questions of a very various and disconnected kind, arranged in accordance with the fancy of those who supported them, and not at all in a careful way, someone placed in his theses the assertion *that the union of soul and body produced not a unity which was an entity on its own account*[1], *but one which was accidental*[2], meaning by an *accidental entity*[3] whatever is composed of two substances altogether different, without at the same time denying the substantial unity by which the mind is joined to the body, nor the natural aptitude or inclination that every individual part has for this union. This we see from the fact that they had added immediately afterwards: *that these substances were termed incomplete by reason of the compound which resulted from their union*; so that nothing remained to reply to either of these propositions, excepting perhaps that they were not expressed after the manner of the Schools.

This seemed indeed to the Theologian and Rector to give a sufficient opportunity for attacking my medical friend on every side, and in order to remove him by this means from his chair if the matter succeeded as he hoped, even in spite of the magistracy. And it was of no avail to the Physician that as soon as he knew that the Rector did not approve of this thesis, he went to see him and the other theological professors, and having explained to them his meaning, assured them that he had no intention of writing anything contrary to their theology, and his. For a few days later the Rector caused these theses to be published to which I am assured he intended to preface this title: *Corollaries propounded for the instruction of students by the authority of the sacred faculty of Theology*; and added *that the opinion of Taurellus whom the*

---

[1] per se.　　　[2] per accidens.　　　[3] ens per accidens.

theologians of Heidelberg termed the Atheist Physician, and that of the foolish young Gorlaeus who says that man is an entity by accident, is in very many ways at variance with Physics, Metaphysics, Philosophy of Spirit[1] *and Theology &c.* So that after having made all the other theological professors and preachers in the place sign these (if they really signed them, for of that I am not informed), he might depute certain of his colleagues who were to tell the magistracy that the physician had been condemned for heresy by an ecclesiastical council and placed in the company of Taurellus and Gorlaeus, authors whom he might possibly never have read, and who for my part are absolutely unknown to me ; and that thus the magistrate could not with the popular goodwill have him longer occupying the chair. But as these theses were still in the press, they fell by chance into the hands of certain of the magistrates who having called to them the Theologian admonished him of his duty, and charged him at least to alter the title and not thus publicly abuse the authority of the Faculty of Theology by resting his calumnies upon it.

Notwithstanding this, he went on with the publication of the theses, and, in imitation of the Reverend Father[2], supported them in disputation for three days. And because they would have had too little matter in them had he not treated of any thing but this verbal question : *whether or not a composition formed of two substances should be called an entity by accident,* he added to this certain others, the principal of which was *concerning the substantial forms of material things,* all of which had been denied by the physician with the exception of the reasonable soul ; he, however, on the contrary, tried to maintain and defend them by every reason in his power, as being the palladium of the Peripatetic School. And in order that you may not here think that it is without cause that I interest myself in the disputes of others, in addition to the fact that in his theses my name was mentioned, as was frequently done by the physician in his, he also mentioned me by name in the course of his disputation, and demanded of his opponent—a man whom I had never seen—if it were not I who suggested to him his arguments ; and availing himself of an odious comparison, he added that those who were dissatisfied with the ordinary method of philosophising expected of me another, as the Jews expected their Elias, to lead them into all truth.

---

[1] Pneumaticam. [2] Bourdin.

When he had thus triumphed for three days, the Physician, who saw very clearly that if he were silent many would imagine him to be vanquished, and if, on the other hand, he defended himself by public disputations, people would not cease as formerly to prevent his being heard, formed the resolution to reply in writing to the theses of the Theologian, in which writing he should refute by good and solid reasons all that had been said against him or his opinions in these theses; but at the same time he should treat their author so gently and respectfully as to try to conciliate, or at least not to exasperate him, inflamed as he was against him[1]. And in truth his reply was such that many of those who read it, believed it to contain nothing of which the Theologian could complain, unless it were, perhaps, that he termed him a man of piety and desirous of opposing every sort of malevolence.

But although he had not been maligned by word of mouth, he yet held that the Doctor had done him a great injury, because he had got the better of him by reasoning, and indeed by reasons that clearly showed him to be a calumniator and ignorant of the matter in hand. And to remedy this evil, he thought he could do no better than make use of his power, and in his own town secure the prohibition of the circulation of a reply which was so odious to him. He may possibly have heard the assertion some people have made about Aristotle, namely, that when he had no good arguments wherewith to refute the opinions of the philosophers who preceded him, he attributed to them others which were quite absurd, that is to say those given in his writings, and, in order to prevent those who came after him from discovering his imposture, he caused all their books to be diligently sought out and burned. Attempting as a faithful Peripatetic to imitate this, our Theologian assembled the Senate of his Academy, and complained of the libel which had been made upon him by one of his colleagues, and said that he must suppress it and at the same time exterminate all this philosophy which disturbed the peace of the Academy. The most assented to this statement. Three of their number[2] were deputed to go to the magistracy and they made to him the same complaints. The magistracy, in order to satisfy them, caused a few copies to be taken from the publisher's shop, which caused the rest to be more greedily sought after, and read with more interest. But as no one

---

[1] This reply by Regius was published Feb. 16, 1642, and was partially written by Descartes himself.

[2] Mætsius, Mathæus and Liræus.

found anything therein of which the Theologian could justly complain, excepting the strength of reasoning which he could not evade, he was made the laughing-stock of all.

He yet gave himself no rest, and assembled his Senatus Academicus every day, in order to acquaint the members with particulars of this infamy. He had a great task in hand: he had to show what were the reasons that he desired the reply of the physician and all his philosophy to be condemned, and he had none to give. Still a judgment finally appeared which was in the name of the Senatus Academicus, but which should be rather attributed to the Rector alone; for as in all the assemblages which he convoked he took his seat in the capacity of judge and at the same time as the most strenuous of accusers, while the Physician was neither heard in his defence nor even summoned, who can doubt that he would easily have drawn the greater part of his colleagues on the side that he desired, and that the large number of votes that he had on his part would have prevailed over the small number of the others? This was evidenced principally by the fact that amongst them there were certain ones who had the same, and even more reason for wishing ill to the physician; and that others who were peaceable men, knowing the ill-temper of their Rector, did not willingly contradict him. And there was this that was remarkable, that not one of them desired to be nominated as approving of this judgment, and there was even one, neither a friend of the physician nor ever known to me[1], who, not desiring to participate in the infamy which he foresaw would fall one day on this action, expressly desired that his name be given as not approving of it.

I shall however here append a copy of this judgment, both because possibly your Reverence may not be sorry to know what passes in these parts between men of letters, and also, so far as I can—when in some years the fragile leaflets on which it is printed have all been dispersed—in order to prevent certain calumniators from making use of their authority by causing it to be believed that the judgment contained reasons sufficiently valid to bring about the condemnation of my philosophy. I shall only omit the name of the University, in case that which occurred through the imprudence of a turbulent Rector just a day or two ago, and which another may perhaps change to-morrow, might disgrace it amongst strangers.

---

[1] Cyprianus Regneri, professor of Law.

JUDGMENT PUBLISHED UNDER THE NAME OF THE SENATUS
ACADEMICUS OF ***[1]

*The Professors of the Academy of *** not having been able to see
without grave regret the pamphlet which was published in the month
of February, 1642, with the title,* Reply about the notes to the
Theological-Philosophical Corollary &c., *and having recognized that
it tended only to the ruin and shame of the University, and that it
could only excite sinister suspicions in the minds of others, judged it
proper to certify to one and all whom it may concern.*

FIRST, *that they do not approve of this proceeding whereby a
colleague publishes books or pamphlets against another of his number,
especially pamphlets in which he is expressly named; and this merely
on the occasion of certain theses or corollaries which have been printed
anonymously, regarding matters of controversy in the University.*

FURTHER, *that they do not approve of this mode of vindicating
a new and assumed philosophy in the said book; especially since it
constantly made use of insolent language, opprobrious to those who
here or elsewhere teach a philosophy contrary to the above, and uphold
the ordinary philosophy which is everywhere received in the Academies
as that which is more true. For example when the author of the
before mentioned pamphlet says:*

Page 6. For it is a long time since I perceived that the great
progress my auditors made in a short time under me, has caused
some people to be jealous.

Page 7. The terms of which the others usually avail themselves
in order to resolve difficulties, never fully satisfy those who have
more clear-sighted intelligence, however little, but merely fill their
minds with mist and darkness.

In the same place. From me men learn much more easily and
quickly to understand the true meaning of a difficulty than is
commonly done from others; this is proved by the experience
of many of my followers who have made an honourable appearance
in public disputes, without having given more than some months
of their time to study under me. Nor have I any doubt that
anyone with any mind at all will allow that there is nothing
to demur to in all this, but on the contrary that all is worthy
of praise.

Page 9. These miserable entities (i.e. the substantial forms
and real qualities) are clearly not of any use at all, unless to blind

---

[1] According to Adam et Tannery Descartes here substituted asterisks for Ultra-
jectini, and in the line below for Ultrajectinae, i.e. of Utrecht (Ultrajectum).

the eyes of those who study, and bring it to pass that in place of this learned ignorance that you so commend, another and haughty sort of ignorance will be obtruded.

Page 15. On the other hand from the beliefs of those who assert the existence of substantial forms, it is easy to fall into the views of those who hold that the soul is corporeal and mortal.

Page 20. It may be asked whether this mode of philosophising which is in the habit of reducing everything to one active principle, i.e. the substantial form, is not merely worthy of being rated as that of a Choræbus[1].

Page 25. From this it clearly follows that it is not those who deny substantial forms, but rather those who maintain them, that may by good reasoning be driven to such a point that they are made to appear atheists or brutes.

Page 39. Because the reasons that have thus far been established by others for the least important of propositions, are for the most part absolutely sterile and untrue, nor do they satisfy a mind which is seeking for truth.

THIRDLY. *That they reject this new philosophy, firstly because it is contrary to the ancient, which has hitherto with good reason been taught in all the Academies of the world, and that it subverts the fundamental principles on which it rests; secondly, because it turns away the young from the study of the old and true philosophy, and prevents them from arriving at the fulness of erudition, because, being once imbued with the principles of this so-called philosophy, they are no longer capable of understanding the terms made use of by authors in their books, or those used by professors in their lectures and disputes; and finally because not only do many false and absurd opinions follow from this philosophy, but an imprudent youth can deduce from it certain opinions which are opposed to the other disciplines and faculties, and above all to the orthodox Theology.*

That for these reasons they express the judgment that all who teach philosophy in this University shall henceforward abstain from the purpose and design of teaching the new philosophy, contenting themselves with that modicum of liberty which is practised here after the example of other most celebrated academies, without for all that destroying the foundations of the old and accepted philosophy, and labouring with all their power in every way to preserve the good

---

[1] A foolish man who tries to count the waves (Suidas).

name and tranquillity of the University. Given this 16th day of March, 1642.

And it is a matter worthy of remark that this judgment was published some time after it had been a subject of derision that the Rector had preferred to suppress the Doctor's book rather than reply to it. Hence it cannot be doubted that, if not all the reasons possible, at least all those that he could invent, in order to excuse his action, are expressed here. Let us then, if you please, run through them all.

First it is asserted, that the physician's book *tends to hurt and disgrace the Academy, and to excite evil principles in the minds of others.* I cannot interpret this otherwise than that from it we might find occasion to suspect, or rather to be assured, that the Rector of the University was imprudent in opposing the manifest truth, as well as malicious, in that having been conquered by reason, he yet tried to conquer by his authority. But this shame and ignominy has waned because he is Rector no longer[1]; and the University suffers less dishonour in still having such a one as a professor, than it is honoured in still having the Physician, provided always that she does not render herself unworthy of him.

It is said secondly *that it is unseemly that a colleague should publish books against another colleague especially one in which he is expressly named.* But on this account the Rector himself, who in this judgment was prosecutor and presiding judge, should be the only one guilty, and the only one to be condemned. For before this, without being provoked to do so, he had caused to be published against his colleague two little books in the form of theses, and had even tried to rest them on the authority of the Sacred Faculty of Theology, in order to assail an innocent man and overthrow him by calumny. And it is absurd for him to excuse himself by the fact that he had not named him, because he quoted the same words that this doctor formerly printed, and so designated him that no one could doubt who was being indicted. But the doctor, on the contrary, replied so moderately, and spoke of his name with such praise, that it might have been believed that it was not against him, but as a friend that he wrote to him, and as a person whose name was even held in honour; and this was really what would have been thought by the world, if the Theologian had availed himself of arguments, however little probable they might be, wherewith to refute the physician. But what is more unjust than to see

---

[1] Voetius' tenure of office ceased on March 16, 1642.

a Rector accuse one of his colleagues of having injured another, for the sole reason that he brought forward reasons so manifest and true to purge himself of the accusation of heresy and atheism which he had made against him, that by this means he prevented his being assailed on all sides?

And certainly the Theologian does not approve this manner of *defending the new and assumed philosophy* of which the Physician avails himself in the pamphlet annexed, *since it contains insolent language designed to bring into opprobrium those who teach the ordinary philosophy which is everywhere received as that which is more true*. But this very moderate man does not observe that he reprehends in another the insolence of his words, as to which I am nevertheless assured that no one could see the slightest indication, if he merely studies those passages here cited, which have most likely been picked purposely in the book of the Physician, as being the most insolent and the best suited to raise up ill-will. Above all is this so if it be likewise observed that there is nothing more usual in the schools of philosophy than to see each one say without any disguise or reserve, that which he thinks, and hence that all the opinions of others are false, and that his alone are true; for the custom philosophers contract in their disputations insensibly habituates them to this liberty, which may seem somewhat rude to those whose lives are more urbane and polished. So the greater part of the expressions which are here cited as having been used in a kind of ill-will against all those who in all places profess philosophy, should not be understood as being said except of our theologian, as is made manifest from the book of the physician; and he spoke in the plural number and third person in order to offend him the less. And finally, as he has made the comparison with Choræbus, and spoken of atheists and beasts, etc., that has not been done spontaneously by the physician, but subsequently to having had thrown at him those injurious opprobrious terms by the theologian, the opprobrium of which he could not repel but by showing by good and evident reasoning that they were totally inapplicable to him, but that they did apply to his adversary. What can you do with a headstrong man like this who arrogates to himself the liberty of calumniating others by calling them atheists and beasts, and who yet cannot endure being refuted by convincing reasoning? But I hasten to matters which concern me more.

He alleges three reasons by which he condemns my new philosophy. The first is that it is *opposed to the ancient*. I do not repeat here what I have said above, that my philosophy is of all others the most ancient, or that there is nothing in the ordinary philosophy which is contrary to it, which is not new. But I only ask whether it is credible that a man is likely to understand a philosophy which he condemns, who is so stupid (or if you wish it, so malicious) as to have desired to bring it under the suspicion of being magical, because it regards figures. I further ask what is the object of the disputations which take place in the Schools. Doubtless, it will be said, by their means to discover the truth. For if it were once discovered, the disputations would grow less frequent, as we see in regard to Geometry, as to which there is usually no dispute. But if this evident truth so long looked for and expected, was at length set before us by an angel, would it not also be rejected for the sole reason that it would seem novel to those accustomed to the disputations of the Schools? But it will possibly be said that the principles which are overturned by the philosophy we assume are not disputed. But why does he thus suffer them to be so easily overturned? And is not their uncertainty sufficiently shown from the fact that nothing has as yet been built up upon them which is certain and assured?

The other reason is *that youth, once imbued with the principles of this so-called philosophy, is no longer capable of understanding the terminology which is in use by authors in their books.* As though it were a necessity that philosophy, which is only instituted for the knowledge of the truth, should teach certain terms of which it itself has no need! Why does he not condemn grammar and rhetoric, because it is rather their function to treat of words, while yet they are so much opposed to the teaching of those scholastic terms that they reject them as barbarous? Were he therefore to complain that *by them youth is turned away from the study of the true philosophy, and prevented from reaching the fulness of erudition,* there would be no reason for laughing at him more than when he says the same of our philosophy; for it is not from it, but from the writings of those who make use of these terms that we should expect their explanation.

The third and last reason has two parts, the one of which is manifestly absurd, and the other insulting and false. For what is there so true or so clear as that it is not easy *for imprudent youth to deduce many false and absurd ideas from it?* But to say that anything follows from my philosophy *which clashes with the orthodox theology,* is clearly false and insulting. And I do not desire to take exception to this statement in that I do not hold his theology to be orthodox : I have never despised anyone for not being of the same sentiments as myself, more especially regarding matters of belief; for I know that faith is a gift of God. Quite otherwise, I even cherish and honour many theologians and preachers who profess the same religion as he. But I have frequently protested that I did not desire to mix myself up with any theological controversies; as inasmuch as I only treat in my philosophy of things clearly known by the light of nature. They cannot be contrary to the theology of anyone, unless this theology is manifestly opposed to the light of reason, which I know no one will allow of the theology professed by himself.

For the rest, in case it is believed that it is without foundation that I assert that the theologian could not refute any of the reasons used by the physician, I shall here bring forward two or three examples to confirm the statement. For there are already two or three little books which have been published on this subject, not in truth by the theologian, but for him, and by persons who, if they had contained anything that was good, would very gladly have attributed to him the credit, nor would he in covering himself as he does with their name, have permitted that these foolish things should have been said, had he had better to say.

The first of these booklets was published under the title of theses by his son who was a professor in the same university[1]. And in it, having done no more than repeat the futile argument which his father had used to establish the substantial forms or add others yet more inane ; and having made no mention at all of the reasoning of the Physician, by which he had already refuted all these arguments, nothing can be concluded but that its author did not understand them, or at least that he was not quick at learning.

The other booklet which comprehends two, appeared under the name of that student who had replied in the seditious dispute which lasted three days under the presidency of the Rector[2]. The title of it is *Prodromus, or a thorough examination of the principles of the orthodox Philosophy, etc.* And it is true that in this booklet all the reasons are placed which could thus far have been collated by its author or by its authors, to refute those of the Physician; for a second part was for the first time added, or a new *Prodromus*, so that nothing might be omitted of all that which came into the mind

---

[1] Paul Voet.   [2] Lambert Waterlaet.

of the author while the first was being printed. But yet we shall see that in these two booklets not even the slightest of the reasons brought forward by the doctor has been, I shall not say thoroughly, but even with probability, refuted. And it would thus appear that the author has had no other design in composing this great volume of pure ineptitudes, and entitling it *Prodromus* in order to make it anticipate another, unless it be to prevent anyone from condescending to reply to it; and by this means to triumph before an ignorant populace, which thinks that books are better the larger they are, and that the loudest and longest talkers, are always adjudged the victors.

But for one who does not look for the good graces of the populace, and who has no other end in view but to give contentment to the honourable and cultured and satisfy his own conscience in defending so far as is possible the truth, I hope to make the futile subtleties and all the other things which our adversaries are accustomed to employ, so open and clear that nobody may be able to use them in future except a man who does not blush at being known by everyone as a calumniator, and as one who does not love truth. And to speak the truth, it has so far served not a little to hold in check the more conscientious, that from the beginning I have asked all who find anything to object to in my writings, to do me the honour of telling me of it, and at the same time I promised that I should not fail to reply to them; for they have seen very clearly that they could say nothing of me before the world with which they had not beforehand made me acquainted, without putting themselves under suspicion of being thought to be calumniators. But it has nevertheless come to pass that many have disregarded this request, and have even secretly censured my writings, even though they found nothing in them that they could convict of falsity, and even sometimes it happened that they had never read them : some indeed have gone so far as to compose entire books, not with a view of publishing them, but what I think much worse, with the view of privately reading them to credulous persons[1]; and they have partially filled them with false reasoning covered with a veil of much ambiguous language, and partially with reasoning which was true, but with which they combated only opinions which have been falsely attributed to me. Now, however, I beg and

---

[1] Descartes here refers to Gassendi, cf. pp. 123 sqq. above.

exhort them all to bring their writings to light. For experience has taught me that this will be better than if they were to address these questions to me, as I asked them to do before, so that, if I did not judge them to be worthy of reply, they should not have reason to complain that I had disdained them, or be able to boast falsely that I could not reply to them. And I should even desire this in order that others whose writings I might publish may be prevented from imagining that I did them an injury by joining my replies to their writings, because (as someone said to me lately about his own case) they would by this means be deprived of the fruit in which they might be able to take pleasure if they had published them themselves, which would cause them to be read everywhere for some months and thus have the possibility of occupying and influencing the minds of many persons, before I had time to reply. I do not desire to grudge them that fruit; nay, I do not promise to reply to them, unless I find that their reasons are such that I fear that they cannot be resolved as they pass from point to point by the readers. For as to those cavillings and revilings, and all the other things said outside the real subject, I shall believe that they are more for me than against me. For this reason I do not think that anyone would employ them in such a cause except he who desires to obtain evidence of more than he can prove by reasons, and who shall show in this matter that he has not sought the truth but is desirous of impugning it and therefore is not a man of probity and honour.

I do not indeed doubt that many good and pious men might hold my opinions in suspicion, both because they see that many reject them, and also because they are supposed to be new, and because few people have so far understood them. And it might even be difficult to find any company in which, if one came to deliberate on my opinions, many more would not be met with who would judge that they should be rejected, than who ventured to approve of them. For reason and prudence dictate that having to give our opinion on something not quite known to us, we should frequently judge of it in accordance with what happens in similar cases: and it has so many times happened that men have introduced new opinions into philosophy which have afterwards been recognized to be no better, but even much more dangerous than those commonly received, that it would not be without reason, if those who do not as yet sufficiently clearly perceive mine, when asked, judge that they should reject them. And so, true as they are, I should yet believe myself to have reason to apprehend that in accordance with the example of the Senate of that Academy of which I have spoken to you above, they might be condemned by all your Society, and generally by all assemblies of those who profess to teach, had I not promised myself that through your goodness and prudence you would take me under your protection. But as you are the head of a Society[1] which can read my essays more easily than many others, the greater part of them being written in French, I do not doubt that you alone can do much in this matter. And I do not ask more of your bounty, than that you will be good enough to examine them yourself, or if greater business prevents your doing that, that you will not hand over the duty to the Reverend Father[2] alone but to others more qualified than he ; and as in the judgments of the law courts, when two or three witnesses worthy of credence say that they have seen something, they are believed rather than a multitude of other men, who, carried away perhaps by simple conjectures, imagine the contrary,—so I beg you to give credence only to those who shall declare that they understand perfectly those things on which they pass judgment ; and the last boon I ask is that if you have certain reasons whereby you judge that I should change my plan of procedure, you will not feel it a burden to tell me of them.

Further in this small number of meditations which I published, all the principles of the philosophy which I am preparing are contained ; and in the Dioptric and Meteors I have deduced from these principles many particular things which show what is my manner of reasoning ; and that is why, although I am not yet setting forth all that philosophy, I yet consider that what I have already given forth, suffices to make known what it will be. Nor do I think that I am without good reason for having preferred to publish first some of my essays, rather than to give my system in its entirety before it was expected. For to speak frankly, although I do not doubt of the truth of it, yet because I know that the truth itself may very easily be condemned by many persons of good understanding, through being impugned by a few envious ones under the plea of novelty, I am not entirely certain that it is desired by all men, nor do I wish to constrain them to receive it. That is why I have given long warning to everyone that I am preparing it ; many individuals wait for and expect it ; one school

[1] Père Dinet as Provincial administered 'the Province of Paris' as it was denominated by the Society of Jesus.
[2] Père Bourdin.

alone has judged that it must reject it; but because I know that it only did so on the solicitation of its Rector, turbulent and foolish as he is, it has not much influence with me. But if perchance some others did not desire it, and had juster reasons for not desiring it, then I do not doubt that their opinions ought to be preferred to those of private individuals. And I even declare sincerely that I should never knowingly do anything contrary to the dictates of prudence, or the wishes of powers that be. And as I do not doubt that the side on which your Society will range itself ought to preponderate over the other, it would be to me the greatest boon if you would tell me your decision and that of your Society; so that as in other things of life I have always honoured and respected you above all others, I now undertake nothing in this affair which I think can be of some importance without having your approval. Farewell.

THE END.

INDEX TO VOLUME II